THE WORLDS OF HERMAN KAHN

THE WORLDS OF HERMAN KAHN

The Intuitive Science of

Thermonuclear War

Sharon Ghamari-Tabrizi

HARVARD UNIVERSITY PRESS
Cambridge, Massachusetts
London, England
2005

Library of Congress Cataloging-in-Publication Data

Ghamari-Tabrizi, Sharon, 1960–
The worlds of Herman Kahn: the intuitive science of thermonuclear war /
Sharon Ghamari-Tabrizi.
p.   cm.
Includes bibliographical references and index.
ISBN 0-674-01714-5
1. Nuclear warfare—Philosophy.   2. Kahn, Herman, 1922–   I. Title.

U263.G49 2005
355.02'17'01—dc22
2004059697

Contents

THE WORLDS OF HERMAN KAHN

*I would not say that the future is necessarily less predict-
able than the past. I think the past was not predictable
when it started.*

DONALD RUMSFELD, 2004

On June 6, 2002, Secretary of Defense Donald Rumsfeld boggled
the world with assurances that Saddam Hussein had weapons of
mass destruction and intended to share them with Al Qaeda. "There
are things we know . . . we know," he remarked nonchalantly. "There
are known unknowns, things . . . we now know we don't know. But
there are also unknown unknowns . . . things we don't know we don't
know." The problem for national security was always the unknown
unknowns. How can you defend against No Discernible Thing? He
struggled to express this pithily. "The absence of evidence is not evidence of absence. It is basically saying the same thing in a different
way. Simply because you do not have evidence that something exists
does not mean that you have evidence that it doesn't exist." The idea
is ticklish, so cryptic and sly it could be a Sufi teaching from Mullah
Nasruddin. How do we interpret this banana peel, Rumsfeld's riddle
of threat assessment?[1]

It wasn't the first time that a high official proposed that Nothing
must be reckoned as the indefinite Something of threat, unless it
could be conclusively proven to be nothing at all. During the cold
war the United States Air Force, believing forces "under concealment," ICBMs "now operational but undetected," insisted that what

could *not* be seen could be assumed to be invisibly in place. In 1960 it concluded that the Soviet arsenal was vastly more formidable than anything the CIA's program of aerial reconnaissance had spotted. Strategic Air Command intelligence officers unhesitatingly identified as missiles every smudge and blot on U-2 photographs—a Crimean War memorial, a medieval tower, even the silhouettes of conventional ammunition depots in the Urals. A year later, they tutored the new President's advisers on how, even with the recent introduction of satellite espionage, missile installations might still elude detection. On the assumption that the Soviets routinely camouflaged their assets, they projected as many as a thousand ICBMs in the Russian inventory, and at least two hundred already squatting on their launchers. Other estimates suggested fifteen. All were wrong. Only four Soviet missiles were operational in 1961.[2]

How could intelligence specialists have been so mistaken? In 1960 Herman Kahn put the problem concisely: "The aggressor has to find one crucial weakness" in his enemy's capabilities, "the defender has to find all of them and in advance." In order to do so, the analyst has to "visualize the possibilities." Not only was this kind of speculative analysis hard to do, it was hard to persuade anyone to listen. Nearly everybody in the defense community was infuriatingly dismissive. Kahn complained, "Any problem that cannot be proved to exist by objective scientific verification or by legal rules of evidence [was] 'hypothetical.'" In the same June 2002 briefing, sounding very much like Kahn, Secretary Rumsfeld pointed out the merits and snares in the idea of possible threats. "All of us in this business read intelligence information. And we read it daily and we think about it and it becomes in our minds essentially what exists. And that's wrong. It is not what exists."[3]

While this book is not about Rumsfeld and the Bush administration's War on Terror, it is precisely about the unknown unknowns of national security. It is about how analysts in the cold war developed ways to fill in the ciphers of strategic uncertainty. It explores the peculiarly inventive quality of strategy, how uncertainty becomes the wellspring of extravagant threat scenarios. However much nuclear war planning—the fighting, termination, and survival of it—was presented to the public during the cold war as a practical question for scientific deliberation, war planning could never be a matter of fact. Whether or not humankind could survive a nuclear war could only be resolved with reference to one's own beliefs about the social and natural world. To flesh out a world where clever men fashioned Something out of Nothing, in this book I offer a tale about Herman Kahn, a virtuoso of the unknown unknowns.

Once you start trolling for possible threats, you begin to flinch, to anticipate. Your fears find corroborative form in the inscrutable flotsam blown this way and that by the world. When I was writing this book, the natural order of things took on the aura of a surprise attack. During summer nights in Atlanta, I was occasionally startled awake by an intolerably bright flash, followed by the house-shuddering crack of thunder nearby. For a microsecond, southern storms were no longer the welcome pulse of water streaming back to earth, but became the light, shock, and blast of a nuclear explosion. As the boom rumbled through my body, something peculiarly historical happened, the improbable yet actual, the hard-to-grasp, hard-to-think-for-more-than-a-moment possibility of nuclear war had arrived. Now. In our present. Not muffled in kitsch design or bygone styles of feeling, but *now*.

In 1998, when I first considered how I might begin this book, I thought the American power to wage nuclear war was a fact of contemporary life that somehow had been repressed. Most people seemed to have forgotten about the existence of nuclear weapons in our world. A few years after the collapse of the USSR, a few ICBM silos were renovated into dwellings for families who reveled in domesticating these terrible hollows. For a moment that now seems irretrievable, the debris of war had become the peacemakers' triumph. With glee and much fanfare, they fashioned the cozy honeycomb of family life—kitchen, den and dining room, bath, bed and study—within the concrete and steel interspaces of missile pods. Housebroken silos may well be relics of the cold war, but unlike the Berlin Wall, nuclear weapons and the strategic threat to use them remain with us.

After the events of September 11, 2001, after the Bush administration's relentless push to generalize vigilante action beyond the frontiers of Afghanistan into a global scourge, and especially in the prelude to the American invasion of Iraq, the menace of weapons of mass destruction unexpectedly lurched into public awareness. Yet even as Bush's deputies invoked the phantom threat of WMD as a goad to subdue skeptics into compliance with his foreign policy, the realities of war waged with these weapons is still hazy even now, a scary Something.

Tens of thousands of nuclear warheads are either already coupled to missiles or could instantly be made ready by the governments of the United States, Russia, China, Great Britain, France, Israel, Pakistan, India, and now, apparently, North Korea. Other states and, allegedly, countless insurgents and militants aspire to devise their own working bombs. Now, as in the cold war, we are menaced by the possibilities of nuclear war touched off by vengeance, pitilessness, dumb chance, or mechanical accident. This actual, this breath-stopping fact—the cataclysmic potential of nuclear war in our world—describes our present. And yet even as you read these pages, it is instantly forgettable.

In 1960 Kahn fixed his attention on this elusive reality. Nuclear war was not improbable but possible, even likely, he said again and again, waylaying anyone who would listen to his unthinkable tidings. But then, and now, "it is almost impossible to get people interested in the tactics and strategy of thermonuclear war." The possibility of nuclear war was harder to think about than one's own death. It meant a death horrifically amplified in the opposing mirrors of the unimaginable millions cut down by such a war and the memory, fresh in 1960, of Hitler's gambling streak with British and French complaisance. Unlike the sacrifices of World War II or Korea, nuclear war offered no consoling wish for the future. Kahn once teased a friend, "I think we can get your daughter through grammar school alive." The man, attuned to his brassy wit, told me he was comforted by the remark. In 1960, most people couldn't bear to hear about nuclear war in the present or future.[4]

Rather than addressing the possibility of war in the tense quaver of mortally frightened peaceniks, Kahn was buoyant and ingratiating. He was appealingly eccentric: grossly fat, a stammerer and wheezer, nearly narcoleptic at times, but, when awake, insatiably chatty. No one knew what to make of him. Was he a bad man but likable? A good man but flawed? A fiend or a gadfly? One reader thought Kahn's book, *On Thermonuclear War*, was "a moral tract on mass murder: how to plan it, how to commit it, how to get away with it, how to justify it." Another thanked him, gulping, "All nonsense about conventional praise aside, the country—probably the world—owes you a great debt." Decades later in his obituary, critics clucked that *On Thermonuclear War* "should properly have caused the sequestration of its author into psychiatric care." Yet the reviewer for a New York chapter of a humanist association praised him for moral excellence. "He determines truth through empirical observation and logical reasoning . . . What else is more akin to the spirit of humanism? Kahn has the courage to face whatever facts are uncovered by his rational search for truth, and to publish the findings despite national furor."[5]

Certainly according to his own lights, Kahn was heroic. He dedicated himself to the most unpalatable crusade imaginable: persuading his neighbors that nuclear war was an immediate peril, and rousing them to prepare to be struck, fight back, and survive. He was fearless and persistent. He was also quixotic, banging together a snuggery of civil defense from a tissue of death-denying wishes. He spoke of Life implacably braving the immensities of weapons effects. He miniaturized the cosmos into human scale by focusing on the practical necessities of survival and recuperation—whether the stock laid aside for the atomic homestead would be enough, whether food and other provisions would hold out. Life, in his view, was not frail, but adaptive and nimble.

Casting nuclear war-fighting and the postwar world into specifics, Kahn worried about genetic mutations in the survivors' children, about soil decontamination and the resumption of agriculture, about an automated deterrence system that could bind the planet into a network of irreversibly computer-triggered bombs. Yet, while he warned America to prepare for nuclear war and repeatedly urged its citizens to accept the legitimacy of striking first should the Red Army threaten NATO countries, he also obsessively enumerated the very uncertainties that dissolved his affirmations of survival into the bracing Nothings of hope. Attaining the summit of prophecy—"any picture of total world annihilation appears to be wrong, irrespective of the military course of events"—he bumptiously reversed himself and pointed out the blind spots in his scenarios of war and reconstruction. Scrupulous and disarming, he repeatedly laid bare the various suppositions that composed his belief in Death-defying Life.[6]

It is painful to imagine in unforgiving detail the unthinkable worst that humanity can do to itself and to the world. For us, this means war waged with biological, chemical, nuclear, and radiological weapons, but also cyber-attacks, climate change, pandemics, species extinction, desertification, drought, population explosion, genocide, resource scarcity, and pollution. These abstractions connote many shapes of shared earthly death, real possibilities but too painful for most of us to examine intently. I do think it was brave for Kahn to ponder the limits of his present moment. But it was folly to downplay the scientific uncertainties that engulfed his prediction of postwar survival. And more than folly to sweep aside the morality of fighting a war with weapons that would vaporize millions of innocent people in a single campaign.

Kahn neatly sidestepped the moral and social costs of fighting with genocidal weapons with a pragmatic murmur, "always abstracting from the humanitarian aspects." Not that he dodged the problem of nuclear casualties. Kahn was nothing if not brazen. He tackled the problem of the social legitimacy of state-sponsored violence head-on. During the years in which he was formulating his arguments about nuclear deterrence, he would regularly demand that his briefing audiences answer the question, "If it is not acceptable to risk the lives of the three billion inhabitants of the earth in order to protect ourselves from surprise attack, then how many people *would* we be willing to risk?" It cut to the heart of his critique of President Eisenhower's strategy of threatening massive retaliation. "It may be too much to promise to kill every Soviet citizen if they act up. I admit it might be too ambitious a program, but you *know* it's too ambitious to promise to kill all the Indians too. They just feel neutral." His audience would laugh, typically, and Kahn, nodding in agreement, would bowl along fearlessly. "You have no idea how aggravated Indonesians and Indians get at our world annihilation stories. It sounds very different when you read it in Hindi. You feel detached. What are these guys doing with my world? It's just not a foreign policy; it's not even a domestic policy."[7]

While defending the legitimacy of using nuclear force with Churchillian stoicism—"Desperate conditions demand desperate living. We did not choose this world; we just live in it"—Kahn was untouched by the problem of the moral deformation of American society, should it authorize the slaughter of millions. He assumed that the United States would be a victim of Soviet aggression. He easily transposed the problem of limiting the numbers of nuclear dead on the other side into a question of domestic civil defense. If nuclear weapons struck the heartland and civil defense measures shielded 40 million Americans who otherwise would have died, he'd exclaim, "We would have done something vastly worth doing!"[8]

By 1973, Kahn prophesied, there might be 50,000 missiles in the world, "each with its own button." He admitted it was "a bit frightening. It is difficult to believe that under these circumstances an occasional button will not get pressed." But still, this didn't portend doom, but a survivable future. He'd shrug, "We may just be going to live in a world in which every now and then a city or town is destroyed or damaged as a result of blackmail, unauthorized behavior, or an accident." Into the breach opened by the unknown unknowns, Kahn professed a philosophy of life that promised a surge of inventive vitality standing down the immensity of death, poison, and a worldwide loss in heritage.[9]

I understand the metaphysics and even have sympathy for it. Yet I break from Kahn on the power of human valor and ingenuity to sustain life and an inherited civilization in the holocaust of all-out war. Too many factors persuade me otherwise: among them, compounding weapons effects that cannot be modeled immaculately, the appearance of unexpected phenomena, the psychic fragility of survivors facing a poisoned wilderness and the annihilation of cities, and my sense that nuclear war surpasses the powers of even the stoutest heart to endure a disaster like no other, blasting our homely social nest into an unbounded world—unroofed, bereft, parched.

Whether nuclear weapons are a legitimate instrument of state power comes down to a matter of belief—whether military means are proportional to their political objectives, whether the sciences underlying calculations of weapons effects are accurate. To threaten to use nuclear weapons is to believe in the robustness of weapons effects models, to assent to extrapolations offered by fallible men and women and equally fallible computer simulations. It is to yield to a belief in the hardness of present facts about weapons effects, and to trust to God the sturdiness of hypothetical models, some of which are quite firm but others merely speculative and untestable. Beyond the uncertainties in the sciences of weapons effects handed up to the commander-in-chief, I am too horror-struck by the degradation of American society that would result from such a war to consent to the combat use of nuclear weapons, however small their yield, however limited the radius of their effects.

Less than a year after Kahn published *On Thermonuclear War*, Carl Kaysen, a special assistant to President Kennedy's national security adviser, urged JFK to be "prepared to initiate general war by our own first strike" in Berlin. While he admitted that "detailed operational studies and exercises" were needed, still he had enough confidence in his war plan to declare "that the assumptions are reasonable, that we have the wherewithal to execute the raid, and that, while a wide range of outcomes is possible, we have a fair probability of achieving a substantial measure of success." A few years later, an operations researcher spilled the beans. You could *never* be sure of your models of nuclear war. "We know that these tests are carried out under controlled conditions. And we know that these conditions will influence the outcome. We also think we know, given information from the test center, what these effects are likely to be. But we can never *really* know. The thing that troubles us is that we don't even *know* if our results are erroneous. We may think they're good. We try to evaluate everything that can affect them . . . All we can hope is that on balance it works out in action as it works out on exercises."[10]

This is not an antiquarian reflection on the old dead cold war. While this book is about the life of the nation at the time of my birth, its world is not cozily sealed off and mastered. It speaks of the actual present and the actual future, of unlikely but not impossible horror. To take sides in the matter of nuclear war-fighting is to pledge oneself to a body of scientific facts, a web of conjecture, a metaphysics underlying prognoses of postwar survival, and a political ethic. From the first days of his administration, President George W. Bush and his coterie pushed for the manufacture of tactical nuclear devices—bunker busters—as well as the invention of new generations of nuclear explosives. In their campaign to rehabilitate nuclear devices as combat weapons, they glossed over geopolitical and scientific uncertainties and shrugged off even the mildest expressions of ethical misgivings as hopelessly naive.

For President Bush, as for Herman Kahn, as for all of us, the matter ultimately turns on faith. For myself, I cannot place my hope optimistically in the sciences underwriting war, whether this is the science that extrapolates the weapons effects of possible wars, the social sciences that shape foreign policy and invent, play, and analyze war games and forecasts, the fantastic imaginary of threat assessment, or science as comic metaphysics—all of which found a merry devotee in Herman Kahn.

Chapter 1

HOW MANY KAHNS CAN THERE BE?

Kahn does for nuclear arms what free-love advocates did
for sex: he speaks candidly of acts about which others whis-
per behind closed doors.

AMITAI ETZIONI, 1961

Is it too soon to pivot round to peer at the half-century just behind us
and contemplate its dreamers, its optimists and crotchets? Too soon
to make out the soap bubble of the cold war that arced over our heads
and seemed as durable as the landmarks that orient our world? This
is a book about a buoyant man, a storyteller and visionary of the thermonuclear era. He masked his stories in the bloodless dialect of
probabilistic risk assessment, but they were stories nonetheless. This
is about world-making, and about someone who happily huddled
with other men at RAND to cast an alternative present and a suite of
alternative futures. Herman Kahn was especially good at imagining
survival against unbearable odds, and at telling stories that detailed
the life or death of the nation. The hero of these tales was not a warrior but the ultra-modern lion of advanced industrial culture, the
civilian defense intellectual. The eggheads at RAND, and this art-
less, sweaty man in particular, did not set out to conquer a world but
to save the future with stories cocooned in numbers, stories of cunning and foresight and daring, of fortuitous invention, and the resurrection of spring.

During the 1950s Kahn worked as a systems analyst at the RAND
Corporation, the air force's nonprofit research institute. We can hear

him briefing visiting air force officers: "I gather you can't see this from the back of the room. You *can* see them? Fine! You've got 20–20 vision though. (He's my boss, and I can't tell him what I think of him. Well, I've got plans under way though, and boy, when I . . .)"[1]

He has a Bronx accent. There's pressure against the sinuses, some wheezing. He stumbles over some words. He gulps in a breath and grins. "You see, ideally, what we would like to do is get the models of your bombers, send them over to Russia, see how many get shot down, how many get through, let them run over their bombing runs, then come back. But you can't get cooperation in doing this. It's the kind of thing which seems to be impracticable currently. I've talked to some people, though, who practically want to try it this way, but even these guys sort of talk very quietly. With more a sort of a feeling of longing, than really believing in doing it."[2]

This chubby young man in eyeglasses, clutching a pointer, tottering at a lectern flanked by easels with charts, perspiring freely, blurts out, "I might mention that—just interrupt me anytime you want with questions, this being really set up as a demonstration–audience participation lecture. We don't want argument, but we're willing to take questions." The audience laughs. "This is serious. I speak as a man who's been wounded. I've got stories to tell which would curl your hair!"[3]

Speaking of World War III, he wags his head. "The Russians aren't dedicated world dominationists. You know, they just sort of want it on account of a sentimental way, you know, but not like 'By God, we got to have it!' It just doesn't make sense for them to really push too hard, you know, but just to push easy." He flips to a drawing of a spindly boy wearing oversized glasses, hugging an ABC primer, and sniffing a daisy. This is the enemy. "The first [mistake] is to assume that he is a sort of cretinoid idiot, who can't see, think, or anything. It might be a fair, if dangerous, assumption that the enemy is at least as stupid as we are." The next picture is a Goliath with four arms, reading a book, lofting a 1000-pound dumbbell, aiming a pistol at a target, painting a picture. The enemy can do everything. "He's a giant, seven feet tall with four arms, each with two biceps. Each arm can, of course, be used independently and simultaneously."[4]

We can tell from the crewcuts and bowties that we've crept up to Kahn sometime in the 1950s. Some men in the audience wear uniforms; others are in suits. Most are in their twenties or thirties. There are a number of women in the back who look like secretaries, but others sit among the ranks of analysts and officers. Here is the lithe daughter of Admiral Nimitz who combs *Pravda* for tidbits. Over there is a woman who spends her days sifting through Japanese signal intercepts collected before the surprise attack on Pearl Harbor.

He ambles along the platform. "Lots of times people say about systems analysis, why don't you guys do an experiment? What the hell are you sitting here figuring things? Why don't you go out and run an experiment? Well, we'd love to run experiments, but there are two difficulties. One, in realistic experiments, people get shot down. That's not the major difficulty. We're willing to do it." The audience laughs. "We are. The real difficulty is we're talking about weapons which aren't in existence yet."[5]

A young man bounds onstage with an armload of charts. Kahn cocks his head and mutters, "Why don't you just split this up a little bit. Put them over there. No, don't just hold it. Well, you just stand. When we first gave this thing, it was sort of a rush job, and he'd been up about 24 hours in a row for quite a while, so he just really couldn't stand." He cackles. "That's no longer the situation. He can stand now. I mean, things have changed. I don't need you anymore."[6]

Kahn whips through the next bit. "If you assume that your job is to defend the 20 largest cities against surprise attacks, this is hopeless unless you assume the enemy is stupid. It doesn't matter what you do, it will not work unless the enemy is stupid. So if you assume this is your mission, you might as well assume the enemy is stupid. But it is not stupid to assume the enemy is stupid, because this is the only [way] this thing could work. Assuming he is stupid, you can save a great deal of money. You design your system against this stupid enemy. [But] *he just ain't that stupid.* He writes in classified papers that he ain't that stupid. He *explains* it to you, understand. So it's very hard to believe that he is. It's a little stupid to believe that he's that stupid."[7]

He nudges his assistant. "Want to give me this next one? Oh. He argues with me. I mean, if a guy is right, he ought to be very polite." The young man flits away. Kahn snorts happily. He's found a great way to talk about pitfalls in modeling hypothetical problems. One of the office secretaries drew a cartoon of a man mamboing with a female dummy. He flips to this drawing and gazes at it. "He is either desperate or guilty of Modelism. We could just as well have shown a young man looking at pin-up pictures, or any situation where somebody is playing with an ideal in preference to the real thing. It may or may not be desirable for a young man to construct his love life around fantasies, but the mature heterosexual male wants a girl!"[8]

He slurps a mouthful of water and races ahead. "One of our colleagues points out that the analogy is unfair to the Systems Analyst. There are delectable girls all around to tempt our 'mature heterosexual adult' away from his dummy, but what can our poor Systems Analyst replace his model with? Another one! Even if he wanted a war, he couldn't have it. Of course, as any psychologist will tell you, the comparison is not so unfair. Some fantasies are nicer than some *real* girls!"[9]

The next cartoon shows a man steering a roadster off a crook in a mountain road, distracted by a buxom woman gazing at the view. He jabs a finger at the drawing and tries to suppress a giggle. "Another mistake which is very very important is over-concentration. This is the kind of thing that, for example, you see: he's just concentrating not on the wrong thing—its worth looking at, but not exclusively. We don't object to you looking at the blonde. We'd look at her ourselves [but] you should look at something else. There's a cliff over here. And the point is look around, look for loopholes, see what's happening."[10]

And there was that novel about pushbutton war. Everyone is talking about launching missiles by mistake. "You're worried about somebody making the wrong connection. You know, he puts the fuse in when he should have taken it out. He turns the dial just for kicks.

He presses the button because he likes to look at the red lights. You know, you people work with computers, you know that people just literally can't resist passing without pressing buttons. I'm one of them myself, I've got to hold myself."[11]

Thinking of the next thing he's going to say, he beams. "You remember there was this legislation passed by Congress saying you can't study surrender. My wife looked at it and said, 'Herman, I got a funny reaction to this.' I said, 'What do you mean?' She said, 'Well, if it ever occurs that I'm cowering in a cellar, and they've hit us, and they've taken out a certain amount of SAC, a lot of air defense, and bombs are dropping near me, I'm sitting there with my two children, I'm going to *consider* the question.'" He shrugs. "I can be funny on the subject of thermonuclear war," he once said to a reporter.[12]

When Kahn's house in New York was being built in 1961, an appreciative producer of seamless concrete cylinders—aware of his zeal for civil defense—offered to donate materials for a family fallout shelter. A hole was excavated near the outer wall of the living room. Before the shelter was installed, Kahn was asked to test its design by wiggling through the pipe that served as its entrance. It was impossible—he was too stout. Infuriated, he ordered his workmen to widen the cavity to accommodate a swimming pool. It was embedded inside the house in a long chamber adjoining the living room. Addicted to swimming, Kahn would slip into the waters of his pool in the mornings before breakfast or late at night.

I picture myself on an early morning in 1962, gazing at draped windows and one glowing spot. A splinter of light darts onto the driveway. The house looks no different from the other ranch houses on the street. Not opulent but comfortable, tucked in a shady cul-de-sac. All is homey and familiar, yet that lamplight discloses a swimming pool encased within the husk of a residential fallout shelter. I imagine Kahn shuttling back and forth, counting laps, daydreaming about the day ahead, the books he's read recently, his current fads and preoccupations. I imagine the fertile seclusion enveloping the swimmer: the flush of sound, water bubbling in the ears, the ringing gurgle and deafness of immersion. The swimming pool is a medium for the fantastic: an earthbound man glides to and fro weightlessly. Swim-

ming in a short pool amplifies the effects of relaxed and flopping effort. Swimming transports man out of niggling little life into the
purest sensations of resolve, unseen and bobbing in water barely
heard, beyond the black façade of daybreak in the suburbs in 1962.

Here is Kahn frisking in the surf on Santa Monica beach. He tum-
bles into the water happily. The ocean suits him, its soft tug, his
sprawl through swells and foam. Here is Kahn counting laps in his
new house in New York. So many people want to find him and talk
to him. A housewife peers out of her window, forlornly blessing the
blue sky. She wonders if she is crazy to brood so much about the end
of the world. "For the last month or so I have seriously been in doubt
as to my sanity," she confides to Kahn. "I weep at the thought of a
surcease of human existence, perhaps of this beautiful earth that I
love so well itself." She feels alone in her fears, she tells him in her
letter. Her friends mock her. "Most people want to know if I am
some 'new kind of nut.'" Those with more finesse say, "If it happens,
it happens." What to do, Mr. Kahn? "I am *afraid*," she whispers. "I
wish to *survive*."[13]

A junior high school teacher snatches a tray of cookies out of
the oven. Inhaling sugar, butter, and chocolate, she frowns, "Is this
enough? Can I bear it?" Having pottered and loafed for days, she
finally sits down to write. "Dear Mr. Kahn," she says, "I have spent a
painful weekend, thinking, watching TV reports, thinking and inter-
mittently seeking relief in cookies, bike rides, not thinking and trite
household chores. I am in the audience of the near-panicked . . . My
intention in writing you is not for you as my 'Fairy Godfather' to
whisk away the problems that cause my fright [and] flight." She
wants help for enduring. "How can I better prepare myself [and my
students] for the task of maintaining mature mental and emotional
attitudes . . . and faith in ourselves as cooperative individuals under
stress (attack or not)?"[14]

The wife of a doctor and mother of three children suddenly real-
izes war could strike at any moment. "I am not afraid to think!" she
wails. "I am a Christian, but I am not hiding behind God, letting
Him take care of things." Even so, realistic preparation for nuclear
war was unspeakably hard to grasp. She works it through: "Suppose

we built a bomb shelter in our yard. Would the days that we could survive there actually help? What would happen when we ran out of food and water? . . . What if I do read articles telling me what to do in case of attack? What good will it do me if everyone else in Los Angeles is dead? My husband's hospital is 20 miles away. How could I, alone, care for three children under three years old?" Yes, nuclear war was a real possibility, but Mr. Kahn, "What are you trying to ask us to do? I feel the urgent need to do something *now*, but what can I do? . . . Please tell me what to do now! What should I read? To whom should I write? If you will give sound advice, I will heed it!"[15]

But maybe preparation for survival will not safeguard the future. Maybe survival was a cosmic daydream. A young man spends his days teaching his kindergarten class, wondering whether his wriggly moppets will grow to adulthood. "No, Mr. Kahn," he admonishes, "it is hard not to feel that in your desire to persuade people to think seriously about nuclear war by persuading them that it may not be as bad as they think, you have skipped over a good many problems." But later that year the young teacher is struck by a joke. A reporter from *The San Francisco Chronicle* asked Kahn to explain his remark that the world after nuclear war "would not preclude normal and happy lives for the majority of survivors." Kahn shot back, "Who's happy or normal right now?" Sensing a whiff of Doomsday, the young man writes a second letter.

> What you seem to me to be thinking, perhaps just hoping, is that . . . life after World War III might be much better than life today. It is as if you thought of yourself as one of a number of Noahs, stepping out into a new world for a fresh start. I don't blame you . . . who would not like to see cleared away . . . the ugliness, horror, and corruption of today's world; who would not like the chance to deal with real problems that might be solved, instead of problems that only lead to more problems, and thence to still more?

But if his life was really abnormal and unhappy, maybe he should redirect his attentions. "If you get tired of making calculations about

100,000,000 dead versus 80,000,000 dead . . . you might try teaching young children. They might convince you that they deserve a chance to make more of their lives than their elders have of theirs."[16]

A band of men and women bearing placards and canteens trudge across the Southern California desert on their way to RAND to talk about the Bomb. It is 1960, and they hope to walk across North America, across Western Europe, and talk to Muscovites too. But first, they arrange to chat with Kahn in a cabana at the Del Mar Hotel and Beach Club. He is the only one from RAND who greets them. "I was surprised at his friendliness and his democracy," one of the marchers remarked. "He wanted to talk with us and he was willing to go out of his way to do so." They talk about World War III. Kahn says he thinks "thermonuclear war likely within ten years if arms control or disarmament agreements couldn't be reached." More than forty years later, Bradford Lyttle, a lifelong peace activist, would single out Kahn for special praise. "I maintain this rather warm feeling in my heart towards Herman Kahn. Even though I felt that many of his ideas were appalling and seemed to be very cold-blooded, personally I found him much more approachable and really more understanding of our position than a number of people in government I talked to."[17]

"Is There Really a Herman Kahn? It Is Hard to Believe"

In the 1960s Herman Kahn was a well-known man. His name alone broadly signified contemporary affairs. Jules Feiffer twitted him in a lampoon of East Coast foreign policy elites. Susan Sontag invoked him in an essay on science fiction films. The composer Luigi Nono even borrowed text from his book *On Escalation* in a work dedicated to the National Liberation Front of Vietnam. Kahn himself quipped, "I am one of the ten most famous obscure Americans."[18]

His first book, *On Thermonuclear War*, published in December 1960, was the first widely circulated study that dramatized how a nuclear war might begin, be fought, and be survived. A reviewer in *The Village Voice* remarked that the book "shocked us into paying serious attention, for the first time, to what our military thinkers, planners, and doubters were thinking, planning, and doubting. Never has so much been publicly written and read about war; never has there been so much open and respected exploration . . . of a nation's military policies."[19]

OTW, as it was popularly known, made Kahn a celebrity. He appeared on TV and radio, in magazines and newspapers, exhorting the nation to muster the will and wherewithal to fight and survive a nuclear war. The book and its author were the subject of editorials, letters-to-the-editor, and college debates. Nearly everything said about him contributed to the feeling that Kahn was a man of the times, but no one could agree on what he represented. Was he a hero-scientist or an American Eichmann? A human computer or a humanist, a patriot or a psychopath? Stacks of letters tipped onto his floor from military and civilian officials, journalists, students, peace activists, veterans, civic organizations, even manufacturers of fallout shelters and survival equipment.

In 1961 it seemed as if everyone wanted to solicit Kahn, argue or plead with him, schedule lectures and meetings, arrange publications and sponsorships. He was invited to address the War College at the Air University, the senior class of the Air Force Academy, and officers attending the National War College. He briefed President Kennedy's assistant secretary of defense for civil defense and met with the Senior Seminar in Foreign Policy at the State Department's Foreign Service Institute. He testified before congressional hearings on civil defense. He addressed members of the U.S. Civil Defense Council in Los Angeles and the Dallas Symposium on Civil Defense. He spent a day hobnobbing with the Lexington Democratic club in Manhattan. He attended the Behavioral Science and Civil Defense conference sponsored by the National Academy of Sciences. At the annual meeting of the American Political Science Association, he joined a panel on "promoting research on war and peace."

Kahn was invited to become an adjunct professor for the UCLA Institute of International and Foreign Studies. He accepted a position on the advisory council to a newly hatched Peace Research Institute in New York. He addressed the Commonwealth Club of California, celebrants at the MIT Centennial festivities, and the students of Oak Ridge High School. The Women's National Press Club and the North Texas Section of the American Nuclear Society engaged him to speak. He debated the wisdom of civil defense with a Harvard philosophy professor and spent a day exploring the possibilities for peace with the American Friends Service Committee at their annual Roundup.[20]

The publisher Frederick Praeger invited him to write a book on foreign affairs. The editor of *Encounter* wanted his thoughts on the furor over *OTW*. The chief of the editorial division of the Organization of American States and the editor of a union periodical asked him for something on civil defense. He corresponded with the peace education secretary of the American Friends Service Committee; the editor of the radical *Committee of Correspondence* newsletter; the director of the Environmental Radiation Laboratory at New York University; a scientist adapting manufacturing processes to the lunar environment; an arms controller reporting on research on radiation absorption in human tissue; and an inventor of a weather control system that would induce rainfall by spreading carbon on the surface of drought-stricken regions. All of this took place during the year that he left RAND and founded his own research organization on the East Coast, the Hudson Institute.[21]

While some readers welcomed his frank exposition of possible war, others pounced on his ethics and mental health. "Mr. Kahn is now cast for the role of Chief Fascist Hyena," scowled a political scientist. He was pelted with a flurry of personal attacks, the first and most famous of which was James Newman's sarcastic review in *Scientific American:* "Is there really a Herman Kahn? It is hard to believe. Doubts cross one's mind almost from the first page of this deplorable book: no one could write like this; no one could think like this." The science correspondent in *The Glasgow Herald* denounced Kahn's book as the work of the devil: "Not the traditional devil, reeking of brimstone and tempting men to old-fashioned sins, but a slick, talcum-scented, contemporary Satan, rationalising hideous emotions by reference to strategic studies, electronic computers, contingency planning, and all the other gimmicks of paranoiac gamesmanship." In his defense, a Berkeley psychoanalyst championed the maturity and courage required to "face the worst fearlessly." In a letter to *The Bulletin of the Atomic Scientists,* Dr. Walter Marseille interpreted antagonism to Kahn as "a widespread and deep-seated emotional resistance against the possibility of nuclear war as part of the reality with which we are living."[22]

Official Washington regarded *OTW* as exemplary work from RAND. While he would never become a Kennedy insider, Kahn's ideas were well known because many of his RAND colleagues had fled into the new administration. Alain Enthoven, the nation's first (deputy assistant) secretary of defense for systems analysis, welcomed *OTW,* writing, "I am most impressed by the scope and the extremely high density of ideas." Reprising his own reasons for quitting, Enthoven regretted that so many "important ideas on strategic problems" had been buried at RAND, "where they are sure to have no beneficial effect on policy. Your book," he concluded flatteringly, "represents an enormous break in the log jam." A year or so later, the secretary of defense's special assistant, Adam Yarmolinsky, greeted an audience at Kahn's new think tank with the comment, "For the past year and a half, we at the Department of Defense have been living off the intellectual capital accumulated by Herman Kahn and others in this audience."[23]

OTW was hotly debated in military circles, especially in the air force. It was the main selection for the air force–sponsored Aerospace Book Club for January 1961 and was offered as a free premium for new members. Among the earliest public notices, the *Bulletin of the North American Air Defense Command* recommended *OTW* as a "reading must." A handful of letters reported that his book had been passed around at military bases, the subject of eager discussion.[24]

Readers were thrilled and alarmed. Some thought *OTW* was hair-raisingly engrossing. "It is the most exciting book I've read in years," exulted a political scientist. "I don't ordinarily write fan letters," began another, "especially to authors of books that keep me from getting to sleep. But I wanted you to know that I've just finished *OTW* and it left me breathless," gasped the editor of *Fortune.* "I think it was a prodigious intellectual achievement." Admirers praised his steady focus on the actual possibility of nuclear war, unwished for but inescapable. The director of foreign policy studies at the Brookings Institution scribbled, "The country owes you quite a debt for being a one-man crusade in this field. No one has done more to awaken the American people to the problem and to urge them to take their head out of the sand and do something about it." The assistant to the director of the Applied Physics Laboratory at Johns Hopkins University carried this further. "The country—probably the world—owes you a great debt for . . . dissecting the malodorous impasse we have so cunningly devised for ourselves . . . How cosmically ridiculous can we humans be with all our self-satisfying posturing about being . . . the Masters of the Universe?"[25]

That some scholars, policy analysts, politicians, and the military toasted Kahn is to be expected. But the real surprise is that prominent segments of the peace movement also approved of him. The Quakers and A. J. Muste, founder of the pacifist Fellowship of Reconciliation, praised him for plotting the grisly details of the postwar world. The disarmament senatorial candidate from Massachusetts, H. Stuart Hughes, remarked, "I think one can say without qualification that Kahn has written one of the great works of our time. Its title sounds like a plagiary of Clausewitz's *On War,* and if Kahn aspires to be the master . . . strategist of the mid-20th century, I . . . know of no better claimant." Even Bertrand Russell, one of the foremost disarmament agitators of the period, paid tribute to *OTW.* In *The Bulletin of the Atomic Scientists* he noted, "The political case for British neutralism has been stated very convincingly by no less a person than Mr. Herman Kahn . . . [His] arguments are valid and should be found convincing even by those British politicians who are uninfluenced by any feeling of abhorrence for nuclear war."[26]

Polemics about *OTW* were so sharp that its very reception was a subject for commentary. The young sociology professor Amitai Etzioni reflected, "*OTW* is not just a book but an event. It has stirred up so many discussions and repercussions, motions and emotions, that it could in itself be a subject of sociological and psychological research." In fact, Kahn's assistant suggested to *Harper's* that one of its staff writers consider "why people react . . . often violently to objective studies of modern war . . . Kahn has become a special kind of lightning rod attracting bouquets and brickbats of this kind."[27]

It was plain that matters which had preoccupied Americans in the 1950s found a concentrated foil in Herman Kahn in 1961. "It is fascinating, I think," mused Hedley Bull, the British political scientist, "to see the variety of things . . . reviewers will say about the same book to such an extent that one begins to ask not Newman's question, does a Herman Kahn exist, but how many Herman Kahns can there be?"[28] The host of Kahns represented different things to different people, depending on their framing perceptions of the reliability of atomic scientists' testimony on technical arcana, the nature of Communist hostility to the West, and the willingness of the United States and NATO to engage in nuclear brinkmanship. Bundling Kahn together with the questions posed to interpret him—whether he was mad or sane, whether his arguments supported or undercut humanist values, whether he was a heroic scientist or an avatar of a new type of American intellectual—lays out a potent force field through which we can explore the welter of meanings of deterrence and nuclear war in this period.

While the squabble about *OTW* spilled from anxiety about the actual possibility of war, the nature and quality of faith in human and earthly continuity lurked behind beliefs about the adaptive power of civilizations to survive the shocks of such a catastrophe. The questions driving this quarrel were fundamental: What keeps humanity alive? Was it human foresight, ingenuity, and good luck? Or was it obedience to commandments laid down by a God with the power to prostrate humanity with cataclysm? We can begin to construe the fantasies, pangs, and political ideas that attached themselves to Kahn in 1961 by sounding the undercurrent of faith that sustained domestic life in these years.

"God Bless You Real Good!"

In the summer of 1957, more than two million people found themselves worshipping Jesus Christ in the streets, pavilions, and lecture halls of New York City. The city's unexpected appetite for mass evangelism set attendance records, surpassing the circus, baseball playoffs, and world championship boxing as the most sought-after spectacle in its history. Billy Graham had burst upon New York in the middle of May. He planned to rent Madison Square Garden for six weeks but tarried the whole summer. "It's a Miracle in Manhattan!" chirped the filmmakers documenting Graham's triumphs. More like "an air-conditioned miracle," sniffed the critics; "it smacks of Madison Avenue."[29]

On the last day of his crusade, you could hear Graham reverberate from banks of loudspeakers strung along Times Square. "Tell the world tonight that our trust is not in our stockpile of atomic and hydrogen bombs but in Almighty God!" he thunders. A half moon drifts up behind the speaker's platform. It is eerie, so many people jammed together. They surge onto Broadway from 37th Street all the way beyond 43rd. You expect New Year's glee, but it's quiet—120,000 people humming, fluttering, sighing, swaying, mewling, wobbling in a vast hush. "Just look at those deadbeats!" snickers a clutch of bystanders. "So he saves you, so we'll be dead anyway in fifty years if we don't get the bomb first." ABC television cameras sweep over the throng looking for beatific tears. A dewy-eyed woman, in close-up, waves her arms in rapture. Another one beams. This one whimpers, and over there a man shivers. Another one glares and clumps off. "I wonder what will happen now," a young man murmurs to his wife as they shuffle to the subway.[30]

For sixteen weeks, more than 18,000 people swarm into Madison Square Garden. Overflow crowds mill around on the sidewalks. Pilgrims rented scores of buses for their journey to New York. A dining car was outfitted with a pipe organ to accommodate a gospel train from Richmond, Virginia. Six nights out of seven Graham preaches. ABC broadcasts his Saturday evening services nationally. He is tireless. He loses eighteen pounds. He devotes a week to the problems of teenagers. He hammers at Jim Crow and the coming atomic Armageddon. All told, he coaxes 66,577 people to come forward and give their lives to Jesus Christ. They are led to the basement of the Garden to commune with counselors and sign cards of conversion.[31]

Between sermons, Graham breakfasted with clergy. He counseled Mayor Wagner, Governor Harriman, Vice President Nixon, and UN General Secretary Dag Hammarskjold. He called for Christian cells in labor and business organizations, prayer meetings at lunch, weeklong revivals after work, paramilitary camps for juvenile offenders, and teenage Centurions for the coming Armageddon. He shuttled uptown to Harlem and over to Brooklyn to press for antisegregation legislation coupled with disinterested love between the races. He urged 17,000 Spanish-speaking New Yorkers to make "decisions for Christ" through an interpreter. He lured 7,000 people into Central Park and corralled a thousand students at Columbia University for prayer. One hundred thousand people crammed the aisles and outfield of Yankee Stadium. He teetered on the steps of the Sub-Treasury Building at Wall and Nassau Streets and trumpeted the Good News to tens of thousands of workers in the financial district. "America doesn't need more nuclear weapons, but more who have faith in God, more who will serve Christ!" People leaned out of office windows and crowded the balconies of the New York Stock Exchange, as his choristers crooned, "I'd rather have Jesus than silver or gold."[32]

Graham rebuked Americans for gorging on sedatives. "We take tranquilizing drugs to keep us steady during the daytime and sleeping pills to put us to sleep at night, with hundreds of aspirins thrown in between." America lolled in "a dream world of dope, drink, tranquilizing pills and entertainment," and the reason for it was the Bomb. Even as the New York crusade picked up momentum, a series of nuclear tests walloped the West's proving grounds. On May 15 Britain had exploded a hydrogen bomb over Christmas Island, becoming the world's third nuclear power. Throughout June, the United States and the USSR bandied drafts of an arms control treaty, which included a provisional halt to bomb tests. On July 2 the United States proffered a ten-month pause. The next day Khrushchev announced that he had shoved Molotov, Malenkov, and Kaganovich out of the Central Committee and Presidium, thereby consolidating his power.[33]

On July 5 the United States set off the largest H-bomb ever detonated on the mainland. The USSR countered with a demand for an immediate suspension of testing. Meanwhile, the Atomic Energy Commission continued vaporizing patches of Yucca Flats, Nevada. On August 21 President Eisenhower agreed to a two-year moratorium. Five days later, the Kremlin announced that it had beat America in the race to launch a long-range missile. Days after that, the Americans, French, and Canadians endorsed a draft of the treaty. The Soviet deputy foreign minister dismissed it. In September, talks broke off.

Throughout the summer Graham warned of the End of Time. While projecting murky tidings in late June—"I have a feeling that something is about to happen—some great thing above all that we ask or think"—by the end of August he foresaw a day "when we will have to pay with our blood for following Christ." The very fact of the H-bomb actualized the reality of Armageddon. "Prepare to meet thy God!" he boomed. "If any generation ever needed to prepare, it's this one. Especially the people of New York. One hydrogen bomb, and you're done." If New Yorkers "remained unrepentant," the city would be razed as Jerusalem had been in ancient days. "Whether or not the technique of mass evangelism is to one's taste," winced *The New York Times*, "there can be no denying that Dr. Graham is its exponent extraordinary . . . providing a faith for the uncertain and the fearful."[34]

Anxiety about the nuclear unthinkable spanned the antipodes marked out by Kahn and Graham. The received view of the 1950s finds only the sunniest gaiety in its greedy and giddy amusements. But from the short, steep prospect of 1961, one man reflected that it was only when he thumbed through the cartoons of Jules Feiffer and Walt Kelley, only when he savored the stabs of Mort Sahl, could he believe he "was not isolated, that there was a widespread underground recognition that things were not jes' fine."[35]

Throughout the decade, despondency seeped from writers of every ideological persuasion. In 1955 *Life* magazine presented with some bewilderment an America "full of confused persons" who feel that there is "something deeply unsatisfying about [their] lives" but who "would have trouble saying what it is and even more trouble . . . discovering what to do about it." They "have a feeling that they have been victimized by life and some . . . are on the way to a crack-up." The nation was "other-directed, hydrogen-haunted, artificially tranquilized and doggedly togethered," spat a disgusted Gore Vidal. If gushing benignity frothed on the surface, it was a fragile cover for angst. "We are *all* harassed," cried the cartoonist Robert Osborn, "whether we know it or not, by interior psychological pressures or exterior bombs and fall-outs. One sees all sorts of people quietly coming apart—or trying to hold things together with alcohol—or behaving as though this was the Age of Beasts . . . I don't think that any amount of smiley advertising and fake togetherness can conceal how little we like to observe the sharpest relations of things."[36]

In 1946 the President and his henchmen, sages and tastemakers, publicists and physicians, priests, pastors, and rabbis had touched off the mood by celebrating the GIs' homecoming with a galling, fidgety heartiness. "We started off, you will recall, by fearing . . . returning sons and brothers . . . The men's own wives and children . . . were nervously coached on how to welcome back the strangers." The anticommunist paroxysms of the late 1940s intensified the uneasiness of a skittish, recovering people. "What came over us?" Archibald MacLeish groaned in a graduation address of June 1950. "How could we fall from ourselves so far? And into such morbid and unmanly fears? . . . Such hysterical suspicion of each other and ourselves? Such neurotic terror of . . . our enemies?"[37]

When the Korean War erupted in late June 1950, and throughout the next year, many Americans felt it was only a matter of time before atom bombs would begin to fall. World War III had begun. It was a time of appalling tension. Describing the atmosphere of futility that "nobody can fail to be conscious of," the essayist Raymond Fosdick sighed, "What is the use, we ask ourselves, of thinking of a better future or even of planning our individual lives if this is . . . the twilight of our age? If the . . . machinery of our civilization is headed for the scrap heap, and if we are to be plunged into anarchy with a clicking abruptness?" The following month, Bertrand Russell coaxed his readers to resist the temptation to relax into despair. "I know many people who feel that the world is doomed to march on to utter tragedy, that everything we have valued is rapidly nearing an end."[38]

During the Korean War, people were dismayed by public affairs. "I only know that much of the world . . . grows increasingly difficult to decipher or . . . make sense of," confessed a scholar. "All too many things . . . contradict our . . . assumptions; . . . all too many things, for that matter, contradict one another." The mood persisted in 1953. An observer writing for *Commonweal* called it *Gotterdammerung:* "What now calls for . . . cure is the contagious mood of universal discouragement spread on every side by a host of Giants of Despair . . . the Defeatists, the . . . sad of mind and sick of heart, the current prophets of inevitable . . . doom." It is their "spirit of fear which threatens to overwhelm us at the moment."[39]

Even with the cease-fire in 1953, people could not shake off "mists of uncertainty, clouds of suspicion, shadows of fear." The next year an essay excoriating "the fears of the intelligentsia" demanded, "Are there any objective grounds for this fear? In what degree are these fears complicated by factors that are personal or professional?" The author shrank from a "unique and shameful feature" of public manners: it is not just "being afraid"; it is "*wallowing* in fear." Just when had timidity become acceptable? Others pursued the theme year after year. In 1955 the "malady of the times" was diagnosed as "a loss of nerve." In 1957 the same man who had traced American anxiety to demobilization scoffed, "It seems to be almost a point of pride . . . today for us to acknowledge openly that our fears are the wellspring of our planning and action, the justification for our sins."[40]

Maybe the problem was postwar well-being. A resilient people had become voluptuous. In 1953 *The Nation* lashed out against American grogginess. "There you have the fog we all stumble in, the dream of comfort. Producing and consuming, we tread our pleasant round, and any pangs or sharp intrusions of reality can be allayed by purchasing a new gadget." A psychiatrist blasted "guilty parents" for pampering themselves and their children. By mid-decade, everyone had heard about tranquilizers called Miltown and Equinal. Millions of people afflicted by "nerves" flocked to their doctors. In 1956, 35 million prescriptions were doled out, a fact that disturbed the editors of *The New Republic.* "In addition to the chemical and biological unknowns" of voracious tranquilizer consumption, they worried, "do we *want* absolute freedom from fear?" "We are irresponsible, apathetic, evasive, shallow and blunted in relation to our fears!" fired off the author of "Atomic Fears and Christian Courage" in 1958. Americans drowsed in downy ease. "The last reason for . . . not facing the focal fear of our time is seen sharply in what we have done with 'comfort' . . . We want to be assured of the outcome before making the effort."[41]

The motif of national decadence appealed to people across the political spectrum. Just prior to declaring his candidacy for President, Senator John F. Kennedy tried out the theme in *The Nation.* "We have gone soft—physically, mentally, spiritually soft. We are in danger of losing our will to fight, to sacrifice, to endure. The slow corrosion of luxury is already beginning to show." While sharing in the recoil from American languor—"We've grown unbelievably prosperous and we maunder along in a stupor of fat"—Eric Goldman diagnosed the problem as smothering complacency. "We live in a heavy, humorless, sanctimonious, stultifying atmosphere" devoid of "self-mockery." Maybe the world wouldn't shatter in cataclysm, he suggested, but expire "with us just sitting solemnly on our lawn chaises, overfed, oversanctified, and overbearing, talking a suicidal stuffiness."[42]

Muscular exhortations to revive American hardiness trailed after the decade-long report on the nation's mood. At the height of the World War III scare in May 1951, a psychiatrist prescribed community service for "atomic jitters." The "knowledge, skill and confidence" cultivated by civil defense offered an antidote to "unrestricted speculation." The associate director of the Institute for Psychosomatic and Psychiatric Research at The Michael Reese Hospital chimed in. Civil defense was indispensable for tiptop mental hygiene. Cobwebby abstractions would be swept away by the fine points of first-aid, rescue, and shelter-taking. The "orderliness and organization" of atomic rehearsal fortified the mind well "beyond the comprehension" of those who are "fascinated by their own nightmarish fantasies."[43]

Other prescriptions for national uplift were spiritual or volitional. Fosdick's "acts of faith" were resurrectional. "In the midst of death," he breathed, "men are vital with life. The preparation for the renewal of life . . . gives sanity and balance to mankind." Bertrand Russell recommended coolness and moderate doses of inattention to the future for those "not compelled by . . . their work to think about military . . . and international affairs." Another counselor advised the restitution of American pluck with a savage collective shake. "Put an end to it!" he roared. First, "we must realize how silly it is and stop running scared . . . Once we stop saying 'Boo!' to each other in the dark, we . . . can get on to manlier things." On the other hand, rather than a militant thrashing, a therapeutically-minded writer for *Christian Century* gently pressed a drooping nation to "face the central fear of our time." Take refuge in one another, he prodded, "person to person, group to group . . . Only the reality of such acceptance and understanding . . . can evoke courage."[44]

The same authors whisked out the most prosaic of consolations. Fosdick cheered the thirty new playgrounds planned for the children of New York City, the astronomers of Mount Palomar who yet peered at the heavens, the scholars at the American School of Classical Studies in Athens who scraped at the ruins of the Agora. For his part, Russell offered the pagan restoratives of "dewy mornings and summer evenings and the sea and the stars . . . love and friendship and music and poetry."[45]

But above all else, there was God. Millions of readers gobbled up *The Power of Positive Thinking* by Norman Vincent Peale. Legislators slipped "under God" into the Pledge of Allegiance and printed "In God We Trust" on postage stamps. While Billy Graham churned up fear and hope, nonevangelical religions were peculiarly elated. A reporter explained the mood. Americans longed "to believe that, despite everything that has happened . . . the world is good, life is good, the human story makes sense and comes out where we want it to come out." Hunger for reassurance could be dated to a surprise hit of 1946, *Peace of Mind,* authored by a young rabbi, which hovered on bestseller lists for 177 weeks. Thereafter, books coaching unmolested serenity with titles such as *The Magic of Believing, Peace of Soul, The Way to Security, Beyond Anxiety, Mind Alive,* and *Guide to Confident Living* perched on countless commuter laps and living room coffee tables. Cashing in on a good thing, Ideal Toy Company manufactured a doll which, when caressed, buckled into a kneeling position.[46]

In pockets of the secular intelligentsia, existentialism enjoyed a vogue. One healthy-minded critic fumed that the so-called "philosophy of the atomic age . . . invites us to wallow in our 'predicament,' with its 'tensions' and its 'anxieties.'" Once humanity had been distinguished by faith and courage, but now "the mark of man is 'fear and trembling.'" While the mass media generally spurned existentialism for currying defeatism, the existential psychotherapy pioneered by Rollo May wrested some sympathy from *Time* magazine. Since "a hydrogen-bomb war could wipe out all life," once-obscure ideas like "Kierkegaard's non-existence and Sartre's nothingness" suddenly percolated into ordinary awareness.[47]

By mid-decade, those Americans who were not inclined to formal religion turned to a science of mind for restoration. It was "the age of neurosis!" sneered an onlooker. "Has there ever been an age so overflowing with neurotic sensibility, with that state of near-shudders, or near-hysteria, or near-nausea, much of it induced by trifles," suffered by a people "at once ill-adjusted and over-civilized?" Newspapers regularly featured self-help articles, personality quizzes, and syndicated columns inviting readers into "The Worry Clinic" and "The Mirror of Your Mind."[48] Ten million pamphlets counseling Americans on *Understanding Yourself, Exploring Your Personality, Growing Up Emotionally, Getting Along with Others, Building Your Marriage,* and *Making the Grade as Dad* littered the lobbies of doctors' offices, clubrooms, and public libraries.

Not only were more and more ordinary people presenting themselves for psychotherapy, but tens of millions swallowed tranquilizers along with their morning coffee. Prescriptions for sedatives tripled between 1955 and 1957. At the time, they were the most immediately successful drugs in American history. Pharmaceutical companies plied physicians with irresistible remedies. For example, a Pfizer brochure touted Atarax's good effects in overcoming "anxiety over interviews or competitive examinations; anxiety over public appearances; . . tension and excitement in noisy environments, among newspaper workers and in the advertising field; . . . anxiety, tension, and excitement among athletes and officials engaging in competitive sports; . . . tension produced by sickness, accidents, weddings, funerals, . . . family separations and differing opinions."[49]

Psychoanalysis appealed to the upper middle class, which entertained "romantically sinister" ideas about the psychoanalyst, as one wag observed, regarding him as "a combination of priest and Pinkerton operative." Freudianism was chic. In 1958 at The Couch in Greenwich Village, New Yorkers could order Psychic Masochist, The Complex, or Dr. Freud cocktails from waiters sporting doctors' smocks. By 1962 psychoanalytic style had become so diffuse that sophisticates felt free to excavate the Oedipal depths of bare acquaintances at dinner parties.[50]

"Is That the Automaton that Smells like the Tear of Grass?"

Just as Billy Graham's crusade laid bare the dread many Americans felt, other feats disclosed anxieties about a technology closely related to the atomic bomb and just as consequential. In 1955 a "John Henry" contest between man and machine was broadcast on television: a Frenchman and a Swedish computer raced to figure out a cube root. Maurice Dagbert beat his rival by eight seconds, and, best of all, the computer botched it. Having won acclaim for humankind, for the next two years Monsieur Dagbert further gratified popular sensibilities (and supported his family) by sight-reading violin music while performing mental computations in variety houses and music halls throughout Europe.[51]

Six years later, at least one computer could piece together evocative verse. R. M. Worthy's Auto-Beatnik machine assembled poems such as:

KITES
Yes, so passionately did my bleak worms live
    underneath the king.
Ah, few sects smell bland.

BASSOONS
Ah, so apologetically did their small rowdies
    cringe beside a tramp.
Beneath a ballad, should a rooster harangue like
    the prostitute?

WHALES
The iron mother's bouquet did rudely call,
Yes, I am as fine as many murmuring crates.
People was braver than snowy hay.
It was dirtiest who bleeds behind the piano.

In 1961 the suitably bearded Mr. Worthy performed these and other automated works at a Los Angeles coffeehouse.[52]

It is hard for us to remember the squirming joy computers elicited in the fifties. In 1954 General Electric introduced a Sperry Rand UNIVAC data processor into a new appliance plant. This was the first commercial use of the new technology. The very fact of digital computers was newsworthy, spawning articles such as "Machines Are This Smart" and "Thinking Machines Take Over!" As late as 1964 someone could write, "Only a [handful] of . . . experts wholly understand the machine; the vast majority of . . . laymen know it mainly as a . . . mysterious twelve-foot refrigerator with blinking lights and whirring tapes."[53]

Computers had originally been marketed to automate payrolls. By 1960 new functions for the machine had arrived: data processing and information storage and retrieval. Futurists immediately leapt to the dream of liberating humankind from stupidity forever. Soon an "information public utility" would offer "a practically unlimited supply of thinking power" to subscribers for time-shared conversation, reference, and information processing. A computer would be able to cross-index "the wisdom of the ages . . . reason without being corrupted by emotion . . . solve more of the world's problems . . . [even] create works of art." As long as humanity could switch it off at will, we need never worry. It was only a matter of time before computers surpassed human ingenuity. "The day cannot be too far off when leading scientific journals will accept papers written by giant brains of the non-human kind."[54]

Inevitably, automation excited fears that computers would replace human beings. After all, here was "a tireless white-collar worker that could inspect, analyze, calculate, keep records, give orders—and not haggle over fringe benefits." Between 1953 and 1960 the evaporation of a million and a half jobs was widely attributed to industrial automation. "Machines Are Taking Over," "Computers Start to Run the Plants," "You Can Be Replaced," hissed the third estate. Anyone browsing through magazines in these years could not fail to stumble across tidings of the automated economy. "When will your husband be obsolete?" demanded *McCall's*. "What will happen to the people now holding the 'doomed' jobs? Just where does your husband's job stand in this changing scene?" Automation's impact on labor swelled into a recognized political problem. President Kennedy declared, "I regard [automation] as the major domestic challenge . . . of the '60s."

New occupations had to be created "to take care of those who are displaced by machines."[55]

Editorialists unraveled the various consequences of data processing and industrial automation. Futurists heralded a utopia where robots and computers dispatched society's dreary jobs, freeing humanity for "learning and teaching, the sciences, arts and letters, the crafts, medicine and its allied works, politics and public service." Others worried that transferring tasks to computers was reckless. "When a machine . . . is capable of operating . . . at a pace . . . we cannot keep," cautioned Norbert Wiener, "we may not know, until too late, when to turn it off." Human oversight was simply too slow. "Whether we like it or not," the geochemist Harrison Brown glumly declared, civilization was yoked to the gadget irrevocably. Not only domestic well-being but survival itself was enmeshed in machine systems. "We have passed a major point-of-no-return."[56]

Experts pondered the ultimate consequence of automated computing: push-button war. In a scant few years, the director of the Jet Propulsion Laboratory predicted, "the decision to destroy an enemy nation . . . will be made by a radar set, a telephone circuit, an electronic computer," without human involvement. Nuclear war touched off by mechanical accident was suddenly a real possibility. He shuddered, "Our very life depends on the . . . reliability of a [computer] in a . . . distant country. The failure of a handful of vacuum tubes and transistors could determine the fate of our civilization."[57]

Computers were not the only villains in the push-button war scenario. "A nervous, psychotic or fanatical launch officer [could] trigger . . . an accidental war almost as easily as a high school boy can smash a revolver cartridge with a hammer," warned Carl Dreher in *The Nation* in 1958. The fantasy of psychotic SAC officers had first been outlined by the Russian Army journal *Red Star* the year before. A piece aimed at Great Britain suggested that an overwrought American based in England could order a bomber to obliterate Moscow. "It is a known fact that there are several million psychologically unbalanced persons in the U.S.," snickered the *Red Star*. "There are some in the army too." Dreher nervously reported that according to one of DuPont's two psychiatrists, in addition to the patients he treated, probably three or four times as many employees *needed* therapy. This amounted to 30 percent of the workforce. He reasoned, "Since DuPont employees are probably representative of employees of large corporations, and these in turn are probably representative of military personnel, the problem of unauthorized use of nuclear weapons and missiles is very real," unless the Pentagon scoured its ranks.[58]

Herman Kahn absorbed all of these concerns. Crowning him the "new civilian militarist," people regarded him as a summarizing symbol of the thermonuclear era. He was a wise counselor to some, not savior but interlocutor, standing on the same ground, glimpsing peril over the horizon. For others, he was a liar and a scoundrel. One woman scrawled to Kahn, "Civil defense is the cruelest deception ever played on any people." It was such "a nonsensical chaos" that it brought "amusement and shame to this country." She continued, arguments justifying *any* scenario of nuclear war were an abomination. "People who say otherwise were plainly suicidal and . . . criminally insane."[59]

An inmate of the Menninger Clinic mocked Kahn's essay "We're Too Scared to Think" in a prank letter. He whispered he had gotten hold of plane tickets to Australia in case nuclear war should break out. Humanity could be salvaged only with the aid of a sperm bank hidden somewhere beyond the reaches of global fallout. Since nuclear war threatened "a crisis in human evolution," the remedy would be to inseminate masses of women outside of the zone of conflict "with the sperm of the most foresighted, vigorous, open-minded and life-desiring males in our population." "The plan is brutal, but"—throwing back Kahn's own words in his "Too Scared to Think" essay—"'unless man does rouse his full mental equipment and masters his technology, he will certainly be in trouble . . . The world may be in danger of annihilation.' No one except *you* has planned honestly enough about nuclear war to know man as a species can survive it. Will you take command of the post-war genetics program?"[60]

The perception that Kahn was an affable psychopath was colored by the proceedings against the Nazi war criminal Adolf Eichmann, whose trial in Jerusalem opened on April 11, 1961. Critics found the equivalence between the two cutting and just. They hurled it at him in town meetings, in debates, in print, and in letters. For example, in a critique of the "fairy-tale simulations" of "the war-simulation gang" in *The Nation,* Hilbert Schenck lumped together "friend Herman Kahn" and "the cool young men of RAND and a hundred other computing centers" as "our Eichmanns-cum-computer."[61]

In a milder vein and privately, the peace education secretary of the American Friends Service Committee also raised parallels between Kahn and Eichmann. Stewart Meacham began by observing that Eichmann's simplicity exasperated the global witnesses to his trial. "If he only had some obvious defect which would separate him from the rest of mankind. But he doesn't." Although proud of having engineered transport into oblivion for millions of Jews, Eichmann also testified that when he once paid a call on a death camp, he was overwhelmed by nausea. "Since he is an ordinary man," Meacham commented, "he reacts to things in an ordinary way." Similarly, the war planners and the compliant citizens who paid for nuclear weapons with their taxes were trapped in the same contradiction. "What are we to say about our present accommodation to the preparations for the slaughter of millions of people in the name of national interest?" Like Eichmann, "none of us could strangle another human being with our bare hands without being sickened by it. But all of us can play numbers games running into the millions with the lives of people."[62]

How did Kahn feel about this? He was nonchalant: "We don't like a person who thinks through a problem in a cool, detached way." But it didn't mean the professional strategist was immoral. "I've been accused of playing an Eichmann-like role in supporting an evil policy. My kind of analysis does make war thinkable, and perhaps I personally over-analyze, but I'd rather err in that direction than the other."[63]

The notoriety of *OTW* branded Kahn as the very personification of the defense intellectual in the modern age. A whiz kid. An eccentric genius. A devil. A bunko artist. It was too much for RAND management. Just as he was being saluted as the ultimate RAND man, its president considered him an inconvenient agitator for civil defense, not a good-will ambassador. Whether he was sacked or he resigned, in 1961 Kahn left California to found his own research organization in New York, the Hudson Institute.

"Herman, Why Do So Many People Regard You as a Monster?"

A writer for the *Village Voice* was bowled over by Kahn's performance. "Listening to him, it was difficult to understand why [he] has been wasting his time on *realpolitikal* research . . . when he would make such a great stand-up comic. Who else can make people laugh about mass annihilation?" People wanted to talk about his personality. What was it about *OTW* that led one woman to began a review by admitting that she had not read it cover to cover? "Frankly, I cannot stomach more than a few chapters of this inhuman document. Nor did I care to look at the end to see how it would turn out, for the only end to what the author proposes is a holocaust too awful to contemplate." Inevitably, friends raced to champion the loveableness of the man who wrote *On Thermonuclear War*. John Strachey of the Institute of Strategic Studies was furious with Kahn's critics. To accuse his colleague of writing a manual of genocide "was sickening." "[He] may be right or wrong, his book may be good or bad, but I, for one, am ready to testify on any witness stand in the world that he is a deeply humane man, permeated by humanist values."[64]

In every profile published in the 1960s, much was made of his jaunty high spirits and irreverence. The oddest thing about Herman Kahn was his gaiety. "This is the jovial man who talks of Doomsday," blazoned the subtitle of "The Real Dr. Strangelove" in the *Daily Mail*. The author was also charmed by the playfulness of Kahn's family, especially his wife. Describing the protesters stumping along in front of their house in New York, she laughed: "They come expecting to see a cold, inhuman monster—and they meet Herman! They have to end up liking him. He knows their arguments better than they do. He knows both sides of the story. He understands why they feel this way, and why they are wrong." When a woman taunted him, "Don't you feel like Hitler or Eichmann?" Kahn's wife fumed, "I could have hit her with a brick, I was so mad. Herman was so nice and so gentle. He never gets upset, never gets annoyed or angry. He doesn't take these things personally . . . There's not a mean bone in his body."[65]

For many observers, the key to the phenomenon of Herman Kahn was that he was conspicuously fat, working-class, Jewish, and from LA. This explained his social location, the gusts and slipstream that yanked and beckoned and smoothed his way. Having determined that he was an unthreatening, pleasant man, journalists dreamed up various droll phrases to describe his appearance. At close to six feet tall and well over three hundred pounds, Kahn was reassuring and somehow comic. He was just "a roly-poly, second-strike Santa Claus," "a thermonuclear Zero Mostel" "with the dimples of Jackie Gleason." One man read working-class style in his unpretentiousness: "a round, jovial scientist who could pass for the owner of a kosher delicatessen." Another emphasized his friendliness, "moonfaced, bespectacled, baldish and graying, effervescent and noddingly agreeable, incorrigibly quick and insanely gregarious, Kahn looks more or less like a retired football tackle, or perhaps a jovial neighborhood grocer." And only an Englishman could drawl archly, "What is he like? If you imagined a Mr. Pickwick who was born in Tel Aviv and gone to the Massachusetts Institute of Technology, that would be near enough . . . He is as clearly fascinated by mega-calories as he is by megatons."[66]

Kahn habitually wore a short-sleeve shirt, disdaining jacket and tie. If pressed, he would grin: "I'm from Southern California. This is my native costume." Always ready to jettison existing realities, he was the consummate futurist, Californian in every particular. Just after being demobilized from the war, his first impulse was to get a real estate license to support himself and his younger brother. Perhaps Kahn's later attachment to civil defense sprang from this Californian sensitivity to real estate. One summer he worked with a structural engineer on the physics of hardening hangars for the Strategic Air Command. The man was Paul Weidlinger, who had designed prefabricated units at the National Housing Agency right after the war. It was but a small step from whizzing past the Quonset hut villages of 1940s LA to assuming that Americans would adapt to underground dormitories and strongholds shuttered by sandbags and protective shielding. All around him neighborhoods were being hoisted and screwed together; houses and apartment buildings were torn down to make way for supermarkets cocooned in acres of parking space. The threadbare boarding house at 1647 Ocean Avenue, former digs of returning sailors and soldiers burning to romance the young men and women traipsing along Santa Monica beach—Tennessee Williams's home in LA—disappears, and up springs RAND on the very spot.[67]

Whole neighborhoods were razed for the expressways of the automobile city. Kahn loved driving his convertible, loved the fluidity of continuous motion; it was like swimming. Coursing through the city in these years must have influenced his notion of the shape and cohesion of the world: it was essentially plastic, provisional, modular. Frances FitzGerald likened Kahn's briefing to a dash along the freeway.

> Herman Kahn begins to speak, slowly at first, and then, as if releasing the brakes on a Mack truck of intellect, faster and faster, until each breath contains a complete paragraph. Trying to understand him is like trying to drive through Los Angeles at rush hour when the cars hurtle bumper-to-bumper along expressways . . . at 70 mph . . Though Kahn must have been small as a baby, he has grown to resemble his adopted Los Angeles, that giant amoeboid city which seems to have no natural boundaries, no structural limits . . . When he speaks, he expresses the junction of three or more mental highways; his sentences ramify into subjunctives and conditionals, which, in their crossing and recrossing over the whole landscape of an issue, form a pattern of cloverleafs.[68]

Kahn nodded with satisfaction. "I'm big, fat and lousy Jewish, and they take it. They take it because they know I'm worried about the country. They take a lot of crap from me which they wouldn't from anyone else. And I'll tell you this: I couldn't happen in any other country." Maybe he couldn't have flourished in any city other than Los Angeles.[69]

His briefings *were* remarkable. They were a marathon, taking three days to deliver. Standing before an audience was meat and drink to Kahn. He'd become so engrossed that he'd plant himself in front of the screen, so that his briefing slides shined on his face and belly. "When he . . . stalks in front of the two screens in a semi-darkened room, words flash across his shirt and broad forehead, escalating Kahn into a self-contained mixed-media display." He had stuttered as a child and still slurred and swallowed his words on the gallop. He abandoned sentences in mid-stream as he scrambled from one idea to the next. He was also a gleeful teller of bad jokes. One man gaped in amazement, "No other strategist could get . . . sane people to laugh at such lines as 'Of course, the system might blow up in the meantime; there's no point in glossing it over.'"[70]

This wasn't a gimmick. Kahn couldn't resist the jokes. "I was trying to shake things up. I wasn't trying to shock, but I did state things provocatively, and sometimes humorously." Whatever profession he might have chosen, he would have poked fun at it. But toying with nuclear war disturbed some of his listeners, while others, once indignant, were gradually disarmed. "In a flash, Herman was off and blubbering, gibbering, snorting, laughing, and the audience sat startled and somewhat embarrassed . . . Within hours they were over the shock; in another day, they were Herman's."[71]

Kahn was deliberately frank, absurd, and horrific: "If 180 million dead is too high a price to pay for punishing the Soviets for their aggression, what price would we be willing to pay?" "How dangerous or hostile a world would we be willing to live in and still call it a reasonable facsimile of a Russian or American standard of living?" "Neutrals and bystanders will inevitably suffer heavily in any thermonuclear war. But there is a difference between damage and annihilation." "I think that any individual who survived . . . should be willing to accept, almost with equanimity, somewhat larger risks than those to which we subject our industrial workers in peacetime."[72]

Kahn's most notorious idea, the Doomsday Machine, was a critique of massive retaliation: "Assume that for, say, $10 billion we could build a device whose only function is to destroy all human life . . . If, say, five nuclear bombs exploded over the United States, the device would be triggered and the earth destroyed. Barring . . . coding errors, [it] would seem to be the 'ideal' . . . deterrent." While he labored to explain why it was unacceptable, Stanley Kubrick excerpted passages about the Doomsday Machine from *OTW* and presented it as an actual weapon in his film *Dr. Strangelove*.[73]

From the debut of Kubrick's film in January 1964, and for the rest of his career, Kahn was inevitably called the *real* Dr. Strangelove. "The gossip . . . going around tells us that Dr. Strangelove . . . is based on Dr. Herman Kahn," bristled an article protesting his good nature and humanity. Journalists in media both high and low found the conceit of Kahn-as-Strangelove to be an effortless lure. The august London *Times* hailed Kahn as "the prototype of Dr. Strangelove," while the *Daily Mail* twittered, "No more jovial man ever stood and talked of the world's balance of terror, of gigantic war, of Doomsday. This is the real-life prototype of Dr. Strangelove." Even Kahn's father's indignant squawk, "How could my son be Dr. Strangelove? He is so warm and considerate," was pulled into a banner caption in a *Life* profile.[74]

Reporters quizzed him about Kubrick's film. "Kubrick is a friend of mine," Kahn assured *Newsweek*. "He told me Dr. Strangelove wasn't supposed to be me." As to being the sinister Dr. Groteschele in *Fail-Safe*, he chirped, "I didn't see the movie and . . . just skimmed the book, but my wife said if the character people say was me weighed more than 220 pounds, she'd sue."[75]

In her review of *Dr. Strangelove*, Midge Decter seized on the affinities between *OTW* and Kubrick's film. Just as Kubrick presented a travesty of massive retaliation, do did Kahn. "For those who know how to read him . . . [Kahn] never fails to imagine all the possibilities for chaos in the positions he offers." He was not particularly aggrieved that distortions of his ideas popped up in *Dr. Strangelove* and *Fail-Safe*. On the contrary. One might have supposed that Kahn would have insisted on distinguishing scientific study from imaginary events. But narratives of future or hypothetical war were essential to grand strategy. Analysts at the Hudson Institute pored over novels such as George's *Red Alert* "to stimulate [their] reason and imagination to cope with history before it happens."[76]

He may have wisecracked and frolicked with his audiences, but Kahn refused to soften his arguments with effusions of pity or sorrow. He freely and cheerfully admitted to all who asked, "It does indeed take an iron will or an unpleasant degree of detachment to go about this task." As a result, in print and in person he was regularly accused of perversity and criminal brutality, if not worse. In turn, he justified his *sang froid* as the comportment proper to a scientist, military expert, and policy analyst. Following the publication of James Newman's scathing and widely discussed review of *OTW* in *Scientific American,* Kahn tried unsuccessfully to persuade its editor to print a rejoinder. Failing that, he elaborated his response over the course of 1961, and in 1962 came out with his second book, *Thinking about the Unthinkable.*[77]

In the book's opening chapter, Kahn compared the self-command of a physician with the nuclear expert. Empathic squeamishness during critical procedures was unseemly. He advised his readers not to trouble a surgeon with photos of his patient's wife and kids. Nor should medical textbooks include reminders, however true, such as "a particularly deplorable tumor," "and now there's a lot of blood," "good health is preferable to this kind of cancer," and "this particular cut really hurts." It was just as ridiculous to demand that strategists hiccup "If, heaven forbid" before they got on with their business.[78]

Defying wave after wave of charges of heartlessness, he would parry with the question, "Would you prefer a warm, human error? . . . a nice emotional mistake?" Political and military affairs could not be hobbled at every turn by the genuflections of the anguished. He protested that nothing would ever become clear if "we are going to label every attempt at detachment as callous, every attempt at objectivity as immoral." Rather than evade the various ways in which war could begin—touched off by accident, unauthorized launch, or miscalculated brinkmanship—it was ultimately more high-minded to ponder them unhurriedly.

Shifting to a less elevated posture, Kahn defended his "normal, neutral, professional, everyday language" against those who insisted that nuclear war be invested with "awe and horror." Awe was too reverential for fruitful analysis. "One cannot do research in a cathedral," he'd often say. "But let me be frank," he sighed, "I prefer to use my normal style of speaking." It would be one thing to guard his tongue for a day or two. "However, I spend full time in this field. It would be too much for me to be artificially solemn all the time."[79]

While Kahn was probably the only nuclear strategist who might have made a go of stand-up comedy, flippant asides peppered many briefings at RAND. During critiquing sessions, in memoranda and corporate communications, and even formal documents people joked about nuclear war, often using Kahn's material. For example, a visiting reporter was given a RAND pamphlet that included the following: "Three fellows are sitting around a table playing pinochle in what is obviously an underground shelter. There is suddenly a terrific shaking. One of the fellows gets up to look at a meter. The other asks, 'How much was it?' The first says, 'About 100 megatons.' The second says, 'I can always tell by the shaking.' Finally the third one says with a great deal of irritation, 'Write it down on the morning report, and sit down and deal.'"[80]

"Thermonuclear war is not a joke," Kahn maintained, "but professional or serious discussion . . . can include humor, at least in Europe and the United States." With the publication of *OTW*, Americans were exposed to the substance and style of professional discussions of war—including the jokes. For the first time, the attitudes of the nation's community of strategists, cultivated in restricted summer studies and the secure briefing rooms at RAND, were exhibited in town meetings, debates, mass publications, television shows, and radio broadcasts. A woman wrote to *The Progressive* to object that in a speech Kahn had snapped, "It is possible, isn't it, that parents will learn to love two-headed children twice as much?" She sniffed, "He is very detached and ironic in discussing twenty to sixty million deaths in nuclear war." Kahn regarded frivolity as a permissible approach to intolerably catastrophic ideas, as did his admirers who, in one way or another, believed it "probably help[ed] both him and his listeners to cope with the terrifying images of his chosen subject."[81]

Kahn's bearing resembled the gallows humor of "sick" comedians such as Mort Sahl, Lenny Bruce, and Jules Feiffer. A thoughtful commentary on their appeal in 1961 suggested that "the sick comedian offers his listener a chance to act as if he had not been shaken, to demonstrate that he is . . . the Good American, because in the face of no matter what madness . . . he 'still is able to laugh' . . . To snicker . . . is to climb out from under the pressure of the inexplicable and the unbearable."[82] Kahn undoubtedly played up the affinities between sick comedy's insouciance and his personal style. In the Afterword to *Thinking about the Unthinkable* he narrated his response to James Newman. (To get the jokes, you should know that Newman wrote *The World of Mathematics*.)

My first reply to Newman's question [Does Herman Kahn exist?] was to gain 10 pounds. This may not seem . . . adequate . . . but it is in many ways appropriate. Actually, when I first read the review I started to laugh because I found it difficult to take seriously. I was startled by the sheer passion of the language. On a second reading I became rather angry. When I got home, I showed it to my wife, who read it and started to laugh . . . After the review appeared I was on a national television program debating the after-effects of thermonuclear war. I decided to ask my opponent, who was a personal friend, to ask me for a comment on the Newman affair. I . . . intended to tell the story I will tell in a moment.

I first checked the . . . good taste of doing this with the producer and some others. They were delighted with the idea. I then called my wife and happened to mention my plan. She became rather excited and said, "The audience will misunderstand." I assured her that this was hardly possible. They might think the "joke" was flat or out of place, but they would not take it seriously. She said that if I was stupid enough to do this thing I shouldn't come home. I replied that I could not be pressured—that this was a matter of integrity. She said, "Remember, I get the children." I said, "You know, this is an illegitimate use of pressure." She said, "*You* get the children." I collapsed and agreed not to tell the story. But now, after long frustration, I have decided to go ahead and tell it:

I was going to describe a solemn ceremony we have at our house. Every evening, after dinner is over, the dishes put away, the children dressed and made ready for bed, and just before the bedtime story, I go to the book case, pull down a volume of Newman's *World of Mathematics,* tear out a page and give it to my seven-year-old girl, Deborah. She takes it to the sink and my wife lights a match. Deborah takes the match and burns the page. While the page is burning, my three-year-old son David, sticks pins in a doll.

We feel that the family that prays together stays together.[83]

One expects him to murmur "But seriously folks . . ." to close the bit, it so much mimics a nightclub *spiel.* Intensely appealing and disturbing in equal measure, Herman Kahn had to be seen and heard if one hoped to fathom his significance and his celebrity in 1961.

Chapter 2

THE COLD WAR AVANT-GARDE AT RAND

*When I now think about RAND, I think about a group of
people who were very peculiar in the sense that they lived
in a world in which you could talk about future in the
plural—there'd be "futures" you could choose from.*

HANS SPEIER, 1988

Star-hopping the recent past, how shall we make out the faint glimmer of RAND in the 1950s? What will orient us? Perhaps the flaring quarrel between civilian scientists and the uniformed services over whose authority was more critical to modern warfare. Which was indispensable—old-fashioned charismatic leadership or the inspired use of mathematic models? Looking back to the techniques he masterminded during World War II, P. M. S. Blackett boasted, "In most of the important cases with which I had personal contact, the really vital problems were found by the operational research groups themselves rather than given to them to solve by the Service . . . staffs." His boss at the British Admiralty agreed that Blackett's crew was wonderfully cunning. The Operations Research Section "proved beyond doubt that the scientifically trained, analytical mind, applied to any problem, could produce invaluable results . . . They frequently surprised me by telling us not only what we did not know, but what otherwise I should never have realized was something we *ought* to know."[1]

But Blackett's smugness was intolerable to the services. Even in an age of wizards' war, martial prowess still presided over the military, however scientifically enhanced it might be. Sir John Slessor protested that the instruments of war didn't win battles; human valor did. "Leadership, morale, courage and skill" could never be stripped down to bare equations.[2]

Operations research, the brainchild conceived in the war years by the young men in the Office of Scientific Research and Development (OSRD), evolved in the 1950s into the speculative fabrications of systems analysis. RAND was its nursery. It was at RAND that the civilian defense intellectual who specialized in systems analysis took form. Within a decade, he wrestled with the military in a furious struggle for dominance. By 1961 the civilians assumed senior posts in the Kennedy administration, and the new secretary of defense, Robert McNamara, enlisted RAND men to brace up the Pentagon's authority over the armed forces. He believed that systems analysis introduced scientific rationality into defense planning, budgeting, and resource allocation.[3]

Once former RAND analysts acquired real political power, relations between the air force and the civilian analysts worsened. Senior officers bitterly resented the RAND youngsters. They thought they were presumptuous and laughably callow. After a briefing from Harold Brown, the 34-year-old director of defense research and development, General Curtis LeMay, who by this time had been promoted to air force assistant chief of staff, burst out, "Why, that son of a bitch was in *junior high school* while I was out bombing Japan!" Retired General Thomas White groaned that under the new regime professional officers would "have to fight under the plans and orders and with the weapons . . . [developed] under the influence of those, often far junior in age and experience, who come into Government, for a few years at most, from colleges and foundations."[4]

You might call this generational strife or a turf war over defense allocations. But its crux was the cocky boast that systems analysis was more insightful than first-hand knowledge. During McNamara's tenure, the authority on which defense policy and strategy were based migrated from the experience of veteran combat officers to the civilian analysts' techniques for simulating combat. This was new and frankly audacious. Throughout the 1950s, RAND analysts insisted that in order to approach nuclear war properly, one had to become a perfect amnesiac, stripped of the intuitions, judgments, and habits cultivated over a lifetime of active duty. So, for example, in 1955 Kahn bragged that the successes of operations research in World War II proved the greater effectiveness of mathematics over time-honored tactics. Systems analysis was unquestionably superior, in his view, despite the common belief that "'experience' has been a better guide than 'theory' in this kind of work."[5]

People at RAND maintained that long familiarity with obsolete or non-atomic weapons systems retarded the military's adaptation to the dynamic threat of the cold war. Kahn pressed home the point. "A civilian analyst is sometimes in a better 'psychological' position than the professional military officer in approaching new long range problems." The RAND economist who became assistant secretary of defense (comptroller), Charlie Hitch, gloated that in decisions regarding weapons systems development such as choosing between long-range bombers with big fuel tanks or short-range bombers with refueling capabilities, "no one can . . . answer by instinct, by feeling his pulse, by drawing on experience." His boys offered a better way. "This is the sort of thing an intellectual, by virtue of his training and his mental disciplines, can do better than a military professional who is not an intellectual."[6]

The uniformed military seethed. General White let it be known that he was "profoundly apprehensive of the pipe-smoking, tree-full-of-owls type of so-called professional 'defense intellectuals' who have been brought into this nation's capital." Their referents for combat were theoretical constructs, not blood and guts. They approached war as if it "could be settled on a chessboard in an ivy-covered Great Hall." It simply wasn't right that the commander who executed the airy notions of untried civilians did not "qualify . . . for a larger role in our strategy-making than he appears to have today."[7]

Atomic weapons inaugurated a colossal shift in authority. They swallowed up the personal wisdom of senior officers rooted in combat experience in favor of intuitions arising from repeated trials of laboratory-staged simulations of future war. When officers objected that Kahn was ill-equipped to speak on military affairs, he'd shoot back, "How many thermonuclear wars have *you* fought recently?" Aside from war games, they admitted, they had no actual experience with these weapons. "OK," Kahn would grin, "then we start out even." While the antagonism between civilian experts and senior officers was openly played out in the Kennedy administration, the real stage for the ascendancy of simulation was RAND.[8]

The Age of Technological Marvels

So what happened in the space of a decade to sweep away the undisputed merits of real life in favor of mastery of simulation techniques? The Hiroshima and Nagasaki atomic strikes of August 1945 meant not only the end of the Pacific war but the beginning of something new. The A-bomb begot a world that could be desolated by city-busting terror weapons, a world where war of unimaginable dimensions could erupt again without warning.

This possibility was dramatized in a lurid cartoon published in *Life* just three months after the Japanese surrender in 1945. It portrayed American cities pounded by atomic rockets guided by radio and radar. The first panel showed an aerial view of metropolitan Washington, D.C. In the foreground an enemy rocket smites the image in two, and behind it an atomic burst obliterates much of the capitol building. In another panel, shrouded men survey the radioactive rubble of a wasteland made recognizable by the remnants of landmark marble lions near the pulverized remains of the New York Public Library. Vaporizing cities "even before surface forces can be deployed," *Life* explained, "the enemy's purpose is . . . to paralyze the US by destroying its people." It would be next to impossible to defend against atomic rockets. Local anti-aircraft batteries would miss some of their targets; and in any case, rockets cut short the defender's response time. While radar offered some warning, "even 30 minutes is too little time for men to control the weapons of an atomic war." Some of the enemy rockets would get through.[9]

What are we to make of this hair-raising tale, absorbed by millions of Americans just weeks after V-J day, as they lounged in barber-shops, diners, college dormitories, shoeshine stands, dentists' waiting rooms, hotel lobbies, factory cafeterias, boarding houses, and sitting rooms? How did it strike the demobilized soldiers crowding every train, plane, ship, and bus? While the enemy blasting the White House and the New York Public Library was unnamed, the point was unmistakable. Rockets collapsed space and time. Even though the war was over, ordinary life could be ripped apart again at any moment. Surprise attack from the air would always be possible, uncoupled from any specific crisis. Nearly everyone—philosophers, scientists, professional strategists, and politicians—agreed that the present world had irrevocably changed and the future itself had been altered. Fear of unprovoked attack literally became a free-floating anxiety.

Reporting on guided missile research in September 1947, Joseph and Stewart Alsop traced America's wariness back to "the Pandora's box" of wartime science. "It is too easy to pretend that the old normal world has revived again. But it has not," they wrote portentously. "A world in which men have . . . weapons of total destruction—the atomic bomb, the radioactive cloud, the dread inventions of chemistry and biology—can never return to its former . . . state." The shock of recent invention was invoked repeatedly throughout the decade. The idea had become so elemental to the conventions of the cold war that by 1958 it could be compressed into the thrilling exhalations of comic book art. The editors of *Atom-Age Combat* breathlessly marveled at the realization of a science-fiction world served by legions of invincible gadgets. "How amazingly powerful and fantastically ingenious our country's atomic defenses are! No matter how fantastic the weapons . . . [appearing in] the following pages appear to be, they are authentic or based on fact! Some already in use . . . Others in their final stages of development! This is the atom age! The unbelievable has already begun to come true!"[10]

Even before the Pacific war staggered to a close, futuristic technologies preoccupied the commander of the army air force, General Henry Arnold. His scientists itched to return to industry and academe. The fear and esprit that had prompted their exertions would no longer inspire them to continue military research in peacetime. Some other enticement would have to be found. Arnold needed to persuade them that the very momentum which carried them through the last stages of the war—the exhilaration of working on avant-garde technologies and ideas—could be enjoyed in peacetime. He planned to tantalize them with the novelty of an absolutely unrestricted charter to plot the future. In fact, unhurried exploration would become the very appeal of Project RAND. Whereas during the war the scientific researchers were "just snowed by immediate emergencies all the time," John Williams recalled, Project RAND offered "an absolutely blue sky contract under which we could do anything that seemed sensible to do."[11]

General Arnold expected future wars to be fought with missiles: "The future Air Force need not . . . have one single [man] in any of its aircraft."[12] The peacetime air force would therefore have to elevate scientists and engineers to an equal footing with the pilot-commanders who had flown the bombers during the war. He believed an air force saddled with lopsided clods who couldn't fly but could design speedy planes was *better* than one governed by pilots only. In order to goad his popeyed officers into adopting a properly deferential regard for his civilian talent, in December 1945 Arnold promoted General LeMay to deputy chief of staff for R&D. LeMay's airmen had scorched Japan in the last months of the war. They firebombed Tokyo and obliterated Hiroshima and Nagasaki. Advancing an unflinching brute like LeMay to the highest possible authority demonstrated Arnold's political shrewdness and underscored his science-based ambitions for the peacetime air force.

The contract for Project RAND stipulated that its employees would carry out "scientific study and research on the broad subject of air warfare with the object of recommending to the Air Forces preferred methods, techniques and instrumentalities." LeMay endorsed RAND's independence. At the close of the contract negotiations, Frank Collbohm, a senior engineer at Douglas Aircraft and one of the founders of RAND, remembered LeMay booming that "the air force is supporting this project because it wants unbiased advice, and in order to be unbiased, he says, 'No one in the air force anywhere is to tell RAND what to do or what not to do. We want them to figure it out.' He made that stick."[13]

Project RAND (acronym for Research ANd Development) was founded in the spring of 1946. Located in a wing of the Douglas plant, RAND was constituted as a fully autonomous research organization under exclusive contract to the air force. In 1947 RAND moved into its own building in Santa Monica, and a year later it established itself as a nonprofit advisory corporation.

Collbohm was appointed RAND's president. John Williams was the first person he hired. Williams had directed the statistical research group in OSRD's Applied Mathematics Panel (AMP). After the strain of war, Williams luxuriated in the opportunity to reflect on the immediate situation. "I had an office in which I could sit and think; generally speaking, nobody would interrupt me . . . from morning to night. I was largely left alone." Now that he had some free time, he mulled over the snags in the AMP's work. "I was having trouble articulating some things I thought I knew." Williams had recruited some of his team to RAND but had concluded that the future ranged well beyond applied mathematics. "It seemed to me that we needed just about every facet of human knowledge to apply to problems . . . we were about to face, and therefore . . . we should staff RAND . . . with that perception." Economics, political science, psychology, every kind of social science would be needed to dream the future for the air force. He advised Collbohm, "In organizing a group, one should have no illusion that pertinent fields of inquiry can . . . be elided from the study, simply because they are difficult to include."[14]

Some weeks later Williams found himself closeted with LeMay. For more than an hour Williams pitched his ideas about RAND. "I said . . . [we needed] every skill known to man, because the problems were too difficult for just us chickens . . . LeMay chewed to death three or four cigars . . . He just stared at me." At length, the general growled that he had a pittance to spend on RAND. What he needed were weapons and aircraft that could be used in the next war, right away if necessary. Williams shot back that the air force had to choose between having "five weapons on the shelf and no well-understood notions about what to do with them" or acquiring fewer systems with practiced strategy and tactics. The general murmured, "Go ahead." The young man jumped to bind him to a promise: "It seems to me you're saying: 'Go ahead, RAND. Study what you think you have to study. Get the kind of people you think you have to get. Pay what you think you have to pay to get them. But remember, we're not made of money; we're poor, so be a little careful and circumspect about it.'" LeMay frowned, "No, God damn it. Spend what you have to spend. And do it *right*." Giddy, Williams bounded back to Santa Monica. From now on, the science of war would include everybody and anybody.[15]

Collbohm was not happy. Being acutely attuned to the air force's culture, needs, and attitudes, he only reluctantly accepted an interdisciplinary model for RAND studies. "He had an absolute conviction that we should work for only one master and that should be the Air Force . . . If you have one master and do a good job for him, he'll protect you. And you can still have intellectual freedom," a colleague recalled. But Williams pushed for absolute exemption from superintendence. He would insist, "We're not competent enough to judge whether [another specialist's] work is competent or not." The study of future war demanded the richest possible mix of expertise, the most expansive field of view. He would say, "What we do is . . . hire the brightest people we can and we leave them alone. We dare not interfere with them."[16]

From its founding to the end of the 1950s, analysts at RAND were generally free from air force oversight. A glass door quarantined the physics department, and only Q security clearance gained entry "behind the glass curtain." But apart from the physics enclave, people likened RAND's research culture to the frank, stimulating atmosphere of a "university without students." In these years, the breadth of possible topics and methods was reverentially, emphatically, and agreeably indefinite. When the economist Sidney Winter, Jr., was hired, his division boss walked him around and suggested offhandedly, "Why don't you talk to a bunch of people here, and ask them what they're doing and read some things and maybe in a couple of months we'll have another discussion about what you're doing." Everyone was expected to generate his own projects and join those of others. "Nobody decided what anybody was doing. It was all a question of individual initiative."[17]

Herman Kahn loved being a part of RAND. He relished the feeling that creative work could be done without the drag of corporate or discipline-based parochialism. He coaxed his friend, the physicist Albert Latter, to seek employment as soon as he completed his Ph.D. "He made it sound exciting," Latter reflected. "The notion of working on problems that might have some bearing on the national security. At the university I was used to working on problems that didn't seem to be very consequential."[18]

Virtually everyone who worked at RAND in these years described it as an inspired moment in their careers. For example, a visitor wrote in 1947, "I have been at RAND for three exciting days and I would like to become part of it. Right now RAND is part solid, part liquid, and part gas." The sociologist Hans Speier recalled, "I had the feeling these are persons with imagination, these are persons who are dedicated to their work, and they are doing important work." The mathematician Olaf Helmer rejoiced in his colleagues' geniality. "If you walked along the corridors . . . you found that most of the doors were open, and you felt free . . . to walk into any [office] . . . and say, 'I have a problem here. This is of interest to you. Would you like to work on this too or do you have any input to provide?'" People were often enticed into areas in which they had no special training. The engineer Bruno Augenstein commented, "Ideas were . . . floating in the atmosphere—and they were people that you could bounce ideas off and get a reaction which you could always use." Everyone gloried in new ideas. He chuckled, "They were not unwilling to give opinions . . . even in fields . . . they were not experts in."[19]

RAND was the nation's first postwar think tank. Shortly after the Korean War began in 1950, an enterprising *Fortune* journalist, John McDonald, requested permission to visit. The debut of RAND in a public medium was overdue. In the years of its anonymity, rumors had circulated about such clandestine activities as "the secret of the flying saucers, man-made satellites encircling the earth in interstellar space, and experimental trips to the moon." In "The War of Wits," McDonald observed that RAND had "become a kind of secular monastery—worldly in rubbing shoulders with the physical and social sciences, industry, and the military . . . yet monastic in its security isolation."[20]

McDonald's article in *Fortune* may well have exposed businessmen to the concept of systems analysis for the first time. He described how RAND's vision of military R&D had widened its focus from the usual scramble for a marvelous widget to an investigation of the totality of warfare to which any one mechanism contributed. His précis of the interdependencies of weapons design, tactics, and hypothetical scenarios was nicely concise. "For any given sum of money and any particular division of this money, and for any particular choice of design characteristics of the weapon, an imaginary war is 'fought' and the damage to targets is computed according to the payoff chosen for the study."[21]

Pleased with *Fortune*'s profile, RAND's administrators set up an office of public relations. Among its first projects was a system of deposit libraries in the United States, Canada, and Western Europe established to circulate the corporation's unclassified documents. In 1955 RAND launched an ad campaign in *Scientific American, Foreign Affairs,* university magazines, and trade journals. From February 1957 through January 1962 *Scientific American* ran full-page ads almost every month. Rather than beckoning recruits directly, the first six ads displayed a close-up photograph of a department head underscored by a solemn dictum about science. For example, the May 1957 issue featured a physicist wreathed with the words "on science and impossibility." The copy expressed RAND's conceit of facilitating advanced work at the cosmic margins. It read, in part, "We can easily imagine physical nonsense . . . Within the limits defined by the impossibilities, there is plenty of room for man's inventiveness to operate. In fact, the game is even more challenging that way."[22]

Another ad was a close-up of Collbohm, his grizzled face up-

turned into a beam of light, mouth pursed, eyes and brow indomitable. Here was the resolute engineer-administrator prepared to super-
vise the exacting and interminable schedule of cold war R&D.
However understated, he flaunted the promise of creative work in
the atomic era. "Uniting the diverse skills of many specialists . . . is
probably the most successful means of discovering realistic, timely,
and original solutions to important problems." The campaign then
tacked into a series of hand-drawn cameos. Beginning with a pen
and ink sketch of Ernst Mach, the next fifty-four ads paraded notable men in the history of mathematics, science, philosophy, and sociology, coupled with the suggestion that RAND heralded the next
step in the cavalcade of great ideas. Clearly, the intent was to en-
twine the corporation with the benefactors of Western scientific civilization.[23]

While RAND fashioned itself after a university rather than an industrial R&D laboratory, it also emanated a self-consciously avant-
garde sensibility at some distance from the sedate chimes of the
Scientific American campaign. Cool jazz could be heard outside somebody's office late at night. Beards sprouted here and there, and pipe-
tobacco was everywhere. More than one man was undergoing psychoanalysis, and at least one was an open homosexual. While one
group of young men performed experiments with digital computers,
another group tallied how many Soviet rubles would be available for
reconstruction after an atomic war. RAND's whiz kids fiddled with
war games, radars, nuclear-powered jet engines, earth-circling satellites, lunar probes. They were all young, the junior officers of World
War II. The culture was breezily informal. There was no dress code
and no established working hours. There were ping-pong tables,
Kriegspiel tourneys, and a putting green. Lunch was eaten outside
under patio umbrellas.[24]

A 1959 photo-essay in *Life* illustrates the sense that the young
men at RAND labored at the cusp of technological marvels. Called
"Valuable Batch of Brains," it presented to America "the first look
ever taken at RAND scientists deep in thought about the nation's security." In all of the images, people are doing something iconically

scientific: a young man in glasses, bowtie, and suspenders squints at the wingspan of a model airplane; two men bicker near a diagram-scored blackboard; a woman pores over *Pravda;* a man writes at his desk; two men steady a model rocket; a man at the beach jiggles "a lunar radio transmitter" stuck into the sand; two men clamber up the pilings of an off-shore oil rig "to see if it could be used as launching platform for missiles"; others shuffle markers in a war game; and steepling his fingers at the tip of his nose, a tousled Kahn chews over "a complicated problem involving defense against atomic attack." The last photo is a group portrait of the new generation of defense intellectuals: a clutch of young men in suits sprawl on the floor of someone's private study. There are prominent visual cues that this is the *mise en scene* for the modern intellectual: along with futuristic chairs and a Japanese paper kite dangling from the ceiling, the image highlights the conspicuous informality of lolling on the floor while debating the life and death of the nation.[25]

While not all of the articles about RAND published in the 1950s exploited popular ideas of scientists as zestfully as *Life,* nevertheless with its futurism, its daily employment of still-impressive computers, its experiments in simulation and gaming, and above all the curious fact that it "manufactures nothing but ideas," RAND was hailed in virtually all public reports as a harbinger of the new world.[26]

Backlash

On August 14, 1958, Richard Russell, the chairman of the Senate Armed Services Committee, proposed a perverse amendment to a supplemental appropriations bill. That morning he had heard on the radio that somebody in the Department of Defense had contracted to study the circumstances under which the United States government might surrender to its enemies in the event of war. What had actually been reported was the publication of a book written by RAND analyst Paul Kecskemeti. He had examined the surrenders in World War II of the French, Italians, Germans, and Japanese. No part of it posed scenarios for a third world war.

Senator Russell admitted he had not read the book, nor had he pursued the matter with anyone at the Pentagon. Nevertheless, he was eager to pass a law forbidding such work in the future. "In this jittery age," he thundered into the well of the Senate chamber, "in no circumstances and in no conditions will . . . [Congress] appropriate one dime of funds" to research that "contemplates the surrender of this country to those who would destroy us!" He thereby touched off a debate about a book nobody had seen. It deflected Congress into a daylong skid, lasting most of the night and much of the following day. Eisenhower shrank from the whole affair, scowling to reporters that hypothetical surrender didn't interest him and that he considered the matter "too ridiculous for any further comment." Ridiculous or not, both the House and the Senate passed the amendment.[27]

Egged on by a petulant military, public uneasiness about the prominence of the civilian defense intellectuals quickened. Even Eisenhower objected to the extension of their authority into political affairs. In his farewell address to the nation in 1961, he denounced the rise of a "military-industrial complex," coining a phrase that quickly passed into common usage. His remarks about the shifting footing between science and the republic are less well known. While academic research was ever more dependent on federal grants, he underlined the second effect, that matters essential to democratic governance were increasingly delegated to technocrats. "We must . . . be alert to the . . . danger that public policy could itself become the captive of a *scientific-technological elite*."[28]

Eisenhower had opened the question. During the next year the Bureau of the Budget and Congress conducted several probes into the pay scale and cost-fixing procedures of nonprofit advisory corporations such as RAND, the Stanford Research Institute, MITRE, and other military-sponsored "think factories." Both the House Space Committee and the Military Operations Subcommittee of the House Government Operations Committee held hearings on the subject. Tidbits snatched from these hearings prompted a stream of articles dissecting the phenomenon of "civilian defense intellectuals."[29]

By 1963 respectful awe for the defense intellectuals associated with the Kennedy administration had slackened. The former chairman of the Atomic Energy Commission, David Lilienthal, furiously pointed out that the systems analysts elevated to senior political offices lacked accountability to any political body. They were "virtually immune" from the public oversight that safeguarded democracy. Not only were the analysts shielded from scrutiny, their vaunted scientific expertise was greatly exaggerated. Lilienthal objected that while systems analysis could resolve technical problems beautifully, it was dreadfully "ill-adapted" to political and social affairs. McNamara's experts had strayed into fields outside of their specialities "with a cocksure confidence that they can find answers—out of their scientific or technical knowledge or intuition—to what cannot be finally and firmly answered at all: the unimaginable complex and shifting *human* problems involved in the threat of nuclear warfare." Kahn's improbable scenarios were especially irresponsible: "How such a technique stimulates the imagination *usefully* I have difficulty in comprehending." Social, political, and technological forecasting was equally fatuous. "How much farther methodologists can wander from the reality of human life than this concept of organized 'expert intuition' I would not care to predict."[30]

Lilienthal's disdain for the speculative breadth of systems analysis marked the faultlines between critics of RAND's futurological mission and its supporters. The passage from the present to the infinite possibilities of the future meant substituting speculative scenarios for combat experience. For every analyst at RAND, the heart and soul of future planning rested in the invention of ways to assign substantive content in the place of the uncertainties of future events. Kahn wrote, "An . . . effort to supplement our . . . analysis with ersatz experience . . . can be most rewarding. In some ways the unrealized and unexperienced, but historically plausible, problems of World Wars III and IV are more valuable than the experienced problems of World Wars I and II." For the corps of analysts at RAND, this was a legitimate application of scientifically disciplined rationality to the indeterminate frontiers of all possible futures.[31]

Even Frank Collbohm, RAND's stolid founder, entertained the dream of all possible futures. In a 1957 address he defined "the real problem" in the cold war as not so much a matter of working out how "to prevent ourselves from being destroyed in some specific manner, but from being destroyed in any way whatsoever. We must therefore consider *all* the possible ways in which an intelligent and determined enemy can attack us."[32]

In 1961 RAND's hometown paper, *The Los Angeles Times,* cooed that the think tank "is the treasure of the new era, the abstract jewels of men's minds, the unleashed thoughts, the soaring, science-spurred image upon which the future floats." For the moment, at least, the future was enfolded in the milky floss of Science, a science as blurred and luminous as spindrift, as alluring and as weightless.[33]

Chapter 3

THE REAL DR. STRANGELOVE

If I were President or Premier, I would appoint him civil-ian overlord in time of war and ideal Santa Claus in time of peace.

STANLEY BURCH, 1965

Herman Kahn always enjoyed himself. He loved nothing better than settling in for a long desultory chat. His pleasure in swatting ideas back and forth was infectious. He was a gadabout, wandering the hallways at RAND, poking his nose in here and there, shambling back into his office an hour later with an armful of papers, two or three ideas for additional studies, and a new joke. "He had a tremendous sense of fun," said one of his collaborators, Max Singer. "In some ways it was a continual frustration at Hudson, because he wanted to talk about something and he would always get diverted onto something else. Not only fun in the sense of 'Ha ha' but in the sense of interesting, amusing." His playfulness was enormously attractive. People wanted to be around him, not only to share his pleasure in work but also because he was witty and fearless. Everyone had a funny Herman Kahn story. "He was irrepressible," observed another friend from RAND, Henry Rowen. "It was just his nature. He just couldn't help it. It was just his bubbling up."[1]

Kahn had been poor as a child, the middle son of immigrants, enraptured with science and science fiction, ebullient and headstrong. He was born in Bayonne, New Jersey, in 1922, the son of a Polish tailor, Abraham Kahn, and his wife, Yetta Koslowsky. The family moved to the Bronx soon after his birth. Although his father had been an observant Jew, Kahn renounced religion while still a boy. He remained agnostic throughout his life, while cultivating a lifelong attachment to Jewish culture and the state of Israel. His parents divorced when he was ten. His mother moved her sons, Irving, Herman, and Morris, to Los Angeles. The family was humble; twice his mother applied for public assistance. During his school years Kahn worked in his aunt's grocery store, the Hollywood Penny Market.

After graduating from Fairfax High School in 1940, Kahn enrolled at the University of Southern California, then transferred to UCLA as a physics major. Besides running the cash register for his aunt, he supported himself during college as a ship's steward, a machinist in a camera shop, and a junior ordnance inspector for the War Department. He and his best friend, Sam Cohen, pre-enlisted in the Army Reserve Corps to snatch a bit more time for school. In May 1943 Kahn was called up to the induction center.[2]

Besides the physical examination, inductees were required to take the army's mental aptitude test. The sergeant cautioned the men not to guess or speed through the test: "No one has ever finished." Kahn had prepared by poring through every IQ test he could find. He ripped through the exam in half an hour, after which, according to Cohen, "he collapses, buries his head in his arms, rests for a few minutes, then he checks it. By now, Herman looked like he was getting ready to go off to a hospital. He was in a state of total collapse from this gargantuan effort." Kahn staggered out of the examination hall. Minutes later, he dashed back. "I made a stupid arithmetic mistake on question 132. I want to change it!" he demanded, furious with himself. "How can I be so stupid?" he wailed as he bustled out of the examination hall. To his complete satisfaction, he later learned that he had achieved the highest score ever recorded in the history of that test.[3]

Cohen and Kahn joined the Army Air Corps and were sent to North Texas for basic training. The weather was unbearable. "God only knows how many pounds Herman lost." He contracted double pneumonia and was packed off to the base hospital. Kahn was a smart-aleck, and taunted his doctor: "You don't know who you are talking to. You are talking to the smartest person in the Army. I got the highest test score ever made!" His doctor threatened to discharge him back into basic training, which Cohen feared might have killed him. By this time, Cohen had a job as an instructor at the base's navigation school. "I went to see the major in charge of this educational detachment. I hold him about Herman and said, 'You need him.'" The major jerked Kahn out of the hospital and appointed him a math teacher.[4]

Kahn and Cohen enrolled in the army's advanced technical training program. Cohen, who had also majored in physics, was dispatched to MIT. Since Kahn hadn't graduated, he was sent to the Oklahoma Agricultural and Mechanical College and West Virginia University to study military science. He was then assigned to the Signal Corps. While he awaited orders, his friend was transferred to the Manhattan Project at Los Alamos. As soon as Cohen arrived, he pleaded with his boss, the physicist Victor Weisskopf, to bring Kahn to Los Alamos. "'Vicky,' I said, 'I've got a friend who is literally the brightest person in the army. We need him here.'" Weisskopf duly submitted his bid for Kahn to join the scientists in Los Alamos. The request came through for him, but by then Kahn was already in the process of shipping out to Burma. Since the authorities wouldn't reveal any details about this alternative mission, he turned it down. Kahn worked as a repeaterman in the Pacific theater, monitoring a Burma-to-Chunking telephone line. In 1945 his brother Irving, an army air force pilot, was killed in combat. Kahn was discharged immediately as a technician, third grade, so that he could help support his mother and younger brother, Morris.[5]

As soon as he was demobilized, Kahn re-enrolled at UCLA and finished his B.A. He then entered the graduate program at the California Institute of Technology. His mother died unexpectedly. He now had to provide for himself and Morris, while still pursuing graduate study. He passed his real estate licensing exam but soon lost interest. In June 1947 he was awarded a masters degree, and the following October Douglas Aircraft hired him for a RAND project. In late December 1947 he became a RAND physicist on the regular payroll. Kahn worked there from 1947 until July 1961.

Pursuant to the Atomic Energy Act of 1946, Kahn was subject to a background check before being allowed to work on atomic projects. His FBI records indicate that, like so many others, he had a family member or friend involved in allegedly leftist activities. This investigation—the first of several—focused on a friend who had attended a July 4th party in 1945 hosted by the Los Angeles County Communist Political Association. But Kahn himself was in no danger of being tagged for radical political activity. His political orientation in these years was liberal and anticommunist. After demobilization, he joined the liberal American Veterans Committee, Americans for Democratic Action, and the American Civil Liberties Union. In late October 1948 the AEC granted him a Q classification, which cleared him for weapons work.[6]

From 1946 to 1951 RAND physicists contributed to an air force project intended to create an aviation function for atomic power. Kahn was hired to help design an atomic propulsion system for an airplane. His experiments with reactor-shielding for the plane led to a job offer from the technical director of the NEPA program at Oak Ridge, Tennessee, in early 1950. NEPA (Nuclear Energy for the Propulsion of Aircraft) was a project created by the army air force in May 1946 as part of its stake in the interservice competition for atomic weapons development. Kahn wisely declined the job. NEPA was a disaster. The design teams could not devise lightweight shielding that would protect the crew from radiation, or scrub the exhaust well enough to avoid irradiating the territories over which the plane flew. The air force reluctantly abandoned the program.[7]

In 1952 Edward Lawrence established the Livermore Laboratory as an affiliate of the University of California. It was meant to be a home for hydrogen bomb research. Members of the RAND physics department—Ernie Plesset, David Griggs, Albert Latter, Richard Latter, and Kahn—shuttled to Berkeley every week to participate. They also contributed to Los Alamos weapons work. Kahn assisted the physicists Edward Teller and Hans Bethe. After Bethe generated various hypotheses, Kahn would check his guesses with formal calculations. They were invariably correct. Kahn told Singer, "It was . . . disappointing because nobody was interested. If it turned out they were wrong, then he would get to give a briefing and that would have been important."[8]

"Kahn set an extraordinarily high bar for himself," added Anthony Wiener. After working side by side with Edward Teller and Bethe, "he realized, 'I'm not going to win a Nobel prize.'" Not only did Teller know the details of every experiment that tested a hypothesis, "'which I didn't know,' he used to say," but he could also reel off details of additional experiments that would confirm his hypothesis. "I didn't know enough to design the new wave of experiments," Kahn told Wiener, "and Eddie did." Because he had to travel to Oak Ridge and Washington, DC, for NEPA, Kahn was granted a leave of absence from Cal Tech from October 1951 to March 1952. He had begun a handful of doctoral projects but dropped each as his interest drifted and wheeled about. Cohen supposed the reason why Kahn never completed his degree was that "he was incapable of writing. There was nobody around willing to help him."[9]

In 1952 Kahn submitted his Monte Carlo studies to Cal Tech as a physics dissertation. But it was rejected on the grounds that academic research must not be commercially sponsored. He pitched his Monte Carlo work to other California universities in hopes of landing a Ph.D. To his dismay, they all insisted that he enroll fulltime for at least a year before they would award him a doctorate. He decided to forgo the degree and remain at RAND.[10]

Sometime in 1950 Kahn began to date a woman who had assisted him briefly, Rosalie Jane Heilner. Jane was a sassy New Yorker with a B.A. in physics who had worked at Cal Tech and RAND as a "computer." This was a job usually performed by women, who manually entered formulas and performed computations for researchers on desk-top calculators. "I worked for Herman for three days," she recalled. "He showed me how to compute three equations simultaneously. I didn't understand a word of what he was saying, and asked to be transferred to a different boss. He was the most creative, brilliant and amusing man I ever met."[11]

In July 1950 Miss Heilner learned that the Army-Navy-Air Force Personnel Security Board had denied her clearance for H-bomb computations. They accused her of being a political radical, or at least having contact with known Communists. She demanded a review of her case. Kahn gallantly stepped in as a character witness at her hearing on January 22, 1951. He testified, in part, that "I am a member of my own Democratic [Party] Club and I am sort of sensitive of how people feel about things. I feel I can recognize a fellow traveler and . . . people who are sympathetic to the aims of the Communist Party. I would unhesitatingly state [she] is not one of these." Heilner was soon after cleared for atomic work.[12]

In addition to courting Heilner, from 1950 to 1953 Kahn spent most of his free time with Andrew Marshall. Marshall had originally joined the social science unit in RAND's Washington office in 1949. By the summer of 1950 he had been persuaded to move to Santa Monica and join the economics department. Bachelors both, Kahn and Marshall soon began to spend evenings and weekends together. Marshall described his friend as a polymath, omnivorously curiously about everything. "We used to talk a lot about economics. He was also very interested in anthropology, in sociology . . . He was a person very interested in . . . how the world really functions." They spent hours weighing the strengths and weaknesses of systems analysis. "Initially he didn't really know that much about it. He was off on these bomb design problems."[13]

Since Marshall had a Q clearance himself, he could wander past the glass partition and into the physics suite to visit Kahn. "With the exception of Herman . . . [the physicists] weren't very interested in what was going on," he recalled. "It was seen as a great sin that Herman was being tempted into this . . . obviously much less rigorous and precise kind of work." In 1952 Kahn and Marshall co-authored the first major systems analysis that incorporated Monte Carlo methods. In it, they examined various combinations of aircraft that could be used in bombing raids against Soviet defenses.[14]

On March 21, 1953, Kahn and Jane were married. Less than three months later, on June 16, 1953, his Oak Ridge and New York clearances were withdrawn, and on July 27 his Q clearance was terminated. The FBI alleged that his wife's sister and husband were "known Communists." That very day, July 27, FBI Director Herbert Hoover ordered a reinvestigation of Kahn's political views and associates. An inquiry revealed that several years earlier an informant for the Los Angeles bureau had reported that Kahn's name and address had appeared in membership files of the Committee for the Protection of the Foreign Born, allegedly a front organization for the Communist Party. Kahn's brother-in-law was a member of its executive board. While Kahn was tagged as a person to watch, it soon became clear that he had no contact with this man. Moreover, his colleagues testified to FBI agents that they had heard him often remark that "a Communist has no place on government security projects." In March 1954 he was cleared once again for access to top-secret documents. His Q rating for atomic research remained suspended while the FBI pressed on with its investigation.[15]

Kahn's case was reviewed at a Personnel Security Board hearing some months later, on July 25, 1954. Before rendering their final decision, the board authorized a further investigation "as to the true reason" why he withdrew from Cal Tech. They suspected his mental health: "The demonstrated instability of Herman Kahn was his admitted inability to complete his work for the Ph.D. in question." Surely this is every dilatory graduate student's worst nightmare— the FBI ordering its agents to interview one's former professors. But all of them at Cal Tech declared Kahn blameless. One professor characterized him as "an average theoretical physicist, but above average in enthusiasm." Another observed that he had been "unorthodox in his approach to his academic work, that he did not like routine . . . [but was] a bright student." No one considered his departure from academic studies objectionable in any way. The board recommended that his Q clearance be reactivated, which it was on June 1, 1955.[16]

While Kahn had followed the evolution of atomic, then nuclear, strategy since he first joined RAND, the suspension of his Q clearance steered him more directly to problems in war-fighting and systems analysis. After years of picking through systems analyses produced by his colleagues, he collaborated with Marshall on several papers. He also became an adviser to the strategist Albert Wohlstetter on nuclear weapons effects on hardened structures. Wohlstetter was already well into his famous analysis of the vulnerability of America's forward staging bases in Europe.[17]

In February 1955 RAND researchers presented the first course on systems analysis to the air force. By then Kahn had lots of ideas. When the course was offered a second time, he was invited to discuss the hidden pitfalls of modeling. His briefings, enlivened with jokes, asides, and stories, were very popular. Marshall credited them with the beginning of his friend's reputation in the air force. "Most people give fairly dull lectures. He became a more widely-known person with a different range of people. Herman was always seen as a phenomenally brilliant person."[18]

Kahn's success in the systems analysis course, combined with his long suspension from bomb design, completed his transformation from weapons scientist to systems analyst and nuclear strategist. As a young man, he had dreamed of being a theoretical physicist. But having recognized the unquestionably superior scientific gifts of the men he assisted, Bethe and Teller, he was already on the lookout for another arena for his talents. He must have been overjoyed by the success of his briefing. "In my view," Marshall reflected, "it was kind of the undoing of Herman. 'Undoing' is the wrong word maybe, but I mean it sent him off in a totally new direction to become almost a kind of public lecturer on a whole bunch of topics."[19]

Kahn's friend Albert Latter thought his metamorphosis was remarkable. They had met while Kahn was taking doctoral-level courses at Cal Tech and negotiating with the department about his dissertation topic. "But as far as I could see his interest was never substantial enough for him to do those things . . . It's pretty clear in hindsight that he had some kind of communion going on with himself, because all of a sudden he emerged as the Herman Kahn that everyone remembers." His physics colleagues were flabbergasted. "I don't think that [they] ever did relate . . . to the new Herman."[20]

While the new Herman initiated most of his own studies, he occasionally joined Wohlstetter's coterie. Wohlstetter's wife, Roberta, who also worked at RAND as a historian, smiled as she recalled Albert saying, "It was great. It was kind of like being joined by a fragmentation bomb." Kahn rapidly absorbed Wohlstetter's arguments and moved to establish his own authority in the field.[21]

Gustave Shubert was there when Wohlstetter, Kahn's sometime mentor, blasted him for writing *On Thermonuclear War*. Shubert had been visiting Wohlstetter in his all-white office, "White rug, white furniture, pristine!" Wohlstetter was lounging with his foot perched on an open desk drawer. Kahn peeked in and asked if he had read his manuscript. "Yes," replied Albert, flicking it at him. "There is only one thing to do with this book. Burn it!" To Wohlstetter's horror, Kahn had poached nearly every one of his major ideas. He was a highly polished man. To read arguments very nearly his own rendered in hopelessly bungled language appalled him. Even so, when colleagues later spurned Kahn, Wohlstetter stood by his friend, loyally indignant when necessary and steadfast during the infancy of the Hudson Institute.[22]

Megalomania, Zoom!

Kahn didn't experiment in a laboratory, but by frolicking and sparring with his colleagues and audiences. He assembled (and compulsively revised) a fat deck of briefing tables. He'd clamber onto the speaker's podium with his charts under his arms, dump them onto easels flanking his lectern, and blast off. In Hudson's first years, he frequently introduced its mission this way: "Basically we want to be the think tank for the Secretary of Defense. We want to be a policy planning group for the Secretary of Defense." Anthony Wiener smiled, recalling the subject, "He loved to say this to an audience, 'That's our agenda for next year. But we need a very intelligent Secretary of Defense in order to be useful to him. The following year, we'll do the same thing for the President. The year after that, for the Secretary General. In the fourth year, God.'" This would always elicit roars of laughter. Kahn invariably added, "At the Hudson Institute, we're proud to say that we stand halfway between *chutzpah* and megalomania." By 1968 he had boiled this down to a concise *schtick*. He told a visitor, "We take God's view. The President's view. Big. Aerial. Global. Galactic. Ethereal. Spatial. Overall. Megalomania is the standard occupational hazard." The joke against himself was irresistible. "Herman Kahn," marveled the reporter, "beaming and at his happiest, began twirling a finger off his desk and into the air toward the ceiling . . . Herman rose out of his chair and suddenly boomed out: 'Megalomania, zoom!'"[23]

"Herman came home, ate his dinner, swam in his pool, and worked. He was too tired to talk about his work," his wife recalled. He was often away traveling, but when he was home, he was great company. "He was very witty, very funny and curious about everything. He was a great conversationalist, fascinated with everything." While an indefatigable talker, his interests always oriented outward. He wasn't in the least introspective. "He didn't talk about himself. He didn't volunteer information unless it was related to the issue at hand. He certainly didn't theorize about why he was the way he was, or why he couldn't lose weight. He didn't talk about his inner process, what moved him this way and that."[24]

Kahn especially liked eccentric people. He deliberately recruited iconoclasts for the Hudson Institute. He explained, "They're very good, but . . . impossible. They are a little bit simplistic, they touch on the hysteric, they come close to demagoguery . . . but they are also extremely interesting." "Herman was never narrow," reflected Wiener, one of Kahn's collaborators. "He surrounded himself with people . . . whose skills complemented his in various ways."[25]

Kahn loved to buttonhole people who disagreed with him. For example, he energetically pursued contacts with the full spectrum of the peace movement, from the anticommunist Robert Pickus, to members of SANE, to religiously oriented pacifists such as Quakers and A. J. Muste, to the academic disarmers of the Committees of

Correspondence in Cambridge, Massachusetts, to the direct-action pacifists of the Committee on Non-Violent Action. Both the strategists and the peaceniks looked forward to these public wrestling matches. Kahn adored these encounters, and some in the peace movement were equally delighted to get on so cordially with a man whose ideas they condemned. The chair of the American Friends' New England Regional Peace Committee in these years suggested that some members of the peace movement were willing to have interactions with Kahn because they wanted to say, "'We have been able to remain in contact with someone with whom we thoroughly disagree.' For a moral sense."[26]

This was certainly the case with the most radical faction of the peace movement whom Kahn met, the pacifists of the Committee on Non-Violent Action. The CNVA not only forswore the draft, refused to sign loyalty oaths, and withheld some or all of their federal taxes, but they also advocated direct action against the instruments of war. They stole into missile bases and onto Polaris submarines, and by the early 1960s battered instrument panels with hammers.

While he was still at RAND, Kahn was contacted by Sam Gottlieb, a filmmaker who was shooting a documentary on the CNVA's San Francisco to Moscow Walk for Peace. Along the way the marchers planned to hold meetings in schools, churches, and public halls, distribute leaflets, and engage fellow citizens on the problems of the cold war at all levels of society, including statesmen. Kahn was the only strategist who agreed to meet with them. When the band arrived in Santa Monica in late December 1960, he met them at the entrance of RAND, "plump, bespectacled, a youthful forty," wrote Bradford Lyttle in his memoir. After introducing himself, Kahn asked if they were the same protesters who had trespassed onto an Atlas missile base the year before. On learning they were, he snickered, "You should have heard what General Powers [the commander of SAC] had to say about you in a briefing session I gave him!"[27]

While they chatted, the afternoon grew dark. Kahn suggested they move to the Del Mar Hotel and Beach Club, of which he was a member. He telephoned the manager for permission to film in the cabana on the beach. Gottlieb's crew lugged their equipment into the outbuilding. Some teenage girls were curious and excited to see the film crew. "Are you making a movie? Can we be in it?" Lyttle gravely explained the purpose of the walk to Moscow and gave them some flyers.

While he and Kahn waited for the cameraman to set up his gear, they discussed the chances that the marchers would be allowed into the Eastern Bloc nations. Kahn was skeptical. Lyttle retorted that he would have been just as doubtful of his group's ability to climb aboard Polaris submarines, which they had done six months before. Kahn pondered this for a moment, then nodded, "I see what you mean. You don't bother to calculate chances. You just do your best, what you think is right." Decades later, Lyttle reflected, "I thought that was a rather sympathetic insight. That was exactly what we were doing."[28]

Suddenly two young men burst in on them, clutching the leaflets and screeching: "Where are these characters? Going to Russia? Boy, they'll sure love you there!" Lyttle murmured that he doubted whether the Communists would be pleased by their call to the masses to practice non-cooperation with military and totalitarian institutions. "You're a nut all right. I know all about you young Communists and fellow travelers!" one fellow shot back. They stormed out of the room. Lyttle and Kahn resumed their conversation while Gottlieb made his final preparations. Suddenly they were interrupted by a posse of men and the hotel manager: "I won't have it! Not here! No! That's all. I won't have it." He evicted them. When Kahn tried to placate him, he howled, "I'll call the police!" "But I'm a member here. I phoned and made arrangements to have this film made here!" "You said this was a film sponsored by RAND." Kahn turned to Lyttle, "I knew you shouldn't have given those girls the leaflets." Gottlieb packed up his equipment. Kahn remained behind to pacify the manager and insist that his membership not be revoked. He also wanted to go for a swim in the pool to calm down. The next morning, he met Lyttle for the interview at the home of a friend of the marchers.[29]

The CNVA was probably the most radical faction of the peace movement that approached Kahn. Robert Pickus, a staff member for the American Friends Service Committee on the West Coast and founder of the anticommunist Acts for Peace, marked out the conservative position among the disarmers. Pickus was to the right of the American Friends; Kahn was clearly in sympathy with him. He wrote to Pickus, "I am so impressed by your Uniting for Peace Movement that I am half-thinking of having the Hudson Institute apply for association." (He described the Hudson Institute as being "a self-announced peace group.")[30]

Kahn also conducted a friendly exchange with the young editor of the Committees of Correspondence Newsletter. Roger Hagan had repeatedly invited him to contribute something to his newsletter. "We need to be reminded that to many of the people you talk to you are as far out as we are, and in the same direction." In reply, Kahn described a meeting of the pro-disarmament Scientists on Survival group. They had focused on the uncertain data of nuclear weapons effects. "I have the distinct impression that the sins that the peace groups accuse the government of, such as dealing in myths and clichés and not coping with reality are as much their sins as the government's . . . I would be willing . . . to stack up the 'reality testing' of the Executive Office and much of the Pentagon with most of what I heard at Scientists on Survival." He proposed an article comparing the realism of the peace movement with the Pentagon. Kahn closed with a comment about his enclosure, a copy of his correspondence with the editor of *Scientific American*, who refused to allow him to rebut the magazine's hostile review of *OTW* by James Newman. "I produce [these] as another example of a standard of behavior which would be intolerable from the right but is considered mildly aberrant [for] . . . peace people."[31]

A few days later, Kahn scribbled a second letter. "I have been thinking about what I wrote . . . and have decided that I am mostly off-base. Someone like myself who is in some sense a member of the 'Establishment' has to have one style of working, speaking, and talking, while a protest group obviously needs a . . . different style, if for no other reason than to get attention. While I believe my comments

. . . [are] correct, I think that their force should be greatly diminished." It was not clear exactly what he had meant to retract, but the fact that he was moved to soften his comments suggests that he cared very much not to alienate Hagan.[32]

Kahn's cordiality with the peace movement did not go unnoticed. In August 1962 he agreed to be interviewed by two FBI agents about his contacts with CNVA and his general relationship with the peace movement. The encounter seems to have been hostile. The agent in charge wrote that his subject "manifested nervousness by stuttering badly which was immediately followed by extremely rapid speech. The writer was forced to ask [him] to repeat his statements." Kahn explained that he wished to form a clear idea of the peace position on various topics. "Organizations such as the CNVA supply a valuable tenseness in our society and they are well meaning individuals. However, he could not condone [their] emotional and irresponsible acts." As director of the Hudson Institute, he defended his regular conversations with disarmers. "It is useful to have people in the peace groups freely express their ideas and objectives to this organization." In fact, he vowed to continue to meet with leftists, as well as liberals and conservatives, in the future. "Such a procedure is necessary in order to obtain the entire spectrum of thinking of all various and opposed groups."[33]

This was no lie. Throughout his life, Kahn befriended people far from him in taste, opinion, and preoccupations. He was fascinated with the counterculture. His sister-in-law's sons were hippies. They had dropped out of college and lived with the Kahn family for close to a year. He occasionally sought out their company, the opinions of their friends, and other ideologically invested young people. Anthony Wiener remembered a trip to the Esalen Institute for a Hudson study on the youth culture. "Herman got along wonderfully with all these people. I found Abby Hoffman for him, Paul Krasner. I identified all of these people. They all wanted to meet Herman. They had a wonderful time. We walked around . . . chatting about dropping acid."[34]

Kahn's engrossment in the counterculture was not wholly theoretical. He confided to a reporter in 1968, "I like the hippies. I've been to Esalen. I've had LSD a couple of times. In some ways I'd like to join them." In 1962 he had volunteered to participate in a study of the effect of LSD on creative people, directed by Sidney Cohen and William McGlothlin at the Veterans Administration Hospital in Los Angeles. In a letter to McGlothlin after the experiment, he wrote exuberantly, "I should probably mention that I really enjoyed the experience and I would be delighted to do it again if you thought it desirable. While I'm not a convert to the LSD movement, I am a convert to LSD, and I would be shocked if I didn't convert to the movement also when I know more about it."[35]

Kahn had a tendency to blurt things outs. His friends repeatedly drew attention to his self-confidence and audacity. Wiener commented, "He said it himself, 'It's not that I'm smarter than other people, it's just that I keep on thinking where other people stop.'" So intent was he on tracking a thought that he exhibited a kind of obtuse effrontery. "Often he would say things very crudely, not in the way that he meant. We had innumerable conversations where I would say, 'Don't you really mean . . . ?' and he would say, 'Yeah that's right.' So afterward, he would say, 'Well, I don't hear the difference. I guess I'm just tone-deaf.'"[36]

Often if he sensed discomfort in his audience, he would go to great lengths to explain himself, but he characteristically resisted attempts to refine his presentation. Jane Kahn recalled that when he had originally created the table correlating the number of millions dead in a nuclear war with the kinds of prewar preparations made, he called it "possible distinguishable post-war states." After some thought he changed it to "tragic but distinguishable post-war states" in order to mollify those who believed that he should pledge his good will. But the table "had nothing to do with feelings," she fumed affectionately, "it was making an analytical distinction!" In order to do this kind of work, "you either have to have an iron will or be very detached. Herman didn't have an iron will. In fact quite the opposite. He tried to diet for 25 years. But he was very detached."[37]

Kahn had no qualms about moving between reality and unreality, fact and fiction, while developing an argument. Early in life he discovered science fiction, and he remained an avid reader throughout adulthood. While it nurtured in him a rich appreciation for plausible possibilities, Wiener observed that Kahn was quite clear about the purposes to which he put his own scenarios. "Herman would say, 'Don't imagine that it's an arbitrary choice as though you were writing science fiction, where every interesting idea is worth exploring.' He would have insisted on that. The scenario must focus attention on a possibility that would be important if it occurred." The heuristic or explanatory value of a scenario mattered more to him than its accuracy.[38]

Many of his friends tell the story of how once, in the course of an anecdote about an incident in World War II, Kahn was cut short by a general: "Excuse me, Mister Kahn, but that's not how it happened." He replied, "How do you know?" The general retorted, "I was there." Kahn paused, then commented, "That bothers me, but not a lot. It doesn't matter how it happened for my purposes. If you will agree with me that it *could* have happened that way, then please understand the point I'm trying to make. And that's enough." This was a regular occurrence. Often somebody in a briefing audience would call attention to an error. "And if you pressed him on this, and challenged him," Wiener noted, "he would say, 'OK, but it doesn't matter.' He was constantly using fiction to make his point. And constantly explaining that that was okay, that this was all heuristic."[39]

Kahn was a fierce debater. Panero remembered, "He would say ten things very fast. Some of them were very strong, no way to attack them. Three were a perception, and two could be flawed in some way, or contingent." In conversation, during the briefings, and even in his printed works, Kahn gave the suggestion of spinning out multidirectional stories that could go on infinitely; each fork in the narrative could render an infinite number of infinite branches. Panero said, "He would think faster and about more subjects when he was trying to talk about one." As Wiener observed, "There was an element in Herman as though he were living out a fantasy of never running out. There was always going to be more: more and more ideas; more and more distinctions to be made. It was important to him psychologically that he keep talking."[40]

Yet Kahn was not a monologist. On the contrary, he generated many of his arguments by engaging with collaborators, and he listened carefully to them. Their contributions stimulated one further remark, one further contradiction, one further variation. While temperamentally good-natured, on occasion, he would become irritated. He would lean forward and sputter, "I can make your argument better than you can, and then I can show you why it's wrong!" "That was one of his favorite things to say to people when he felt like putting them down," Wiener said. "Then he would demonstrate it, if you would ask him to."[41]

He would rapidly assert a number of independently valid statements, all of which were not quite to the point. "While you're still worrying about the first one, he's gone on to 2, 3, 4, and 5. Afterwards you can reconstruct the whole thing and you can come back to him and say, 'Look, Herman, every one of the points you made was true but irrelevant.'" His rejoinder would be to generate another group of statements radiating even finer distinctions, or remoter connections to the original question. "It became an endless process." Wiener reflected that what was "characteristic of Herman in these arguments was the speed with which he would come up with all of these things to say." Recalling these sessions, Panero added, "You really could not move Herman to integrate while he was talking. You just had to annotate them in your head and then try to separate what was right from what was wrong, and what you believe. If you started arguing with him, he'd develop the subject at a higher rate of speed than you could. And better. So you would end up losing, even having started from a valid point."[42]

While Kahn might evade rebuttal by changing the subject, switching arguments, or overstating his facts, his zest for dialogue was so appealing, his gaiety so disarming, that most of his assistants were recruited to work on projects in these very same encounters. Sidney Winter, Jr., remembered Kahn bursting into his office blazing with some idea. "Well, I have been thinking about such and such, and I'd concluded so and so. What do you think of that?" Winter would pop back, "I think it's flat wrong." "Well we did this calculation, we did that calculation, and it came out this way. So why is it wrong?" The numbers were off. "And pretty soon, you'd be in a position where you had agreed to do some calculations yourself in order to fend him off the next time he came around."[43]

Kahn always enlisted collaborators for his projects. Panero called him "an idea sponge," luring antagonists into debate about problems that interested him but of which he was unsure. "He would go around until he found a young guy in his twenties who was brilliant, had very good grades and was quick. And in a sense, he'd seduce this young man, pull him in, and argue . . . with him." In their first encounter, the young opponent would air all of his ideas. Afterward, Kahn would scour the research literature to find data and arguments to support his and his sparring partner's positions. Having had his say the first time around, the young man would be vanquished when Kahn ambushed him. "In my time with Herman, I watched him burn out a series of young men who thought they were brilliant when they arrived and left with their tails between their legs. I mean just absolutely destroyed."[44]

Even in his earliest years at RAND, Kahn made use of collaborators such as the physicists G. Goertzel and I. R. Latter, as well as Andrew Marshall. He hired his first collaborator, the mathematician Irwin Mann, in 1954 to help him pull his Monte Carlo studies into a book. With adjoining offices, Kahn relied on Mann (or one of the secretaries) to transcribe dictaphone tapes. He avoided writing as much as possible, preferring to speak into a tape recorder. Later on, he would have one of his collaborators record his briefings and use these transcripts as the basis of texts, which they revised. Mann edited, amended, and liberally rewrote Kahn's words, but Kahn generated almost all of the ideas for the projects on which they worked, though he "never pulled rank," Mann commented. "It was not an equal partnership in those things we co-authored. It is true in some sense that Herman could have done [it] by himself and I couldn't."[45]

Distracted, disorganized, and mercurial, Kahn would abandon a study and begin something new well before Mann thought the first had been properly completed. From 1948 to 1956, Kahn plugged away on a handbook, *Applications of Monte Carlo,* but eventually discarded it. Mann sighed, "We broke on the issue of how finished something had to be. Nothing was ever finished. It was terribly sloppy. It was an enormous myth that anything was studied. Nothing was studied. Not really. He didn't study anything. He was enormously smart. Dangerous on facts when cornered." By 1958 Kahn moved on to civil defense and left Mann behind.[46]

Kahn's next collaborator was Robert Panero. As an engineering consultant to RAND, Panero had given a paper on underground installations at the First Protective Construction Symposium. Kahn was interested in every aspect of the problem, from siting industrial plants underground to various ways of hardening communication facilities. Panero spent a good deal of time with him from 1957 to 1959. He proposed siting components of the North American Air Defense Command (NORAD) in a series of unconnected strata underneath Cheyenne Mountain. Kahn and Panero briefed General LeMay (who at this time headed Strategic Air Command) on the benefits of relocating NORAD deep underground. Panero also devoted much of 1957 to a feasibility study of evacuating the population of Manhattan to a mass shelter installed 2,000 feet underground in the island's impermeable rock.[47]

Max Singer came next. He was a young lawyer who had worked in the General Counsel's office of the Atomic Energy Commission for two and a half years before quitting to work on the Kennedy campaign. He met Kahn during a summer study in Cambridge, Massachusetts. Kahn invited Singer to work for him on a project called "The Next President's Study," which was intended to be a set of national security briefings that would be delivered to whoever won the election in November 1960. Singer's first assignment was to read the galleys of *OTW* to familiarize himself with Kahn's ideas. Within six months, he and Kahn were laying plans to create the Hudson Institute.

A few months after Singer moved to Santa Monica, Kahn acquired Anthony Wiener as another collaborator. A classmate of Singer's from Harvard Law School, Wiener was an instructor in the political science department at MIT, as well as a research associate at the Center for International Studies. On one of his jaunts through Cambridge in 1960, Kahn telephoned Wiener. "I still remember how he sounded because I never heard anyone speak this way, he spoke so rapidly, he slurred his speech. It was hard to follow." "This is Herman Kahn. Max Singer told me that you would be a good person to meet. I'm coming to Cambridge, can you spend two days with me?"[48]

Curious about Singer's new boss, Wiener met him for breakfast: "And there's this great big 300-odd pound guy sitting across this small table in the hotel . . . chortling and joking . . . He's kidding around about everything. It was part of the very informal, relaxed, give-and-take style that he cultivated." Kahn had scheduled two public gatherings, a lecture, and a debate, as well as meetings with faculty groups at Harvard and MIT. Wiener accompanied him throughout his trip. "What impressed me was that he had a different interesting story on a different topic for each one of these groups. Most people have only one story." Some months later, Singer telephoned his friend and asked if he would consider coming out to RAND to work with him and Kahn. Wiener wanted to stay on the East Coast. A few months later, Singer called again. He and Kahn were going to found their own institute on the East Coast, and they were inviting him to join them. Wiener took a leave of absence from MIT, and in July 1961 the three men opened the Hudson Institute.[49]

These young men were vitally important to Kahn. While he generated ideas in dialogue, he desperately needed their skills to translate crude outlines or the raw transcripts of his briefings into articles, reports, and books. His first book from Hudson, *Thinking about the Unthinkable*, was written in collaboration with Singer, Wiener, and John Caplan, a law professor at Stanford. "He talked it out into a recorder. He listed the main points into dictaphone or tape recorder; someone transcribed his partly garbled speech; the team received a transcription; we'd take it, elaborate it, amplify." His collaborators produced drafts and handed them back to him. "And he would say,

'Well I don't agree with that' or 'Yeah, that's good, that makes me think of something else' . . . He would just pass it back and forth . . . Often there would be four or five people doing this and then it would just grow." Kahn compulsively inserted qualifiers such as "more or less" or "mostly." "Herman reflected the real ambiguity of the things he talked about. He did equivocate a lot as a result."[50]

Kahn displayed and elaborated hundreds of charts during his briefings. "Standing there expanding out to the huge waistline of his belt. With these charts up. He had these two screens . . . and a pointer . . . And you go very fast." He spoke in a blur, "extremely imperfect English, flow-of-consciousness type stuff," added Winter. He delivered each briefing between thirty and fifty times. The briefing would evolve from a mélange of inchoate and old well-formed arguments to new, fully elaborated material. His audiences offered rebuttals and corrections, to which he would develop counter-arguments. "So if he got in trouble, that was a great stimulus to new ideas. They would all get incorporated."[51]

Kahn deliberately elicited strong responses from his audience. "You've got to startle them so they would pay attention," he would instruct Wiener. "Here you threw away this point. You threw it away by making it sound too reasonable." Marshall reflected that "being a kind of performer tended to push him in the direction of developing striking formulations of things to get ideas across in this lecture platform. It also tended to push him in the direction of trying to find a humorous and catchy formulation."[52]

Kennedy's assistant secretary of defense for civil defense, Steuart Pittman, was fond of Kahn, but understood why so many people were offended by him. "He was trying to communicate complex ideas. You sacrifice elegance for being . . . understood when you're doing that." The topic itself repelled people. "[You] walk right into the Dr. Strangelove reaction and there's no way to deal with it without being exposed to [outrage]." Pittman thought Kahn's delivery was a more formidable problem. "The trouble with Herman . . . was that his mind worked so fast, he leapt from crag to crag, to keep up with him was difficult. A lot of people who didn't keep up with him would say the guy is throwing things around irresponsibly. He's throwing ideas around that are unconnected, leaping from one thing to another." Bewildered by his rattling effusion, skeptics and the fearful were not disarmed by his affability.[53]

"When he would go giving the basic thermonuclear war thesis," Cohen remarked, "people would scream at him, 'You monster you! What right do you have to talk this way? You should be locked up!'" There was one rabbi who bawled, "How can a Jew behave the way you're behaving?" Kahn relished the incident. Cohen thought he basked in notoriety. "At least as important as adulation was condemnation. He really wanted to be cursed and damned. He just gloried in it."[54]

Unlike nearly everybody else, Kahn did not toady to the air force. Imagine the effect of this disheveled, giddy dumpling needling a room full of officers: "Now the enemy has a third choice. He can just take that road. He didn't have to go past the fort. The enemy may figure this way. After all, if you put the fort there you must have had a reason; he'll attack it. We refer to this as the military mind—the *Army* military mind. We're very clear on that. So you have a problem here. You don't want to rely on the enemy being stupid even though you feel in your bones he is. He's at least as stupid as you I mean, for example."[55]

"They would look at him in fascination," said Wiener, "but generally speaking with a mixture of horror and awe. Part of the way he got their attention was that they had never seen anybody like this. They had never heard anybody talk this way." That was the brunt of Kahn's critique of Wiener's briefings—"That I sounded too reasonable. That I sounded too much like other people, and that wasn't good. I should really be distinctive, be really different." "Herman was such a phenomenon, a thing I never would have imagined," marveled Winter. The spectacle of his pumpkin body, his gibbering fluency, his giggle and gags with his unspeakable, unthinkable emphasis on the immediate danger of contemporary life made him a gazing-stock and a wonder.

Chapter 4

AN OPERATIONAL BUT UNDETECTED CAPABILITY

*You sort of plead with yourself—he can't make a bomb, he
can't make a jet fighter, he can't do this; you go to Korea
and the thing's flying around—what the hell?—mirages!*

HERMAN KAHN, 1955

Kahn once joked, "Most Americans find it very hard to believe in enemies . . . Neither can I. I have difficulty. I train myself every morning to try to do it." Not only did Americans shrink from the idea of a hatred so grinding that an enemy would willingly assault the United States with genocidal weapons, but it was hard to imagine a scenario in which waging all-out war against the United States and NATO would make military or political sense. Kahn implored (or begged) his readers not to muffle the likelihood of nuclear war "with an air of hypotheticalness, unreality or improbability." "I suspect," he remarked, "that many in the West are guilty of the worst kind of wishful thinking when, in discussing deterrence, they identify the unpleasant with the impossible." As long as the nation opposed Communist aggression with a promise of nuclear retaliation, nuclear war had to be recognized as an actual possibility, even though everything about it was conjectural. "In this field," he sighed, "everybody is a theorist."[1]

Persuading people to regard hypothetical threats attentively in a spirit of solemn anxiety seemed impossible. Kahn lampooned the unconcern he expected to find in politicians and bureaucrats. It had three voices.

- The problem is *hypothetical.* You cannot *prove* it exists. There is no need to get hysterical.
- The problem is there, but there are many other problems. In your parochialism and naiveté, you have gotten hysterical. We have known about the problem for some time and we are not hysterical. Why are you?
- The problem is there. It is insoluble. (Or, it is too late to do anything.) For God's sake don't rock the (political or public relations) boat.[2]

Nuclear war couldn't be grasped because it was unreal. It could only be approached with the imagination born of a faith that leapt across the abyss between the present and the post-attack world. In this chapter we're going to fix our attention precisely on the no-man's land between positively known reality and impossibilities—the frontier of improbable but not impossible events. While folk beliefs in ghostly apparitions gradually yielded to faith in the splotches, spirals, and tallies of modern scientific evidence, phantoms did not disappear from our world. The horrified suspicions gripping the men and women who squinted above and beyond their hometowns in the 1950s were prompted by the jittery uncertainties of the Cold War. They jumped when they heard the whine of a plane, snatched their binoculars, looked up, and hesitated: Is that an incoming Soviet bomber, one of our own, or a smear in my lens?

The history of the cold war has become petrified into a kitsch montage of mass hysteria. One need only think of the vile House Un-American Activities Committee's investigations of entertainment professionals, McCarthyite book-burnings in libraries and schools, the angst caused by *Sputnik* as it sailed above American skies.

Paranoia wriggled and curled in the sporadic surges of enthusiasm for civil defense, from the intricate plans to billet urban evacuees in rural villages that were drawn up during the Korean War, to the boomlet in fallout shelter construction during the Berlin Crisis in 1961. If you wanted to gather evidence of a national mood of unstable excitability, and even delusions of persecution in these years, you could make a plausible case. But this ironic shorthand blunts the urgency, terror, moral seriousness, and despair that clutched American society in these years. We can more sensitively explore the cold war by referring to a shape of feeling. If we foreground the cognitive and emotional palette of these years rather than its pathology, we can enter vitally into its world.

The Postwar Uncanny

The atmospheric mood and style of the cold war open themselves to us by way of Freud's notion of the *unheimlich* or the uncanny. The uncanny is something that is closely known but lost from memory until the instant of its reappearance—it is "nothing new or foreign, but something familiar and old-established in the mind that has been estranged only by the process of repression." For people not directly concerned with national security in the 1950s, atomic war had just this kind of familiar-but-forgotten quality—something known to all but passed over. However much people gawked at atomic tests in movie newsreels and on television, atomic weapons and war were remote from the workaday world—immense, secret, and infernal, too cosmic for the prosaic stuff of life. World war fought with atomic weapons could not be tested against everyday reality. Its existential possibility was known to all, yet known with even more abstraction than the stars and the planets were known.[3]

Signs of the national mood more concrete than this are hard to gather in the long stretch of time from 1947 to 1961. Daily life altered repeatedly in these years, and people at different strata of society dreaded atomic war more or less acutely. Relatively few Americans volunteered for the civil defense corps' fire, police, and rescue squadrons or built fallout shelters. More to the point, fear of atomic war did not often flicker at the forefront of people's daily worries. Poll after poll confirming general apathy mortified civil defense boosters. But rather than assuming this proved indifference, one could suppose that fear about a horror that most Americans felt they couldn't influence and couldn't survive might *not* express itself behaviorally, might *not* articulate itself to pollsters. It might nevertheless scratch out traces across the cultural horizon.[4]

Tucked into the dominant satisfactions of daily life in these years, we can espy the traces of a catastrophe that could befall America at any moment. These were nearly invisible, both familiar and inconspicuous. Here, a shop window poster encouraging citizens to volunteer for the local civil defense organization; there, a newsreel about American hydrogen bomb tests in the Pacific. A fallout shelter display erected in the parking lot of a supermarket. The weekly blast of a warning siren. An addendum to a nursing textbook about first aid for radiation burns. A toy ballistic missile unwrapped on Christmas morning. Highway billboards designating city arteries as emergency evacuation routes. A flock of high school students excitedly waving to friends from atop a Ground Observer Corps parade float.

From farmers peering into a blank sky with binoculars, awaiting a bomber whose rumble could already be heard, to intelligence officers poring over mushy images in high-altitude photographs, most Americans knew little about their enemy. For much of the 1950s, the USSR was a closed society, and very little leaked out. Analysts probed the Soviet speech and action available to them, dissecting every comma in edicts, the graphic layout of *Pravda*, pleasantries Russian diplomats bandied with their hosts at Georgetown cocktail parties. They brooded over the patterned significance invested in Soviet parades and other public spectacles. Virtually anything, a bagatelle, a ceremony, a cough and a wink, might let slip their enemy's intentions or capabilities.

The intelligence community knew quite a lot about the Soviet atomic complex itself. In the first half of the 1950s, Spurgeon Keeny ran an office in air force intelligence HQ that followed Soviet nuclear development. He recalled, "We had Air Force bases in the Far North. The Soviets didn't have landlines in a large part of Siberia. They used radio telephones. We could hear everything. By the early 1950s we knew the location of every one of their important facilities." Keeny briefed the secretary of defense in 1953 and 1954 on "all of the major sites, where they were and what they were doing. We had a clear picture of the structure of the Soviet atomic production complex. We knew their Oak Ridge, their Hanford, and their Los Alamos."[5] Not only did they know the layout of the Soviet production complex, they had a pretty good idea about their atomic and nuclear bombs themselves. American intelligence monitored uranium extraction in Czechoslovakia and East Germany. AEC scientists gathered debris from atmospheric tests and from this deduced the design and yield of the Soviet bomb. "All of the information we knew about their tests made it clear that they had succeeded in making an explosive device and were weaponizing it." The mystery lay in the numbers of bombs they had and the Kremlin's intentions to use them. American intelligence officials knew the locations of the major sites in the USSR but didn't have any photographs of them. Photographs would help resolve the question of how many bombs and delivery vehicles—long-range bombers and, later, missiles—they had. Moreover, the Pentagon wanted *reliable intelligence* about Soviet intentions. No one knew whether or not the enemy could or would realize his threats.[6]

Did the Soviets really want to annihilate the West? As soon as possible? Was it true that New York and Washington might be vaporized one sunny day? Was World War III right around the corner? These questions are not as preposterous as they sound. In two separate polls conducted in 1950, more than half the people surveyed believed that U.S. involvement in the Korean War meant that World War III had *already begun.* Three years later, the chairman of the joint chiefs of staff rebuked his countrymen for describing current realities as World War III. In an address at Rollins College in February 1953, General Omar Bradley objected to the "unchallenged" currency of the remark, "Let's face the facts, we are already in World War III." "Personally," he protested, "I don't believe that we have reached that stage."[7]

Still, it was hard to shake the feeling that world war would come eventually. In another poll taken on July 18, 1956, 59 percent of the young and middle-aged adults surveyed believed that the United States would fight another world war in their lifetimes. Just days before, the Soviet Party Secretary Nikita Khrushchev had declared, "I would like to emphasize that war between the Arab states and Israel would mean World War III." Today, we are hardly accustomed to hearing statesmen pronounce threats of world war. To our ears, the phrase "World War III" is so provocative that its utterance is taboo in the mouths of presidents and prime ministers. In the 1950s, statesmen experimented with the effect of employing such coercive language in their dealings with one another.[8]

Such threats were more than mere rhetoric. Dispatching atomic forces to crisis hot spots was a real option. Not only were warnings of World War III delivered to and fro, but several times during the 1950s both President Truman and President Eisenhower seriously considered deploying their strategic forces. Eisenhower deployed his strategic forces to forward positions in response to Khrushchev's threats of World War III during the simultaneous Polish, Hungarian, and Suez Canal crises of the second half of 1956. Several times, Soviet leaders repeated their warnings of impending world war, throwing Americans into perplexity as to the meaning of their remarks.[9]

In late 1955, border skirmishes took place almost daily in the Gaza Strip. On January 22, 1956, the UN Security Council censured Israel for the ferocity of its retaliatory attacks in response to Arab border violations. So fierce were its reprisals that many observers anticipated an Israeli preventive war against her neighbors in the immediate future. It began on July 26, when Egyptian President Colonel Gamal Nasser proclaimed that he had nationalized the Suez Canal. On October 29, with military assistance from France, Israel launched an attack across the Sinai Peninsula. Without American approval, British and French troops soon joined forces with the Israelis. Just days *before* the Israeli mobilization, the reformist Polish Premier Oscar Gomulka ordered his Stalinist minister of defense to resign. Khrushchev flew to Warsaw to intimidate Gomulka's faction in the Central Committee into retaining his minister. Gomulka stood down the pressure tactics. Khrushchev withdrew but ordered a division of the Red Army to pour into Warsaw. By October 22 demonstrations had erupted in cities all over Poland. As word of the Polish insurgence spread to Hungary, student protesters swarmed Budapest, demanding the expulsion of Soviet forces from *their* territory. By October 24 the USSR had dispatched troops, tanks, and armored cars to the Hungarian capital to smother the rebellion.

Whereas the Red Army smashed the uprisings in Poland and Hungary, the British, French, and Israelis made a strong stand in the Sinai and the Canal Zone. The situation couldn't be more explosive. On November 5 Soviet Premier Bulganin cautioned the West that the USSR was "prepared to use force to crush the aggressors" in Egypt. Should the Red Army be introduced into the conflict, hostilities could lead to World War III. He proposed sending a joint Soviet–American force into the theater to compel peace. Bulganin admonished Eisenhower privately, "If this war is not stopped, it is fraught with danger and can grow into a Third World War."[10]

The European assault on Suez prompted Khrushchev to utter his infamous prophecy "We will bury you!" at a reception on November 18. Gomulka had scuttled to Moscow to propitiate the Kremlin. Framing his remarks as a toast to his Polish underling, Khrushchev exclaimed, "The bandit-like attack by Britain, France, and their puppet, Israel, on Egypt is a desperate attempt by colonizers to regain their lost position . . . But the time has passed when imperialists could seize weak countries with impunity." Building to a climax, he couldn't resist goading his guests. "*We* base ourselves on the idea that we must peacefully co-exist. About the capitalist states, it doesn't depend on *you* whether or not we exist. If you don't like us, don't accept our invitations and don't invite us to come to see you. Whether you like it or not, history is on our side. We will bury you!" Emissaries of twelve NATO countries and the Israeli chargé d'affaires waited until Gomulka made a brief reply and then flounced out of the reception hall.[11]

On the same day as Khrushchev's outburst, the Kremlin invited NATO members to a disarmament conference. Its message began, "The armed attack of Britain, France, and Israel on Egypt has created a situation dangerous for peace and has confronted the peoples with the threat of a third world war in all its acuteness." The West was preparing its citizens for a "plunge . . . into the abyss of another world war" for the sake of "fabulous" war profits. The only sensible road was a peace summit. At nearly the same hour, the Soviet news agency *Tass* announced that Russian scientists had exploded their first hydrogen bomb.[12]

On the very next night, November 19, Khrushchev added another dollop to his stew of threat and conciliation. To underscore the earnestness of his support for Nasser, he resumed his tirade against the Western forces arrayed in Egypt, browbeating the British and French for "having cut the throats of the Egyptians" under the guise of restoring order with a police action. "What kind of order is this?" he bellowed. "It is the order of colonizers, the order of enslavement, domination of the strong over the weak!" Once again, the European and Israeli diplomats marched out of the party secretary's presence.[13]

Several months later Khrushchev recast his threat in a spirit of friendly competition. "Recalling a remark about the 'burying' of capitalism that he made recently," one journalist wrote, "Mr. Khrushchev said he had meant that capitalism would 'die a natural death without any violence on our part.' He added, 'Of course, we will contribute to it what we can.'"[14]

Khrushchev was taunting and intemperate. But he was also funny. He could spit out one-liners on the spot. For example, during his trip to the United States in the fall of 1959, he compared an American cocktail with Russian vodka: "They have only just invented this drink and already they are diluting it." On his distaste for the French can-can performed at a Hollywood soundstage: "A person's face is more beautiful than his backside." On the merits of American welfare provisions, he retorted with the proverb, "Only a grave can correct a hunchback." On the Hungarian revolt of 1956 he snapped, "The question of Hungary has stuck in some people's throat like a dead rat. They feel it is unpleasant and yet they cannot spit it out."[15]

Khrushchev was capricious. His notorious capers at the UN General Assembly in 1960 are a case in point. Crowds hissed at him wherever he went. He shrugged it off. "I'm not afraid of it," he told the press. "I was in the Civil War for three years at the front and that was booing—real booing." As he made his way out of his hotel to return to the Soviet UN mission, a throng of nearly three thousand people shouted catcalls at him. He planted himself in the hotel foyer, waggled his hands, and simpered. When he returned later in the day, some elderly women in the lobby jeered him energetically. On his way to the elevator, Khrushchev pivoted, faced the clutch of ladies, and trumpeted, "BOOOOOOO!"[16]

During a speech at the UN in which he chastised President Eisenhower for allowing a U-2 spy plane to penetrate Soviet air space, Khrushchev spoofed an American television commercial. Within moments of beginning, he paused and poured a glass of water. He looked up and grinned, "This is fine Soviet water. I recommend it highly to all who have not tried it." The assembly burst into laughter. Later, he took a sip, held the glass aloft and murmured, "Excellent water." Toward the end of his speech, he exclaimed, "I'm drinking my Borzhom to the bottom!"[17]

Khrushchev hooted at the British prime minister. He heckled an address delivered by General Secretary Dag Hammarskjold. At one point in the secretary's remarks he began to pummel his desk with his fist. Other members of the Soviet delegation soon began to hammer their desks, followed by the delegates from the Warsaw Pact nations, all pounding away in unison.

Seizing a gesture that magnified the dramatic possibilities of the occasion, the Soviet premier wrenched off his shoe and banged it wildly during a debate on colonialism. Lorenzo Sumulong, a member of the Philippine delegation, had been in the midst of urging the assembly to introduce into its anti-colonialist declaration a defense of "the inalienable right to independence of the peoples of Eastern Europe and elsewhere who are deprived of their political and civil rights, and have been swallowed up by the Soviet Union." The deputy foreign minister of Romania, Eduard Menzincescu, bobbed up and objected that the delegates of the UN shouldn't be insulted. The acting chair of the session, an Irish delegate, overruled him.

At this point, Khrushchev lunged onto the rostrum. Sumulong shrank back. Khrushchev waved him aside, muttering "jerk" and "lackey of Western imperialism" in Russian. The chairman again silenced the premier, who stalked back to his seat. Sumulong resumed speaking. Within minutes, Khrushchev tugged off his shoe, leapt up, and brandished it. He slammed his shoe onto his desk and left it there. A moment later, he battered his desk with both fists, which the Soviet delegation immediately mimicked. Sumulong was dumbstruck. The chairman pressed him to continue "in the interest of the dignity of the debate." Switching tactics, Khrushchev cordially addressed the Philippine delegate, whom he called "not a bad man," and invited him to visit the Soviet Union and see for himself how free its peoples were.[18]

Later in the day, Khrushchev again snatched up his shoe, waved his arms, and howled during a speech by the American assistant secretary of state, who had reintroduced the subject of the Soviet domination of Eastern Europe. Khrushchev glowered for a moment, then sat down. Menzincescu scolded Chairman Boland for not having muzzled the American. Besides, he added, the Northern Irish people surely longed for political freedom as much as anyone else. The enraged Boland banged his gavel so violently that its head broke off and arced over his head. "Because of the scene you have just witnessed," he sputtered, "I think the Assembly had better adjourn!" Afterward, an aide announced that the chairman had already begun to adjourn the meeting before Menzincescu had so much as mentioned Northern Ireland. The Romanian sniffed that he'd gladly celebrate Irish emancipation, but hardly thought he had spoken out of turn.[19]

Reporters rushed at Khrushchev. What did he make of the session? Had he changed his mind on the importance of disarmament? He countered cryptically, "If I were to disarm every day, I'd be totally disarmed." He patted his jacket and pulled out his eyeglass case. "This is my only arm." He produced a penknife out of his pocket and remarked, "I have this. Can you puncture such a sack as Wadsworth [James J. Wadsworth, permanent U.S. delegate to the UN] with this?" When asked why no vote had been taken on his proposals for disarmament, Khrushchev smirked, "The main instrument of the president of the General Assembly broke. He rapped his gavel and it broke. How can he proceed without a gavel?"[20]

The next day Sumulong took the floor to object to "the unparliamentary and unkind remarks" by the Soviet premier, who "did not see anything wrong when he called my humble person a 'stooge.'" Khrushchev let loose a great guffaw which was echoed by the Soviet delegation and Communist-bloc members in the Assembly Hall.[21]

What was he up to? Was he mad? Shrewd? Simply joking? Boorish and impertinent, Khrushchev ruptured the distinction between popular speech and diplomatic niceties. By breaching the repertoire of a head of state, he contributed to the uneasy feeling that the times were both ludicrous and sinister.

The Cold War Fantastic

Among the various actors in different strata of American society, who can we find to light up something as evanescent as a mood of nervous uncertainty about the threat of atomic war? Sifting through the population, first we recognize the ordinary folks who comfortably tolerated the repressed threat. Communist aggression, atomic war, bombers, rockets, radiation burns, and fallout lurked in the cultural landscape but were not easily cut out of the background for careful attention, except by worriers like the civil defenders, the world federalists, the disarmers, and the atomic scientists.

Next, we separate out politically-minded citizens directly engaged in the cold war—writers and journalists, some industrialists, the military and the political classes. After the settlement of the Korean War, these Americans had little definite proof of immediate Communist intentions on which to focus their anxieties. They dreaded an indistinct, improbable Something. The fuzziness of the threat meant "the real problem is not to prevent ourselves from being destroyed in some specific manner, but from being destroyed *in any way whatsoever.*" Without reliable intelligence of the Kremlin's aims, all possible scenarios were valid. America would have to prepare not for one future but for all possible futures.[22]

Certainly our man Kahn took this principle to heart. He insisted that the very idea of a Soviet strike out of the blue was not macabre. "I have found among too many people the utmost resistance to taking seriously the idea of 'gambling' or 'reckless' Russians. I do not believe such resistance to be based on sound intuition . . . Under the new conditions of the Soviet counter-deterrent [that is, the presumed Russian strategic advantage of the missile gap], the past may be a poor guide to the future." The very supposition of unexpected events opened the door to phantasmagoria. In the face of uncertainty, Kahn argued, not only must one study the transparent facts that commanded attention, but worry far more about the situation's indefinite qualities. In this connection, Max Singer pointed out, "He often talked about the advantages of a good paranoid, who could smell out not only things that weren't there, but there might be some things that *were* there that others wouldn't notice."[23]

Whereas everybody was absolutely uncertain about Soviet intentions, and less than certain about the speed, schedule, and output of the Soviet weapons production program, some smaller fraction of defense professionals groped further outside of the visible spectrum into the twilight realm where Seeming is Being. The air force's argument—that one couldn't prove that missiles aren't on launchers just because they couldn't be seen—defines the outer reaches of cold war perception. If by 1961 other intelligence analysts had forsaken the idea of a crash missile program in the USSR, how could SAC officers have been so preposterously mistaken? Perhaps this was only bootstrapping, in which the more missiles the other side has, the more the air force would have to acquire to outperform them. While this was undoubtedly a factor, so too was the anxiety excited by uncertainty itself. Spurred on by the indefinite Something of Soviet hostility, SAC officers felt compelled to speculate about unseen, undetectable possibilities.

We can turn to literature to show us on how panic and dread aroused by uncertainty prepares the mind for haunting disturbances. Stories conforming to the genre of the fantastic characteristically explore the hysteria and hesitancies provoked by uncertainty. What distinguishes the fantastic genre from fantasy and suspense is that it lingers at the point of irresolution. The things that menace a hero could be visitors from the spirit world, which would put the story squarely into the fantasy genre, or they could be the shenanigans of a mortal foe, or hallucinations induced by illness, drugs, or dreams, all of which would make the story a thriller. But fantastic stories hover between the mundane and imaginary worlds. Once a decision is made about the nature of the menace, it resolves into a footprint of the actual world, or collapses into marvelous froth.[24]

There are two other qualities of the fantastic genre that throw light on the impulse toward extravagant speculation among some intelligence analysts. The first has to do with uncertainty about what one sees. In classic fantastic stories, there is always some kind of perceptual trouble. The object world is murky and can only be viewed with the aid of some kind of instrument: a mirror, a field-glass, a keyhole, a pair of spectacles. One can't be sure if the thing is really there, or seems to be there because of a scratch in an instrument lens, or maybe it's just the cock-eyed hiccup from a bad dinner and a glass or two of sour wine.

The other motif from the fantastic genre worth highlighting has to do with the world from which the menace springs. Fantastic stories split the world into two: the mundane world, where uncertainties resolve into explainable phenomena, and the magical world of gods, spirits, and dead souls. Until a decision is made about the nature of the menace, fantastic stories give us the picture of a hero wandering in and out of daily life into the nether world. Probable and improbable worlds are both present to him during the interval of his uncertainty.

We can find both motifs in cold war speculations. Intelligence analysts labored over indistinct images snapped by cameras dangling from air force balloons, from impossibly high flights of the U-2 plane, and the first generation of spy satellites. And we could look to Kahn for samples of the double world of the fantastic. He moved easily between the peacetime present and the postwar world. Where an ordinary man saw a subway tunnel, Kahn saw a subway *and* a dormitory for postwar survivors. Where an ordinary woman saw the medical miracles of chest x-rays and penicillin, Kahn saw the march of progress *and* proof that postwar survivors would do just fine.

For Kahn, the proper referents for nuclear planning were the twinned realms of the status quo and the improbable but not impossible world of nuclear war. The analyst therefore had to transpose his perception of the bomb as a peacetime deterrent into the means for fighting and winning an all-out war. Most men could not make the shift. Kahn repeatedly reproached his readers for thinking of nuclear war as an unreality that could not even be pictured in the imagination. "Thermonuclear war seems so horrible that it is difficult for most people to imagine that such events can—and do—occur." Even war planners had "enormous psychological difficulty" in admitting a thermonuclear war could be "a disaster that may be experienced and recovered from."[25]

The very cipher of nuclear war—its horrific lack of content—swept the concept into the uncertainties of the fantastic. And yet, time and again, drowsing in the all-too-somnolent placidity of a sunny day, the all-too-gentle rustle of eventide, people would startle to awareness and wonder whether the next moment would bleach the world white in a long-dreaded, long-forgotten surprise attack on American cities.

A Feeling of Inevitability

The felt worlds of 1945, 1951, and 1960 were unlike. However, a continuous thread ran through the war scare of 1948, the World War III scare during the Korean War, the convulsions of McCarthyism, the crises in Poland, Hungary, and the Suez Canal, the launch of *Sputnik* in 1957, up to the collapse of the Geneva Summit and Khrushchev's shoe-banging episodes at the General Assembly in 1960. Throughout it all, free-floating dread twisted the bowels of many Americans. Some identified fear of atomic cataclysm as being behind it all.

The present was often characterized as "the possible and intellectually probable end of mankind." In his book *The Atom Bomb and the Future of Man*, Karl Jaspers argued that the bomb necessitated "a new way of thinking." Physical scientists had been the first observers to mark this world-historic upheaval in human possibility. The physicist Max Born articulated for Jaspers the change. He had written, "Today we do not have much time left; it is up to our generation to succeed in thinking differently. If we fail, the days of civilized humanity are numbered."[26]

Atomic weapons seemed to draw cosmic forces down into the evanescent present. At the Trinity test at Los Alamos in July 1945 the physicist Enrico Fermi wondered aloud whether the blast would ignite the atmosphere. Eleven years later, Senator Estes Kefauver announced that an H-bomb blast could jolt the earth off its rotational axis by sixteen degrees. Uttered by social actors with varying political and scientific perceptions of their present moment, we can find traces of the feelings expressed by the comic book editors: "This is the atom age! The unbelievable has already begun to come true!" The A-bomb oriented dazzled and uneasy minds toward technical and scientific inventions. Radar, jet engines, rockets, automated systems, and digital computers defined the unbelievable dimensions of the present.[27]

Possible atomic Armageddon excited widespread movements for the establishment of a world federalist government, or at least for international control over atomic research and development. However, not everyone in the United States adopted a transcendental outlook. Stoicism was by far the prevailing public emotion in the United States. More than a year into the Korean War, *Time* magazine presented the results of a national survey of youth between the ages of eighteen and twenty-eight. Young people were "waiting for the hand of fate to fall on [their] shoulders, meanwhile working fairly hard and saying almost nothing." Looking at patterns of education, work, marriage, childrearing, and carousing, the reporters seemed dismayed by the peculiar impassivity of American youth:

> Intellectually, today's young people already seem a bit stodgy. Their adventures of the mind are apt to be mild and safe . . . Young people seem to have no militant beliefs. They do not speak out for anything . . . The only two issues about which

> the younger generation seems to get worked up are race rela-
> tions and world government; but neither of these issues rouses
> anything approaching an absorbing faith . . . GI Joe's younger
> brother . . . does not go in for heroics or believe in them. He is
> short on ideals, lacks self-reliance, is for personal security at
> any price. He singularly lacks flame.[28]

Since they had no active part in thwarting the danger of war, young people assumed an attitude of subdued forbearance. *Time*'s portrait closed on a cheerless note. "The best thing that can be said for American youth," concluded the writers (who must have congratulated themselves for having been jollier in *their* twenties) "is that it has learned that it must try to make the best of a bad and difficult job . . . The fact of this world is war, uncertainty, the need for work, courage, sacrifice . . . Youth today has little cynicism, because it never hoped for much."[29]

Those who *could* perform a role in the cold war—the analysts, military leaders, and politicians who cut for themselves a part in the ordeal—became aroused to hyper-vigilance. The uncertain factors shaping an inevitable future war fomented an occult view of the present. Analysts anxiously scanned the proclamations of Soviet leaders, Continental Air Defense anxiously scanned the American frontier for incoming bombers, and McCarthyite tribunals anxiously scanned the dossiers of potential subversives for clues about the intentions of the bosses of the Comintern. Putting the *Time* survey together with Kremlinology, we can define the feeling-state of the engaged cold war public: credulity offset by fatalistic forbearance.

The activities of the volunteers in the civilian Ground Observer Corps enacted this skittish fortitude by combing the skies for Red bombers. From 1952 to 1957 Americans were pelted with shop-window posters, newspaper and magazine advertisements, radio announcements, and even leaflets dropped from planes exhorting them to "Look to the Skies!" and "Wake Up, Sign Up, Look Up!" and join the civilian Ground Observer Corps. The GOC sought publicity everywhere. Floats appeared in holiday parades; celebrities such as

Bing Crosby, Joan Crawford, and Nat King Cole pitched GOC volunteerism on radio programs or in person. Highway billboards and movie shorts solicited GOC volunteers. Local chapters hosted talent shows, beauty pageants, square dances, ice cream socials, and bake sales. They were sponsored by city and county councils, churches and high schools, labor unions and private firms, men's service organizations, veterans associations, Chambers of Commerce, Boy Scouts, Girl Scouts, Air Scouts, Eagle Scouts, Sea Scouts, Explorer Scouts, and Ladies Auxiliary service groups. At its peak in 1956, more than 400,000 people were enrolled nationwide as cadres in the Ground Observer Corps.[30]

Families established observation posts in their homes, while young people formed clubs to inspect the skies around the clock. Whole cities threw themselves into GOC work. Stories of dedicated attendance abounded. A World War I veteran devoted seventeen hours each day to Skywatch observation. Twice weekly a housewife traipsed three miles at midnight to operate the local observation post until eight o'clock the next morning. Boys as young as nine and ten operated a twenty-four hour watch at their school. Volunteers for a not-yet-built observation post in Colorado participated in three alerts during winter blizzards by keeping watch near a bonfire lit in the middle of their town's main street.[31]

At times, enthusiasm for ground observing was heartbreakingly comic. Whenever a plane flew over the South Dakota village of Yale, a small crowd sprinted to the post office to compete for the chance to file a report to the nearest filter center. So great was the general concern not to let air traffic go by without identification that one woman installed a loudspeaker in her home so that she could hear planes eight miles away. Another woman regularly roused herself from sleep (with help from her indoor amplifier), grabbed her binoculars, and dashed into her yard to identify overhead planes. A farm wife canvassed the skies while milking her cows. Even pet dogs and farmyard geese and ducks were enrolled as aircraft spotters.[32]

What motivated people to devote themselves to ground observing? Certainly, the pleasure in sociable effort shouldn't be minimized.

The GOC's dances, beauty pageants, parties, and award ceremonies played a role in attracting volunteers. "I love the work," said one woman, "and I know that others would too if they only knew how they are needed." Yet civic conviviality was not the principal reason that thousands of Americans hoisted binoculars to follow the vapor trail of every plane that streaked by. Over and over again, the GOC magazine reported testimonies of alarm. People felt defenseless in their homes, schools, offices, factories, and farms. After she learned how a low-flying Soviet bomber might slip through the radar net without anyone's notice, another woman "thought to myself, 'This could happen to us, and if I can help, I will.'" Another woman remarked, "I haven't forgotten how frightened we were in Bremerton [Washington] at the time of Pearl Harbor." And frightened was what the GOC volunteers seemed to be. World War III could erupt at any moment. Only unbroken watchfulness from every point in the nation's interior could ensure a secure air defense.[33]

The Ground Observer Corps was inaugurated on June 1, 1950, by the Continental Air Command. The air force had recognized its need for human "gap-fillers" in the warning network as early as November 1949. Radar could not detect aircraft flying at altitudes lower than four thousand feet. There were also holes in the radar coverage of the North American perimeter. In 1951, with the assistance of the Civil Aeronautics Administration, the air force authorized an Air Defense Identification Zone at the borders of the United States, in which all aircraft flying higher than four thousand feet would be required to identify themselves. The volunteers of the GOC were tasked to identify multiengine aircraft flying *below* this altitude. (Whence the term "unidentified flying object" for nonstandard or unrecognizable craft espied from the ground.)

Originally, the plan was to station civilian volunteers eight miles apart throughout the nation. Upon hearing the whine of a turboprop plane, the volunteer would get a fix on the plane's trajectory, identify it by shape and markings, and phone the information to a regional filter center. From there, if requested by local civil aeronautics authorities, the filter center would forward the information to the local

Air Defense base, which would scramble planes skyward for further reconnaissance.

As of July 1, 1950, only 402 of the needed eight thousand observation posts were staffed. But soon after, American mobilization for the Korean War aroused the public, and by year's end volunteers filled more than half of the posts in the Eastern and Western Defense Force areas. However, air force officers supervising the GOC noted drooping enthusiasm among their corps in the Eastern and Central Air Defense regions. After the excitement of training, volunteers found the absence of air traffic a letdown. To inspire them, the air force invited members of the Civil Air Patrol to fly over areas where local flights could not be arranged in order to relieve the ground observers' boredom.

In October 1951 the Air Defense Command remedied its problems in recruitment, morale, and retention. Henceforth, a perimeter zone from one hundred to two hundred miles in depth around the borders of the continent would be created, within which the Ground Observer Corps would be put on twenty-four-hour alert. The remaining posts were shunted to reserve status. Cadres for Operation Skywatch were given intensive indoctrination, quasi-military uniforms, and a more prominent public relations profile. General Hoyt Vandenberg, the air force chief of staff, announced the inauguration of the Skywatch program on April 23, 1952. When round-the-clock surveillance began in July, of the 200,000 GOC members, 150,000 enrolled in Skywatch service.[34]

Alas, Skywatch was a disappointment. In the Central Air Defense area, there was little activity to entertain the round-the-clock ground observers, who volunteered for shifts as long as twelve hours at a stretch. On the other hand, air traffic in the Eastern Air Defense area was so dense that it was impossible to identify the speed, direction, and type of every multiengine aircraft overhead. The Eastern Air Defense command soon dropped the idea of compelling identification of all air traffic. Instead, civilian observers were instructed to look out for unusual phenomena. (Eventually, observation posts in New York City, New Jersey, and other congested air corridors were retired to standby status.) As a sign of the suspense (and tedium) of observers across the nation, the reports that the GOC *did* pass on through the volunteer-run filter centers to the Air Defense Command were often erroneous. A 1953 study noted "an excessive number of manifestly friendly tracks were being reported . . . to the overtaxed radar network."[35]

Skywatch was intended to be a transitional measure until improvements such as additional interceptors, ground-to-air missiles, gap-filler radars, offshore Texas Towers and picket ships, the Distant Early Warning (DEW) Line, the Airborne Early Warning and Control program, and the Semi-Automatic Ground Environment (SAGE) system were installed later in the decade. By the end of 1957, the Skywatch program was terminated, and the GOC was phased out on January 31, 1959.[36]

While in absolute numbers the Ground Observer Corps represented a scant fraction of the population, it attracted extraordinary participation. In addition to the usual civic volunteers of the period—housewives, retirees, church and city boosters—the GOC recruited people ordinarily regarded as marginal to the public life of the nation: boys and girls in state reformatories, prisoners, Native Americans on reservations, Alaskans, teenagers, mothers of young children, Catholic monks, people with disabilities. Geese and wide-awake dogs played their part by helpfully alerting their human keepers to approaching flights. When more observers were needed, other groups were roped in. State and federal forest service personnel manned observation posts, as did members of the Coast Guard, the National Wildlife and Park Services, government weather stations, and fish hatcheries.[37]

The cadres of the Ground Observer Corps reads like a Whitmanesque muster: lumbermen in the Pacific Northwest; fishermen in the mid-Atlantic states and in the Great Lakes; offshore merchant marines along the East Coast; ferry pilots on the Mississippi River; engineers running the rural electric cooperatives of Montana and Minnesota; tugboat captains from Seattle to Alaska; rig operators for the Sun Oil Company's Pennsylvania pumping stations; section and depot crews of the Chicago, Burlington, Quincy, Rock Island, Northwestern, Western Pacific, Gulf-Mobile, and Ohio railroads—all were enrolled in the GOC. Dam tenders for the Ohio River and the Imperial Dam in Yuma, more than a hundred bridge attendants in North Carolina, and toll collectors at the New York State and Ohio Turnpikes watched the skies. Taxicab drivers working the late shift in Marshalltown, Iowa, kept track of flights over the city. The State Highway Patrol in North Dakota and Wisconsin and the police organizations of Indiana and Michigan kept a lookout. Inmates at the West Virginia Prison for Women at Pence Springs and the men's honor camp of the West Virginia State Penitentiary, four Northern Michigan prison camps, the California State Prison at Folsom, Attica State Prison in New York, the Nevada State Prison in Carson City, the Delaware New Castle Workhouse, the Virginia State Penitentiary, the Statesville Penitentiary in Joliet, Illinois, and forty-eight prison camps in North Carolina were trained for ground observer work. So were the nurses of Mercy Hospital in Dubuque, Iowa, the guards at the Iowa State Penitentiary in Fort Madison, Iowa, and the Navajo Tribal Police in Tuba City, Arizona.

It is tempting but wrong to confuse the Americans who hurtled out of their beds and into their yards to inspect an overhead plane with the vigilantes of horror movies who feverishly scoured the horizon for Godzilla or other atomic mutants. Rather than giving way to an all-too-easy disdain for the futile watchfulness of the Ground Observer Corps, one can't help but be awed by the mosaic of people scattered across the country who volunteered for Skywatch. The fact that so many different kinds of people joined the GOC demonstrates the somber involvement in the next catastrophe that many Americans must have felt.

The Korean War and World War III

So preoccupied have we been with mood and style up to this point, we have neglected to register the principal events of the cold war period. Here is a summary.

The USSR padded its frontier by establishing outlying satellite states, beginning with Finland in March 1946 and Poland the following January. On March 12, 1947, President Truman declared America's determination to check Communist expansion into Europe. However, the Soviets annexed Hungary and Bulgaria that September, Romania in December, and Czechoslovakia in February 1948.

In late June 1948 the USSR barricaded all surface approaches to the Western sectors of Berlin. The United States responded with a massive airlift, shuttling food and basic necessities to West Berliners for close to a year. The Western allies founded the North American Treaty Organization (NATO) on April 4, 1949, as a bulwark in Europe against further Communist penetration.

The occupying powers established the Federal Republic of Germany on May 23, 1949. The following October, East German Communists announced the establishment of the Soviet-dominated German Democratic Republic. In Asia, civil war erupted in China in May 1946. By October 1949 Mao Zedung proclaimed the People's Republic of China. Kim Il Sung founded North Korea in February 1948 and promptly accepted aid from the USSR.

On the home front, the Truman administration prowled after Communists allegedly infiltrating unions, schools, entertainment, and journalism. Loyalty investigations of federal employees began in March 1947. In the following October, the House Committee on Un-American Activities opened an inquisition into radicals suspected of contaminating the entertainment industry. In February 1950 Senator Joseph McCarthy gloated that he had unearthed 205 subversives in the State Department.

Finally, perhaps the single most important fact to be registered as background to the ascendancy of the bomb was the demobilization of American forces in 1945 and the subsequent contraction of military expenditures to peacetime levels. From 1945 to 1950 President Truman imposed budget ceilings on defense appropriations. His thrift resulted in perceived shortages in manpower, weaponry, and supplies in all three armed services. Given his tight-fisted economies and the fact that the Red Army could marshal infinitely more ground forces than the United States and NATO, by 1949 the President and the joint chiefs resolved that atomic weapons would be the lynchpin of an American strategy that threatened atomic war in response to Soviet adventures in Europe.

Conservatives in Western intelligence circles guessed that it would take the Soviets as long as twenty years to master atomic weapons science. On September 23, 1949, Truman announced that the Russians had successfully detonated their first bomb, dubbed Joe-1. Four months later, the President authorized the inauguration of H-bomb research, which would increase the explosive magnitude of The Bomb a thousandfold. Given the fact that the atomic monopoly had been broken, hydrogen (thermonuclear) weapons research seemed to satisfy the demand for moderating defense expenditures while stiffening national security.

As wave after wave of crises from 1947 to 1949 unnerved Americans—especially the blockade of Berlin in 1948, Joe-1 in 1949, and Mao's victory in the same year—the Korean War looked like the opening gambit of a Communist strategy to incite World War III. On June 25 North Korean troops bolted into South Korea. On June 27 the President ordered the air force and navy into the theater to beef up the Republic of Korea's army. Some weeks later Truman asked Congress to institute a draft. Having a practical basis for complaint, the joint chiefs of staff could now press their demands for more funds. From $10.5 billion for fiscal year 1950, Congress authorized $48 billion to pay for troop mobilization. Still, Truman confided to his budget director that he "had no desire to put any more money than necessary . . . into the hands of the military." Whereas the JCS repeatedly asked for double, then triple the pre–Korean War defense budget, the President demurred, waiting to see how events unfolded in Asia and elsewhere.[38]

His real worry was that Kim Il Sung's invasion of the South might be a Communist ploy to ensnare America's troops in Asia, thereby clearing the way for a new phase of global war. The next move might be to snatch petroleum reserves in the Persian Gulf, or mobilize the

Red Army around Berlin. During the summer of 1950 American analysts scrutinized Soviet activity around the world for clues. A CIA intelligence memorandum of June 30 foretold "strong provocative actions" in Berlin and Vienna as part of a Soviet "war-of-nerves" calculated to scatter American might.[39]

During the summer and fall of 1950 South Korean and international forces routed Kim's army. By October UN forces crossed the South Korean border and began pushing the Korean People's Army (KPA) northward. The KPA yielded Pyongyang on October 19. General MacArthur's troops pursued them to the Chinese–Korean border. With the surrender of their capital city, the North Korean regime seemed close to collapse.

But in late October thirty-six divisions of the Chinese People's Volunteers (about 300,000 troops) surged into Korean territory, fortified by twelve wings and air defense divisions of the Soviet air force. Just when the conflict looked as though it was nearing a terminal point in mid-October, the Chinese entry into the conflict intensified the danger of general war. Even so, holding firm against his military, Truman forbade the bombing of Chinese staging bases in Manchuria and any other escalating tactics.

In early December the Chinese repulsed the UN troops across the 38th parallel and pushed them back into southern territories. At this point, Truman felt compelled to yield to pressure from the joint chiefs. While the crisis forced the President to allow greater defense expenditures, most of these increases were for troops stationed not in Korea but elsewhere. Europe remained America's primary security commitment. It was still vulnerable to Soviet aggression. Procurement for the Strategic Air Command was given the highest priority, even though the air force had immediate needs in Korea.

By summer 1951 the opposing forces in Korea faced an impasse. But the Soviets had not swept into Western Europe as analysts had feared. America sent word to China, the USSR, and North Korea that it wished to open peace talks. It looked as though the war might draw to a close shortly. Hostilities maundered on for two more years, concluding in stalemate in 1953.

Even though the Chinese entry into Korea had been expected, the event itself stunned Truman: "I've worked for peace for five years and six months, and it looks like World War III is here," he wrote in his diary. Kim's invasion of South Korea gave the long-suppressed uneasiness of the American people a definite focus. Robert Patterson, the former secretary of war, petitioned the President to divert a full quarter of the GNP into a crash mobilization, urging Truman to prepare the nation for the "total danger" of war.[40]

In a speech in Dallas on June 13, 1950, Secretary of State Dean Acheson rejected the option of preventive war. But by August, there were cries on many sides for America to pounce on the USSR immediately. On August 10 congressional leaders met with Secretary Acheson to press for preventive war. "Sentiment" for American aggression "through the country [is] building up," declared Senator Estes Kefauver. The commandant of the Air War College, Major General Orvil Anderson, publicly pleaded with the President to take the initiative. "Give me the order to do it and I can break up Russia's five A-bomb nests in a week!" Secretary of the Navy Francis Mathews urged the nation to adopt a "peace-seeking policy" that would "cast us in a character new to a true democracy—an initiator of a war of aggression. It would win for us a proud and popular title. We would become the first aggressors for peace." Mathews was uncompromisingly clear about what he meant by being an "aggressor for peace," namely, "instituting a war to compel cooperation for peace." It was the only way to "effect the salvation of the free world." (Neither demand went down well with Truman: Anderson was bumped from the war college; Mathews was humiliatingly reprimanded.)[41]

At the height of the widespread anxiety about world war, Soviet Premier Joseph Stalin stepped forward in February 1951 to discuss the international scene for the first time in two years. In answer to a question whether another world war was inevitable, he replied, "[At] the present time it cannot be considered inevitable. Of course, in the United States of America, in Britain, as also in France, there are aggressive forces thirsting for a new war." Nerves were so jangled that these spare comments mollified many observers.[42]

A year later, in 1952, at the Lisbon convocation of NATO, journalists reported "strong indications that Moscow does not really believe in any possibility of peaceful co-existence between the capitalist and Communist systems." Nevertheless, while yet pursuing "the program of Stalinist world revolution," NATO ministers concluded that the Kremlin sought "at all costs to avoid 'excessive risk' to the Soviet Union itself." They therefore decided that rearming West Germany under NATO command was not provocative enough to oblige the Russians "to initiate actions that might risk a third world war." At the meeting, Secretary Acheson firmly reiterated that the United States absolutely rejected a policy of preventive war.[43]

Still, the impulse to jumpstart World War III could not be squelched in a single stroke. "It seems to me the time is ripe for a blow this year," mused the military attaché in Moscow in his diary in 1951. To his everlasting chagrin, General Robert Gow's jottings were published in an East German newspaper and in a book written by a British Communist. Someone had nabbed his diary from his Frankfurt hotel room, photographed it, and returned it without his knowledge. Gow had scrawled such lines as "War! As soon as possible! Now!" "We need a voice to lead us without equivocation: Communism must be destroyed!" "We must understand that this war is total and is fought with all weapons." As soon as the story broke, he was yanked from the American embassy in Moscow and sent packing.[44]

The Will to Believe

While the impulse to get it over with was an irritable tic on the part of some Americans, let's consider the assessment of the worldwide danger of the Korean War set forth by more circumspect observers. Having canvassed the threat perceptions of ordinary citizens and impatient militants for preventive war, we can turn to the National Intelligence Estimates of the threat of atomic war and see for ourselves the uncertainty with which even the best informed people sought to construe the events of 1950.

During the first six months of the Korean War, the CIA wondered whether the Chinese army would fight or limit their activity to offering staging areas for the KPA. And what would have to happen for Stalin to commit Red Army troops? Let's have a look at these threat assessments in order to familiarize ourselves with the drift of political-military inference during the early years of cold war.

As soon as they were founded in 1948, both the Republic of Korea and the Democratic People's Republic of Korea announced that the first business of their governments would be to reunify the peninsula, following the withdrawal of occupation forces. Throughout the rest of 1948 and all of 1949, intelligence analysts expected civil war to break out at any time. Just before Kim's invasion of South Korea, a CIA assessment reviewed his military capabilities. The authors believed that it was unlikely that Kim could single-handedly conquer the South. Moreover, the Soviets and Chinese would not fight alongside Kim "except as a last resort." Clearly, the Soviets understood that their presence in Korea would escalate a local conflict into a major provocation of the United States and her allies.[45]

On the heels of Kim's southern campaign, in June 1950 the Truman administration sought the views of everyone in a position of responsibility. Analysts stationed at the American embassy in Moscow interpreted the situation as an unambiguous challenge to the United States, "which should be answered firmly and swiftly because it constitutes a direct threat to US leadership of the free world against Soviet Communist imperialism." Should the West shirk its obligation to assist Syngman Rhee in South Korea, they felt sure that the Kremlin would interpret this as Western sufferance of an expanded Communist presence in East Asia.[46]

The CIA concurred, noting that Stalin had "probably calculated that no firm or effective countermeasures would be taken by the West." The basis for assuming American indifference in East Asia was Secretary Acheson's remarks to the National Press Club on January 12, 1950, in which he affirmed that a "new day has dawned" in the Asian Pacific. Henceforth, the United States would not shelter these territories. "It is a day in which the Asian peoples are on their own and know it and intend to continue on their own."[47]

It was one thing to be confronted with civil war in Asia; it was another to face a Soviet invasion of Western Europe. If the Communists seemed ready to advance against West Berlin or Vienna, then the Korean affair must be regarded as the opening move of world war. However, reports in late June found "no evidence . . . indicating Soviet preparations for military operations in the West European theater." The CIA concluded that the Korean adventure was harassment only. The Soviets wanted "to make the US effort . . . as difficult and costly as possible."[48]

Even two weeks into the conflict, the CIA was still in the dark about Soviet aims. "The world [is] still waiting for some indication of Soviet intentions . . . At the moment, the Soviet and Communist propaganda line offers no clue." Should the South Korean and UN forces drive back the KPA, would the Soviets rally to assist Kim? "All evidence available leads to the conclusion that the USSR is not ready for war." The authors suggested that Stalin was more likely to protract the war for as long as possible, and perhaps "initiate hostilities elsewhere." Perhaps the mobilization of American forces had, in fact, moderated the ambitions of the Kremlin.[49]

While intelligence officers were confident that Stalin would avoid committing his soldiers to battle, they were less sure about Mao. As early as July 7 Chinese troops were reported near the Korean border. By September, UN forces had so routed the KPA that Soviet or Chinese forces would be needed to avert defeat. A series of intelligence briefs speculated whether and when the Chinese, who had begun to amass in Manchuria, would enter combat. Should they do so, they would "substantially increase the risk of general war."[50]

General MacArthur's landing at Inchon on September 15 squeezed the Soviets ever more sharply as he drove northward. The CIA repeatedly argued that the danger of general war presented "compelling reasons" for the Soviets to withhold their forces, even it meant allowing Kim's regime to be overthrown. (As we now know from Khrushchev, as recounted by a Russian historian, on October 13, 1950, "Stalin . . . was willing to abandon North Korea and allow the United States to become the USSR's neighbor, with its troops deployed in Korea, if this was the price to pay for avoiding direct military confrontation with the US at that time.")[51]

Throughout September and October reports filtered in regarding the Chinese decision to intervene in Korea. Yet even on the last day of October, the CIA hesitated about Chinese involvement. By November 3 there at last could be no doubt that Mao's troops had joined forces with the KPA. While many people were panic-stricken about pending global war, an early assessment of the Chinese action was nicely circumspect. While "the Chinese Communists . . . have accepted a grave risk of US–UN retaliation and general war," the report made much of the "limited extent of their intervention" and suggested that it was more likely "defensive in nature."[52]

Five months into the war, the CIA established the Office of National Estimates. On November 15, 1950, it delivered its first national intelligence estimate (NIE) to President Truman. While recognizing that solid information was missing, the NIE stated, "It must be recognized, however, that a grave danger of general war exists now." The possibility of a sudden strike against the United States and her allies remained ever-present should Stalin conclude he could obliterate the West in a disarming blow.[53]

The August estimate of the following year (1951) began with the credo, "We believe that . . . [the Kremlin is persuaded that] an armed conflict between [the West and the USSR] is eventually inevitable." The USSR would scramble to match any development in Western military capabilities and maintain "an advanced state of war-readiness." The authors regretted that they couldn't offer the President a definite finding of whether or not the Soviets *intended* to precipitate war. Instead, they surmised that "the USSR has the capability to launch general war . . . The international situation is so tense that at any time some issue might develop to a point beyond control."[54]

The CIA had prophesied the cusp of 1952 as the summit of danger. While assuming the Communists expected "an ultimate frightful collision" between the West and East, the January 1952 NIE admitted that a surprise attack in the near future was improbable, given the fact that the Red Army had not stormed Western Europe. Even so, the authors couldn't refrain from suggesting that the Soviets *might* pulverize their enemies. They wrote menacingly, if uncertainly: "The possibility of deliberate initiation of general war cannot be excluded at any time merely because such initiation would contradict past Soviet political strategy. Further, the possibility of deliberate initiation of general war cannot be excluded even if, judged from the outside, it seemed certain that the interests of the USSR would be better served by other courses of action." While cautiously phrased, the postulate that the Kremlin was determined to wage an aggressive war against reason and available evidence is plainly perverse.[55]

The Missile Gap, 1957–1961

With the stalemate of the Korean War and both sides' invention of a working hydrogen weapon in 1953, the next focal object in the arms race was the production of a delivery vehicle for the bomb. For the remainder of the decade, analysts assumed that Soviet aggression was inhibited only by this lack.

The Korean War gave intelligence analysts real events to scrutinize. With the stalemate of 1951, threat perception regressed to divination. Lacking definitive information, analysts filled in the outlines of the Red Menace with mirror images. As early as 1948 the chairman of the Atomic Energy Commission deplored "the way the intelligence agencies deal with the meager stuff they have. It is chiefly a matter of reasoning from our own American experience, guessing how much longer it will take Russia using our methods and based upon our problems of achieving weapons."[56]

If the threat assessments of the Korean War were marginally defensible inferences of Communist intentions, the missile gap of the second half of the 1950s shows how analysts educed the worst possible prognosis for impending war. Soviet missile superiority seemed to realize the promise of the V-2 rocket threat, which had been cast since 1945 as the apocalyptic medium of the next catastrophe. The details underlying guesses about the rate of Soviet missile production are actually decisive. Measuring the magnitude of the threat takes us right into the No Man's Land of fantastic credulity. In the missile gap, analysts detected missiles in the ectoplasmic traces of Nothing At All.

The story begins with signals intelligence. Wartime technologies for eavesdropping on the enemy's radio, telephone, and telegraph communications were refined in the late 1940s. By monitoring Soviet communications, analysts discovered the existence of a missile testing facility that had been established to develop the rocket technology pried from kidnapped German engineers immediately after the war. The CIA became aware of Kapustin Yar in the spring of 1947. Otherwise, most of the reliable intelligence about bases, railroads, and other strategic targets within the USSR was known from World War II–era Luftwaffe aerial photographs. However, since the Germans had been concerned mainly with the western front, huge swathes of the Soviet Far East were unknown to Western intelligence agencies.[57]

Engineers scrambled to devise technologies that could augment the crumbs of human intelligence gleaned from behind the Iron Curtain. This is the gadgety stuff of spy novels. Unbelievably, the air force thought it might snoop on its enemies with high-altitude balloons. Project Genetrix disseminated camera-carrying balloons that were meant to waft over the Soviet Bloc countries and the People's Republic of China. Steeled by the air force's emphatic guarantee that the balloons could not be discovered by radar, seized, or intercepted, President Eisenhower reluctantly approved their release in late December 1955.

By the end of February 516 balloons were launched to float east on the trade winds from Western Europe. They tended to drift south rather than eastward, alighting in the Chinese desert, the Black Sea, Southern Europe, and the Mediterranean. Some were shot down, and others landed thousands of miles away from their targets. The Russian press gleefully displayed American cameras, transmitters, and polyethylene gasbags to the international media. The Kremlin accused the United States of going to the brink of war by secretly releasing these balloons over its territory. The air force sheepishly rejoined that the balloons had been used for weather research spon-sored by the International Geophysical Year. Eisenhower quashed the program *tout de suite*.[58]

Amazingly, this random operation yielded the richest booty of images of the interior of the Soviet Union since the captured Luftwaffe photographs of the previous decade. Of the 516 balloons, 34 succeeded in photographing Russian or Chinese terrain. Even odder than that, the bar on the balloon from which hung the camera and ballast equipment happened to resonate with a Soviet radar fre-quency used for early warning and ground-controlled interception. When Soviet radar pulses connected with the bar of the balloon, it vibrated in such a way that American and NATO intelligence per-sonnel could locate these air-defense radar installations. The result was that, at the end of the two-month operation, NATO had gath-ered a cornucopia of information on Soviet Bloc radar nets and ground-controlled interception technologies.[59]

The air force couldn't resist the sneaky allure of more balloon espionage. On July 7, 1958, they launched three additional camera-carrying balloons from an aircraft carrier in the Bering Sea. The bal-loons touched down in Poland and the USSR. In addition to formal protests of the violation of their airspace, the Soviets again exhibited the recovered aircraft and cameras to a wondering international audi-ence.[60]

When the National Security Agency introduced radar for intelli-gence gathering, it was a welcome reliable asset. It captured the speed and thrust of missile trajectories and determined whether or not tests had been successes. In 1955, the NSA established its first radar sta-tion near Samsoun, Turkey. The Turkish radar tracked Soviet inter-mediate-range ballistic missile (IRBM) test launches at the R&D fa-cility at Kapustin Yar. By late 1956 it detected forty to fifty test shots for an intercontinental ballistic missile (ICBM).[61]

On July 27, 1955, the CIA began preliminary trials of its se-cret high-altitude reconnaissance plane, the U-2. Soon thereafter, square-jawed unflappable commercial pilots began to report substantial numbers of UFOs to air traffic controllers and to federal civil and air force aviation authorities. The silver-painted U-2, flying 40,000 to 50,000 feet higher than commercial aircraft, scintillated in the beams of a setting sun. Air Force Project Blue Book investigators routinely crosschecked UFO sightings against the flight logs maintained by the CIA's project staff. While most sightings were resolved with reference to U-2 flight paths, the air force could not disclose the truth about the glowing object in the sky to complainants or the press.[62]

President Eisenhower had been just as loath to approve the civilian U-2 program as he had the air force's balloon scheme. He worried that the planes could be tracked by radar, or—heaven forbid—intercepted. "If uniformed personnel of the armed services of the United States fly over Russia, it is an act of war—legally—and I don't want any part of it." U-2 was intended to be a short-term program. Its handlers assumed that within a year or two Soviet radar technology would attain enough accuracy to intercept the flights. Actually, American estimates of the tempo of Russian radar development were naive. From the beginning of the program, every mission was tracked by Soviet radar and duly protested.[63]

The missile arms race opened up in 1955. The National Security Council reviewed progress on intermediate and long-range ballistic missile research in July. The following September President Eisenhower resolved that the long-range (intercontinental) missile program should dominate his military R&D agenda. Two months later he added the intermediate range program to the highest priority list. On April 24, 1956, Khrushchev announced that the USSR planned to deploy long-range guided missiles tipped with hydrogen warheads. Hot-headed congressmen instantly accused the President of allowing the missile program to lag behind the Russians. The President reacted phlegmatically.[64]

The CIA informed the President that he should expect a series of Soviet ICBM test flights in the spring. From May to August 1957 the CIA monitored eight long-distance flights, two with ranges of 3,500 nautical miles. In addition to Kapustin Yar, the U-2 discovered another missile installation, Tyuratam, in August. The second U-2 flight of the 1957 summer season reconnoitered the nuclear proving grounds in Semipalatinsk. Here, photo-interpreters found evidence of a recent low-yield nuclear test.[65]

Eisenhower was not at all surprised when, on August 26, *Tass* announced that "a super-long-range multistage ballistic rocket" had been successfully tested and that the next rocket would carry a satellite payload. On September 10 another U-2 mission overflew Kapustin Yar and captured images of a large medium-range missile sitting on its launcher. Consequently, when on October 4 the first earth satellite, *Sputnik,* was launched by the Russians, the President received the news nonchalantly. He assured the nation that *Sputnik* had not upset the balance of power in the missile arms race. America was not in any acute danger of surprise attack. Eisenhower also adjusted the missile program to an accelerated footing. What he did not do is divulge to the American people the source of his abiding calm.

In the wake of the commotion over *Sputnik,* on November 15 Khrushchev bragged that Soviet ingenuity exceeded American skill. "Let's have a peaceful rocket contest just like a rifle-shooting match, and they'll see for themselves." Within months, quite without confirmed proof, the office of the chief of staff for intelligence for the air force began a four-year campaign to persuade decision-makers that the USSR had *already* amassed hundreds of operational ICBMs.[66]

Even in the first year of the missile gap, we can find references to phantom evidence. In a November 1957 NIE, the authors admitted that "positive intelligence" was "minimal." Their estimate could offer "only a possible Soviet program, but one which is . . . both feasible and reasonable." Nevertheless, the NIE maintained the assumption of a missile threat with reference to empty possibility. An accompanying document stated that although "firm evidence" was lacking, "we believe that employment of missiles launched from aircraft or submarines is within present Soviet capabilities."[67]

From November 1957 to November 1958 the CIA acquired substantive data of enemy missile development. They could finally confirm the existence of an ICBM program, as well as find evidence of nine IRBM missile systems being readied for operational use. Notwithstanding this information, the 1958 November estimate pointed to "serious intelligence gaps." In areas where solid facts were absent, analysts guessed Soviet force sizes by extrapolating from American missile R&D. They predicted that the Soviets would field ten prototype ICBMs by 1959. The number ten was a shot in the dark. "These numbers are selected arbitrarily in order to provide some measure of the Soviet capacity to produce and deploy ICBMs; they do not represent an estimate of probable Soviet requirements or stockpiles."[68]

Given the overheated anticipation of a Soviet crash program in missile R&D, something perverse happened—or, rather, failed to happen. While it made no mention of the lapse, the next NIE was issued in early November 1958, that is, roughly seven months *after* the Turkish radar had last detected missile tests at Tyuratam. By April 1958 the number of test shots, including aborted missions, totaled between ten and fifteen, none of which extended farther than 3,700 miles, hardly intercontinental distances. Russia launched *Sputnik III* in May. Thereafter, missile tests at the Tyuratam facility were suspended for close to a year.

The pause was confounding, since on December 4, 1958, at the Geneva Conference on Surprise Attack, a Russian delegate let it be known that "Soviet ICBMs are at present in mass production." The following February Khrushchev announced to the Soviet Communist Party Congress that "serial production of intercontinental ballistic rockets has been organized." Likewise, the Soviet defense minister affirmed that "our army is equipped with a whole series of intercontinental, continental, and other rockets of long, medium, and short range."[69]

After almost a year, in March 1959 NSA's Turkish radar picked up the resumption of ICBM testing at a rate of about four trials a month. The U-2 flight schedule resumed on July 9, 1959, more than sixteen months after its last mission over the USSR. Among other targets, it overflew the Tyuratam facility and discovered two more launch pads under construction. However, the summer flights also determined that Tyuratam and Kapustin Yar were the only active missile bases in the USSR. Notwithstanding the discrepancy between the long pause in testing and Russian boasts of missile mobilization, in November of 1959 Khrushchev exulted, "In one year, 250 rockets with hydrogen warheads came off the assembly line in the factory we visited." Some analysts, including the intelligence officers of SAC and the air force, readily believed him. We know now that the Kremlin had been fed copies of the NIEs until 1961. An army intelligence officer working for the joint chiefs of staff, Colonel William H. Whalen, had slippped virtually all of the NIEs of Soviet capability to the KGB from the late 1950s until some time in 1961.[70]

The long pause between tests was ambiguous. The air force aggressively shaped every datum into evidence for Soviet crash mobilization. Absence of activity meant that testing had terminated and series production of the SS-6 had begun. On the other hand, the CIA's Office of Scientific Intelligence argued that the pause meant that the missile program had probably stalled.[71]

"Every present indication," began the November 1959 NIE, "suggests" that the Soviets had embarked on an intense program of rapid ICBM development. To this relatively moderate remark, the air force assistant chief of staff for intelligence footnoted the more hair-raising prediction of a Soviet race to achieve global military dominance by mid-1961 or earlier. He believed that the Kremlin desired to achieve "at the earliest practicable date a military superiority over the United States . . . so decisive as to enable them either to force their will on the United States through threat of destruction or to launch such devastating attacks against the United States that, at the cost of acceptable levels of damage to themselves, the United States as a world power would cease to exist." Echoing Khrushchev's claim, he added that the Soviets would attain the technical and economic capacity to produce 250 ICBMs, with 185 ready on their launchers by 1961.[72]

As to an operational ICBM, "for planning purposes" the NIE suggested that the Pentagon should expect an initial operational capability of about ten ICBMs by January 1960. The problem was guessing how rapidly the Soviets could be expected to amass a missile force into a pre-emptive strike capability. The year 1961 loomed as the moment when the Soviets would attain "a decided military, political, and psychology advantage over the US."[73]

Although the authors of the NIE acknowledged the humble reality of ordinary production delays due to bottlenecks and other slowdowns, they ignored this. In fact, they assumed that the Kremlin would devote a *second* plant to missile production and assembly. Allowing for a production build-up and factoring in a learning curve, the high-end estimates supported by the chief officers for the State Department, the air force, and the joint chiefs forecast two hundred missiles sitting on their launchers by mid-1961. Since anyone could see that this was the best means for gaining strategic advantage, they argued that it would be a reasonable course to follow: "Soviet planners would regard the advantages to be gained as justifying additional effort."[74]

In April 1959 Turkish radar picked up the resumption of missile testing, which continued throughout the rest of the year. This included the first full-range 5,000 nautical-mile test, which proved the intercontinental power of their technology. However, the radar also detected a handful of failures at launch or during flight. It was hardly evidence of a fully fledged missile production program.[75]

In addition to the U-2 flights and the Turkish radar, in 1959 the NSA added electronic and communications eavesdropping stations in Norway, Italy, Greece, Ethiopia, and Peshawar, Pakistan. This last was critical for eavesdropping on the Tyuratam installation, the nuclear test site at Semipalatinsk, and Chinese tests at their nuclear facility at Lop Nor.

By January 1960 Tyuratam was still the only major site for SS-6 deployment. Had there been other missile launch facilities in the USSR, they would have been readily identifiable. The SS-6 rocket was liquid-fueled and inconveniently heavy. It could only be transported by rail. Surveillance of railways would reveal whether or not the SS-6 ICBMs were being shuttled about for active deployment. None was found.

By the end of 1959, members of the intelligence community

were thoroughly exasperated with the air force's interpretation of the available material. Secretary of Defense Thomas Gates testified to a House Armed Services Committee that henceforth the NIE would focus on what the Soviets "probably *will* do" rather than what they *could* do. The change meant counting operational launchers rather than guessing the total capability of the missile production plant of the USSR.[76]

The 1960 NIE couldn't wring a consensus from the three services, the joint chiefs, the secretary of state, and the CIA. While the authors surmised that the Soviets had probably begun to move from missile prototype to series production in early 1959, they had "no direct evidence of the present or planned future rate of production." They could find no launching sites for the putative rocket force or any support facilities. Nonetheless, they insisted that ten operational missiles would exist by January 1, 1960. They based their estimate on extrapolations from Soviet military doctrine, Russian production norms, and guesses at how enemy planners might conceive their missile requirements.[77]

Trailing after the main text were a series of footnoted objections. The army protested that *direct evidence* of missile strength was critical to a credible estimate. Since "much of this evidence constitutes negative indications," placing too much faith in these extrapolations "leads to unrealistic overestimation." The air force parried that to the contrary, one should assume that Soviet planners wished to acquire a missile force that would "enable them . . . to force their will on the US."[78]

The CIA pressed Eisenhower to approve a U-2 flight over an alleged base at Plesetsk. The aircraft was shot down on May 1, 1960, before the Americans had the opportunity to corroborate the purpose of the facility. Given the President's concern that a Soviet intercept of a penetration flight might provoke war, it is a historical curiosity that Eisenhower was already sheltered in an underground bunker rehearsing the first stages of nuclear war in the national civil defense exercise, Operation Alert, when word came of the downed U-2. Within days of learning that the pilot was alive and had confessed to spying, Eisenhower cancelled the rest of the flights scheduled for that year. On May 11 he publicly disclosed the nature of the U-2 operation, in the course of which he acknowledged that he had indeed authorized covert reconnaissance flights over enemy territory.

A little more than a month after Francis Gary Powers's plane was shot down, the nation's first satellite was launched by the CIA. After partial successes and aborted missions, the thirteenth *Discoverer* satellite, launched on August 18, 1960, acquired more photographic coverage of the USSR than the output of the U-2 program altogether. Its initial objectives were the Soviet missile launching complexes, which the U-2 had failed to get. The satellite also identified previously unconfirmed missile test ranges such as the Plesetsk site, as well as the main test center for the submarine-launched missile facility at Severodvinsk. These photographs resolved the question as to what an actual Soviet ICBM launch site looked like. Plesetsk looked like Tyuratam.[79]

Based on the information retrieved from the *Discoverer* missions, the NIE of September 21, 1961, was finally able to offer positive intelligence about the Soviet missile program. "We are still unable to confirm the location of any ICBM launching facilities other than those at the test range." However, "on reasonably good evidence," two to four operational ICBM sites could be said to exist in the USSR. On this basis, the authors projected a missile force of between fifty and a hundred ICBMs for mid-1961, situated in ten to fifteen missile bases, in spite of the satellite evidence of only two to four sites. The additional bases were a "general approximation" based on a judgment "as to the relationship between what we have detected and what we are likely to have missed."[80]

It is worth reading the air force's dissenting footnote in full to get a flavor of its credulity and antagonism.

The Assistant Chief of Staff, Intelligence, USAF does not concur . . . In his judgment the Soviet leaders recognize that the ultimate elimination of the US, as the chief power blocking their aim of a Communist world, requires a clear preponderance in military capabilities. He believes that this consideration is the major determining factor in the continuing development of Soviet military force goals. This factor and the available evidence considered in light of extreme Soviet security and the great lack of intelligence coverage of large suspect deployment areas in the USSR, leads him to believe that there are at least 120, and quite possibly an even greater number of operational ICBM launchers in mid-1961.[81]

The next *Discoverer* mission passed over suspected missile sites in the USSR, confirming that areas that had been included as possible launch facilities were innocent of missile activity. A subsequent NIE suggested that probable sites included in earlier estimates might also be empty of missiles. Even so, unbelievably, its authors did not challenge the air force numbers. Rather, they also assumed undiscovered sites, and therefore proposed ten to twenty-five missiles sitting on enemy launch pads. "The high side takes into account the limitations of our coverage and allows for the existence of a few other complexes . . now operational but undetected." We know now that even though the 1961 NIE had postulated ten missiles, only four of these ICBMs were actually deployed.[82]

Herman Kahn brooded, "Are we taking one chance out of a hundred that the Russians have a disguised program we do not know about? Is it one in ten, or one in three, or what?" However much he cajoled his audiences to consider improbable possibilities, he was by no means alone. All the strategists at RAND partook of this occult business. RAND was a creature of the air force, battened on air force largess, propelled by air force hungers and urges, and guided by the air force mission in the cold war. Not only did RAND enjoy privileged consultation with senior command officers, it fed its minions from the royal jelly of air force intelligence.[83]

Having been battered by Congress after reports of the secret Gaither study were leaked to the press, in 1958 President Eisenhower withheld *all* further intelligence from his widest circle of advisers. The Pentagon's civilian contracting firms were stricken from the NIE distribution list. The result was that RAND analysts continued to believe in the spurious missile gap well after it had been disproved. From then on, the only intelligence about Soviet strategic capability available to RAND originated in the air force. Therefore, they did not know, could not know, how swollen their numbers were, nor the extent to which air force reckoning had strayed from common sense.

The story of the missile gap illustrates how far credulity can wing us into unknown unknowns. While his election campaign blared the bad news of Soviet missile superiority, by the time President Kennedy bearded Khrushchev in Berlin in 1961 and Cuba the following year, he knew better. The prospect of hundreds of "operational but undetected" missiles no longer stabbed at his imagination. Yet precisely because the *Discoverer* missions found only a handful of enemy missiles, in the summer of 1961 Kennedy aides drew up a war plan for a preventive strike against the USSR. They reasoned, "If the Soviets had only a few nuclear weapons and terrible air defenses, maybe the United States could knock out the whole Soviet nuclear arsenal in a very small sneak attack." While the President explored the idea of a limited first strike, he worried about the possibility for escalation into general war such a move would open. He queried his military advisers in mid-September: "I am concerned over my ability to control our military effort once a war begins. I assume I can stop the strategic attack at any time, should I receive word the enemy has capitulated. Is this correct?" No one responded directly to his concerns. On the contrary, SAC Commander General Tommy Power burst out, "The time of our greatest danger of a Soviet surprise attack is now . . . If a general atomic war is inevitable, the US should strike first." Luckily for us, President Kennedy did not consider preventive war to be urgent or necessary. As risky as the two nuclear crises of the early 1960s were, surely we would have found ourselves nearer to the lip of Doom had zealotry been allowed to elide possible threats into probable ones and thence into achieved reality.[84]

Chapter 5

HOW TO BUILD A WORLD WITH ARTFUL INTUITION

*You're trying to decide today what the conditions will be
eight to fifteen years in the future, and just what type of
things you should develop. Under these circumstances it
turns out that competent honest people often don't do very
well. That doesn't mean we want incompetent or dishon-
est people! At least not deliberately.*

HERMAN KAHN, 1955

RAND researchers tried to transpose the defense community's feelings of reverence for senior military officers into blithe disregard. In
their view, the expertise needed to plan for nuclear war shifted the lo-
cus of authority from veterans of the last war to practitioners of the
new technologies of simulation. Nuclear war was unlike anything the
world had seen before. Imagining how it would be fought was a science fiction, a hypothetical physical, military, and social construct.
How could America plan for something that would be unexampled,
catastrophic, and accessible only through experiments, models, and
simulations?

Military decisions have always been grounded in an unstructured,
inarticulate, and unimprovable mix of instinct, bias, and personality.
One convert to the new sciences wrote, "In past years . . . risks were
taken by military commanders who used judgment and experience
to estimate an enemy's intentions." In contrast to the vernacular
grooves of tradition, what did the modern science of war look like? It
glided forward on the skids of computation. By 1956 we can read the
already naturalized maxim: "In the old war game, professional opinion and subjective qualitative information are supreme . . . [Now,]

analysis and objective quantitative data tell the tale." Propelled by impersonal quantification, the science of war rocketed into the future. Scientists, the simulationists insisted with a swagger, "reach dispassionate, objective conclusions." The practitioners of the new techniques liked to boast, "At RAND, we tend to have faith that systems analysis can do a much better job on many problems than . . . staff work in the military."[1]

During World War II, operations researchers in the United States and England fiddled with weapons systems already in use. Their spectacular interventions moved John Williams to wonder whether the scientific analysis of military problems could be abstracted as a general approach. In 1946, writing to Project RAND's director about the OSRD's Applied Mathematics Panel, he commented that "isolated components of the theory of warfare suggest the possibility of similarly treating the *entire* subject." He later reflected, "My notion of what Project RAND represented was an opportunity to do more fundamental studies of warfare [than] had been done before." While the operations researchers had demonstrated the insight engineers, mathematicians, and physicists could bring to combat, Williams proposed a *futurological inversion* for RAND.[2]

Atomic wars would be short and intense. Any new weapon system, as well as the strategy and tactics for its use, had to be projected ten or fifteen years ahead. This condition snagged the simulationists in an inextricable contradiction. In light of the uncertainties inherent in modeling hypotheticals, no one could deliver a definitive study. During the 1950s the simulationists justified their work by reminding their audiences that the validity of hypothetical analysis rested on the oracular cunning of *anyone* who dared to model the future. But the air force founded RAND as a scientifically based institute dedicated to improving on the hunches of the old campaigners. Scientists had proven their value during the war; it was the virtues of unsparing and probative science that were wanted. How, then, could the simulationists mediate between the demands for a quantitative rationality and the unstable hypotheticals of any imaginary future? How could they construct an indefinite, intuitively rendered science?

The men at RAND had elevated the experience and knowledge they gained by long practice with Monte Carlo, systems analysis, war games, and man–machine simulation over the generals' wisdom derived from actual combat. In contrast to the creaky habits of the officer corps, they believed that their own march up to future war had sharpened intuition, stimulated creativity, offered insight into complex interactions, and heightened sensitivity to their own blind spots. But having thus distinguished their approach from the uniformed military, the simulationists wrangled over competing techniques. The economists squabbled with the systems analysts; others rebuked them both for methodological folly; and the physicists snubbed everyone.

The Pulse of Creative Thought

Rather than tease apart the details of these disputes, I want to heap together all of the methods for simulating future war and approach them not as a science but as a style, a mood, and an aesthetic. Practitioners of these arts, along with their historians, justly insist on preserving the ramparts that enclose and differentiate their chosen fields. But what I'm looking for are the traces of an aesthetic, which scientific practices surely bear in much the same way that a society's fine arts, politics, and ephemera do.

What I have in mind is something like Nietzsche's musical understanding of the pulse of creative thought. An amateur musician himself, Nietzsche, in *Beyond Good and Evil,* spoke of "the tempo of style" and "the average tempo of its metabolism." When I leaf through RAND publications from this period, I catch sight of typical shapes of problem formulation. The themes of open serial study, branching forms, the rejection of realism, untiring stress on insight, intuition, creativity, tacit knowledge—all blend into a distinct genre. I'd like to extract these motifs in order to situate Kahn's thoughts about the plotting and planning of nuclear war into the larger stream of futurological ideas at RAND. What would later be read as repugnant eccentricities in *On Thermonuclear War* deviated very little from the general flow of studies produced by his colleagues.

A glance at threat assessment in our own time throws light on the cold war character of the simulation genre at RAND, as well as its transhistorical potential. Secretary Donald Rumsfeld's shorthand spree through the core concepts of risk assessment—his unknown unknowns, his absence of evidence and evidence of absence—borrows liberally from strategic futurology. He defines the threat in a manner that everyone at RAND, from Frank Collbohm to Herman Kahn, would have recognized. "A terrorist can attack at any time, in any place, and using any technique . . . It's physically impossible to defend in every place, at every time against every technique." His description of the pitfalls of intelligence gathering echoes complaints CIA analysts made about the USSR in the 1950s. "Their task is to penetrate closed societies . . . and learn things our adversaries don't want them to know . . . often not knowing precisely what it is that we need to know, while our adversaries know . . . what it is that they don't want us to know."

The terrorist threat of today resembles the cold war fear of a sudden strike from the air and hence drives the impulse toward extravagant speculation. "Intelligence agencies are operating in an era of surprise when new threats can emerge suddenly with little or no warning, as happened on September 11th." Because they have no means to confirm their suspicions, intelligence analysts, goaded by an uncertain menace, stitch together threat estimates impetuously, sometimes feverishly. "It is their task to try to connect the dots *before* the fact." Since intelligence will *always* be imperfect, Rumsfeld counseled decision-makers to take hypothetical threats seriously. "We do not, will not, and cannot know everything that's going on . . . [If] we mistake intelligence for irrefutable evidence, analysts might [hesitate] to inform policymakers of what they think they know and what they know . . . they don't know, and even what they think [that is, guess]."[3]

In the 1950s, the RAND simulationists preened themselves on being the avant-garde of the defense community. But what, exactly, makes simulation techniques so iconoclastic, so *modern?* The men designing Monte Carlo samples, systems analyses, and war games believed that atomic war *instantly* nullified military experience. Indeed, after reading about Hiroshima in the newspaper, the military historian Bernard Brodie burst out, "Everything that I have written is obsolete." All of warfare had to be created anew under the sign of the bomb. But the modernism at RAND wasn't extreme; unlike the scientific dissenters, the disarmers, and the internationalists who argued that the bomb made war itself obsolete the RAND simulationists comprised an avant-garde comfortably settled within the framework of cold war politics—a cold war avant-garde.[4]

Let's look at the motifs of the simulationists and see whether we can make out a coherent pattern. The first formal feature was a marked preference for the open form of serial study. Research on future war bumped along provisionally. Rather than fishing for an optimal solution to any problem, from 1950 onward RAND analysts stole up to the future in successive, rudimentary, non-analytic trials. They emphasized their studies' dynamism and learning curve. They tutored their sponsors in tolerance for uncertainty. In an age where scenarios for war were tethered to successive generations of weaponry, soon to be displaced by the next cycle of the arms race, the watchwords of the day were flexibility, adaptability, alterability.

The serial study excused the simulationists from ultimate conclusions, which left them free to map out the totality of future war. By temperament or training, they gravitated to opposing forms: compact studies correlating limited combat objectives with fixed budgets, or grandly speculative affairs spiraling around society, nature, and war. The quantitative studies often aimed toward an ideal of omniscient information management. Its opposing pole invoked an intuitive holistic gestalt.

Another motif worth mentioning is the representation of manifold alternatives in branching forms and correlative graphs and columns. Following the zig-zaggery of fragmentary alternatives was the only way to survey possible events and phenomena. It was ubiquitous—in the multiple trials of Monte Carlo samples, in the correlation of alternatives in systems analysis, in the consecutive rounds of war games. It was a critical component of RAND futurology. Kahn compressed the methodological ideal into a few sentences, coupling the will to circumscribe the totality of future war while simultaneously splintering any single conjecture into almost infinite variations: "We must try to think a war right through to its termination. This does not mean . . . we can predict the details of what will happen, but only that it is valuable to think through many possible wars to their termination points." This branching impulse was so contagious that we can glimpse it even in the work of someone who despised speculative futurology. In a 1959 paper, Richard Bellman, an irascible critic of systems analyses, characterized dynamic programming as "not so much any fixed set of concepts and techniques as *a state of mind* [that favored] a multi-stage decision process."[5]

Since everything about future nuclear war was new, people at RAND floundered, trying this and that. The studies were conspicuously provisional. In Monte Carlo estimates, systems analyses, role-playing games, and man–machine simulations, the definition of the problem, the design of the model, and the collection of data happened simultaneously. It was a process in which "conclusions will emerge and become more certain as the volume and quality of the facts improve with further study." In other words, they made it up as they went along. In a report on his man–machine simulations, Murray Geisler reflected, "Right at the beginning we had to put our money and time on a problem of uncertain outcome. Therefore, we could not be sure that we would be testing important research hypotheses."[6]

The provisionality, open form, and simultaneous shapes of many possible wars suggested the absence of a consensus on the core techniques of systems analysis. The *Fortune* reporter who visited RAND in 1951 was mystified. He wrote, "Systems analysis is understood in sixteen different ways by sixteen different people, and yet they all do it together like a jazz band playing around an unexpressed four-four beat . . . It provides a pattern on which numerous and diverse specialists can cooperate . . . Some see it as a unique analytical method, others as a familiar scientific attitude." When Malcolm Hoag delivered an orientation lecture to a gaggle of visiting officers in 1956, he warned them that RAND futurology wasn't a formulaic business: "One can only repeat: 'Systems Analysis is no substitute for good sense,' and 'There are neither prescriptions nor substitutes for inge-nuity in analysis.'"[7]

In virtually every paper on future war, the role of intuition and art-fulness in model design was endlessly and compulsively emphasized. One author instructed his readers that the analyst "must . . . construct a model as best he can, where both the structure of the model and its numerical inputs may be based merely on intuitive insight and lim-ited practical experience." "In these analyses," observed another, "we have to do some things that we think are right but that are not verifiable, that we cannot really justify, and that are never checked in the output of the work."[8]

Another motif was the fabricated quality of the simulations. Models could be distorted to magnify unlikely events. Andrew Marshall de-lighted in Monte Carlo's pliancy: "Their synthetic character gener-ates an additional, and very flexible, degree of freedom. This added degree of freedom can be exploited, sometimes to an extraordinary extent." Sensitivity to error followed from this: "The degree of ap-proximation to reality of the models used in these synthetic experi-ments is often not known." Indeed, everyone agreed that the undis-coverable correspondence between a model and its referent was the most significant (and worrisome) dimension of simulation.[9]

In virtually every major paper, analysts ritually acknowledged the fictitious nature of simulations of war. Kahn exposed the artifices of the model-maker more bluntly than most. "Take this curve over here. What it says is that if a certain number of bombers hit your area de-fense, this is the probability that those bombers will get through. Now you get a curve like this in several ways. We got it just by draw-ing it. That's one way. It's practically the classical way." More soberly, he remarked in another memo, "Hopefully, the understanding thus gained will guide our intuition even where the known theorems do not directly apply. It will . . . be as interesting to see what cannot . . . be done by mathematics as what can, so that our ambitions will be curbed." Otherwise, the model was neither predictive nor offered "precise rules for specific realistic situations."[10]

While insisting that the value of any model relied on its de-

signer's finesse, Kahn and his colleagues just as vehemently and pi-
ously affirmed the scientific qualities of their simulations. Quantified
guesses were superior to perfunctory ones. As Kahn expressed it,
"The best we can claim for our results is that they are plausible.
Many, possibly all, of the numerical results can be expected to
change with further study. But even so, most of them should be
better than the intuitive feelings and preconceptions almost everyone
has at present."[11]

Malcolm Hoag shared this tendency. Rather than regretting the
insecure foundations of model design, Kahn's colleague flourished his
anxiety as the mark of conscientious professionalism: "The man who
solves complex problems in the space of five minutes on the intuitive
basis of 'sound' military . . . judgment and experience . . . [may] sleep
easily at night," whereas the civilian analyst who devoted two years
to the same topic "may sleep badly, but only because he has become acutely aware of all the pitfalls in the problem." The analyst's
recommendations will be more astute, more accurate, and more decisive than those of his military counterpart. "If you take . . . people
who are scientifically trained . . . detached from the [problem and]
. . . have no bias . . . and give them ample time . . . [they] ought to be
able to do considerably better than one harassed Indian [that is, staff
officer] . . . [given] three months to solve an impossibly big problem
with little assistance." To his air force audience he did concede that
"systems analysis as currently practiced . . . is much more an art than
a science . . . [The analyst's] operations . . . are not characteristic of
'science' with a capital S."[12]

Finally, as our last motif, the simulationists dreamed up worst-case
scenarios and improbable threats. Even before RAND was founded,
on the last day of 1945, the physicist Harold Urey worried that "an
enemy who put twenty bombs . . . into twenty trunks, and checked
one in the baggage room of the main railroad station in . . . twenty
leading American cities could wipe this country off the map so far as
military defense is concerned." The expectation of surprise attack has
engrossed vigilant imaginations ever since. At nearly every turn Albert Wohlstetter twitted the duffers at the Pentagon for being shift-

less and feeble-minded. It was folly, he'd say, to assume that the Soviets would employ strategies in the next war that could be conveniently countered by American capabilities, when there was an *infinity* of ways to smite the United States.[13]

RAND's injunction to ransack the universe for these possibilities confirmed in Kahn a tendency to wallow in eccentric scenarios. As a discovery method, he believed that war games should thresh out unlikely but "interesting" possibilities. "The scenarios are not designed to describe 'most probable' or necessarily 'fairly likely' courses of events, although each is intended to be 'not impossible.'" The aim was to throw light on these events "not simply because one thinks they are most likely to happen." In virtually every briefing, he implored his audiences not to shrug off his ideas. "In more casual days one could dismiss a bizarre-sounding notion with a snort . . . about [its] being impractical or implausible." But the absolute horizon of nuclear war invited "crackpot or unrealistic" speculations. "We must take seriously the hypothetical possibility of either direct attack or extreme provocation . . . long before the challenge materializes."[14]

Monte Carlo

Kahn, *sans* Ph.D., made canny use of the commanding authority of science. When pressing home an argument, he didn't shrink from claiming to know the facts. He arrayed "even intuitive notions" in quantitative garb in order to express himself "with accuracy." The Monte Carlo studies of his earliest years were recognizable as science. But in his transit to systems analysis in the mid-1950s, Kahn's science became science fiction, an exercise that derived political and military policy—discrete, authoritative, partisan—from the vagaries of simulations concocted with good guesses. For Kahn, it was but a few steps from devising a "system of fictitious particles treated by an electronic computer" to scenarios of future war that "stimulate our imagination . . . [by bringing] less probable possibilities into focus."[15]

His first years at RAND were devoted to simulating the activity of elementary particles and gamma rays that might penetrate various thicknesses of protective shields in nuclear reactors. He delivered papers on this topic at all three of the major unclassified conferences that introduced the Monte Carlo technique to the physics, engineering, mathematics, computing, and operations research communities in 1949 and 1954.[16]

Monte Carlo was intimately related to the development of the electronic computer. If we wanted to identify the moment when empirically based experience was supplanted by synthetic data, we could do no better than look to John von Neumann's meteorological conundrums during the war. He conceived the germ of Monte Carlo while mulling over the physics of colliding atmospheric gases, but he elaborated and refined the idea between 1944 and 1948 on problems of a neutron's behavior as it encounters plutonium or some other radioactive substance. An individual particle might recoil from the plutonium nucleus, be absorbed by it, or split itself, releasing more neutrons. Whereas each of these possibilities had a specific probability at specific temperatures, the actual behavior of neutrons was random. Purely abstract calculations couldn't capture this phenomenon in detail. Nor could laboratory apparatus withstand the intense heat and pressure of a fusion reaction. It was therefore necessary to represent neutron activity in a simulated space. The only way to estimate the ratios of neutron scattering, fusion, and fission en masse was to track a representative sample of these particles. A roulette wheel, later a table of "pseudo-random" numbers, could be used to generate the path any one particle would follow. (Hence the name Monte Carlo.) What emerged was the *shape*—the upper and lower boundaries—of the probabilistic distribution of the event.[17]

It was truly a machine representation. Publicly introducing Monte Carlo in 1949, Nicholas Metropolis and Stanislaw Ulam announced, "These experiments will . . . be performed not with any physical apparatus, but theoretically." They added, "We want to point out that modern computing machines are extremely well suited to perform the procedures described." Thus, the field for the physics experiments critical for hydrogen bomb design migrated from the laboratory bench to ENIAC, the first electronic computer. Certainly, the most revolutionary claim for Monte Carlo was that mathematical models subject to repeated trials of random sequences were equivalent to empirical experiments. They were, to quote one physicist, "numerical experiments with the program as the apparatus." This idea quickly became axiomatic. In their 1949 paper, Kahn and Goertzel put it this way: "One is not carrying out a mathematical computation in the usual [analytic] sense, but . . . carrying out a mathematical experiment with the aid of tables of random digits."[18]

Electronic computers enabled countless repetitions of the "random walks" of individual particles. As its enthusiasts claimed, "The tremendous volume of logical, numerical and bookkeeping operations that must be performed . . . makes this . . . a very natural application for digital computers." The data were begotten by the sample size, the boundaries of the model, and the capabilities of the machine. That is to say, the output of a Monte Carlo simulation was literally "descriptive of the performance of a given configuration of the system."[19]

As in every statistical study, the sample size had a direct bearing on its outcome: if it wasn't large enough, anomalies would throw off the result. Even when a computer ran thousands of trials, its representation in any simulation would always be relatively minuscule compared to the real physics of billions of elementary particles. A statistical fluctuation could warp the data. To offset this possibility, Monte Carlo designers added a bias to their models so that the random walks would "tend in the direction required." They would then correct for this by calculating the differences between unbiased and biased random walks. It was this refinement, called variance reduction and importance sampling, on which Kahn first exercised his formal imagination.[20]

Monte Carlo occupied an intermediate space between laboratory physics, where experiments on real substances and processes occur in actual space and time, and theoretical physics, which acts upon conceptual entities. Invented by physicists, used for hydrogen bomb design, Monte Carlo seemed to have real referents in the world. Certainly its brainchild, the thermonuclear weapon, had real consequences for the world. But even so, Monte Carlo models hovered above empirical reality. They could offer only approximations of neutron behavior. In every Monte Carlo simulation, it was always possible that design errors might never be detected.[21]

Monte Carlo made sense to the men behind the glass door at RAND. During his early years there, Kahn "seemed to be a physicist. He worked on physics problems," remarked a colleague. But when he turned to systems analysis, "it seemed to most of us that he had departed from our world." In spite of the fact that the Physics Department thought he had sailed off the edge of legitimate science in search of the Happy Isles of futurological conjecture, there were continuities between Kahn's Monte Carlo studies and his nuclear strategy. In fact, all of the motifs of the simulation genre crop up in his Monte Carlo papers and remained forever after as the architecture of his imagination.[22]

The fact that the simulation need not emulate a physical process but could sample a distorted, biased, or even wholly unnatural event is the first wonder of Monte Carlo. It could mimic an actual process or deviate from it considerably. Ideally, a sample would trace typical life histories of neutrons flitting through a plane slab. But in practice this was too computationally demanding. Honing the sample size was the real design problem. Kahn insisted that these refinements were, "to a certain extent, *arbitrary*." He counseled the simulationist to expend his efforts contriving efficiencies that lessened the computational load rather than straining to create a model that faithfully hugged the lineaments of the elemental world. The simulation needn't be analogous at all. What was needed was the physical intuition of an expert model builder. Model design was artisanal and subjective: "The ability to set up an efficient Monte Carlo problem depends more on the intuition of the computer [the human analyst] than on being able to evaluate the formulae given."[23]

In a 1957 paper Kahn reprised the theme of the insight afforded by non-natural representation. He exulted in the "complete control" that allowed him to tinker with probabilistic events. Like genies tumbling out of bottles, improbable events sprang forth and frolicked on command. "If, for example [the model-builder] were to want a green-eyed pig with curly hair and six toes, and if this event had a non-zero probability, then the Monte Carlo experimenter, unlike the agriculturist, could immediately produce the animal."[24]

While glorying in the plasticity of Monte Carlo, Kahn immediately called attention to the potential for error this enjoined. "The calculator is, of course, confronted with the problem of how far to go in altering the sampling." He observed, "The decision about what aspects to concentrate on must be made early and therefore may easily be made wrongly." As early as 1949, he worried about the ways things could go wrong. Given statistical fluctuations, the computer might not register activity in lesser but significant regions. "The estimate of the probable error may be small so that the computer will have no indication that things have gone wrong." The investigator wouldn't stumble across the error. He might believe the findings of what he assumed was a roughly accurate estimate. To ensure against this, the sample had to include "any possibly important but neglected regions of the phase space" so that these outer reaches can "influence the result."[25]

In November 1952 Kahn and his friend Andrew Marshall delivered an address on Monte Carlo at a Washington conference. They transposed the field of application from physics to war. It was the first time their audience had heard of the technique. Presenting as much an advertisement as a tutorial, Kahn and Marshall flourished the indispensability of the method for problems involving multiple uncertainties. It offered the analyst the freedom to choose the parameters, sample size, and importance functions of his simulation.

In their paper, Kahn and Marshall laid out design principles for Monte Carlo that unerringly anticipated the motifs of the simulation genre: (1) the model is a non-natural representation: "the amount of covariation of two processes is to a large extent under our control"; (2) the model is highly manipulable: "success . . . depends on being able to discover and exploit . . . opportunities for . . . increasing the correlation between the outcomes of the two processes"; (3) the model depends on the skill of the designer: "all that can . . . be done is to *approximate* this . . . distribution function . . . arrived at by the use of physical intuition"; and (4) there was a danger of underestimating the variance of the phenomena in the sample, which could result in latent errors: "one appears to have a good estimate on the basis of the information at hand when in fact he has a very bad one."[26]

There is no end to speculation. As Metropolis and Ulam recognized in 1949, "The 'space' in which our process takes place is the collection of all possible chains of events, or infinite branching graphs." When he bolted from physics to systems analysis, Kahn carried his methodological preoccupations—the intuitive nature of model design, anxiety about undetectable errors, the manipulability of the simulation, the correlative comparison of alternatives, the rejection of realism in improbable but critical events—into the scenario technique for authoring possible worlds.[27]

Systems Analysis

Systems analysis was as provisional and fictitious as Monte Carlo. Because it toyed with the same elastic probabilities that begot Kahn's green-eyed curly-haired pig, systems analysis looked like science fiction. You could imagine any totality you pleased. In fact, the first systems analyses at RAND attempted to cram every conceivable variable into master frameworks of future war. These rudimentary studies whirled into confusion, and the air force eventually checked the group's grandiose ambitions. Over the course of the 1950s, the systems analysts tinkered with the method and acquired more experience with its shortcomings, but they never disowned its speculative kernel.

During RAND's first decade, its analysts bickered over the best way to imagine future war. Their immediate problem was agreeing on a method for representing and assessing multiple future systems. On the one hand, Samuel Wilks pressed for a matrix of quantifiable phenomena such as damage and target coverage coordinated with different budgets for weapons delivery. Olaf Helmer countered with the case for folding political, economic, and psychological factors, along with historical study, into the prospectus for any future weapon system. As head of the section, John Williams favored the big picture. While regretting that "the complexity of the subject [was] almost boundless," he called for "a frame of reference which adequately encompasses the subject matter." Still, the ordeal of juggling the variables comprising the totality overwhelmed everybody. Complaints bubbled up in nearly every one of these early studies. By 1948 the tension between the quantified and gestalt models resulted in the reorganization of the Military Worth section into separate departments of social science and economics.[28]

By May 1949 the analysts felt that they were close to arriving at a science of war. They had laced together offensive and defensive systems studies into "a master systems analysis [that] would provide, for any given time within the study's horizon, the optimal allocation of resources between attack and defense." The method for assembling the totality had by now become clear. RAND's vice-president, Lawrence Henderson, spelled out the royal road to the guiding synthesis in a December memorandum.[29]

First, the big picture would have to be sketched out. "The pertinent factors comprising aerial offensive and defensive systems must be identified, put in quantitative form, and the effect of their variation on the results established." The analyst must then "consider the interrelation of all these factors simultaneously." He should evaluate alternative weapons systems with a "mini-max calculation," determining which offered "a maximum pay-off (in terms of utility or military worth) for a given expenditure of resources, or a given pay-off for a minimum expenditure of resources." Henderson's ideal was exhaustive and impossible. "Thus," he wound up, "systems analysis seeks to cover the full range of possible future weapons characteristics and simultaneously analyze each set of possible characteristics in all possible tactics and strategies of employment." Many of the motifs of the futurological genre are already here: the will to represent the totality, and the simultaneity, modularity, and combinatorial pattern of its components.[30]

The air force abrasively challenged these studies. By 1951 the simulationists concluded they had been grossly over ambitious. Not every element in a problem could be quantified. Four years after RAND's founding, the problem of the intangibles of future war had yet to be resolved. Senior management thereupon decreed that titanic attempts to scale the totality of future war would no longer be welcome. Henceforth, staff energies would be confined to the precincts of sub-optimization studies.[31]

This was understood as a move toward component analyses. Still, people argued that even though the Olympian view had been officially renounced, in the course of checking any one component against alternatives the analyst was obliged to venture beyond the frontiers of his study to assess its impact on other subsystems in the ensemble. In a 1952 paper Hitch protested he couldn't avoid sidling toward the totality. Merely comparing one component against another "wasn't good enough." In order to test the worthiness of the criteria used for evaluating lower-level alternatives, any self-respecting analyst *had* to steal into the big picture.[32]

A year later Roland McKean seconded Hitch's injunction to stray beyond the enclave of sub-optimization "for possible gains to other operations as a result of the ones under consideration." After all, what was the principal objective of the business at hand? One had to sift through "all possible alternatives and all possible allocations of one's resources among those alternatives . . . [weighing] the possible impacts of . . . all events not under the optimizer's control and expectations." McKean served up a résumé of the other motifs of the simulation genre. The choice of model variables was a headache, depending, as always, on the cunning of the designer. Intuition was indispensable for systems analysis (which looked less and less like the science of warfare). "The methods of science will not magically or automatically reveal optimal choices," he remarked. "It will always be necessary to use great care and good judgment in picking out the partial optimizations that look promising and to set up appropriate criteria [for assessing] . . . alternative policies or courses of action."[33]

On this last point, the economists quarreled furiously with the systems analysts. Armen Alchian, Reuben Kessel, Burton Klein, Kenneth Arrow, and Richard Nelson disdained the fussy coordination of pinning the one best criterion to the one best component analysis as a terrible way to approach the future. It put a crimp in what should be an expansive survey of possibilities. Given the plasticity of weapons system components during feasibility and R&D phases, Alchian and Kessel argued that a genuine optimization of all the possible technologies necessitated a proliferation of research. Since "optimal diversity in concrete situations cannot be ascertained," it was best to crown the principle of maximal diversity as "the optimal principle of choice." In other words, the Pentagon should pay for competing, even redundant, R&D programs. Only if it could be made to tolerate the indeterminacy of embryonic innovation could the most efficient advances emerge. By 1958 the economists' arguments crystallized into the thesis that the pace and direction of innovation could not be planned in advance, and therefore the air force should permit (and pay for) "more competition, duplication, and 'confusion.'"[34]

Kahn smacked his lips at this prospect. This was just the warrant he needed for an exquisitely far-reaching futurology. He commented with delight, "On the whole, the non-technical people have done better than the technical people." The visionaries "just drew fairytales," while the poor, conservative engineers objected that "we can't say that this is going to happen in ten years, we don't know how to do it; if we knew how to do it, we'd just do it today." Precisely because the dreamers had no responsibility for materializing their ideas, they could promise anything. It was always best to shun the engineers. "If you're talking about things which are two, three, four generations away, you've just got to take it into account. You've got to be ridiculous—you've got to look at ridiculous extremes."[35]

While any simulation was only as good as the wits of its designer, its findings had to be quantitative, defensible, and grounded in statistically valid norms. Everyone was preoccupied with the problem of exercising good judgment in the unstructured spaces of future war. The primers on systems analysis produced at RAND during the 1950s convey the double gesture of an appeal to the dynamism of intuitive, occasionally quixotic reasoning, counterpoised by the demand—at times an imploring entreaty—to concede that systems analysis was more scientific than the crotchety recommendations put forward by the gaffers in HQ. The major figures at RAND who wrote papers on systems analysis in this period—Hitch, Hoag, Marshall, Williams, Wohlstetter, Edward Quade, and Richard Specht—repeatedly advised their readers to make allowances for gusts of intuition. Let the whiz kids have flashes of divination. Call it an art, not a technique. In short, much of the discussion revolved around the obligatory incorporation of the irrational into the science of war.

In a 1955 paper entitled "An Appreciation of Systems Analysis," Hitch outlined a number of themes touching on the notorious complexity of simulations of future war. Projected fifteen years ahead, choices about the elements of weapons systems, operational parameters, tactics, and practical assumptions were at the mercy of the riptides of inspiration. "Some are . . . subject to our control, some are . . . subject to the enemy's control, some are subject to nobody's control." Tempted and overwhelmed by an infinity of elements, the analyst factored out variables that deserved individual treatment and mashed the rest together into an aggregation. He cautioned, "Distinguishing problems that we can successfully factor out is an art." According to what principle should this operation be performed? "Preliminary analyses and tests" could carry you some of the way, "but for the most part," deciding what to do was driven "by sheer judgment." It was a delicate matter. "It is hard to do; it amounts to no less than deciding what is important and what is not."[36]

Picking his way through the snares of the "advisory art with many limitations," he groaned, "one may well ask, in view of this long catalogue of difficulties, dangers, and limitations, and the rather obvious possibilities of abuse they open up, whether military systems analysis is worth supporting and continuing." His answer was modest and faithful. Long-range planning was hard, guessing "intelligent behavior under uncertainty is *really* hard." The galaxy of meaningful elements easily swamped the model and model-maker. The problem could be simplified "only by escaping from reality."[37]

All right then, systems analysis was a scouting operation, not a science. Still, it had its uses. It could "enable us to focus the intuition of experts on a manageable technical problem." In the genre's agile two-step, Hitch exposed the fragility of the business but humbly touted its merits. "One would have to say that the case for analysis in broad context problems is comparatively unproved." But even the most speculative analysis could help decision-makers. Future war required study; it couldn't be guided by charismatic authority. "We trust a man's intuition in a field in which he is expert . . . No one is an expert in more than one or two of the sub-fields; no one is an expert in the field as a whole and the interrelations. So no one's unsupported intuitions in such a field can be trusted." Therefore, an attempt to weave together the postulates of a rabble of experts would produce something surpassing the wisdom of any one man.[38]

Hitch wasn't happy. The following year, provoked by somebody's paper on systems analysis, he flew off into a well-bred little tantrum. He was all for intuition, weren't they all, but artistic abandon had its limits. The most important part of designing a simulation—choosing the criterion according to which an array of alternatives would be compared—was typically undertaken in an impetuous gallop. The analyst "takes the first obvious criterion which pops into his mind and dashes on to the less important but more congenial aspects of his job." But wasn't the criterion the key to any study's intelligibility? The historian David Hounshell explained the significance of criterion choice for a systems analysis: "Exactly what was being optimized (maximized or minimized)? What *should* be optimized? How could one be certain that optimization was possible given . . . [the] extreme uncertainty in very large, highly dynamic systems such as global nuclear warfare?" While descriptions of the critical activity of comparing alternatives had changed over time from "evaluation of military worth" to "criterion specification," the *basis* for comparison remained the chief problem for systems analysis in 1956. Its resolution would not be easy or elegant. Hitch closed his paper gloomily, if cryptically. "The only road to good theory . . . is by way of bad theory. So we had better get on with developing the theory we need, even though, for a time, it is likely to be bad as well as distasteful." The simulationists dodged the issue with an artistic shrug.[39]

Systems analysis was the emblematic practice of the simulation aesthetic. It modeled future war with an adversary whose intentions were not fathomable and whose capabilities could not be ascertained by extrapolating combat performance from prototype or not-yet-existing weapons. The obsolescence or latent error of present information always threatened the validity of recent studies. The modular quality of the total system meant that one could assemble, reassemble, adjust, and alter the elements, perimeters, budgets, objectives, strategies, tactics, operations, and performance of weapons systems at will and infinitely. Protean, ephemeral, and credulous, it perfectly captured the transient tempo of the atomic age.[40]

The Simulation Aesthetic and the Zeitgeist

Did RAND's futurological motifs bear any stylistic resemblance to the avant-garde in the fine arts? A cultural historian, Daniel Belgrad, distilled the *Zeitgeist* of the postwar years by sifting through the works of the beat and Black Mountain poets, bebop jazz, abstract expressionist painting, modern dance, ceramic sculpture, and critical psychotherapy in order to assemble the "formal vocabulary" of the cold war aesthetic of spontaneity. "To see spontaneity as embodying a cultural stance is to grasp that what is most significant about spontaneous art, music, and literature is the world view (or *mentalité*) it communicates."[41]

Many artists in the 1950s abandoned fussy conventions of refinement in their crafts. The poet Allen Ginsberg remembered a distinct "element of improvisation and spontaneity and open form" in the fine arts of the period. Some RAND motifs do map onto this aesthetic. Futurology's seriality and provisionality correspond to the deliberately unfinished works of visual artists, musicians, and writers, their rejection of descriptive realism, and their attempts (through drugs and other means) to ferret out insights not readily available to ordinary awareness. But surely the greatest overlap between the fine arts avant-garde and the cold-war simulationists were the role-playing war games at RAND. The beat authors contemplated the rhythms of desire and reserve, approach and collision, commingling and retreat in dialogue. Belgrad shows that in many beat works, the contours of the cultural surround are suddenly thrown into relief by a truly intimate encounter.[42]

This resonated with reports from role-playing war games. The gamers argued that insights arose from immersion in play. In 1956 Joseph Goldsen noted that the war game demonstrated "the organic nature of the complex relationships" that daily transactions obscured. War-gaming gripped its participants, whipping up the convulsions of diplomacy "more forcefully . . . than could be experienced through lectures or books." All of its practitioners in one way or another protested that narrative accounts were colorless imposters for gaming experience. Olaf Helmer commented ruefully, "Just about the only . . . way for the potential user of gaming to learn enough about the subject to . . . judge its utility is to . . . go through the motions of constructing a game . . . playing it, and . . . applying the outcome to the real world . . . [This paper] cannot replace this kind of experience."[43]

Belgrad suggested that the spontaneous aesthetic of the fine arts avant-garde ushered in the counterculture of the 1960s. The role-playing games at RAND were one wellspring of the tendency that would flower in the 1960s into experiments in group behavior, such as the transmission of role-playing games to schools and universities, encounter groups, psychodrama, and happenings. By 1965 at least two war-gamers associated with MIT elided the Human Potential Movement's discourse of personal growth with the decade-old promise of war-gaming. They celebrated role-playing as "a 'sensitizing' device [for] illuminating, intensifying and contrasting" the preoccupations and blind spots of the players. It hung upon the "the raw intellectual and attitudinal materials" of its players. For an expert participant, the game was a marvel, "widening the boundaries of his imagination and preconceptions and leaving him a more flexible and aware individual."[44]

As a lark, and because the question is irresistible, let's see how Kahn stacks up against Belgrad's taxonomy of the aesthetic of spontaneity. There are so many ways in which his ideas share no common ground with the worldview of the beats and abstract expressionist painters that they defy any attempt to straddle RAND and the fine arts. Still, a filament floats between them.

First, Kahn was a working-class Jew who had shirked his Ph.D. Belgrad made much of the ethnic and social marginality of the fine arts avant-garde. While lacking an advanced degree meant less in the 1950s than it does now, Kahn stood the greatest chance of success in a profession where social pieties could be swept aside. RAND futurology fit him better than the gray-flannel-suit culture of the postwar boom.[45]

While Kahn's ideas about individual and social psychology were behaviorist and not particularly inspired, his personal style fell in step with humanistic psychology. The fine arts avant-garde represented human experience as a physical-emotional-cognitive flux. The productive generalities of the psychologist Paul Goodman articulate this motif most sharply. Instead of conceiving man as a discrete mind tucked in a fleshly envelope, extending unreliable feelers out to the world, Goodman characterized human beings as a "social-animal-physical field." The body was "the site of an unarticulated struggle between the faulty social order and human possibility." Goodman was interested in the self's pursuit and recoil from the world, its wandering attention: What is happening? What is being perceived? What is being felt?

In his 1951 book *Gestalt Therapy,* Goodman explored the inconstancy of social objectivity. The self seizes on a focal point from the eddies of happening—in Goodman's terms, a "figure" against a "ground." In the gestalt understanding, "only the interplay of organism and the environment constitutes the psychological situation, not the organism and environment taken separately." In a healthy self, awareness soars and dawdles and scampers in the whirligig of attention. But the social order stiffens awareness into neurosis: a lurching gait, cloying pleasantry, sleepy rigmarole. Goodman's gestalt therapy aimed to expose and soften these rigidities so that "attention would be released for active engagement with the gestalt formation."[46]

It is right here that Kahn departs from Goodman's gestalt. In the spontaneous aesthetic, Belgrad places the accent on invention occasioned by bodily instinct, emotion, and the unconscious. All three played no manifest part in the RAND simulation aesthetic. Kahn's professional demeanor enacted a certain kind of American masculinity—ambitious, stoic, but conspicuously disembodied. There was one exception: his exuberance was physical and cognitive. "Kahn's body shook, sending up endless amounts of energy, moving like lightning through his briefing charts." Here is common ground. "The content of abstract expressionism," Robert Motherwell reflected, "has to do with energy . . . All that we abstract expressionists were doing was shifting . . . [to an] emphasis on *process.*"[47]

A critic of *On Thermonuclear War* commented that Kahn "arranges certain sets of figures in a form that would delight a Dada poet." While he would not have welcomed the tone and its implied antirationalism, Kahn wouldn't have minded the fact that someone likened his ideas to art. The tables in *OTW* were spangled with numbers but they measured nothing—they described shapes of hypothetical events. He cheerfully admitted that this was a kind of science fiction: "What you are doing today fundamentally is organizing a Utopian society. You are sitting down and deciding on paper how a society at war looks." He invited his Princeton audience to enter into the spirit of his explorations or challenge him in the same vein.[48]

In a Hudson Institute paper from 1963 he demanded, "Is there a danger of bringing too much imagination to these problems? Do we risk losing ourselves in a maze of bizarre improbabilities?" On the contrary. "It has usually been lack of imagination, rather than excess of it, that caused unfortunate decisions and missed opportunities." His futurology was determinedly "liberating and suggestive." For Kahn perhaps more than the other simulationists, war-gaming and role-playing scenarios opened the door to many possible future worlds. Since the future was unknowable, "it is hard to see how critics can be so certain there is a sure divorce from a reality which does not yet exist and may yet surprise them."[49]

Paralleling the many worlds cooked up in Santa Monica, Jackson Pollock's gesture–field paintings and Charles Olson's poems of the early 1950s teetered between figure and ground in "multiple foci of attention in a constantly changing field." The American fine arts avant-garde inherited from earlier modernists the collapse of individual perspective. Regarding shifting standpoints "without priority or sequence," Belgrad wrote, "the meaning of the whole is different from that of each image presented singly, or from that which would be created by a simple sequential arrangement suggestive of a linear narrative." We can tie this to Kahn's compulsion to tack into variations and inversions of the many possible worlds. In the same Hudson memo that extolled the merits of priming the imagination with scenarios, he stated, "To be fully aware of the shape of reality it is necessary to glance beyond its boundaries on all sides." In his work after 1962, his explorations might plausibly have been influenced by memories of LSD derangement.[50]

The beat poets adored the hilarity and liberties of long ranting bouts patterned after bebop jam sessions, where "reality was understood to emerge through a conversational dynamic." Even the revival of public reading in these years nudged the pleasure in poetry away from the quiet savor of words on the page to the exhilaration churned up in community gatherings. Kahn's elation was not, in my view, the giddy effect of exhibiting himself before others but was rather the genuine pleasure he took in dialogue. Because he couldn't bear to write, he relied on his assistants, co-authors, and audiences to disentangle and polish his ideas. He evolved new material by improvising a claim or scenario during a briefing, heeding rebuttals, and gradually weaving it into his repertoire. Delight in live performance and banter are surely qualities he shared with the fine arts avant-garde.[51]

Kahn scrambled to lasso the totality. In a gesture of insatiable, virtually illimitable discrimination, he strained toward exhaustive breadth in every study. Marshall regarded this as a critical weakness. For example, he begged Kahn not to cite certain authors who Marshall knew, from secret intelligence on Soviet capabilities, were mistaken. "I used to tell him, Herman, you know, these guys . . . are not very good . . . Why are you citing x, y, and z? Who both you and I know are probably wrong?" Marshall guessed he used these tainted sources in spite of the warnings because "he was *driven* by a self-imposed requirement for . . . comprehensive treatment." While burning to circumscribe whatever interested him, Kahn always sauntered off to some other enticement. Slogging to completion seemed not to appeal to him. Futurology's provisionality allowed him to break off in midstream with the sheepish coda, "More research needs to be done."[52]

BY THE MARBLE LIONS OF NEW YORK'S PUBLIC
LIBRARY, U. S. TECHNICIANS TEST THE RUBBLE
OF THE SHATTERED CITY FOR RADIOACTIVITY

Soon after the end of World War II, Americans began to worry about the next war, which would be fought with atomic rockets. "The 36-Hour War," *Life,* November 19, 1945. Used with permission of Getty Images.

Local chapters of the civilian Ground Observer Corps attracted members with ice cream socials and beauty pageants. *The Aircraft Flash*, July 1954.

The Ground Observer Corps recruited its skywatchers from diverse social groups: mothers of small children, boy scouts, teenagers, prison inmates, native peoples, handicapped people, monks, ferry and barge operators, taxi drivers, train conductors, foresters, toll collectors, and dam tenders. *The Aircraft Flash,* December 1955 (top), September 1955 (bottom).

Cover, *The Aircraft Flash*, December 1955.

Top: "Farm and home-type posts provide much of the Canadian Ground Observer Corps surveillance; families at such posts are invaluable. Here, a Quebec farmwoman pauses from her chores to look to the skies." Bottom: "A native Eskimo boy teaches a group of younger native children some identification procedures at Saint Mary's Mission located on the Yukon River." *The Aircraft Flash*, December 1957 (top), February 1956 (bottom).

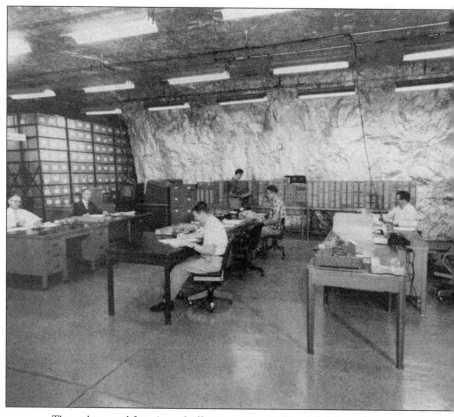

The underground factories and office spaces imagined by civil defense planners would look something like U.S. Steel's record storage facility. "Civil Defense Is Possible," *Fortune*, December 1958.

FOR YEARS THOSE OF US WHO HAVE TOILED IN THE VINEYARDS OF SUBURBAN CIVIL DEFENSE HAVE BEEN CONCERNED WITH THE PROBLEM OF HOW TO MAINTAIN LAW AND ORDER FOLLOWING A NUCLEAR ASSAULT.

THE BIG CITIES WOULD, OF COURSE, BE ANNIHILATED, THEREBY SIMPLIFYING **THEIR** CIVIL DEFENSE PROBLEMS IMMEASURABLY. HOWEVER, FOR THOSE OF US IN **SUBURBIA** THERE ARE **BOUND** TO BE COMPLICATIONS.

WE WOULD BE SUBJECT TO MASS ONSLAUGHTS OF REFUGEES FROM THE CITY. WHILE OUR HEARTS, AS ALL HEARTS MUST, GO OUT TO THESE VICTIMS THEY **DO** POSE A THREAT TO OUR CAREFULLY PLANNED PROGRAM.

HOW CAN ONE TELL A RADIO-ACTIVE MOB THAT THEY WOULDN'T BE HAPPY IN OUR TOWN? NO, WE CAN ONLY PRESERVE OUR WAY OF LIFE BY BARRICADING OUR STREETS AND RE-DIRECTING ALL MIGRANT TRAFFIC TO THE PUBLIC HIGH-WAYS, AIDING THEM PERHAPS, WITH IMPROVED DIRECTIONAL SIGNS AND FREE ROAD MAPS.

BUT WHEN MAN'S SURVIVAL IS AT STAKE HE MAY WELL SURRENDER TO THE **BASER** INSTINCTS. OUR BARRICADES MIGHT HAVE TO BE DEFENDED BY **FORCE OF ARMS.** BUT JUST AS WE ARE WILLING TO GO TO WAR TO DEFEND OUR FREEDOM SO WE SHALL BE WILLING TO DEFEND WHAT'S LEFT OF IT BY MANNING THE SUBURBAN BARRICADES!

IN SUBURBAN CIVIL DEFENSE OUR MOTTO IS: IF YOU CAN'T GET YOURSELF A RUSSIAN, SETTLE FOR AN AMERICAN.

Jules Feiffer was one of the rare humorists who poked fun at civil defense. Used with permission of Jules Feiffer.

"Want To Know How It Ends?"

This cartoon appeared in the *Washington Post* on the last day of 1956. Herblock was the only editorial cartoonist who regularly skewered the nation's nuclear weapons programs. "Want to Know How It Ends?" from *Herblock's Special for Today* (Simon & Schuster: New York, 1958). Used with permission of The Herb Block Foundation.

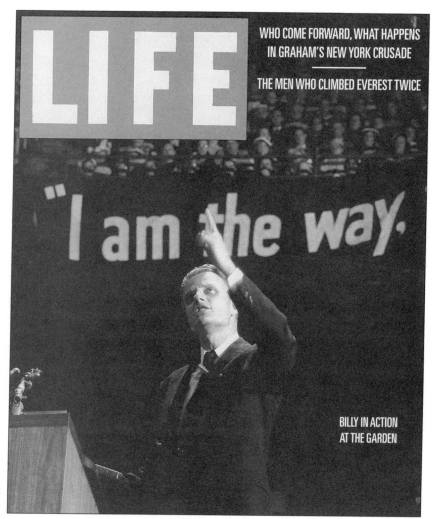

In the summer of 1957, Billy Graham preached to more than two million people in his New York crusade. *Life*, July 1, 1957. Used with permission of Getty Images.

Used with permission of Jules Feiffer.

Radar, jet engines, rockets, automated systems, and digital computers defined the unbelievable dimensions of the present. From *Atom-Age Combat*, February 1958. Used with permission of Michigan State University.

These drawings illustrated Herman Kahn's
memorandum, *Ten Pitfalls of Modeling*.

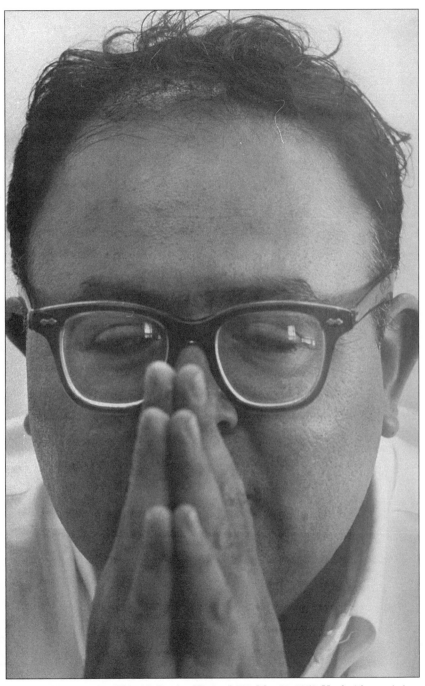

Herman Kahn in 1959. "Valuable Batch of Brains," *Life*, May 11, 1959. Used with permission of Getty Images.

Playing a war game at RAND, two teams of RAND scientists were separated by a low wall. Star-shaped pieces in the foreground represent enemy bomb bursts. Round pieces represent U.S. aircraft. Daniel Ellsberg is in the center foreground. "Valuable Batch of Brains," *Life*, May 11, 1959. Used with permission of Getty Images.

The comic strip which leaked the fact that the Pentagon had begun crisis war gaming. *Steve Canyon*, June 9, 1963. Milton Caniff Collection, The Ohio State University Cartoon Research Library. Reprinted with permission of the Caniff Estate.

TAYNO

...on science and research

"In every field of science, advances in knowledge are forcing more and more specialization. As disciplines become narrower and their interactions harder to discern, communication among specialists becomes more difficult. At the same time, the relevance of political, economic, and social factors in the broad application of physics, chemistry, and mechanics to major practical problems is increasingly evident. Many such problems, unlike research at the frontiers of the specialties, are too broad in their implications and too complex in detail to be solved by any expert working alone. The research team, uniting the diverse skills of many specialists, and using the best mathematical tools — theoretical and computational — is probably the most successful means of discovering realistic, timely, and original solutions to important problems of public welfare and security."

— *F. R. Collbohm, President*

THE RAND CORPORATION, SANTA MONICA, CALIFORNIA
A nonprofit organization engaged in research on problems related to national security and the public interest

Top: RAND's president, Frank Collbohm, from its public relations campaign in *Scientific American.* This photo appeared in July 1957. Bottom: The RAND Corporation Building in Santa Monica. Used with permission of RAND Corporate Archives.

Afterhours in Albert Wohlstetter's den. "Valuable Batch of Brains," *Life*, May 11, 1959. Used with permission of Getty Images.

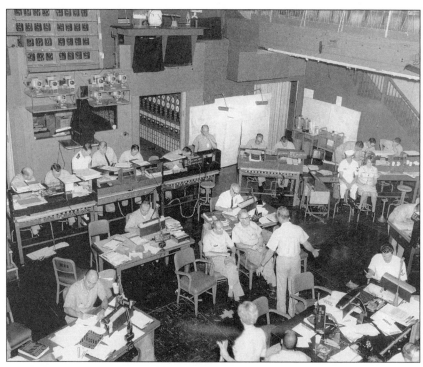

Top: War Damage Computer for Naval Electronic Warfare Simulator (NEWS), 1958. Bottom: NEWS at Naval War College. Photographs courtesy of the Naval War College Archive.

From the Naval Electronic Warfare Simulator. Photograph courtesy of the Naval War College Archive.

Announcing...

THE GREATEST
MISSILE
EVER BUILT

With this article, MAD scoops all other leading scientific publications and lifts the veil of secrecy on a fantastic new missile now being readied for its final test. (Unfortunately, we are not at liberty to reveal which nation has this ultimate weapon, but that sort of adds to the excitement!)

PICTURES BY
WALLACE WOOD

WHY THIS MISSILE WAS DEVELOPED

Pictures of present day ordinary missiles show need for new approach

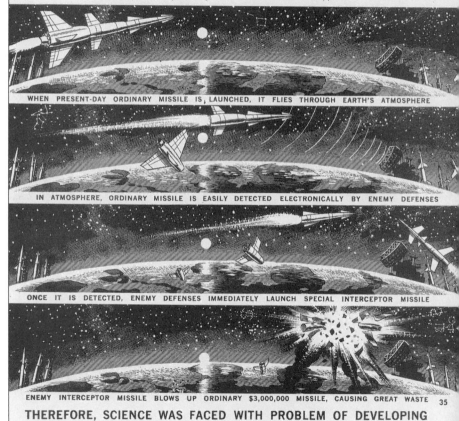

WHEN PRESENT-DAY ORDINARY MISSILE IS LAUNCHED, IT FLIES THROUGH EARTH'S ATMOSPHERE

IN ATMOSPHERE, ORDINARY MISSILE IS EASILY DETECTED ELECTRONICALLY BY ENEMY DEFENSES

ONCE IT IS DETECTED, ENEMY DEFENSES IMMEDIATELY LAUNCH SPECIAL INTERCEPTOR MISSILE

ENEMY INTERCEPTOR MISSILE BLOWS UP ORDINARY $3,000,000 MISSILE, CAUSING GREAT WASTE

35

THEREFORE, SCIENCE WAS FACED WITH PROBLEM OF DEVELOPING UNDETECTABLE MISSILE! FOR SUCCESSFUL RESULTS, TURN PAGE:

*HOME BEFORE DARK with OIL FOR THE LAMPS OF CHINA

Mad Magazine, June 1959. Used with permission of E.C. Comics.

GREATEST MISSILE EVER BUILT BLASTS RIGHT CLEAR THROUGH THE EARTH!

SIMPLY AIM IT ANYWHERE!

The Inner Space Guided Missile is simplicity itself. All that is necessary is to decide upon the country you want to blow off the face of the Earth, calculate the aim, and fire!

THE PERFECT GUIDED MISSILE
IT'S UNDETECTABLE, UNPREDICTABLE, AND IMPOSSIBLE TO DEFEND AGAINST!
(DON'T YOU WISH YOU KNEW **WHO** HAS IT?—CHUCKLE!)

MAD COMES TO THE DEFENSE OF OUR MUCH-MALIGNED

WHAT OUR TEENAGERS REALLY THINK ABOUT

Most adults assume that all teenage girls ever think about is *boys!*

THIS IS NOT TRUE!

ART—BOB CLARK

Like F'rinstance I got somethin' to say about 'secret ingredients'!

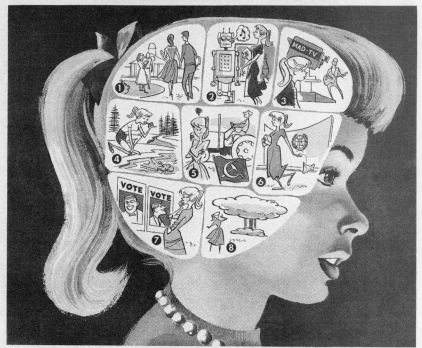

Actually, teenage girls think about important things like national, international, scientific and cultural problems of today, such as:

¹ SEGREGATION	² AUTOMATION	³ ELECTRONICS	⁴ NATURAL RESOURCES
A teenage girl thinks about segregation in schools, for it's no fun in classes where boys and girls are separated.	A teenage girl worries about automation because she would hate to see somebody invent a machine to replace a boy.	A teenage girl is interested in electronics because where else but on TV can she see all those cute boy singers?	A teenage girl is anxious about the development of her natural resources so all the boys will begin noticing her.

⁵ COMMUNISM	⁶ UNITED NATIONS	⁷ POLITICS	⁸ THE ATOMIC BOMB
A teenage girl is opposed to Communism because she'd hate living where boys think more of their tractors than of girls.	A teenage girl supports the United Nations because she knows that boys from other countries can be cute, too.	A teenage girl is interested in politics because recently there have been really cute fellers running for office.	A teenage girl is concerned about the atomic bomb as a weapon of destruction since it could wipe out all boys.

Mad Magazine, October 1959. Used with permission of E.C. Comics.

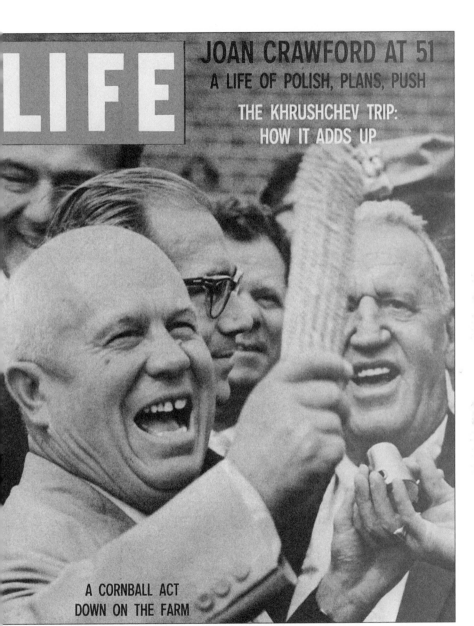

LIFE

JOAN CRAWFORD AT 51
A LIFE OF POLISH, PLANS, PUSH

THE KHRUSHCHEV TRIP:
HOW IT ADDS UP

A CORNBALL ACT
DOWN ON THE FARM

Cover, *Life,* October 5, 1959. Used with permission of Getty Images.

Top: The San Francisco to Moscow peace march. Bottom: Kahn and Bradford Lyttle, a member of the Committee for Non-Violent Action. From Bradford Lyttle, *You Come with Naked Hands* (Raymond, NH: Greenleaf Books, 1966). Used with permission of Bradford Lyttle.

Widely available tranquilizers helped the urban middle class "get through the day" in the mid-1950s. © Tee and Charles Addams Foundation.

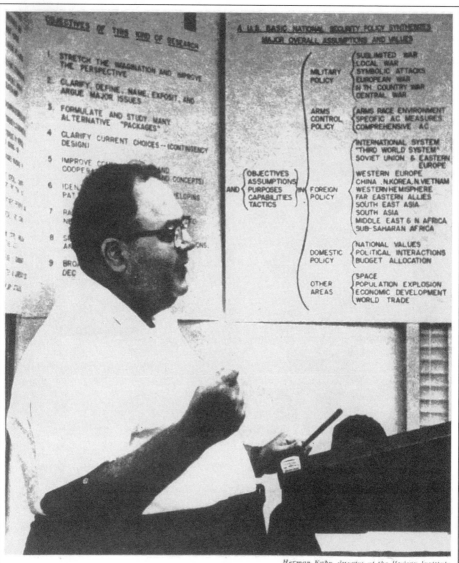

"The business of giving the Government advice has made war and peace virtually a new academic discipline."

Herman Kahn, director of the Hudson Institute

Report on a 'Think Factory'

Kahn surrounded by his briefing charts. From Arthur Herzog, "Report on a Think Factory," *New York Times Magazine,* November 10, 1963.

Ed Koren's "SuperKahn" cartoon appeared in the satirical periodical *The Outsider's Newsletter*, 1963. Used with permission of Ed Koren.

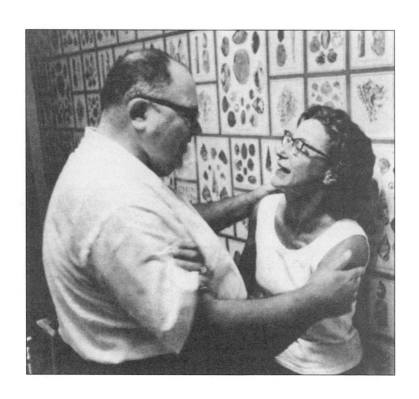

Kahn and his wife Jane, and Kahn capering on the grounds of the Hudson Institute, 1968. From William A. McWhirter, "I Am One of the 10 Most Famous Obscure Americans," *Life*, December 6, 1968. Photos by Henry Groffman.

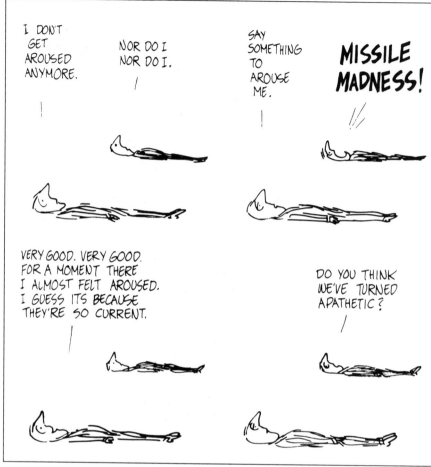

Jules Feiffer's cartoon meditations on faith in the scientific experts appeared in the *Village Voice* in the late 1950s. This one (which should be read left to right across two pages) was published in 1960. Used with permission of Jules Feiffer.

MISSILE MADNESS. YES, THAT'S A GOOD ONE. THAT CERTAINLY SHOULD HAVE AROUSED ME. BUT NO IT DOESN'T.

ATOMIC HOLOCAUST!

AH, THAT USED TO BE A VERY EFFECTIVE ONE. YEARS AGO I GOT AROUSED ALL THE TIME ON ATOMIC HOLOCAUST. BUT NOW—

BRINKS-MANSHIP! GUNBOAT DIPLOMACY! QUEMOY! MATSU!

APATHY IS SUCH A **BAD** WORD. I'D HATE TO THINK ITS APATHY WE SUFFER FROM.

LETS JUST CALL IT FAITH.

"HOW TO WIN ARGUMENTS ON YOUR SUMMER TOUR OF EUROPE" OR "A GUIDE TO CONVERSATIONAL COUNTERFORCE"

ENGLAND: WHEN THEY BRING UP HERMAN KAHN, EDWARD TELLER AND NUCLEAR DETERRENCE (85 POINTS), COUNTER WITH ROY WELENSKY, SOUTHERN RHODESIA AND THE CONTINUED SALE OF ARMS TO SOUTH AFRICA. (90 POINTS)

FRANCE: WHEN THEY BRING UP THE C.I.A., CIVIL RIGHTS AND THE RADICAL RIGHT (80 POINTS), COUNTER WITH THE O.A.S., SUPPRESSION OF THE PRESS AND PLASTIC BOMBS. (85 POINTS)

RUSSIA: WHEN THEY BRING UP THE STOCK MARKET, THE DECLINE OF CAPITALISM AND THE CUBAN FIASCO (75 POINTS), COUNTER WITH HUNGARY, FAILING CROPS AND MAO TSE-TUNG. (85 POINTS)

GERMANY: WHEN THEY BRING UP ALLIED INDECISION ON WEST BERLIN (35 POINTS), YOU MAY COUNTER WITH LATENT NAZISM AND THE FEAR OF A NEW HITLER-BUT IT WILL SCORE YOU NO POINTS - THEY HAVE NEVER HEARD OF EITHER.

A FINAL WORD OF ADVICE: THE BEST WAY TO ESCAPE TROUBLE ON YOUR TOUR OF EUROPE IS TO AVOID SPEAKING TO ANYONE WHO UNDERSTANDS ENGLISH.

ALOHA!

Chapter 6

FAITH AND INSIGHT IN WAR-GAMING

Modern war has become too complex to be entrusted to the intuition of even the most experienced military commander. Only our giant brains can calculate all the possibilities.

JOHN KEMENY, 1961

It is dreadfully hard to wrap one's mind around the *mise en scène* of nuclear war. One's attention dulls and slides away. Daydream beckons. The strategist Bernard Brodie complained it was impossible to imagine the details of a post-attack world. "Even if the spirit were willing," he sighed, "the data and the imagination would be much too weak." He couldn't grasp the *reality* of nuclear war. "To make an intellectual prediction of the likelihood of war is one thing, to project oneself imaginatively and seriously into an expected war situation is quite another."[1]

Brodie wasn't inhibited or shocked by matters publicists in and out of RAND flaunted as the most advanced, most modern of developments. After all, he wasn't ashamed to talk to his colleagues about his psychoanalysis. But he was too snugly burrowed in the liberal arts to enjoy the gyrations of simulation. His instruments of research were antiquated: no computers, no interdisciplinary teams, just his noggin, the library, table-talk, and the occasional colloquy. While Brodie sat out the vogue for the science of war, others at RAND eagerly threw themselves into the jet stream of novelty.

To enter into the spirit of the cold war avant-garde, you must imagine the moods and hopes driving the simulationists. Imagine founts of zeal for electronic computers, ambitions for a view from simulation's balcony, for an overview of the social, economic, military, and political totality. Imagine their exultation in the speedy dynamism of American ingenuity. Imagine postwar gaming and simulation as a craze and a bubble. Throughout the 1950s, here and there, commands and individual officers adopted many of the motifs of the simulation genre. We can see this in a profile about the Combat Operations Research Group (CORG) in a February 1956 issue of *Army* magazine. The army's director of war-gaming had to sell the promiscuous commingling of advanced research to an audience indoctrinated in the clean segregation of combat specialties. Reconnoitering "almost all corners of the intellectual world," he wrote, "CORG . . . brings together mathematicians, physicists, historians, psychologists, all of whom have something to offer the modern warrior. To join [them] CORG brings military officers with the widest possible variety of experience." Equipped with a pleasingly compact microcosm of human intelligence and skill, the army ventured into the territory cleared for them by RAND. "Now, in the early days of the Atomic Age, there is developing a scientist-soldier team whose joint function is to outguess any conceivable enemy in any conceivable future situation . . . Huddled around an electric brain that helps the fighter to fight and the thinker to think, they are beginning to work—or 'play'—together in the most elaborate war game imaginable."[2]

Electronic computers and systems analysis were the great novelties of the first postwar decade. As with all enthusiasms, exaggerated hopes were laid before these new capabilities. While the technical literature was awash with tributes to "the breathless awe inspired by the meteoric advent of the electronic computing machine," the same observer remarked, "The spectacular increase in computational speed and capacity brought about in the last fifteen years has not come without the confusion, the false hopes, and the excesses that seem, inevitably, to accompany a brilliant new development." The reception of these new techniques has all the earmarks of anxious faith. The war-gamers openly worried about the uncertainty of their simulations. So how did they invest their faith in war games? How did they both tout and distrust the promise of synthetic experience?[3]

During the 1950s and well into the 1960s, manual war games—here we're including conventional as well as nuclear war games—were played on boards, maps, charts, or terrain models. Combat forces were represented by miniatures, pins, symbols, or markers. Players were divided into opposing teams representing multi-state alliances, individual states, or the command authority of one of the divisional levels of the service hierarchy. There was a separate role for the game director or Control Group, who orchestrated each round of play. The game director played secondary actors as well as "nature," whose function was to introduce chance events into the game. Control, the game's author-director, was its "all-seeing, all-knowing, strictly impartial deity."[4]

The players moved on the basis of intelligence given to them by the Control Group, the situation on the ground, and strategic doctrine. The teams signaled their moves by declaration, filling out a form for delivery or telephoning Control. The resulting encounter—detection, interdiction, hits, damage, and casualties—was determined by the umpires or by reference to rules, tables, graphs, formulas, and dice.

There were some variations in game organization. In one-map games, players and umpires clustered around a single terrain model, map, or game board. It was more usual to segregate the teams with a curtain or screen, or isolate them in separate rooms. In a two-map game, each team could see only its own schematic of the theater of operations. Knowledge of the enemy's capabilities was confined to the intelligence doled out by the game director. In the more usual variant, a third map offered the total picture to the Control Group. This was called a three-map or three-room game.

The politico-military desk game was an exercise involving two or more teams of experts and referees. Here, players role-played the major political and military actors in a crisis. The game opened with a crisis scenario, a sheaf of background papers, and a few rules of engagement. They gathered around a conference table and played against Control, who would communicate the moves of the enemy side, or against another team in another room. Senior members of the State Department and the Pentagon participated in games of this type, played at the request of the joint chiefs of staff. Often, a senior State Department official at the Soviet desk would represent a member of the Soviet Central Committee.

In theory, role-playing induced sympathy for the people who were being impersonated. In one of the first unclassified comments about the JCS exercises, in 1964 a game director remarked, "Role playing in the Pentagon games project State, Defense, and other department officials into the shoes and war-rooms of foreign leaders to think as an opponent might think—to view the world through pink-tinted glasses." While no one could "really be made to think like a Soviet politician," it nevertheless pushed "him some distance in that direction." By role-playing one's counterparts, the experience offered "insights into the pressures and limitations on foreign generals and statesmen."[5]

While seminar games were staged without props or scenery, other simulations duplicated a combat information processing center, situation room, or communications hub. Their designers called these exercises "man–machine" simulations. Drawing on the tradition of training combat personnel on analogue devices such as the Link flight simulator, the man–machine game reproduced the physical layout and equipment of an actual facility. The apparatus usually included screens and projectors for the display of forces, inputs for sensors, radar, and communications, and damage calculators. For example, the Navy Electronic Warfare Simulator, which was introduced in 1957, consisted of command centers, control rooms for umpires and spectators, as well as backstage data processing rooms. Man–machine simulations were training devices and, to a lesser degree, experimental environments.[6]

By the late 1950s war games were also played on analogue and digital computers. Since human players could not make decisions about the choice of moves—that is, they didn't actually *play* the game—purists quibbled that computer simulations shouldn't be called games at all. In 1955 the first national Symposium on War Games threshed out the question to everyone's exhausted satisfaction. The assembly concluded that computer simulations could be called games if the number of actors was reasonably small, if the model excluded psychosocial, political, and economic variables, and if the computational limits of the machine were factored into the resulting analysis. But, clearly, these first-generation computer simulations lacked the *sine qua non* of war-gaming: the *experience* of dynamic play.[7]

Role-Playing Crisis Games

In the first two decades of the twentieth century, professors at the Navy War College had been fond of war games but eventually cast them aside. Role-playing crisis games seem to have originated at RAND. These experiments excited a great deal of interest from academics and the State Department. Even before the conclusion of the series of political games played at mid-decade, RAND fielded requests for briefings on war games. It seemed to many people that a potentially important research technique had arrived on the scene.

In 1948 and 1949 a few mathematicians at RAND concocted three rudimentary games. The second of the three was the most promising: the date of the scenario was 1953, and the game assumed that Stalin was dead and the Red Army had poured into Scandinavia. But RAND soon cast aside crisis gaming in favor of systems analysis and Monte Carlo simulation. Then in 1954 a handful of mathematicians began to toy with a computer game. Their efforts attracted attention from Air War College staff and the State Department, who recommended incorporating political and economic factors into the model. The result was the first genuine cold war game, staged in December 1954. While the designers consulted with a few social scientists, their game clumsily quantified a smattering of political and economic variables.[8]

Herbert Goldhamer of the Social Science Division believed that a war game should represent the mazy scramble of real life. Frustrated with the mathematicians' fumbling, he and a colleague put together a game according to the recognizable motifs of the simulation genre: "minimal formalization" (moves would not be fettered by rules and conditions); "incomplete and incorrect information" (to mimic the uncertainties of actual crises; "contingent factors" (introduced by the referee's role as "nature"); "plausibility of game events" (the determination of moves would be left to the players and referees); "clarification" (the game was intended to unearth latent biases, interdependencies, confusion, and ignorance); and "exploration of novel strategies" (during the pre-game orientation, players received briefing documents that prodded them to consider less hackneyed possibilities).[9]

Four role-playing exercises were played during 1955 and 1956. The first two ran for a few days, and the third ran the course of the summer of 1955. The fourth and final game swallowed up the energies of twenty participants for three weeks in April 1956. This would be the most elaborate war game of the decade, and the model to which later political exercises would refer. A team from the Social Science Division posed a number of questions which they hoped the unfolding month of gaming would resolve. Chief among them was whether gaming could be used as a forecasting technique "for sharpening our estimates of the probable consequences of policies pursued by various governments." Would gaming spark "political inventiveness," and, more importantly, how did it compare to conventional policy analysis? Did gaming uncover problems that would otherwise be neglected? And, invoking the emerging touchstone of intuition, did the experience impart to policy analysts and researchers "a heightened sensitivity to problems of political strategy and policy consequences?"[10]

The first three games were a bust. Procedural quagmires muddied the players' perceptions of the games' worth. The question remained whether role-playing crisis games could be a genuine research method. It was hoped that the fourth round would settle the issue once and for all. The game scenario was projected nine months into the future. Since it was an attempt to explore the research possibilities of gaming rather than conform to Eisenhower policies, the U.S. team was encouraged to try out any and all tactics available to the executive branch of government. The other teams played moves reflecting the doctrines of their respective governments.

The game was played with reference to carefully prepared background, strategy, and game-classified papers. Each side wrote up its move in a policy note, including extensive justification, and passed it to the referees, who assessed its credibility. In addition to introducing acts of God into the unfolding dynamic, the referees leaked intelligence and unsubstantiated rumors through a pipeline of covert agents and a free press.

At the close of the fourth round the game director circulated a complete dossier to the participants for critique. Was the role-playing game a useful proving ground for political-military ideas? The group concluded, "It is our judgment that the results which might be achieved [were not] . . . worth the sacrifice of the time, money, energy and neglect of other pressing problems." To equate the game with a social science experiment, researchers would have had not only to evaluate the crisscross of a completed game but to compare it with variations. Multiple trials would have been necessary to sort out branching alternatives. Clearly this wasn't practical. Not only was such an experiment time-consuming, it was simply too taxing. The game historian remarked, "Even the short periods of game activity elicit[ed] a considerable drain on [participants'] intellectual capital and resources."[11]

Falling back to something less exacting than a formal experiment, they wondered whether games could be used for brainstorming. But even here they decided that game play was so intricate that no single strategy could be scrutinized with the care it deserved. Had the scenario been confined to a subset of a crisis, maybe the hopes for gaming's stimulus to invention might have been better realized. As it was, the result was inconclusive, anticlimactic, and frankly disappointing. "The players agreed that in a strict sense no fundamentally new insight or scientific 'breakthrough' was produced by the play itself. Nor was it at all certain that the 'knowledge' . . . generated could not have been yielded by . . . conventional and less expensive procedures." With a shrug of exhausted irritation, they recommended that no fulltime games be played at RAND ever again. Instead, maybe tightly circumscribed, problem-oriented games could be conducted on occasion.[12]

But on second thought, maybe *something* fleeting and flimsy and vaguely interesting happened during the fourth round. The game had imposed a crisis gestalt on the players in which they scrambled to work out the next move in the eddy of vying interests. Maybe the game's value was the *experience* of strategy formulation, rather than the outcome of play. Perhaps the war game offered a middle ground between rigorous analysis and the daily hurry-skurry of men responsible for plotting short-term policies. Indeed, the team from the State Department was especially pleased. "Its impact was far greater than that which could have been produced by . . . reading . . . research studies."[13]

Even before the fourth round had concluded, news of war-gaming wafted to elite institutions. Invitations were forthcoming. In the summer of 1956 Hans Speier gave a briefing to a Social Science Research Council summer institute and in 1957 to the fellows at the Center for Advanced Study in the Behavioral Sciences at Stanford University. In the years between 1956 and 1958 Joseph Goldsen delivered a lecture on gaming at Yale and at a conference sponsored by the Carnegie Endowment for International Peace at Princeton. Herbert Goldhamer briefed the Army War College, and in September 1959 delivered a paper on gaming at the annual conference of the Political Science Association. Other members of the RAND team addressed audiences at the Department of State, the Center for International Affairs at Harvard, the Brookings Institution, Northwestern University, and MIT.[14]

War-gaming became the vogue of the moment. In 1957, independently of RAND, Professors Harold Guetzkow and Richard Snyder devised a game they called the Inter-Nation Simulation for use in their courses at Northwestern University. The following year Professor Oliver Benson of the University of Oklahoma programmed Guetzkow and Snyder's game for a digital computer. More importantly, RAND personnel transmitted the technique during visits to MIT in 1957 and 1958. W. Phillips Davison spent the academic year at MIT, in the course of which he played a modified cold war game in his graduate seminar on international communications. Later that year Professors Lucian Pye and Warner Schilling, also at MIT, experimented with it in a course on American diplomacy. The following year (1958–59), several RAND analysts consulted with Professor Lincoln Bloomfield about game design, and in September Paul Kecskemeti, a participant in all of RAND's political-military games, bundled off to MIT to assist in Bloomfield's game sponsored by the United Nations Project at the Center for International Studies. In this one lineage—Goldhamer to Kecskemeti to Bloomfield—war-gaming passed from RAND to MIT to the State Department and the JCS.[15]

Bloomfield had been a State Department official for eleven years before he moved to the MIT Center for International Studies in spring 1957. He observed, "My previous [years] . . . had convinced me that the government badly needed a better way to anticipate foreign policy crises." He embarked on a series of games with and for the government, as well as some pedagogical exercises with undergraduates. Beginning in 1958 and extending over the course of the next thirteen years, Bloomfield directed twelve senior-level war games at MIT. He and Harvard professor and RAND associate Thomas Schelling jointly developed the basic game design.[16]

The first game, dubbed the Endicott House game after the MIT facility where it was held, was sponsored by the UN Project at the Center for International Studies. Involving senior faculty and researchers from MIT, Harvard, Yale, and Columbia, the Endicott House game attempted to question whether a role-playing exercise "would produce significant predictive indications" in a cold war crisis. During January, March, and April of 1959, Bloomfield conducted two undergraduate games focusing on the current state of the Berlin Crisis. In these games, he wanted to compare the results of gaming with conventional college instruction.[17]

In their review of the three MIT exercises, Bloomfield and his colleague Norman Padelford concluded that the role-playing crisis game was not particularly useful for foreign policy specialists. "This kind of operation is their *métier,* they do not need simulation." However, like the RAND social scientists, they were thunderstruck by the atmosphere induced by role-playing. "The game does supply a personal kind of experience of self-awareness . . . and of a heightened sense of reactions produced out of the dynamics of the game." This was also instrumental in the games' successes as undergraduate vehicles. "Simulated experience for the student of political science is a form of vicarious learning seldom afforded by the more orthodox teaching methods." But undergraduates should not be exposed to role-playing games until after they had thoroughly studied diplomacy and the political process. "Otherwise," they cautioned, "the gaming is likely to become artificial, pursued largely on the basis of hunches or intuitions rather than of knowledge and understanding." (The very same shortcoming, playing by hunch and intuition, would be imputed to the professional tier of war-gamers.)[18]

Bloomfield's exercises attracted attention throughout the foreign policy community. In 1961 the joint chiefs of staff established the Joint War Games Group, a Pentagon-level gaming agency. Henry Rowen, a former RAND analyst, who was an aide to John McNaughton, the assistant secretary of defense for international security affairs in the Kennedy administration, recommended that the RAND-MIT crisis game be adopted by the JCS.[19]

Very soon afterward, during the tense September of 1961, the Pentagon sponsored two war games on the Berlin Crisis. Schelling recalled, "At dinner at the home of Charles Hitch, then Comptroller of the Department of Defense, as I was en route to spend a summer at RAND, Walt Rostow urged me to develop the Berlin game; actually to give up my RAND summer developing the Berlin game; I did, and we staged it in September." Directed by Schelling, senior government officials impersonated the leadership of the Blue (US) and Red (USSR) states. The scenario for both games involved military threats over Berlin. Despite Schelling's demonic inducements for either side to escalate to war, they adroitly sidestepped his provocations.[20]

Neither President Kennedy nor his brother Robert participated in Schelling's exercises. During the Cuban Missile Crisis, Daniel Ellsberg recalled, "On this Saturday morning, we were in . . . the Policy Planning Room. There were various cables coming in from minute to minute. One of them looked almost identical to one of the cables of the year before. Namely that students were rioting and demonstrating in Berlin. It looked very much like the message from the [Berlin] game. I tapped Walt Rostow on the shoulder and I said, 'Read this.' He read it. I said, 'This shows how realistic the Berlin game was.' He said, 'Or how unrealistic this is.'"[21]

President Kennedy did not take part in any of the Pentagon games conducted during his administration. His brother Robert was intrigued with the technique, however. The President, had he survived, might well have agreed to observe, if not play, a war game. On Halloween 1963 Schelling directed several crisis games simultaneously. His players included the chairman of the JCS, the director of the U.S. budget, the commander of the Marine Corps, and several others, including Attorney General Robert Kennedy. In the post-game session, the President's brother excitedly proposed gaming civil rights. He suggested that the President might glean something from it. "We also talked about getting the President to observe—not participate in—a brink-of-nuclear-war game for a whole day or two," Schelling recalled. "I took that to imply that John Kennedy had never participated or even considered it. I'm quite sure he died before he ever had a chance."[22]

Serious Play

War-gaming in America was a somewhat clandestine affair. While not an official secret, gaming was acknowledged only reluctantly in the public media. It would be unseemly to advertise the fact that the nation's military was rehearsing the next war with miniatures and markers, stage sets and role-playing dramas that "offer . . . the whole world as a theatre." President Eisenhower's acting secretary of state, Christian Herter, was quite willing to sponsor political-military war games at MIT in 1958, "provided that he did not have to tell Congress the State Department was 'playing games.'"[23]

Similarly, the Office of the Joint Chiefs of Staff did not publicize the establishment of its war-gaming group in 1961. Analysts traveling within the RAND-Cambridge-Pentagon nexus would have heard of war games played at RAND and MIT and doubtless anticipated the establishment of a JCS-level research group. But the public at large remained unaware of this development until news of the Pentagon games was leaked by Milton Caniff in his nationally syndicated comic strip *Steve Canyon* on June 9, 1963.

Because Steve Canyon was a gallant air force hero, Caniff was regularly briefed on service matters as possible material for his comic strip saga. Sometime in 1963 Caniff was invited to observe a Pentagon exercise, which he subsequently dramatized in his June 9th strip. The JCS were dumbfounded by the unexpected disclosure. While the comic strip did not excite national attention as they feared, Lincoln Bloomfield chuckled, "When, to their chagrin, [Caniff] went public and the strip hit the street, it also hit the fan. The embarrassment (and extensive kidding) they endured in-house caused the folks in the Pentagon basement to vow never again to make the mistake of allowing an uncleared round-bottomed civilian on the premises."[24]

Participants were reluctant to use the word "game" to describe these exercises (preferring "simulation"), since game seemed an unsuitable name for rehearsals of conventional, limited, or all-out nuclear war. The phrase "serious play" characterized war-gaming in the heaps of articles introducing it to military audiences. Serious play connoted the solemnity, the expense of buying computer time and assembling gaming facilities, and the time and effort of scores of researchers who devoted months to game design and preparation. Grim as war games were, they were also enormously enthralling. Lincoln Bloomfield marveled, "To someone who is not a psychological expert, it is nothing short of astonishing to see grown men abandon their families, forget their worldly obligations, and engage their personalities and intellects so completely in a simulated role. Perhaps show business learned this a long time ago."[25]

While everyone made valiant attempts to cast crisis and war-gaming as a sober research method, Bloomfield and other early observers conceded that role-playing was also make-believe. They themselves called it "a political psychological art form," "the process of creating an imaginary universe," "social science fiction," "stagecraft." In fact, Bloomfield wrote that during its first decade, gaming's "only truly demonstrable value . . . was entertainment." War-gaming's resemblance to theater could not be evaded. In the same public discussion of JCS war-gaming, its director quipped, "I'm afraid that before I finish, you will associate our efforts more with those of Cecil B. DeMille than John von Neumann, but that would be too harsh a judgment." For the most part, the exponents of war-gaming refrained from drawing from the larger cultural meanings of play, such as symbol-making, dreams, and jokes.[26]

The quality from which the war game derived its realism was its dynamism, that is, its "process and playability." This was the first meaning of serious play. Operations researchers Clayton Thomas and Walter Deemer, Jr., noted, "We feel that the essence of operational gaming lies . . . in its emphasis on the *playing of a game*. Playing to formulate a game, playing to solve a game, and playing to impart present knowledge of a game." Bloomfield described the process of gaming as "setting into motion . . . a self-sustaining chain reaction which develops a life and a momentum of its own."[27]

Implicit in the vitality of play was the idea that the outcome of any game was uncertain, however constrained by the rules and opening scenario. "The sequential interaction of the actors . . . lead[s] them to unforeseen choice-points." Like the violent rush of real crises, one couldn't anticipate the consequences of the teams' moves until they unfolded in completed play. Clark Abt, one of the most formidable game designers of the period, explained, "Gaming is a series of if-then decisions structured like a tree. There is uncertainty at every branch of a decision-making tree." The more intricately designed the game is, the greater the semblance of contingency and therefore the greater realism of play. Just as importantly, "The more complex the branching structure is, the greater the likelihood that an unexpected outcome will result."[28]

Gaming as Synthetic Experience

Typically, players finessed the problem of gaming's validity by emphasizing the intensity of the *experience*, itself an untidy anti-concept.

For example, RAND analyst Robert Specht interrupted himself with the aside, "A war game teaches both intellectually and emotionally—it is an experience one lives through. You and I should not be talking about a war game—we should be playing one." Following Specht's lead, let's inspect the qualities of the game experience. It has been characterized as a spur to group creativity, a training of intuition, the creation of a parallel world, and synthetic history.[29]

Gaming's power to stimulate creativity was frequently emphasized in the literature: "Gaming stretches the limits of one's imagination, of one's notions of the plausible and the possible, and one's awareness of the role of the unanticipated in international affairs," remarked Richard Barringer and Barton Whaley. Whereas the accent on group creativity led gamers to probe novel situations, gaming also stimulated insight, another topic of interest to the cold war avant-garde. Insight was ritually invoked in every discussion of gaming in the period, and yet what was it exactly?[30]

The Behavioral Sciences Subpanel of President Kennedy's Science Advisory Committee defined insight as "the achievement of understanding, particularly when it takes place suddenly and dramatically. It is a genuine, if elusive, phenomenon." In some gaming formulations, insight seemed to mean lucidly grasping the dynamic operation of components of a total system. W. L. Archer used it this way. "The tactical game provides a simulated battle experience for the military players from which it is possible to gain considerable insight into the key factors and critical interaction between the major tactical systems." On the other hand, insight was sometimes treated as an indefinable good, the fruit of the players' tacit knowledge. Clayton Thomas proposed the game as "a mechanism for eliciting 'buried' knowledge from experts, files, latent sources of all kinds, and then assembling it into a coherent totality that provides a test context."[31]

During the 1950s, the stimulation of a player's intuition was a shibboleth among game enthusiasts, but no one could define it sharply. Let's sample a number of statements about gaming intuition to get a feel for its use. In 1957 Thomas and Deemer wrote, "Although there are no formal criteria to indicate when the game has been adequately solved, [the analyst] will judge intuitively when it is safe to draw conclusions. Meanwhile, with each successive play, his feeling for the game increases." In 1964, at the Second War Games Symposium, a navy analyst commented, "Because of the rapid changes taking place in the nature of weapons systems and, therefore, in the nature of warfare, a considerable amount of intuition enters into [decision makers'] judgment." And finally, from 1965, Barringer and Whaley wrote, "It is believed that the planner will acquire more of a 'feel' for the timing, logistics, political implications, and other aspects of the problem than he would in the absence of the game experience."[32]

By foregrounding intuition, strategy drifted away from the conventions of policy analysis. What can we make of statements that justified themselves by an inexplicable feeling for the dynamic of play? Dreaming up a game, simulation, or model meant drafting a world-picture of the cold war. Grasping the tangle of influence and disruption wrought by incompatible interests resembled the world of a novel, a painting, a drama. While not every author exploited the affinity between war games and the fine arts, certainly within the operations research literature, the war game, systems analysis, or simulation were regularly described as an ingenious fabrication with few leading principles. Dalkey observed, "At present, the construction of a simulation is almost entirely an intuitive art." Helmer elaborated, "There is no theory of operational gaming . . . [Gaming] is still very much in the nature of a craft and thus calls for an artisan's approach to be understood and appreciated." Thirty years later, the naval operations researcher Peter Perla remarked, "Game design has no real formalisms. Instead, it is dominated by individual style and by fashion, and in that respect is more like painting than the other arts."[33]

While game intuition was often understood to project a world-picture of a cold war crisis filtered through the personalities of the players and the organizational culture of the sponsoring institution, the actual experience of playing the game produced more than a feeling for the crisis gestalt. Nearly everyone marveled at its distinctive emotional intensity. Bloomfield's colleagues at MIT surveyed participants in nine games conducted at the Center for International Studies, beginning in 1958. Asked to quantify the intensity of player involvement, 64.9 percent of the respondents marked the variable "extreme or intense." In other words, role-playing seemed to elicit the same behavior they would probably display during a real crisis. Bloomfield and an associate mused, "The single most highly valued quality of the political exercise is that professional players are seen to act *essentially* as they act in real life." A respondent in the 1965 survey reasoned, "You're looking at live people who are your peers coping with genuine problems as they might arise, and doing so under strong competitive and professional pressure to perform well." So enthralling was the game world that players broke away reluctantly. "Coming out of a role is a little like coming out of a deep sleep afer a particularly vivid dream," Bloomfield wrote. "It takes time for the carry-over of emotional content from the game to reality to wear off."[34]

Its very intensity made the game a special kind of lived experience. Bloomfield called the war game "a laboratory in which [crisis] events can be lived through experimentally." Abt suggested that gaming provided "anticipatory experience." Simulation had long been recognized as an instrument for training. But unlike field experiments, war games could elicit behavior unavailable in any other forum. A colonel in the Air Command and Staff College wrote, "It is . . . [now] possible to glimpse the elusive and manifold shape of future conflicts and to harden, by fictional exposure, the officers who may some day come face to face with the hideous visage of the real thing." Many gamers used the term "synthetic experience" to describe game-play, and justified it along these lines: "The requirement to prepare for potential conflicts with weapons of a radically new sort, where previous experience gives little guidance, imposed the necessity for developing a substitute for experience; and simulation is precisely a technique for creating synthetic experience."[35]

Gamers regarded the total event—designing the game scenario and reference papers, the experience of play itself, and the subsequent record of game transactions, up to and including post-game assessment—as forecasted or synthetic history. (Adding a Hegelian nuance to the proceedings, war games even acquired a daily newspaper called *Weltbild*, composed by Bloomfield and company at MIT in 1958. Like Scheherazade forestalling the cataclysm each night with the embroidery of complications, the *Weltbild* "present[ed] to the players at the beginning of each day the hypothetical events which had taken place overnight and would seriously affect their plans for the day.")[36]

The shift from synthetic history to future history was not a great leap. From 1961 onward, Kahn and his collaborators devised a series of Alternative Future Worlds as "substitutes for relevant knowledge, experiment, judgment, perception, insight, and intuition." He believed that these imaginative forays should properly be understood as "artificial 'case histories' and 'historical anecdotes' to make up to some degree for the paucity of actual examples."[37]

The Problem of Realism

The narrative framework for synthetic history, the scenario, was the kernel of the war game. Providing a forum for experience, the invention of the scenario presented the designer with a literary problem. In a contemporary primer on war-gaming, Perla expressed the idea most succinctly: "Designing a war game is more akin to writing an historical novel than proving an algebraic theorem."[38]

Early in the 1950s analysts recognized the categorical difference between mathematically informed games and an unstructured exercise. For example, in 1954 Alexander Mood described the game as "a method for solving problems previously thought to be . . . answerable only by appeal to the judgment of experts. [These] problems . . . cannot be detached, for purposes of investigation, from their natural context." Certainly, we can recognize a parallel between game scenarios and literary art. Scenarios could not be plucked from their cultural and historical situation. They were oriented toward the totality, and like a novel, they dramatized several streams of interaction simultaneously. Analysts inched up to the idea. Rauner and Steger observed, "By providing a detailed, tangible representation of reality, game-simulations make it easier for planners to understand the over-all model than if it is more abstractly drawn." Kahn stressed the gestalt of scenario. "[Scenarios] help to illuminate the interaction of psychological, social, political, and military factors, including the in-fluence of individual political personalities . . . and they do so in a form which permits the comprehension of many interacting ele-ments at once." But on this very point, critics argued that game sce-narios suffered from the analytic deficits of narrative history. "The scenario writer constructs the behavior of adversaries in a crisis with-out many of the constraints that operate on decision makers in a cri-sis . . . In other words, both the scenario writer and the historian attack crisis studies from the outside, looking in."[39]

Gaming was approached with as much caution as enthusiasm, for how could group story-telling resolve operational conundrums? Re-garding "the general uncertainty of the results of research," Clayton Thomas of the air force's Operations Analysis Office remarked, "The three-room war game . . . is properly restricted in its employment to those problems where it seems that 'nothing else will work.' In a typi-cal application, prior efforts to simplify the problem further have failed and the residual formulation is full of complexities."[40]

Ambivalence about gaming's resemblance to literature was not limited to the scenario. Following the thread of systems thinking, the gamers tried to shoehorn everything of importance into game design and play. Since a major war would batter every department of life, they were tempted to expand their model into infinitely complex de-tails in the simulation of reality. But at the same time, they were de-termined to set upper and lower boundaries, limits, and constraints of every kind onto that surging impulse toward the *Weltbild*. In other words, in war game design, one makes out a wish to cast a richly fur-nished world, but one sealed off like a terrarium or a tableau in a pa-perweight. This snug little world, in which the totality could be grasped all at once, encompasses the universe of miniature life. The behavioral experiments staged in the ingenious enclosures of sub-marines and arctic bases, the maps, chits, and rule-books of board games, the intricate array of model railroad networks, and the plaster-molded, landscaped table-top terrains of toy soldiering all contributed to the propriety and ultimate acceptance of the game-world microcosm.

The congruence between the model and future war was typically posed as a question of the game's realism. Analysts of the period recognized this as a genuine problem. Mood wrote in 1954, "Most games now in existence need further development and refinement before they can be said to represent reality well enough to provide a basis for decisions. And until that time comes, one cannot be certain of what the games will accomplish." In 1958 Specht remarked, "We have not settled the question of the realism of a war game. This is a problem that . . . runs far deeper than the superficial aspects of rich detail or enormous complexity." Three years later, Churchman elevated its importance into being the leading puzzle of the field: "We can say that now the most significant problem of operations research is the problem of realism." The following year another analyst admitted, "The search for an elusive and seemingly very desirable attribute called 'realism' continues to preoccupy many of us."[41]

Game design stalled on the range and degree of detail necessary to flesh out the scenario. How much was warranted? How much was obfuscatory? The designers' preoccupation with instilling a sense of reality among players by piling on political, social, and operational details opened the question of determining what sort of realism was pertinent to the game world. For Thomas and Deemer, authors of the Operations Research Society's prize-winning essay of 1957, the "appearance of realism" was both a benefit and an encumbrance. For one thing, the authenticity of the game experience aroused enthusiasm and a commitment to the lessons derived from the particulars of play. Thomas wrote elsewhere, "All of these emotional responses evidence a striving for reality." The fact that it was an experience—an event—risked assigning too much weight to the insights elicited in a game: "One is fascinated by the appearance of real events unfolding before one's eyes, and may forget that the appearance does not in itself prove or disprove the reality or faithfulness of the representation." Thomas and Deemer repeatedly despaired of the conviction players felt while extrapolating general principles from a single trial of a game scenario. "Despite the absence of logical proof," they remarked, "operational gaming inspires its practitioners with a remarkable confidence in its results. Sometimes an implausible result is accepted with special relish *because* of its implausibility."[42]

For Thomas and Deemer, as for most gamers, realism "induce[d] an ambivalent attitude towards elaboration." More ominously, they cautioned that the urge to festoon the scenario with secondary issues was a "temptation" that "court[ed] delusion." What they meant by realism was piling on the details and refinements that contributed to the simulation's verisimilitude. Game designers believed that by heaping up variables and irregularities, they were conveying the ineffables of politico-military conflict. They seemed to draw from an anecdotal sensibility in which a jumble of details, revealed in episodic moves, in an atmosphere of uncertainty and incomplete information, evoked a sense of reality.[43]

Yet, for many game designers, simulation was not literature, but an *experiment* and should therefore conform to the criteria of scientific realism. Over against the thick description of story-telling, long-standing experimental principles counseled representing only the essential structure of a phenomenon, even if the isolation distorted its verisimilitude. One couldn't achieve a semblance of reality because the phenomenon to be gamed made it proof against a meticulously empirical, contextual representation. Clearly, there could be no one-to-one correspondence between a simulation of nuclear war and reality; the weight of uncertainty blocked this possibility.

Given that simulations of war would necessarily be idealized, for Thomas and Deemer the scientific realism aspired to by war-gamers aimed for an unadorned, quantified schematic of combat. The scientifically real captured the essence but not its documentary appearance. It would be quantified, aggregated, and subject to analytic solution. Thus, in the course of protesting the incoherent findings of role-playing, they offered the striking difference between the stark configuration of the scientifically real and the quasi-literary refinements of war-gaming. In war-gaming, "one has no such sure guide to the adequacy of a proposed solution." As a result, one can't really assess the value of any particular game outcome. Moreover, in the absence of a reliable sensitivity analysis, game designers tended to "overemphasize the desirability of elaboration."[44]

Other war-gamers echoed the idea that literary realism was a trap "which," Archer complained, "may gave the player a false sense of security." This was not a professional secret, but openly acknowledged. Gaming enthusiasts and critics struggled with the problem in eager discussions at briefings, post-game assessment sessions, conferences, and symposia.[45]

Arguments about the merits of gaming became so much the norm at professional meetings that RAND's Ed Paxson reproduced them in a research memorandum on war-gaming. His "Critic" accused players of being too credulous, and designers of "confusing their model with reality" and providing spurious details that could not be checked against field experiments or other data. His "Protagonist" retorted, "War-gaming is not an exercise in mass self-hypnosis. But the players do become convinced that a war game is an experiment, undoubtedly imperfect. They know that intuition and judgment intervene."[46]

Given the fact that war games were regarded both as synthetic history and laboratory experiments, eventually they were used to generate operational data. The events taking place in the course of play, as well as game outcomes, acquired the aura of well-founded fact in the absence of empirical sources. "As we recede from such sources of empirical data as World War II and Korea, an ability to generate synthetic battlefield facts becomes increasingly important." Sterne reflected, "Such game outputs are valuable through being, often, the only operational details that can be obtained about novel military actions, or with novel forces, or under novel conditions." Hausrath told the story of a field experiment requested by army game designers when they discovered that there was no available information about how to pinpoint fire from an anti-tank weapon. A field experiment was performed, and the resulting data were plugged into a war game.

"Here was an example of a game that established a requirement for field tests. The field tests in turn yielded data that enabled the game to solve problems not previously within the capability of operations research analytical study."[47]

Clearly, simulations could be justifiably used for planning. But the gaming community split on the soundness of "synthetic operational data." Would they be able to sift through the gamed phenomena linked to rules, conditions, and aggregated data, and make out data resulting from game-play? Archer pointed out that it was a "subtle and complex problem" to distinguish the substantive outcome of a game from phenomena flowing from the scenario and rules. Any outcome was just as likely to be a consequence of design, and not the result of player participation. He warned that there were "definite limits to the resolution" of the war game. In other words, game outcomes corresponded to the game logic, and only secondarily, or indirectly, to the actual world. There seemed to be no positive grounds for evaluating the result. Abt pointed out that while clearly invalid games could be discredited by reference to real-world phenomena, "there does not seem to be any objective method for determining the degree of validity of not completely *in*valid models." Ultimately, the problem could be resolved only by resort to the final decision-maker's intuition and judgment.[48]

Discussants at the Second War Games Symposium in 1964 heatedly debated the question. George Pugh, the deputy assistant director for weapons evaluation and control at the Arms Control and Disarmament Agency, asserted that in reviewing game results the supervisor's intuition played a central role. In cases where findings from computer simulations "didn't jibe" with his intuition, he ordered his team to rework their model. Often they uncovered mistakes. Just as often, after revisiting their design, his team would return to explain the vagaries of the result with him in depth, which in turn "revised" his intuition. Contrary to Pugh's standpoint as the ultimate arbiter of his researchers' findings, an army operations analyst responded that in his opinion, "The most valuable answers from any OR [operations research] technique, including games, [were] correct answers that disagreed with the intuition of the military." The counter-intuitive results of war games were their raison d'être. "We are coming up with something that they just wouldn't have ever gotten around to by themselves."[49]

Into this round-robin of self-congratulation, the chief of the Air Battle Analysis Center interjected that he was uneasy about relying on intuition "because you have to worry about the station in life of the person exercising the intuition." Only a few years earlier, a decision-maker with no experience with war games and computer simulations would habitually discredit these findings—he "would believe nothing in which he had not personally participated." Whereas intuition had acted as an impediment to the advancement of long-range planning, now war-gamers worked for decision-makers who "believed everything without questions."[50]

They broached the tricky problem of whether or not to believe the results of a game as though it were a simple output from an impenetrable black box. The chief of the Joint War Games Agency, Rear Admiral Clyde Van Arsdall, declared that he had no choice but to defer to the findings of the professional gamers. When he first became chief of the new agency, some analysts on his staff counseled him to "trust the people who knew the routines and technical details." It would be a great mistake to "get lost in the guts of a computer, which was not my business." It was good advice, he told his audience. "I could care less about how one of your programmers starts at the beginning and comes out at the end, because I think you know more about that than we do. If we can pose the problem and you can run a routine that will give us the answers, fine."[51]

But not everyone shared his faith in the professionals. A discussant from IBM countered that game sponsors often protested, "When I play the game . . . I have to take some egghead's word that these models are realistic and accurate. I don't really understand the model, and no matter how you try to convince me, I will always have some doubt about how I can use the results for decision making." They begged him to build "simple-minded games" whose assumptions and routines were intelligible to laymen. Only then could they make an informed evaluation of its results, saying: "I then might feel more confident about using the results for actual decision-making."[52]

Was it a matter of deciphering game design, managerial incompetence, or lack of time? One panelist remarked, "Perhaps the biggest problem that exists today is that a war game model is extremely difficult to understand. Years are spent in their development, and when someone is in a hurry for an analysis, he can't spend the time to learn all vital details of the model." Another discussant accused decision-makers of abandoning their responsibility to probe gaming results. "They will not look at the assumptions that constrain the model, and they will not take the time to read through the explanatory appendices, particularly those that have all the integrals worked out." Clearly, not everybody could appreciate the explanatory appendices. The last speaker of the symposium pondered the detail into which the decision-maker needed to delve in the black box of game design. No senior official had the time to inquire into every finding. He concluded affably, "Here perhaps more than anywhere else in gaming is the user of games required to exercise his judgment and intuition: in choosing judiciously which 'black boxes' to accept without opening, which ones to examine in detail, and which ones to accept after a careful description by the author."[53]

Gaming was the vogue of the moment. Its very ambiguity elicited ardor and skepticism in the defense community. Given the atmosphere of heightened interest bordering on anxiety regarding its utility, it is not surprising that everyone felt obliged to catalogue the benefits and pitfalls of war games, to offer caution in its use, and stake a position regarding its ultimate value to strategic planning, analysis, and research.

A number of analysts addressed gaming's correspondence to reality, then compared its defects with more conventional techniques. In these contests, war-gaming gained in richness, subtlety, and intelligibility. For example, Robert Davis commended role-playing games for their ability to represent the complex environment of arms control "rather than abstract[ing] it away." Moreover, the players "respond to a situation which resembles as nearly as possible 'real life.'" Davis nevertheless disconfirmed any comfortable congruence between the simulation and reality. He asked, "Has the real system been so violated . . . that there is not a reasonable degree of similarity between our conceptual model of reality and the real world?" He opined morosely, "Not one of the techniques described is . . . adequate; not one of them can be operationally traced back to the bedrock of reality." Gaming and simulation were as flawed as other research techniques.[54]

Bloomfield and Whaley worried, "Can reality ever be . . . approximated under laboratory conditions, however skillfully attempted? Does what happens in a game bear any demonstrable relationship to what will happen in real life?" They tempered the skeptical reach of such a question with the reminder that all research simplified the world's "infinite number of variables." They offered a modest vote of confidence for gaming. "On some issues, but not on all," they concluded, "it comes closer to reality than . . . other methods."[55]

In his "Introduction to War Games," Weiner noted the absence of real experience and data for new weapons systems as well as the pitfalls of drawing inferences from demonstration tests, field exercises, games, and simulations. Since games and simulations posited specific cases, it would be impossible to know how actual future combat conditions differed from hypothetical studies. "We have no acceptable and precise way of relating [test conditions] to combat." Bloomfield, for his part, doubted whether "culture-bound Americans," even foreign policy experts, could accurately role-play their Soviet counterparts. Archer protested that game models were too simple to afford statistical confidence in their outcomes. Other critics presented a hodge-podge of complaints: the absence of firm facts, the inadequacy of modeling imponderables such as group morale, leadership, and enemy response. And everybody objected to the roiling atmosphere of game design, arbitration, and play.[56]

A trio of British observers offered a sly impression of the craze for gaming. "At first sight, simulation or gaming may appear to the European . . . as dangerous, esoteric, pompous, behaviouralist and American, yet its frequent use in varied fields in the United States commands attention." Deploring the "evident and manifold" limitations of war games, they nevertheless yielded to the Pascalian wager with the concession, "Yet the alternatives are inadequate, as the state of 'conventional wisdom' at the moment unhappily bears witness." Dipping into the gambling idiom themselves, after listing the various constraints and defects of gaming, they suggested its chief liability was "the absence of a sense of high stakes." It could never be real enough. No simulation could possibly attain the burden of gravity assumed by decision-makers in a real nuclear crisis.[57]

In a retrospective article, Bloomfield and Gearin concluded that their early games had been more like "a political-psychological art form" than a fully articulated research technique. "The point was to present players with a horrendous crisis problem and turn them loose in order to 'see what would happen.'" It was a fruitful technique for brainstorming. For policy analysis, "the PE [political exercise] was, at best, a form of organized mind-blowing, with serendipity the chief objective."[58]

Its very amorphism excited criticism from social scientists. They charged Bloomfield with having exerted "little effort . . . to define inputs and measure results in other than gross or intuitive terms." Hostile social scientists demanded scholarly reference to ongoing social psychology, political science theory, quantification of inputs and outputs, and mathematized analysis. In its current form, resting on a narrative and performative structure, "the lack of rigorous controls made it impossible to conduct a controlled test of specific hypotheses except in the most general way." In turn, Bloomfield and Gearin defended group exploration of a "plausible" reality against the "excessive scientism" of their critics. "It would . . . be a shame to distort the values that already inhere in the PE [political exercise]," they retorted, "for the sake of fidelity to often imperfect and sometimes dubious theory."[59]

The Wager of War Games

Hopes for the computer's contributions to military planning predated the invention of the digital electronic computer. In 1946 Warren Weaver, the chief of the Applied Mathematics Panel of the

Office of Scientific Research and Development, dreamed of a "great Tactical-Strategic Computer" that would compute the optimal war plan. "You begin to twiddle the decision variable dials," he wrote wistfully. Adjusting the "military worth dial" automatically rotated the "decision variable dials." Modifying the plan this way and that allowed the analyst to "observe directly whether the change is for the better or for the worse." In order to arrive at the optimum plan, he speculated, the computer would have "a mechanism which . . . shifts all the decision dials through cycles of accessible values, the resulting values of M.W. [military worth] being recorded so that the maximum can be located and the corresponding set of optimum values of the decision variables determined."[60]

Defense analysts were the first computer addicts who originated much of the lore of the computer's exalted capability. Fantasy that strategic and tactical inputs could be programmed into the black box and the desired plan or even the war itself would thereby be rendered was not merely a quixotic desire afloat in a void. When computers appeared in defense, corporate, and government spheres in the mid-1950s, they excited powerful fantasies within the culture. If not openly expressed in the technical literature, popular descriptions abounded with the hope that bloodless simulations would become a substitute for war.

For example, the mathematician John Kemeny, expressed the yearning to be rescued from war that was popularly invested in the computer. In the future, he wished, wars would be conducted at "great simulations laboratories at the United Nations." The war would take place "on the largest and most expensive computing machine ever constructed by Man. After twenty-four hours of computation, both sides are informed of the outcome. The victor can then rejoice, and the defeated country—after paying due reparations—can start arming for the next simulated war." The idea was repeatedly invoked. Several years later, in "The First Battle of World War III," George Boehm prophesied that it was "not wholly inconceivable" that major wars would be played at some international computer laboratory. "All that will remain to be done on the fateful morning will be to push the 'start' button and wait for the computer to wage war 10,000 times." Studying the printouts of the outcomes, "we can envision one commander-in-chief . . . [saying,] 'Okay. You wiped us out 9,327 times. I'll tell my Prime Minister to pull out of the Balkans. Now, how about a Martini before lunch?'"[61]

As early as 1956 the new technology had attracted a circle of fervid operations researchers whom Bernard Koopman playfully admonished for suffering from *mechanitis*, "the occupational disease of one who is so impressed with modern computing machinery that he believes that a mathematical problem, which he can neither solve nor even formulate, can readily be answered, once he has access to a sufficiently expensive machine." Reflecting operations researchers' faith in the computer's powers, one author observed, "This preoccupation with machine gaming was further fostered and encouraged by an appreciation for the complexity of the new weapons systems available. Indeed, the speed with which these weapons could react, each to the other, seemed to indicate that only a machine with vast memory and instant response could be expected to indicate a successful counter strategy in sufficient time to be useful."[62]

While Koopman parodied computer enthusiasm in 1956, by the end of the decade a number of systems analysts sought to cool the mania. For example, in 1958 Robert Specht tried to refocus professional interest in model design and analysis by reproving his readers, "It is important for us to remember that there is nothing magic about a computing machine . . . Regardless of the machinery used, it is to the assumptions that we must turn when we ask for an explanation of the results of the game." Three years later Clayton Thomas noted that a mystique had long beguiled researchers concerning the digital computer's "machine virtues" such as automaticity, transferability, and speed. "When one hears of the flexibility of computing machines that 'can do anything,' one sometimes forgets that a machine solves no problem entirely by itself, in some magical, automatic way of its own."[63]

By 1964 analysts had accumulated enough experience with computer-aided gaming, computer games, and computer simulations to moderate their ardor. "There was a tendency two or three years ago for us to become a slave to the computer," remarked the chief of the air force's premier gaming office, the Air Battle Analysis Center. But now military wisdom had regained some of its luster. He continued, "Whatever the place of the machine, we cannot function without the operational experience of man and the application of sound military judgment in any of our games and analyses."[64]

Just as some sectors of the armed forces were wildly enthusiastic about war-gaming, we can observe a backlash among the senior and middle-level military officers hostile to computer-dependent weapons systems, systems analysis, and war-gaming. It was inevitable that conflict would break out between civilian analysts and the venerable senior staff of the armed services. In a 1960 article, Robert Roy matter-of-factly laid out the structural antagonism between the practitioners of the new analytic techniques and their reluctant clients. Operations researchers typically aroused hostility at their field sites. "The notion that a group of outsiders, themselves incapable of performing an operation, can tell veteran, expert operators how to do better is . . . preposterously contrary to our own notions about ourselves." He counseled his readers to be mindful of the injured pride their studies invariably provoked, and "to learn to practice the art of persuasion to the n-th degree."[65]

Alas, most analysts were hardly discreet in their assault on the old guard. We can readily sense the aggrieved indignation felt by military traditionalists in the remarks made in 1961 by a British Labour Party MP. Richard Crossman commented waspishly to an audience at the Royal United Services Institute, "One of the strangest features of American life in the 1950s—which no doubt will continue throughout the 1960s—is that many of the experts who lead the discussion on the nature of war have no experience in it or training for it." He described his encounter with a civilian defense analyst whom he had accosted in a recent trip to the United States. "I said to him . . . 'Did you ever in your life go near the Army or hear a shot fired in anger?' 'Of course not,' he said, 'one would hardly get to my position if one had.'" It was a joke, of course, but Crossman declared, "it's a remarkable fact that . . . the war gamester, in fact, is a human computer." In contrast, he was pleased to compare the enlightened military of the United Kingdom. "Here in Britain, thank goodness," he murmured, "we still realize that, although scientific and technological development may substitute the machine and the computer for human activity, it still remains true that the final decisions must be taken by human beings, and the humble study of human nature still remains the criterion of wisdom, whether in a general or a politician."[66]

Senior American (and NATO) officers eagerly demonstrated the fallacy of replacing military wisdom with the findings of civilian systems analysts and war-gamers. For every article suggesting that answers to problems of strategic planning could be found in simulation, one could find screeds such as Lieutenant Commander Frank Haak's 1961 piece for the *Proceedings* of the U.S. Naval Institute. Systems analysis "should be employed to refine human judgment rather than replace it." While acknowledging the transformation of warfare, the senior officer must nevertheless reclaim his ultimate authority for combat decisions and "avoid the dangerous practice of accepting on blind faith the scientists' findings." Haak intoned, "The military field is his profession, not the scientist's." In manifest rebellion against Secretary of Defense Robert McNamara's reforms, he called upon his fellow officers to restore the supremacy of military judgment and intuition against the prevailing methodism of the civilian technicians. "The time is ripe for the man with the military mind to reaffirm his ability to satisfy those demands and put the scientists back to work in areas where their own professional qualifications are best suited."[67]

While Haak regarded decision-making as the essence of command authority, an accent on the irrational art of war foregrounded the exceedingly romantic *cri de coeur* of a senior French operations analyst, which appeared in the August 1962 issue of the U.S. Army magazine *Military Review*. In "The Soldier and Technical Warfare," Ferdinand Otto Miksche argued that the modern military had substituted "technical routine" for the "creative intelligence" employed by seasoned combat soldiers. In the mechanized, automated, centralized military, "soldiers are no longer fighters but specialists in the use of certain instruments." Miksche characterized the implementation of war plans via man–machine weapons systems as a soulless, technicist, and inflexible approach to warfare. "It is no more possible to win battles solely with technical means than to paint worthwhile pictures with a machine whose electronic brain is able to select colors." He most particularly derided the most advanced electronic, radar, and computerized capabilities of the modern armed forces. "The atomic general, dressed like a robot, follows the course of the battle on the screen of his televisor with fixed gaze. An electronic brain will furnish him the data for his decisions." For Miksche, this wasn't soldiering but machine-tending. "A soldier must be able to act instinctively, without having to stop to reflect." Like his American counterparts, he concluded that the root of the decline of martial authority lay in the "exaggerated hopes" invested in machines whose capabilities had supplanted "confirmed experience."[68]

For many observers of the professional craze for war-gaming, its validity was as haplessly imperfect as expert intuition, and as likely to err. Two prominent exponents of game theory and decision analysis, Duncan Luce and Howard Raiffa, seem to have expressed the operations research community's mood when they wrote rather sagely in 1957, "[We should like] to see if under any conditions, however limited, the postulates of the model can be confirmed and, if not, to see how they may be modified to accord better at least with those cases. It will be an act of faith to postulate the general existence of these new constructs, but somehow one feels less cavalier if he knows that there are two or three cases where the postulates have actually been verified." In the case of gaming nuclear war, the model's assumptions could not satisfy these modest demands for verification.[69]

Hence we arrive at the conundrum of simulating nuclear war. There was no independent way to validate the findings from any game. One could only submit to an act of faith. In 1961 Schelling reflected, "We are poor in alternative ways of studying the phenomena empirically . . . The knowledge we can get from experimenting with a game may not be comprehensive or terribly reliable, but, compared with what we have or can get in any other way, it looks good."

This was the essence of the futurological wager. Then, as now, advocates of biological, chemical, and nuclear weapons for deterrence declared that it was simply not true that using weapons of mass destruction would lead to global annihilation. The result was as variable as the modeling assumptions underlying any simulation of such a war. Planetary life or death could be derived by extrapolating from the conditions of a strike, a war's termination, weather variables, and a host of imponderables. Teetering on the Pascalian dime, they defied the mortally fearful to prove otherwise.[70]

Chapter 7

THE MINESHAFT GAP

*One can almost hear the President saying to his advisors,
"How can I go to war [when] almost all American cities
will be destroyed?" And the answer ought to be, in essence,
"That's not entirely fatal, we've built some spares."*

HERMAN KAHN, 1960

Uncertainty presents a double face to the world: callous and narrowly practical, or unpredictable and feverish. This accounts for the moods of strategy. If you had to make life-saving decisions with imperfect or doubtful information and no power to alter the outcome, how might you appear to others? If one is stern, one will be expressionless. A more romantic soul might be silkily nonchalant. Immediately, we can see the parallel between the exchange of threats in crisis maneuvering and Dostoevskian gambling.

"To be taken seriously by those who wield power," observed Anatol Rapoport, one must "accept the game paradigm . . . [to show] one knows what it means to 'play the game in a man's world.'" Given the impossibility of picturing World War III, Elliott Fremont-Smith chimed in, "How else is one to think about war if not in terms of chess, poker, and Tactics?" People at RAND assumed the faces of high-stakes gambling: an insensible mask, lightened occasionally by a gay willingness to risk the highest consequences. "It is at first hard to understand the obvious satisfaction these chess players . . . get in this weird game," mused Norman Thomas. "On reflection one can understand that . . . strategy has its own fascination, especially if one can train oneself to think in terms of nations and statistics, not human beings." Another observer was struck by the alluring grandiosity of power politics. The "awfulness" of strategy, he remarked, "has a certain magnetism."[1]

There was pleasure in spinning out a catalogue of possibilities, hatching intrigues and feints, plotting campaigns, playing out the ultimate contest. Strategy could induce paroxysms of roguish jauntiness. It offered the exhilarating emotional palette of a certain type of boy's world: a virtuous people menaced by evil zealots, the fate of millions concentrated in the hands of a daring few.

Kahn carried the thrilling convulsions of the strategic imagination to feats of civil defense. He wanted to know how people could be shielded from blast and fallout. Maybe factories could be erected in mines. Three years of foodstuffs could be squirreled away. There was no real reason why people in target cities couldn't flee into subterranean shelters. Since America's enemies taunted it with nuclear weapons, surely it made sense to launch a Manhattan Project on postwar survival and reconstruction.

A member of Kahn's civil defense team at RAND mapped out a plan for cocooning New Yorkers in dormitories erected in the natural caverns that sprawled beneath the subway tunnels and sewer and utility strata of Manhattan Island. For ninety days, people could tarry in these dens "with no . . . access to the outside world," waiting out the decay in the radioactivity of the rubble up above. Robert Panero's engineering firm concluded that "such shelters seem to be feasible" at a cost of $500 to $800 per shelter space. Extrapolating from the 1948 census, they estimated that approximately 750 million square feet of available underground space in the United States was ripe for civil defense construction.[2]

Burning with the highest hopes, Kahn raced to Washington to tell Spurgeon Keeny's working group on civil defense the good news. He implored them to advise the President to install 50 million underground berths for targeted populations, 50 million less-hardened shelters for second-tier city dwellers and suburbanites, and an additional 100 million spaces of fallout protection for the rest of the nation. From an imaginary pot of $200 billion, he suggested $30 billion be set aside for buying up "immediately usable factory space underground." Not only would these facilities offer protection during a war, but they had the additional merit of providing "radiation-protected working and living space" during reconstruction.[3]

The men in Washington were flabbergasted by Kahn's vision of a post-attack world. He had grossly overestimated their willingness to entertain world-rebuilding ideas. "The biggest influence Kahn had on me," Keeny remarked many years later, "was showing what a huge undertaking civil defense was, and many of the limitations of what it could do." There were so many headaches: hustling people underground, shuttling others to rural reception areas, provisioning shelters. "I had never really thought about it quantitatively. As one studied it in some detail, the utility of blast shelters became increasingly dubious." As the group digested Kahn's assurances that with adequate stocks and training, New Yorkers could survive a nuclear war and climb back up into a humanly supportable world, one member recalled, "We became increasingly convinced that the distortion of society [by such a civil defense initiative] would be such [that] no one would tolerate it."[4]

While they shrank from the deformation civil defense initiatives would inflict on American democracy, Kahn aimed straight for it. He recognized the stupendous tear in the social fabric posed by the threat of nuclear war. He nonetheless toyed with ideas that others regarded as cranky or perverse. Civil defense opened up an administrative utopia. Consider the immensities of the problem: one had to imagine a socio-technical organizational structure that could be established in peacetime but endure into the postwar world, a nationally coordinated plan promulgated in peacetime but enabled after the war by emergency elites and cadres and executed by millions of people who had been compulsorily drilled during peacetime in the proper responses to the impact of a nuclear strike, confinement underground, and resurrection into an irradiated world. Surely this is a fantastic undertaking, weaving the parallel worlds of the peacetime present and the postwar situation. The possibilities were mind-boggling. For Kahn, the enormity of civil defense cried out for his kind of realism. It was also a fount of hope. "Because a war is so horrible, it takes an act of imagination to visualize one starting. It should not take a further act of imagination to believe that it will end." With careful preparation, "it is difficult to see how the military forces themselves can be totally destroyed."[5]

His approach to civil defense displays the hallmarks of the RAND futurological aesthetic. It epitomized the totality; estimates of the post-attack environment were biased toward health and recuperation; model parameters were chosen for ease of computation; models were designed by feel and judgment; their numbers merely animated speculative ideas. The postwar world spun into a desultory tangle of multiple paths issuing from a single stem of the many-branched potentials of civil defense. The model's potential for undetectable error inspired in Kahn an exhaustive cascade of variables and variations.[6]

In comparison with systems analyses, civil defense was both more mythic in its invocations of end-time narratives and more substantively historical. The hardiness of American pioneers, the strike out of the blue at Pearl Harbor, the doughtiness of the British during the Blitz, Soviet resilience after the depredations of the Nazis—all were reference points in Kahn's civil defense imagination. Yet while civil defense incorporated more exacting social phenomena than systems analysis, it was far more speculative. Nuclear war-fighting was not the only basis for envisioning its unfolding, but one among many. The viability of the economy, the integrity of the social order, the constitution of the survivors, and the biosphere itself were problems that civil defense had to address and solve.

Protection against Enemy Action

Immediately after the war's end, teams of social scientists combed through the ruins of Axis cities to assess the effects of aerial bombardment. The resulting *U.S. Strategic Bombing Survey (USSBS)* became the chief source of ideas and data for atomic civil defense. The author of the volume *The Effects of Atomic Bombs on Hiroshima and Nagasaki*, Paul Nitze, spelled out rudimentary civil defense ideas for the postwar era: America should disperse its industry into the hinterland, erect a national blast shelter system, and lay plans to evacuate city dwellers to rural reception centers in the advent of war.[7]

In any conceivable future war, at least one bomber would penetrate national defenses. Civil defense seemed to offer prudent insurance against enemy action. From the immediate postwar period through the 1950s, blue ribbon panels, advisory boards, and classified summer studies were periodically convened to examine the economic, scientific-technical, and political feasibility of massive civil defense programs. Usually with some urgency, they all recommended the immediate inauguration of a national program.

In light of widespread anxiety about Soviet long-range bomber capabilities, a Technological Capabilities Panel was convened in 1954 to assess the American and Soviet potential for fighting World War III. Informally called the Killian Panel after its chairman, James Killian, Jr., the committee delivered its report, *Meeting the Threat of Surprise Attack,* to President Eisenhower on February 14, 1955. Invoking the shibboleths of the atomic age, the committee affirmed that without military and civil defense, America's vulnerability *invited* surprise attack. The only way forward was to acquire defensive capabilities of every conceivable type with as much effort, money, and ingenuity as the nation could muster. They pressed President Eisenhower to speed up missile development. But he didn't particularly fancy rocket war. Eisenhower admitted he did "not think too much of the ballistic missiles as military weapons." He deferred to the Killian recommendations only because of the "psychological importance" of missiles.[8]

Skeptical about the efficacy of even a robust national civil defense program, on January 12, 1956, the President directed his National Security Council to consider the "chaos and destruction" resulting from a thermonuclear war. He wanted to acquaint himself with the magnitude of ruin occasioned by these weapons and the degree to which military and civil defense could mitigate such a catastrophe. Specifically, he asked them to sketch out the worst possible outcome of a likely scenario of war, the point at which "we will have passed the limits of what human beings can endure." The NSC reported back that even with advance warning, a Soviet attack could still prostrate the United States. While American forces could retaliate against the enemy's heartland, Eisenhower reflected in his diary, "There was little we could do during the month of warning in the way of dispersal of population, of industries, or of perfecting defenses that would cut down losses."[9]

A few months later, he convened a secret committee to evaluate civil defense in light of these trends. Officially called the Security Resources Panel, it became known as the Gaither Commission after its chairman, president of the Ford Foundation and RAND board chairman H. Rowan Gaither. Eisenhower addressed its first meeting in August 1956. He asked them simply, "If you make the assumption that there is going to be a nuclear war, what should I do?" This disposed the committee to enlarge the scope of its study from the merits of civil defense to the current and near-future state of America's ability to deter, fight, and survive a nuclear war.[10]

On December 21, 1956, the Federal Civil Defense Agency's director, Val Peterson, presented a proposal for an elaborate blast and fallout shelter program to the National Security Council. Estimated at $32.4 billion, it would provide state-of-the-art blast protection up to 30 pounds per square inch (psi) for people in presumptive target cities and fallout protection for the rest of the population. Several weeks later, the NSC met to evaluate Peterson's idea. Several questions would first have to be resolved in order to make sense of his bewilderingly great allocation: was the United States *really* vulnerable to surprise attack? What was the effect of such a program on the economy? And more importantly, if a $20 to $40 billion shelter program seemed necessary to protect Americans, would it be better to use the same money to strengthen offensive forces?[11]

Herman Kahn enters the story as an informal consultant to the Gaither Commission. The roots of this relationship go back to fall 1952, when an informal RAND group that included Bernard Brodie, James Digby, Charlie Hitch, Victor Hunt, Arnold Kramish, Andrew Marshall, Alex Mood, and John Williams began meeting at lunchtime to discuss strategy and to wrangle over the problem of limiting damage in atomic war. As a consequence of his close relationship with Marshall and his budding friendship with Wohlstetter, Kahn became a regular participant in these sessions. Then in 1956 RAND began a major study on the composition of strategic bomber forces. As an adjunct to the project, Kahn decided to launch a little study on civil defense. While some people had touched the subject before, it was scorned by senior management and the air force.

Kahn pushed his study over the objections of his superiors: "The president of RAND [Collbohm] had ideological objections to civil defense, as did the Air Force, and his objections were very personal— he was director of civil defense at Douglas [Aircraft during WWII] and had done some very stupid things." By the mid-1950s, civil defense had acquired a politically liberal aura: "In general, the Right was anti-civil defense before our study and the Left was pro–civil defense because civil defense cared about people—it was warm, human, soft. The Right didn't like the idea of being scared, so they opposed it." Kahn wheedled a vice president to approve it with the proviso that the air force didn't pay for it. Ultimately, it was funded by a Ford Foundation grant to RAND for small-scale, non–air force research.[12]

The Gaither Commission sorted its members into working groups on different aspects of thermonuclear war. Each committee invited experts to brief them on their assigned topic. Then they wrote a background paper that was passed to the members of the steering committee. One or two members of the steering committee ultimately drafted the final report to President Eisenhower. Spurgeon Keeny was the chairman of the civil defense working group. He had been tapped for the position since he had directed the air force's intelligence office on the Soviet nuclear weapons program for several years.

In the summer of 1957 Kahn briefed Keeny's team on the major arguments for civil defense. They were appalled by the political consequences of Kahn's technical fix. "There was no longer any question but that in a nuclear war you would lose the whole society, even though you could save lives with fallout shelters. The whole experience was extremely disturbing to me and many of the other participants. Was this really a way to solve the problem? The proposed solution seemed to lead to a garrison state." Keeny authored the group's recommendations on civil defense, and submitted them to steering committee members William Webster and James Perkins, whom he assumed would incorporate their ideas into the final report.[13]

Kahn also briefed Keeny's group on Wohlstetter's famous RAND report, *Protecting U.S. Power to Strike Back in the 1950s and 1960s.* Wohlstetter had studied American vulnerability to Soviet surprise strikes. He had recommended placing SAC bombers in hardened blast shelters, dispersing and hardening hangars and other critical buildings, building more airfields for returning bombers, and augmenting the radar warning network. Drawing heavily on Wohlstetter's work and influenced by his discussions with Kahn, Keeny wrote a background paper on SAC vulnerability and passed it forward to Perkins and Webster. The steering committee also heard directly from Wohlstetter himself. Since his ideas echoed the perspective of the Killian panelists, to whom the acting chair of the Gaither Commission, Robert Sprague, had been a consultant, Wohlstetter's notion of strategic vulnerability was received with great sympathy. Wohlstetter had consulted with Rowan Gaither privately before the committee's formation and had urged him to widen the scope of the study from civil defense to a general examination of strategic vulnerability. But they turned their attention to problems of offensive nuclear war-fighting only after his formal appearance before the commission.[14]

The steering committee directed their attention to strategic vulnerability. Following Wohlstetter's lead, they worried about the exposure of the bomber fleet. They roughed out an analysis which determined that on a typical day, all of the bombers in the Strategic Air Command were concentrated on a handful of bases, and few, if any, were on strip alert. Sprague and Foster flew out to SAC headquarters in Nebraska and confronted General Curtis LeMay with the news that the offensive force was unlikely to deploy within the warning time of an impending attack. An exercise testing SAC readiness had demonstrated, according to a memorandum written by Eisenhower's aide, General Andrew Goodpaster, that "not a single plane could have left the ground within six hours except for a few that were by chance in the air on a test at the time."[15]

Apoplectic that a civilian advisory committee dared to counsel or guide him, LeMay blurted out that if he received confirmed intelligence of forces massing for an imminent attack, he would order a preemptive strike against Soviet air bases. The unprotected bomber fleet was a moot issue. This was a shocking admission. In essence, he announced that he planned to defy the United States' official war plans and follow an autonomous policy of striking on warning.[16]

Two further developments exacerbated the steering committee's perception of the urgency of the threat. On August 26, 1957, the Kremlin announced that it had conducted the first successful flight test of an ICBM over its missile test range. And on October 4 the Soviets launched *Sputnik* into space. Neither event was a surprise to President Eisenhower. Since the summer of 1955 the NSA intelligence had monitored the missile test site at Kapustin Yar from a listening post in Turkey. Moreover, U-2 spy planes had been overflying the USSR since July 1956. By the following spring they detected a second installation in Tyuratam, whose range extended over three thousand miles, putting the continental United States almost within range of Red Army missiles. Eisenhower was satisfied that the Soviets were only months ahead of the United States in missile development. This could hardly put America's deterrent forces at immediate risk.

He called a press conference to assure the nation that the *Sputnik* launch did not imperil America. The Communists had technical problems with missile guidance and re-entry that had yet to be worked out. For the present and the near future, he declared, manned bombers would remain America's deterrent. Besides, Americans would be testing their own missiles very soon.

But in late September, when an American Atlas rocket exploded on its launch pad, Congress fretted that the Russians were pulling ahead in the arms race. To make matters worse, *Sputnik* demonstrated that the Soviets had developed the capability to propel a missile over five thousand miles. *Sputnik* seemed to confirm that the Kremlin was pursuing a crash program of missile R&D. While members of the Gaither steering committee almost certainly had access to radar and non–U-2 spy flight intelligence, and therefore would have known that the Russians had not taken a commanding lead in missile technology, they were ideologically committed to pushing the President to authorize an aggressive schedule of missile R&D. As a consequence, the authors of the final report of the Gaither Commission magnified the risk of America's vulnerability to surprise attack. Given the imminent danger of the next two years, they stressed, "If we fail to act at once, the risk, in our opinion, will be unacceptable."[17]

On November 7, 1957, the steering committee presented its findings to the President. It concluded with the opinion that "by 1959, the USSR may be able to launch an attack with ICBMs carrying megaton warheads, against which SAC will be almost completely vulnerable under present programs." They also endorsed civil defense in terms calculated to please the joint chiefs and the President. "The main protection of our civil population against a Soviet nuclear attack has been and will continue to be the deterrent power of our armed forces." But the deterrent would never be adequate unless it was bolstered with shelters. "As long as the U.S. population is wide open to Soviet attack, both the Russians and our allies may believe that we shall feel increasing reluctance to employ SAC [except] . . . when the United States is directly attacked."[18]

The panel advised that active and passive defense be inaugurated "with all possible speed." ("Active defense" meant defensive weapons systems; "passive defense" meant structural measures such as armoring and hardening buildings; "civil defense" referred exclusively to the protection of noncombatants.) While the committee did not endorse a major blast shelter program, it proposed $25 billion for fallout shelters, since no other measure was "likely to save more lives for the same money in the event of a nuclear attack." Whether or not Kahn directly influenced Nitze or Sprague, the authors of the final report promoted civil defense as an indispensable safeguard for the deterrent and retaliatory mission of the armed forces. Fallout shelters fortified deterrence "by discouraging the enemy from attempting an attack on what might otherwise seem to him a temptingly unprepared target; second, by reinforcing his belief in our readiness to use, if necessary, our strategic retaliatory power."[19]

In order to pressure Eisenhower to accelerate missile R&D, after having briefed the President on the report but before he could formulate his response properly, someone on the Gaither steering committee leaked excerpts of their recommendations to a reporter at *The Washington Post*. Eisenhower was furious. Keeny recalled, "He felt that it was an unprincipled act of insubordination of the panel, which was supposed to be working for him." The President thereupon directed the CIA to bar RAND and other civilian contractors from access to raw intelligence or direct contact with intelligence professionals. While RAND analysts continued to receive the NIEs, they were not exposed to the feverish debates raging within the intelligence community. The result was that, with the exception of Andrew Marshall and Joseph Loftus, they simply echoed the air force's extravagant assessments. Their conception of the Soviet threat were wholly unchecked by countervailing opinions.[20]

While incensed by the leak, the President was neither alarmed by nor sold on the committee's proposals. "I did not agree with all of the panel's hypothetical figures," he wrote in his memoir. "Moreover, the panel had failed to take into account certain vital information and other considerations." For one thing, in spite of congressional charges that he was complacent in the face of Soviet technological advances, he had decided not to expose the U-2 program, which would have proven that their worst fears were unfounded. Second, he considered the suggested expenditures to be excessive. They would have distorted the economy toward an overemphasis on arms production. Moreover, Eisenhower loathed civil defense. A national fallout shelter program, complete with mandatory civilian training, would hamstring a free and independent people: "Given the atmosphere of the time, 'We must neither panic nor become complacent,' I told my associates . . . Our security depended on a set of associated and difficult objectives: to maintain a defense . . . [but] we could not turn the nation into a garrison state."[21]

As a matter of principled reflection, rather than contemplation of the various scientific construals of nuclear weapons effects data, Eisenhower did not believe that American society could survive and reconstruct from a nuclear war. As he thanked members of the Gaither Commission for their efforts, Eisenhower's parting comments were dismaying and poignant. Hearkening back to his original request for the study, he said he now realized he had asked the wrong question. "You can't have this kind of war. There just aren't enough bulldozers to scrape the bodies off the streets."[22]

The United States was not falling behind the Soviets in the arms race; it was merely losing its lead. Eisenhower fully trusted the strategic value of the manned bomber force. He declared to his NSC, "Until an enemy [has] enough operational capability to destroy most of our bases simultaneously and thus prevent retaliation by us, our deterrence remains effective." While rejecting the alarums of the Gaither Report, he agreed to extend the nation's tactical warning systems. In January 1958 the Ballistic Missile Early Warning System (BMEWS) was authorized as a supplement to the Distant Early Warning Line, which had entered service the previous August.[23]

Eisenhower's cool response to the Gaither recommendations fomented a split in the strategic community. Two groups emerged: the old stalwarts, who continued to push for advances in offensive and defensive strategic systems in the never-ending arms race, and a new sort of strategist, men who abandoned their campaign for superhardened, super-accurate weapons systems in favor of arms control. For example, Jerome Wiesner, who would become President Kennedy's science adviser, had advocated defensive systems installed in the periphery of SAC bases. But now he was struck with "the inherent futility" of defensive measures against atomic attack. "It became clear that if you were certain that war was going to occur you'd take a lot of costly steps. But even then you couldn't do much."[24]

For Keeny, the six months he worked on the Gaither study was a defining moment. Weeks of assembling materials for committee members had unsettled his notion that technical solutions could be found to mitigate a nuclear catastrophe. It had become clear that a political, not a technocratic solution, was the only way to manage the cold war: "[We] had a real concern as to whether the technological response to a worst-case analysis of the threat was the right way to go as opposed to a diplomatic approach including constraints on the threat by arms control."[25]

Similarly, Herbert York, director of the Lawrence Livermore Laboratory, who had been instrumental in developing the ICBM, experienced a change of heart: "There were three events that contributed to changing my views. The first was the Gaither Panel, but that was the least important . . . As soon as we got seriously working on arms control, I saw the light . . . Arms control and technology were alternative ways of approaching national security." The second factor that critically shaped his views was participation in the President's Science Advisory Committee (PSAC), formed in December 1957. And finally, York had been appointed director of defense research and engineering, a position he held during the last three year's of Eisenhower's administration. "It was my experience as DDRE that finally taught me the futility of the technical approach." By 1963 York declared that the cold war could not be managed by the arms race. He stated publicly that by relying on "technical solutions" to a political problem, "the result will be a steady and inexorable worsening of this situation . . . I believe that there is absolutely no solution to be found within the areas of science and technology."[26]

In 1958 Eisenhower initiated the Geneva Conference of Experts on Nuclear Test Detection, the Conference on the Discontinuance of Nuclear Weapons Tests, and the Surprise Attack Conference. Keeny observed, "There was a close continuity of events between the Gaither study, Eisenhower's reaction to it, his decision to go ahead with the Test Ban Treaty and the Surprise Attack conference. His reaction to it was . . . you're gonna have to explore other ways to deal with this, because this [active, passive, and civil defense] is leading to a disaster. Eisenhower didn't like the picture that the Gaither study painted of the future any more than Wiesner, or Herb York, or I liked it."[27]

The RAND Civil Defense Study

During his last four years at RAND, Kahn immersed himself in civil defense research. In August 1957 he presented his first briefing on the topic. Recoiling from the belief that nuclear war meant the collapse of world civilization, he maintained that "the limits on the magnitude of the catastrophe seem to be closely dependent on what kinds of preparations have been made, and how the war is started and fought." Accordingly, he framed his research as a response to the query, "How would the country look five or ten years after the war as a function of various preparations?" Formulating the question this way enacted his characteristic preference for regarding a future problem as a nested structure that embedded one conditional within another.[28]

The report, *Some Specific Suggestions for Achieving Early Non-Military Defense Capabilities and Initiating Long-Range Programs,* was the result of several months of work by a sixteen-man team directed by Kahn. In it, he proposed a $500 million budget to establish a national civil defense program and underwrite research and development in "all aspects of the state of the art of non-military defense." He advised the government to gather critical stockpiles; prepare existing mine space for storage, industrial production, and civilian use, including dormitories; enlist the energies of professional societies and universities in scientific research; and, mirroring the long-range plans of the armed services, institute comprehensive federal planning for postwar survival and recovery.[29]

He was determined to persuade anyone who would listen that the chief problem of civil defense was properly understanding it. Kahn's 1958 report opened with his basic thesis: given the tempo and magnitude of nuclear war, it would be impossible to improvise protection in the brief interval of a mounting crisis, or worse, in the wake of a nuclear strike. Therefore, government attention should be redirected from a World War II–era policy of recruiting industry and civilians after a war has begun to ensuring the nation's survival by peacetime preparations for war. In the nuclear age, the nation's survival could be ensured only by mobilizing citizens for war during peacetime. He described his "prewar mobilization" idea as a "starter set" for national reconstruction. By warehousing surplus goods, the economy and society could convert at a moment's notice to wartime readiness. Kahn's scheme protected civilians and property; accumulated critical stockpiles; offered detailed plans for crash mobilization during prolonged crises; and suggested measures to aid postwar recuperation and reconstruction.[30]

He sketched out four progressively more lavish budgets, from a "Cheap Starter Set" at $200 million, to a "Luxurious" program of $20 billion. He admitted that the parameters of the four plans were "orienting and educational, and not . . . estimates or recommendations." More precise numbers would require "more work and resources than we gave to the problem." Kahn's luxurious starter set not only offered "very high standards of habitability and protection," but was "over-designed as a hedge against the enemy's threat becoming worse or our reconstruction plans going awry." His "austere" plan was a nationwide network of blast and fallout shelters built to "minimal standards." His "minimum" plan provided fallout shelters to everybody. Finally, his "cheap" program provided fallout protection to citizens in target cities and "wherever [else] it is . . . desirable."[31]

Kahn scaled back his ambitions for civil defense in order to demonstrate what could be done with a cheap program. Whereas most of his lavish budget was spent hoarding and hardening assets, a cheap civil defense program would be a "legacy for any later and larger programs." Such a program "might save from 10 to 50 million lives, limit . . . damage to property, and markedly facilitate our ability to recuperate." By offering imperfect fallout protection for a limited range of strike scenarios, Kahn showed atypical political sensitivity. "Realism in this case," he allowed, "means not trying to do too much and, as a result, failing totally, but rather trying to get those capabilities that might be useful in special circumstances even if the range of circumstances is not complete."[32]

He pressed the government to draw up detailed plans for post-attack damage control (such as shutting down utilities), emergency repair, and communications and electricity patch-up. It should distribute manuals for urban and rural decontamination. In order "to provide a reasonably dispersed population target," urban evacuation plans should be reinstated. Existing surpluses should be inventoried. Strategic raw materials, war-reserve tools, Commodity Credit Corporation stocks, and obsolete materiel should be consolidated in a centralized registry. Suitable fallout shelters should be identified through a survey of underground space throughout the nation, which would certify that subways, sewers, tunnels, and sub-basements of urban buildings, along with mines and caverns in the countryside, were fallout-proof. Improvements to these structures could be made with "sandbags [or] shutters . . . either before or after the attack, wherever it seemed desirable or cheap." The most expensive item in Kahn's plan was the universal distribution of radiation dosimeters. "Such meters," he observed, "would be invaluable as a recuperation aid . . . Without [them] . . . it is likely that restoration would be very difficult, if not paralyzed."[33]

He airily suggested that the government sell property insurance against nuclear war. It was a cunning idea. The promise of guaranteed compensation would give contractors an incentive to build blast and fallout protection into new or remodeled buildings. And insurance premiums could finance the recuperation stockpiles.[34]

If so many remedies could be implemented, why did civil defense fail to arouse enthusiasm among the nation's citizens, Congress, or the administration? Kahn suspected that "until the feasibility of recovery is settled, it will be difficult to arouse real interest in attempts to alleviate the consequences of war." Not only had various shelter configurations not been thoroughly studied, but most of the other problems associated with "preserving a civilization and a standard of living have not been examined even superficially." There was simply not enough information about the real conditions of the post-attack environment. Kahn therefore proposed $200 million for a major program of research, development, systems analysis, planning, and technical design. Asking point-blank, "Is $200 million an unreasonably large sum?" he compared the R&D budgets of aircraft and missile development with civil defense. If the Pentagon annually spent $5 billion on military hardware, surely civil defense was "at least as complicated as an interceptor aircraft."[35]

Since research was cheap, every suggestive possibility should be pursued. Otherwise, "there may be disastrous inadequacies, or even complete lacunae, in the program." He hastened to explain that his sums were "relatively arbitrary": "The numbers are intended to communicate quantitatively our intuitive and preliminary thinking." In fact, "in several categories [such as] anti-contamination . . . we have no real feeling as to what reasonable expenditures are."[36]

The ensuing discussion makes plain Kahn's sense of the speculative possibilities of reworking the social, political, and economic totality in light of civil defense needs. This ranged from basic explorations that would propel further "imaginative work" once research had begun, to suggesting programs for industrial and governmental activities in underground shelters in mines, caverns, quarries, and deep-rock structures. This last was one of his most notorious ideas, appearing in *Dr. Strangelove* as "the mineshaft gap."[37]

Kahn's study paid particular attention to the protective qualities of deep underground structures. Mines could have multiple uses: as emergency personnel housing in the event of evacuation and dispersal of the population and industry; as warehouses; as industrial sites for commercial and office activities; as postwar civilian housing. They could serve all of these functions in sequence: "For example, we might outfit a mine as an emergency shelter for evacuees, use it later for stockpiling, and finally convert it for use as a permanent underground installation of some sort."[38]

He therefore proposed an exhaustive research agenda for mines: (1) surveying existing underground space, "including . . . adapting the mine [into] shelters, . . . location of transportation, utilities, and labor force"; (2) surveying existing quarries as cheap resources for converting already excavated sites into future underground shelters and tunnels; (3) encouraging the private sector to construct underground plants; "for example, we might wish to encourage very deep mining under urban areas"; (4) promoting research "to develop new uses for crushed rock" and other mining products in order to create new incentives for the expansion of mining ("If these studies were even mildly successful, they might make very important changes in our capability. We concede, of course, that some of the studies might be very speculative."); (5) surveying the geological composition of the United States in order to identify new sites for underground facilities; (6) underwriting the design of various underground industrial, military, and civilian facilities; (7) creating a federal clearinghouse on protective structures and making its technical assistance widely available to industry and local government.[39]

Kahn had equally ambitious plans for investigating reconstruction, since "almost no work has been done on the problem of restoring a prewar society." As a demonstration of the feasibility of construction projects that had both peacetime and postwar uses, he suggested that ten to twenty prototype factories for underground plant operations be erected with the cooperation of private firms. Military and civilian installations such as "communication facilities, specialized commercial and office space, and possibly civil defense headquarters should be tested for relocation underground." Studies of shelter ventilation, humidity, waste disposal, sanitary engineering, and overcrowding should also be initiated.[40]

Kahn consistently minimized the weapons effects, suggesting that "abruptly abandoned plants that did not suffer blast damage but were subjected to fallout" could soon be up and running as production sites in the postwar period. He therefore advised researchers to estimate what degree of blast damage plants could suffer and still operate. Economists and engineers should "design an emergency 'temporary' reconstruction program that would restore production quickly, use salvaged materials and equipment, and substitute less-scarce for more-scarce materials." Or, varying the notion, economists should consider how industry could assemble stockpiles of new and obsolete construction elements for use in new plant construction. In another twist on pre-attack mobilization, Kahn suggested that industrial plants be redesigned so that they could be located underground or built within blast-proof shelters. "This would mean economizing on space . . . minimizing ventilation and air-conditioning problems, minimizing noise problems, and exploiting special features of mines."[41]

With such a far-ranging program, Kahn anticipated an economic boom touched off by civil defense research. Just imagine the products, services, and technologies that civil defense needed and which the market could provide: excavating and tunneling equipment; mass construction; shock absorbers; ventilation; damage control; digging-out equipment for emergency use in deep shelters; shelter utilities; non-food shelter supplies; communication techniques; storage and preservation; postwar building technology; gasoline substitutes; warning systems; rapid movement of masses of people; blast doors; stockpile connectors; shielded vehicles for moving people in contaminated areas; methods and materials for modifying conventional vehicles.[42]

Decontamination would be another growth industry. Kahn proposed a $30 million budget for research into mitigating fallout during and after the war. In addition to basic studies in the phenomenology of fallout, procedures for decontaminating food, water, and soil should also be thoroughly investigated. Moreover, the possibilities of concocting "synthetic food" from uncontaminated stockpiled material (such as hydroponic and algae cultivation) and "therapeutic agents that could be added to food to prevent retention of fission products in the body" (presumably in the form of calcium and potassium pills) should be explored. Scientists and engineers should delve into innovative technologies such as nuclear waste disposal systems as well as "vacuum cleaners, sweepers, bulldozers, scrapers, and wash-down systems."[43]

RAND studies in the 1950s did not address the ecological problems of a post-attack environment. In *OTW*, Kahn remarked, "The war may have important and totally unsuspected ecological consequences." He acknowledged that radiation would disturb the balance between bird and insect populations as well as radically disrupt weather patterns. While confident that the amount of radiation released by a comparatively "small attack" would not injure the biosphere, he admitted that a large attack might possibly "sear a very large area of the country by thermal radiation; and either attack could cause cataclysmic tidal waves, floods, and fires." For all that, Kahn allowed that his research team "did not look at the interaction among the [weapons] effects we did study." It was only in August 1961 that someone at RAND produced a paper on the ecology of nuclear war. An analyst trained as a physician observed that ecology "has been strangely neglected . . . and detailed research is conspicuously absent . . . not part of the intellectual equipment of people ordinarily concerned with civil defense and postwar recovery."[44]

Kahn's study paid special attention to the production, processing, storage, and distribution of food. He guessed that surplus food inventories should be sufficient to meet the needs of the surviving population for the first postwar year. Expressing a systems orientation toward the economic totality, he suggested that national food stocks be inventoried and updated so that postwar distribution patterns could be studied. The main task would be providing rations to the population until sufficiently clean crops could be cultivated and animals could graze on uncontaminated pastures, or pure food could be imported. Stockpiles of unprocessed foodstuffs could also be warehoused in underground facilities for long-term postwar consumption. Kahn urged provisioning the nation's shelters with a three-month supply of food as well as stockpiling several years' worth of vitamins.[45]

He proposed $10 million for studying communicable diseases that might afflict shelter residents, such as respiratory viruses and "antibiotic prophylactic studies." Likewise, he recommended research for determining the highest human tolerance to short-term radiation exposure in order to plan the activities of emergency workers. This included "a search for and the screening of promising drugs that might prevent the acute radiation syndrome." Psychiatric and social psychological casualties should not be neglected, especially morale, family separation, panic, and the stress of shelter life. "Various measures (work therapy, sedation, recreation, segregated activity or discipline areas, etc.) ought to be studied and prepared in order to maintain shelter discipline, to lessen the mental strain, and to minimize the incidence of psychological aftereffects."[46]

Finally, the government should encourage parallel efforts by the private sector. In the universities, protective requirements should be routinely incorporated into the professional curricula of engineering and architecture students. Rather than enjoining volunteer effort from professional societies (such as the National Association of Manufacturers, American Society for Heating and Ventilating, American Society for Testing of Materials, American Society of Civil Engineers, American Concrete Institute, American Institute of Architects, American Association of Railroads, American Medical Association), civil defense research among these private groups should be federally coordinated.

Kahn's study closed with a comparison between the apocalyptic conception of nuclear war and his group's findings. While most Americans believed that a nuclear war would be "so annihilating that nothing useful could be done to mitigate its consequences . . . we have demonstrated that, subject to uncertainties, the above view is wrong, for at least the next five or ten years." While sensitive to the myriad unknowns and unknown unknowns crowning the problem, he entertained a rosy prognosis for a postwar world for the rest of his life.[47]

In March 1959 Kahn delivered the lecture, "Why Go Deep Underground?" at the Second Protective Construction Symposium at RAND. In this paper, which he wrote while delivering the *OTW* briefings around the country, we can observe just how faithful, how provisional and anxiously credulous his investments in civil defense were. He observed that the design challenges of underground construction involved "new or esoteric principles." The architect and engineer would "find his reserves of experience, knowledge, ingenuity, and technique strained to the limits . . . The experience of the most readily available designers may not be even remotely appropriate."

Accordingly, in order to enter into the speculative domain of the post-attack world, he advised the engineer to overdesign the structure, heeding all the known weapons effects phenomena, "and then hope for the best."[48]

Kahn closed his remarks with the disconcertingly hapless wager of strategic futurology: "All we can do is just face the fact that to some extent the working of our installations depends upon faith."[49]

Chapter 8

ON THERMONUCLEAR WAR

To stay cheerful when involved in a gloomy and exceed-
ingly responsible business is no inconsiderable art: yet
what could be more necessary than cheerfulness? Nothing
succeeds in which high spirits play no part.

FRIEDRICH NIETZSCHE, 1889

"Is it really true that only an insane man would initiate a thermonuclear war?" Herman Kahn would ask. "Or are there circumstances in
which the leaders of a country might rationally decide that thermonuclear war is the least undesirable of the available alternatives?" As
Kahn gnawed at these questions, his answers skittered over an exhaustive array of topics. Fond as he was of tidy schematics, ticking off
each item in a cascade of charts, his briefings were mazes, his digres-
sions abstruse and associational.[1]

Brooding about war awakens the story-telling imp. *On Thermonuclear War* hums with motifs of world cataclysm, resurrection, and
miracle. While sometimes resembling a sales pitch or a comic *spiel,*
Kahn's expository style was an experiment in historical narrative. His
zigzags, pockets of scenario detail, and lists resembled the herky-
jerky pulse of an epic poem. This was the case not just because the
book dealt in the near-cosmic rebirth of a nation. Keep in mind the
exhilaration of being thrust into the appalling demands of the here-
and-now. Among other things, *On Thermonuclear War* was a live performance. When addressing awful matters and exhibiting the absolute freedom and absolute terror of nuclear war to all the world,
Kahn radiated the nervy bravura of an actor. It is here, in the en-

counter between an audience and a man willing to storm the citadel of the unthinkable that the energies of *OTW* and the epic style converge.

Kahn's dynamism advanced from point to point on the stepping stones of epic strings of variables. With its pageantry of World Wars I through VIII, *On Thermonuclear War* had a Scheherazade-like architecture of nested stories that promised to continue indefinitely, there being no end either to the scenarios or, seemingly, to the discussion itself. Thinking about the unthinkable seems to be related to this quality of endlessness. Kahn once mentioned to McWhirter that the *Tales of the 1001 Nights* was one of his favorite stories. The reporter reflected, "Herman Kahn may feel that, by inventing one Scenario after another, he is holding back the changes that would seal our doom."[2]

At RAND, Kahn was not responsible for designing actual plans for the air force. He was paid to ruminate about hypothetical crises. But if we look at historical contingency planning for a moment, we will recognize in it the temptation to sketch out every variation in the course of drafting a decision tree of a political–military crisis. We can contextualize Kahn's dynamism by listening to men reminiscing about their work as they made detailed plans for escalating moves ultimately resulting in nuclear strikes during the Berlin Crisis of 1961.

In 1991 several Kennedy administration officials described their planning activities during that event. Given that the Berlin plans originated as a critique of massive retaliation, they closely resemble Kahn's effort. The story began in 1959, when General DeWitt Armstrong was assigned to the International and Policy Planning Division in the Army General Staff. He was the action officer responsible for the army's role in the Joint Task Force on NATO and Berlin. Essentially this meant that as the support officer to the national security planner, he was the army's contingency planner for Berlin. Armstrong was struck by the "strong general-nuclear-war coloration" of existing Berlin strategy. In the event of a crisis, he recalled, in a few small steps "the United States faced the question of whether to undertake a massive nuclear action or not." His colleagues assumed that deterrence would inhibit the Soviets "from anything but a very brief blockage of the *autobahn*, if even that. But just suppose it did not?"[3]

If the Soviets challenged the Allies in Berlin, there was no plan at the ready. Because intermediate steps between doing nothing and doing too much had not been formulated, it seemed to Armstrong that there was a genuine risk "the U.S. might collapse early" in a contest of wills in Berlin.[4]

Armstrong tried to coax his air force colleagues to accept the necessity of introducing flexibility into strategic doctrine. "There were a lot of true believers in the Air Force, guys that were really convinced, first, that the deterrent will deter, and, second, that nothing must be done to interfere with the capability of this massive nuclear retaliation threat to work its magic on the aggressor." In frustration, around the time of the 1960 elections he drew up a safer alternative. It was a complex scenario that explored possible developments that could occur should the Soviets block the *autobahn* at Helmstedt. In sharp contrast to the hypnotic vagueness of existing plans, Armstrong dramatized the various trains of events that might unfold. Like a good war game designer, he specified the numbers and kinds of vehicles, weapons, and command and control capabilities of the major players. At every stage of the scenario, he presented a sheaf of options, each one of which was filled out with details of their political, diplomatic, and strategic ramifications.[5]

The thrust of his analysis was to demonstrate the effectiveness of a graduated approach to military conflict. Rather than imposing a catastrophic ultimatum on the enemy, Armstrong's scheme retarded the process of crisis decision-making by allowing intervals for diplomacy and information-gathering. "Each of these new increments by the allies would force upon the Soviet Union a new high-level decision. They had to decide, well, are we going to raise that bet, or are we going to buy out? And as this program of mounting pressures ran up the ramp, each time they could see, Jesus, these guys are more serious than we thought. And then would come the next one." With each phase of escalation, the possibility for nuclear war drew nearer but would not immediately overwhelm the antagonists.[6]

Several months after he had completed this study, in May 1961

Armstrong was transferred to the Office of International Security Affairs (ISA) to work as the action officer on Berlin planning for Assistant Secretary of Defense Paul Nitze. Armstrong translated his paper into a colossal graph known as "the horse blanket." This was army jargon for plans inscribed on enormous sheets of paper. Admiral John Lee of Nitze's staff condensed Armstrong's diagram into "the pony blanket."[7]

President Kennedy warned the nation about the dangerous crises escalating in Berlin in a televised address on July 25, 1961. Immediately after his speech, NATO foreign ministers gathered in Paris. In an address to the NATO Council on August 8, Secretary of State Dean Rusk articulated the administration's Berlin plan. Armstrong had authored Rusk's text. In due time the Berlin contingency plan was delegated to an interagency military group supporting NATO. This last committee digested the pony blanket into the executive "poodle blanket." On October 10 President Kennedy met with his Cabinet, generals, and national security adviser to discuss the evolution of war plans for Berlin. Before the meeting, Nitze had circulated a memorandum, "Preferred Sequence of Military Actions in a Berlin Conflict," to the principals. It laid out four unfolding scenarios. Its outline form and options escalating to "general nuclear war" suggest that Nitze's memo was based on the poodle-blanket document.[8]

The lineage of Berlin contingency plans conveys the formidable reach of the original horse blanket design. Dreaming up future history seems to induce this kind of giddy expansiveness. "I was hypothesizing in this thing, not predicting," explained Armstrong. "You can do this endlessly without exhausting the possibilities." Likewise, Lee remarked, "The permutations quickly approached infinity. Fortunately things got repetitive; there's a limit to what you can do." If the extravagant possibilities for Berlin dismayed actual war planners, we can appreciate how much more unbounded was the vortex of possibilities which engrossed Kahn's imagination.[9]

In 1959 Kahn took a leave of absence from RAND and spent a semester at the Center of International Studies at Princeton University. He also crisscrossed the country delivering a three-day-long briefing,

"Three Lectures on Thermonuclear War in the 1960–1970 Period" to more than five thousand policy-makers and advisers. By July 1959 transcripts were well in hand. His secretary circulated copies to seventeen colleagues at RAND for editorial assistance. While it was a small thing to recruit friends to help refine his text, persuading the air force and RAND management to release the book for publication was harder. The air force cleared *OTW* just one month before RAND instituted a publication review process intended to smother works defying cherished air force positions. The new policy stipulated that manuscripts had to be cleared by every relevant air force office and other federal agency, with an eye to suppressing "anything that could embarrass anybody in the government or services."[10]

In April 1959 Kahn requested guidance for clearing the manuscript of *OTW*. There should be "little to arrange," he assured his boss. "I am doing this as an employee of Princeton University and private citizen and am relying on unclassified sources completely." In the course of directing him to send the final manuscript to the Office of Security Review, the vice president of RAND, L. J. Henderson, Jr., instructed Kahn to attach a cover letter attesting that the book was a private affair "and not a RAND book in any sense." Should any conflict with the air force arise, it would be "a personal problem for Herman Kahn and . . . entirely your own responsibility." While management did not approve of *OTW*, it couldn't object to the book's release under the imprimatur of Princeton University Press. While he didn't agree with many of Kahn's ideas, Henderson sighed, he did think the book might "serve to promote discussion" about neglected problems. Kahn handed the galleys to Max Singer for one last revision. The book was published on December 8, 1960.[11]

Kahn was among the pack of analysts who railed against President Eisenhower's policy of threatening massive retaliation against Soviet aggression. Like Truman, Eisenhower wanted to buy a ferocious national defense without straining the economy. His secretary of state, John Foster Dulles, announced the doctrine in a nationally broadcast speech to the Council on Foreign Relations on January 12, 1954. Dulles characterized the cold war in terms of "the long haul," a notion that had been proposed the previous April at a NATO Council meeting. As America turned away from the crash mobilization in Asia and Europe during the first two years of the Korean War, national security would henceforth have to offer "a maximum deterrent at a bearable cost."[12]

Rather than answering local aggression with the might of any one European state (all of which were still recovering from World War II), the collective security afforded by NATO would stiffen regional defense with "the further deterrent of [the] massive retaliatory power" of the United States. Deterrence would be ubiquitous and indeterminate. "The way to deter aggression," in Dulles's view, was "to be willing and able to respond . . . at places and with means of [our] own choosing." Those means principally involved "a great capacity to retaliate instantly."[13]

By the mid 1950s, strategists in and out of RAND began to pronounce the threat essentially unbelievable. Given the collaborative culture of research at RAND, Kahn's contribution to the debate is difficult to assess. His ideas about flexible war plans, limiting nuclear war, strategic vulnerability, credible first strike capability, and intrawar bargaining synthesized arguments that had evolved at RAND over a number of years.

In the brawl trailing the publication of *OTW,* the question whether Kahn was a typical RAND specimen was occasionally lobbed into play. For example, the RAND mathematician Richard Bellman pelted *Commentary, Fortune, Harper's, The Nation, The New Republic, Newsweek, The New York Times, The Progressive, The Reporter, Saturday Review, Time, The Washington Post,* and the director of Princeton University Press with letters spurning Kahn. *OTW* did *not* express the consensus on nuclear war-fighting: "I can report that a number of senior members [at RAND] . . . who have examined these questions . . . do *not* share Kahn's views, and I myself do not have these troglodytic, apocalyptic visions of Kahn."[14]

In one sense, he was right. Senior management and the air force chafed at Kahn's identification with RAND. Their mutual discomfort resulted in his departure the following year. But neither Bellman nor senior management were among the coterie of men who spent their days mulling over the details of hypothetical nuclear war. "RAND is not a monolithic organization," Kahn remarked in 1955. "One of the nice things about this place is that people can think in different ways and nobody falls on them like a ton of bricks. When I say we, I'm talking about me and my friends." His circle included the most prominent strategists of the period: Bernard Brodie, Albert Wohlstetter, and Thomas Schelling, among others. Virtually every substantive argument Kahn made about deterrence could be found in pages written by these men. *OTW* was not a grotesque sideshow.[15]

The Right Way to Think about Nuclear Deterrence

Having cast *On Thermonuclear War* as a near-encyclopedia of proliferating scenarios, branching forms, and kaleidoscopic intuitions, how shall we gather momentum to make our long leap into its pages? The book is prolix, repetitive, gargantuan. In what follows, I will not attempt to survey all of Kahn's arguments. Instead I'll restrict my discussion to his critique of deterrence, projections for postwar survival and reconstruction, and his methodological comments. It's not possible to follow him concisely; yet there *is* a red thread braided into its many topics.

Kahn was determined to prove to his audience that most ideas about nuclear war were maudlin, sleepy, badly formulated, and factually wrong. To that end, nearly every page addressed the questions: What's the best approach to the possibility of nuclear war in our present and future? How shall we feel about this? If it were possible to survive such a war, what can we do now to protect ourselves and ensure recovery? The single most important idea coursing through *OTW* was the thesis that the magnitude of death and ruin in a nuclear war depended on "the preparations made before war, the way the war started, and the course of military events." Of the three, prewar preparation was the dominant factor that would shape the post-attack world. Holding this assertion in mind helps us cut a path through the labyrinth.[16]

Kahn parsed America's threat against its enemy into three classes of deterrence, each of which required different weapons systems. Type I deterred the Soviets from a direct assault against U.S. territory. It was an "automatic and unthinking" policy of immediate massive retaliation. Type II checked Soviet aggression against NATO countries and other U.S. allies. Type III inhibited the enemy from provocative actions through a graduated escalation of diplomatic and military moves. In a nutshell, for Kahn, unless the United States drew up plans to fight a "3–30 day war," fortified its air defense, and shielded society and the economy by throwing up a massive civil defense infrastructure, then the threat of nuclear war—the very underpinning of American diplomatic and military activity—was an empty show.[17]

Deterrence worked on "the enemy's mind rather than . . . his body." The puzzle was to work out how far one needed go to impress the enemy that bad actions would be punished with the hell bomb. What does the United States have to do to be persuasive? To answer that, you had to flip the question and ask, What does *not* being persuasive look like? And how can we fix it?[18]

This was a methodological issue. How do you evaluate deterrence? Simply promising retaliation was not an adequate threat. "Even a frown" might startle "a complacent and cautious enemy." Likening a deterrence system to a massive building, Kahn stipulated that you shouldn't ask how it will fare on a balmy day but how well it survives floods, hurricanes, tornados, earthquakes, and blizzards. It was an engineer's question. Worst-case scenarios tested the resiliency of deterrence. "We may not be able to predict the loads [the deterrent system] will have to carry, but we can be certain that there will be loads of unexpected or implausible severity." In other words, Kahn posed the question: what would the deterrent system have to look like so that even when the stability of the USSR and its satellite states was challenged, the Kremlin would *still* refrain from attacking the United States with nuclear weapons?[19]

He illustrated the idea by reconstructing the Kremlin's temptation to strike American targets preemptively, had the United States intervened in the Hungarian revolt of 1956. If we suppose that the Russians faced American ground forces in Hungary and Poland, they had three options. They could do nothing and risk losing their satellites. Not likely. As a second option, they could retaliate. If the Americans fought conventionally, they would wonder why we hadn't used the H-bomb. Were we keeping the theater free of radiation so that we could burst across the Russian frontier? The Kremlin would be tempted to drop atomic bombs on American positions in Hungary to eliminate that possibility. On the other hand, if the United States *had* exploded a tactical atomic bomb in Europe, the Kremlin would think this limited action necessitated reprisals. In either case, retaliation would inevitably escalate into all-out war.

As a third and plausible option, rather than do nothing or wait for the next bad thing to happen, the Kremlin could blast American targets preemptively, which would give it strategic advantage over an enemy whom it assumed would eventually obliterate Moscow. Knowing that the Soviet Union faced these three options, the United States chose not to intervene in 1956. The Hungarian crisis suggested one of many scenarios in which the Red Army could traipse around the world without fear of Western intervention. America's threat to blow up the USSR as punishment against local bad acts was simply not credible. Kahn packed *OTW* with scenarios demonstrating this idea.[20]

To dramatize the flimsiness of a threat to move—in one step—from doing nothing to using the most powerful weapon in the American arsenal, Kahn unveiled the Doomsday Machine. "Assume that for, say, $10 billion we could build a device whose only function is to destroy all human life." It would be connected to a cat's cradle of sensors planted around the nation and a computer. "If, say, five nuclear bombs exploded over the United States, the device would be triggered and the earth destroyed." Should Khrushchev attack, the USSR "would be automatically and efficiently annihilated."[21]

To be awe-inspiring, a deterrent system had to be "frightening, inexorable, persuasive, cheap, non-accident prone, [and] controllable." On these grounds, it looked as though the Doomsday Machine outstripped every other system. "Now, on first sight,[the Doomsday Machine] is better than any other system we've talked about." But, Kahn confided coyly, he was astonished by the disgust it excited. "Why? [Because] it's not controllable. It kills too many people too flippantly. It kills them frivolously and it kills too many." Nobody wanted an automatic world-annihilating machine to be the guarantor of world peace, because a system malfunction "would cause the death of one or two billion people."[22]

The Doomsday Machine threw light on the problem of defining a tolerable threat in peacetime. Kahn insisted that Americans must consider how many of the world's people they could acceptably kill in a war protecting themselves and NATO citizens. "How many is acceptable? It's an important question. You have to ask that." It also underscored the notion that if one promised to do something awful in response to bad acts, it had better be persuasive. The United States had done nothing to ensure the survival of its citizens. Without readying the nation for fighting, terminating, surviving, and reconstructing from a nuclear war, who could possibly believe that an American President would order the Strategic Air Command to bomb Moscow? To elaborate the point, Kahn unspooled a continuum of deterrence ideas that ranged from the simple custody of the bomb all the way to fielding an invulnerable first strike force. He moved incrementally closer to acquiring a lavishly equipped capability for waging nuclear war *in peacetime* by pointing out the lack of credibility for each posture that was less than a fully ready warfighting kit.[23]

From the bare possession of nuclear weapons, the next point in his deterrence continuum inched closer to acknowledging a rationale for nuclear war-fighting. Here he probed the reliability of the threat. How good was deterrence if the strategic forces could be obliterated by a sudden strike? Admitting the vulnerability of the bomber fleet parked on the SAC tarmac or in unshielded hangars meant that for deterrence to be effective the United States needed enough strategic power "to cover *all* contingencies." In other words, to ensure against surprise attacks on vulnerable capabilities, you needed nuclear redundancy. Practically speaking, this meant enlarging the offensive forces of all three services to include submarine-launched ballistic missiles, bombers, and ground-based missiles.[24]

The next step was defending the deterrent. The strategy of *counterforce* typically targeted the enemy's installations and forces on the ground. Kahn amplified the idea to include anything that might "counter the use or effectiveness of the enemy's forces." Critics objected that counterforce was destabilizing. Wouldn't an offensive force be scary enough to inhibit an enemy from attacking? Wouldn't the refusal to add defensive measures assure the world that the United States had tasked its forces for a retaliatory mission only? Kahn rejoined that without shielding its strategic forces and population from attack, deterrence was little more than "a facade to impress the enemy." The problem lay in its lack of realism. Operational plans for war-fighting and war-surviving had not been thought out and put into readiness. He sniffed, "The planners seem to care less about what happens after the buttons are pressed than they do about looking 'presentable' before the event . . . If deterrence should fail, they . . . could not be less interested in the details of what happens—so long as the retaliatory strike is launched."[25]

If the nation rested its security on the threat to pulverize the Soviet Union with its inventory of thermonuclear weapons, then some thought should go into the problems of war-fighting. One had to work out how much and what kind of counterforce capability was needed. Kahn's notion of counterforce encompassed offensive capabilities, targeting the enemy's bases and command and control; passive defense, dispersing and hardening the strategic forces and putting them on alert; civil defense, establishing a nationwide fallout shelter system and compulsory civil defense training, stockpiling industrial materials, universally distributing calcium pills and dosimeters, and investing heavily in decontamination research. All of these measures were counterforce insofar as they lessened the severity of an enemy attack.

For Kahn, any mitigating measure was counterforce, including medical supplies for the post-attack environment. Modern warriors should be as "concerned with bone cancer, leukemia, and genetic malformations as they are with the range of a B-52 or the accuracy of an Atlas missile." While war planners fixed their attention on deterring and fighting, everybody else focused on survival.[26]

Since negligence in amassing stores for post-attack conditions could be fatal, counterforce meant assembling a "preattack mobilization base" well in advance of any conflict. It readied the armed forces, the economy, and civil society to mobilize rapidly for war so that emergency resources would be immediately available. "Unless the President believes that the postwar world will be worth living in, he will in all likelihood be deterred from living up to our alliance obligations." The brunt of his argument was to show that a fully outfitted war-fighting posture was the most persuasive way to keep the cold war peace. If you were going to keep your enemy from blowing you up by threatening to blow up him up in retaliation, you had better look like you mean business.[27]

The merits of fielding war-fighting capabilities ran through all of Kahn's ideas. While building up a first strike capability sounds like war-fighting, he classified it as a *peacetime* policy. In the absence of these capabilities (including hardening, burying, and dispersing offensive forces, evacuating the population, and disseminating civil defense measures throughout the economy and society), it might appear to the Kremlin that the preferred American strategy in a growing crisis would be to get the first nuclear strike in, for fear that its forces and population might not survive otherwise. This was the hitch in a second-strike policy. If SAC had to wait until it received secure confirmation of the loss of the nation's capital, its fleet would not survive the assault.

In other words, America's strategic vulnerability amounted to an invitation to the Soviets to strike first. This was the creed of the nuclear war-fighter: "Under some circumstances, our vulnerability to a Russian first strike would *both tempt the Russians* to initiate a war and at the same time *compel them*, because they might feel that we would be tempted to preempt for our own protection." If both East and

West were vulnerable to a first strike, the fear of surprise attack ratcheted up the pressure to preempt.[28]

Thomas Schelling's description of trigger-happy reciprocity captured this idea. "Suppose that my nervousness depends on how frightened I am, and my fright depends on how likely I think that he may shoot me; and suppose he acts the same way. Then when I consider the . . . probability that he may shoot me out of sheer preference, it makes me nervous; this nervousness enhances the likelihood that I may shoot him even though I prefer not to. He sees my nervousness and gets nervous himself; that scares me more, and I am even more likely to shoot." Accordingly, Kahn explained, if the United States believed that the Soviets were deterred by the invulnerability of American offensive forces so that they were "not . . . tempted by our vulnerability to solve . . . [their] problems by quick action," neither would the American defender feel compelled to strike preemptively at forces which it feared were preparing to strike first. Hence, counterintuitively, Kahn argued that acquiring an invulnerable first strike capability made the world *safer* from the risk of nuclear war.[29]

One might think he had exhausted the deterrence continuum at this point. But Kahn wanted to make room for crises in which retaliation would be an act of will. The accent was on limited nuclear exchanges. For the sake of fortifying the reach of American power to protect U.S. allies and client states, he wanted to legitimate tactical nuclear war-fighting—that is, limited bombing that would not give way, in one move, to total world war. He called these capabilities Type II and Type III deterrence systems. He opened the topic with the chilling words, "I am now going to ask the reader for an unpleasant feat of imagination, one which very few Westerners seem willing to achieve—to try to project himself into a future wartime situation and . . . ponder the questions seriously . . . How might a thermonuclear war be initiated? . . . [How might such] a war be fought and terminated?"[30]

Under what circumstances would the President be obliged to make a political decision to use nuclear weapons? Type II deterrence crises referred to attacks against the territories of American allies. Unless the United States threatened nuclear reprisal, the Soviets might assume that apart from striking the American heartland, they had virtual freedom of movement in Europe and the rest of the world. What mattered was the Kremlin's estimate of American responses to a sudden irruption. "The Soviet planner asks himself, 'If I make this very provocative move, will the Americans strike us?'"[31]

The United States needed to be able to fight a small atomic war in Europe; otherwise, NATO was jeopardized. The Type II deterrent force would "limit limited wars." The idea was that the United States could pacify the Soviets by putting into readiness such forces as would enable the Europeans to survive war on their soil, if necessary. "If the West is to have the resolve, in a time of need, to stand firm, the United States needs to have capabilities and war plans designed to give a reasonably credible and *explainable* possibility that our allies will be able psychologically to endure the strain of a prolonged crisis and physically to survive the war which might result from a failure of Type II Deterrence." Unless the United States extended civil defense and tactical nuclear cover to its allies, the Soviets could try to "strain the alliance to the breaking point."[32]

Fighting was the best way to be persuasive: "Resolve is best shown by action." Therefore, Kahn recommended laying out a series of escalating moves between the first clash of arms and total war. Even after combat has begun, he believed it should be possible to limit its scope by building thresholds between the opening blow and all-out fury. Type III deterrence parried enemy moves with ever-sharper countermeasures so "that the net effect of the aggressor's action is to cause him to lose in position." Called tit-for-tat deterrence, this kind of intra-war bargaining tightened the screw little by little. Pre-attack mobilization played a critical role in this scheme. Facing an inconvenienced, pettish, aroused society, the enemy would likely be discouraged from experimenting with American military resolve.[33]

While strafing the enemy or evacuating his own citizens from cities were actual moves available to the commander-in-chief—not mere promises but actions on the ground—they were also psychological operations when coupled with the threat to do worse. They flogged the enemy's mind as well as his body. At bottom, for Kahn the best way to think about deterrence was as a fretwork of incrementally more violent threats, actions, and reprisals. This was better than shrieking "Take it or leave it!" Behaving "like a force of nature that cannot be influenced or reasoned with" was too clumsy, since maneuvering in a crisis was never a soliloquy. "The enemy also can threaten us, and he will . . . refuse to believe that we will ignore his threats. If we believe the enemy is listening to our threats, then somehow we have to believe that he thinks we are listening to his threats. Even if we think we are sincere in our irrevocable commitments . . . when the time comes to act it just will not be worth it."[34]

A war of nerves was a tooth-grinding gamble, but madness could be mesmerizing. Kahn suggested, dangerously, that maybe the best way to inspire compliance was to appear "slightly mad, intemperate or emotional." In the game of deterrence, the player who looks as though he has committed himself "irrevocably" is more likely to win a bargaining contest than his demure partner. This, then, was the point at which the rationality of irrationality comes into play. Pretending to be fanatically committed to an irrational policy could be the best possible strategy in a crisis. As always, the problem was credibility. Kahn pointed out, "If we wish to have our strategic air force contribute to . . . deterrence, it must be credible that we are willing to take one or more . . . actions. Usually the most convincing way to *look* willing is to *be* willing."[35]

This was equivocal business. "Life, liberty, and security may depend on playing . . . the game of 'Chicken,'" he mused. "Short of an objective arbiter . . . to decide disputes . . . one must be willing to play the 'game' . . . or surrender." Let's stop right here and consider what is being said. Kahn insisted that in order to *look* willing to fight a nuclear war, you had to *be* willing to fight a nuclear war. Was this martial bluster or a program for nuclear war-fighting? On the one hand, he suggested that the United States had, ultimately, to make a limited tactical strike to show its enemies that it was indeed willing to cross the nuclear threshold. "Resolve is best shown by action. The use of Controlled Reprisal is a direct matching of our resolve against his." On the other hand, he maintained that it was "desirable" to keep American intentions ambiguous by pretending to be irrationally committed to all-out war. "If we refuse to use such strategies, we will be giving up an important set of options that may cause us very serious handicaps."[36]

In the briefing he delivered at Princeton University, Kahn reeled off a little parody of the contradictions involved in having to look resolved to punish bad acts demonically, while assuring the enemy that the war could be limited.

> Let me tell you my solution to the whole problem . . . You make the SAC commander's job hereditary and put a guy like . . . General LeMay in charge who really is going to hit them hard, you know, and he is really irrevocable. You make his assistant's job hereditary and his job is to shoot LeMay at the outbreak of war. So you have a sensible strategy . . .
>
> You have to have a spy in Russia so that after they've made the irrevocable decision to go to war, to tell them: Look be sensible about your targets because the Americans really won't hit you. See they think LeMay's going to be in charge . . . So you've got a spy in Russia to tell them what the situation is after they've made the irrevocable decision to go to war . . .
>
> You also . . . buy a fantastic number of IRBMs [intermediate range ballistic missiles] and put them in Europe. Alert. Ready to go. And this is bad because it makes the Russians trigger-happy. You know, they want to hit them, take them out. So you put [Bertrand Russell] in charge of [them]. You know they'll never be used. You make his assistant's job hereditary. Comes the crisis, he shoots Bertrand.
>
> It isn't finished yet. You now need a whole series of spies in the various countries of Europe to release exactly the right

amount of information . . . There's a little sociological problem which I'll leave to you.[37]

The Radioactive Postwar Environment

Kahn often teased his audiences about the postwar world. After laying out a scenario, he'd say, "The straightforward factor by which we
exceed the National Academy of Science standards [for exposure to
radiation] is now really horrifying." "How does a country look on the
day of the war? The only answer a reasonable person can give is 'awful.'" He'd nod agreeably, "It takes an iron will . . . to distinguish
among the possible degrees of awfulness." With these words, he
opened the scandal of thinking about the unthinkable that would
forever after cling to his name and work.[38]

Kahn was annoyed by blubbering heavings about survival. He'd insist, "In describing the aftermath of a war it is not . . . illuminating to
use words such as 'intolerable,' 'catastrophic,' 'total destruction,' 'annihilating retaliation.'" If postwar states differed, then it was "important to get a 'feel' for what the levels of damage might really be under
various conditions . . . The only way in which we can communicate
even intuitive notions with any accuracy is to use quantitative measures." A friend of his recalled, "He'd always ask, 'How can we possibly size this problem?' Somebody would say, this effect exists, he'd
want to know how big is it?"[39]

He envisioned a range of postwar conditions whose degrees of awfulness were a function of prewar preparations. Civil defense could
make a difference between 100 million deaths and 50 million. Critics
hissed that only a depraved man could draw such distinctions in an
absolute catastrophe. "It is not that the problems are not inherently
emotional," he protested, "they are!" But anxiety shouldn't drive policy; it should only prod men to swallow realities they'd rather not
confront.[40]

Kahn was exasperated by the idea that nuclear war meant world
annihilation. To believe that any military engagement involving nu-

clear weapons of any magnitude would automatically obliterate the world's peoples certainly simplified the problem immensely. But its flaw was its necessity. Believing that nuclear weapons were world-destroying was effortless. "There is obviously a difference between damage and annihilation. It is high time that the distinction was drummed into many key minds in our society."[41]

Nuclear weapons simply couldn't snuff out the earth's creatures. His 1958 civil defense studies had determined that until 1970, "any picture of total world annihilation appears to be wrong, irrespective of the military course of events." Assuming this was true, effusions of repugnance were beside the point. Rather than evoking a blurry tableau of post-attack desolation, Kahn tried to bear down on the details of several postwar worlds. "But surely one can ask a more specific question," he would protest. Overcoming the tendency to focus on a single horrific picture, he would ask, "How does a country look five or ten years after the close of war?" as a result of various prewar preparations.[42]

Kahn's notorious table of "tragic but distinguishable states" dramatized his conviction that prewar preparations limited deaths, limited damage, and fostered postwar recuperation. If 40 million people died in a nuclear blast and then another 40 million expired from radiation exposure during subsequent weeks or months, those radiation deaths would be "an unnecessary additional disaster."[43]

In 1959 he once saw an ad for the SANE antinuclear coalition in both *The New York Times* and *The Herald Tribune*. It read, "What kind of insane person would take comfort from decreasing casualties from three-quarters to a half?" This seemed to be a garbled variant of something he said, so he telephoned a friend at SANE. "That sounds like you're sort of quoting me." "Yeah, we call that the Herman Kahn ad." He was indignant. Not only was the math wrong—"I talk about going from going from three-quarters to three-eighths . . . a factor of two"—but it missed the point altogether. If civil defense could save a quarter of America's population from needless death, about 40 million people, that was a good thing, wasn't it? "Not to take comfort from that is somehow curious. I mean, you should, clearly." Yet he allowed, "On the other hand, I do have some sympathy with the ad in the sense that if we happen to go from 160 to 120 [million deaths] it would be hard to somehow take comfort . . . You would find it difficult."[44]

Kahn reflected, "It is in some sense true that one may never recuperate from a thermonuclear war. The world may be permanently (i.e., for perhaps 10,000 years) more hostile to human life." If the proper and only question about nuclear war was "Can we restore the prewar conditions of life?" then "the answer must be 'No!'" But that wasn't the best approach. It was better to ask: "How much more hostile will the environment be?" "How happy or normal a life can the survivors and their descendants hope to have?" His assurances were pert and pompous. "Despite a widespread belief to the contrary, objective studies indicate that even though the amount of human tragedy would be greatly increased in the postwar world, the increase would not preclude normal and happy lives for the majority of survivors and their descendants."[45]

To add some meat to the postwar world picture, he posed the worst possible thing people feared. What would that be? Godzilla, the mutant child. Would the bomb sterilize survivors? Would radiation exposure beget monstrous offspring? He translated this into a homelier problem: "How much damage would be done if everybody received a radiation dose to his reproductive organs as large as that considered acceptable by the National Academy of Sciences?" If everyone were bombarded with ten roentgens, he estimated there would be a 0.04 percent increase of mutants born into the postwar world, increasing to 0.4 percent with each new generation.[46]

Birth defects were tragic for parents, he remarked coolly, but these risks were socially legitimate in modern society. On average, Americans had absorbed half of the maximum permissible dosage of radiation from medical X-rays alone. In fact, given their education and tendency to consult doctors twice as often as the average person, the readers of On Thermonuclear War might have absorbed the NAS limit *already*. "The resulting damage," he shrugged, "is just part of the price we have to pay to live in a civilization with nuclear power plants, X-rays, fluoroscopes, tracer elements, weapons tests, and so on."[47]

If every survivor of nuclear attack received 25 times the permissible dose, birth defects would increase by 1 percent. "It was possible that an American president might be willing to accept the high risk of an additional 1 percent of our children being born deformed if that meant not giving up Europe to Soviet Russia." At this point in a public lecture, a woman in the audience stood up and wailed, "I don't want to live in your world in which 1 percent of the children are born defective!" "My answer was rather brutal, I fear," Kahn smirked. "'It is not *my* world,' I observed." Besides, "she had a real problem, since 4 percent of the children are born defective *now*."[48]

Society already tolerated birth defects resulting from exposure to weapons test radiation, he maintained; the mutants were just kept out of sight. Adding "a further 1 percent would be terrible," but it wouldn't be a hardship. It was hypocritical to say otherwise. "We not only bear this relatively high rate of tragedy; we come close to ignoring it." If genetic mutations from postwar radiation were comparable to the radiation risks that industrial workers *already* endured, then "most people will be able to live with such increased risks." As a sop, he added the prophecy of a miracle cure. In addition to "natural decontamination," Kahn slipped in future developments of which we know nothing today but which one could hope for. Who knew what human cleverness might dream up to protect reproductive tissues from radiation?[49]

While Kahn was resigned to birth defects, he also probed the problem with great ingenuity. This was how he counteracted strontium-90 contamination in the post-attack environment. If swallowed, strontium-90 (Sr-90) irradiates bone cells and marrow, thereby increasing the likelihood that the exposed person will eventually develop cancer or one of the leukemias. Fortunately, Sr-90 is chemically similar to calcium. When calcium is ingested along with contaminated food, the body appears to prefer to absorb the calcium first, and correspondingly less strontium.[50]

Kahn addressed the problem of genetic injury by starting with the maximum permissible amount of Sr-90 that adults could safely absorb. According to the International Committee on Radiation Protection, it was 67 strontium units. While many scientists thought this was too high, he pointed out that industrial workers were allowed 2,000 strontium units. Next, how much Sr-90 might a post-attack environment have? He presented the worst case: assume fallout contamination of 0.002 kiloton per square mile; assume 1 unit of strontium per person; assume the amount of fallout translates directly into the amount of Sr-90 in human bone; and assume people would not eat contaminated food that produced more than 67 strontium units in new bone, then how bad was the postwar situation? If fallout alighted over a million square miles, then only 13 megatons of fission (.013 kiloton per square mile) would "make the food unfit for human consumption." "If you use dirty bombs, the ground will get so contaminated that there will no agriculture for 40 years. You understand that's a long time between breakfast and lunch—40 years."[51]

But here he flourished his special magic. The variables of the problem—the amount of fallout in the environment and the permissible dosages of Sr-90 exposure—could be adjusted. Owing to the fact that fallout does not settle uniformly, and with passing weather and time radioactive particles decay, the contamination in the environment would safely decrease by a factor between 50 and 100.

Peacetime exposure standards could also be liberalized "to the point that the incidence of cancer begins to change average life expectancy by a significant amount." Why not ration contaminated agricultural products according to how much strontium they contained? The purest food, Grade A, could be rationed for children and pregnant women. Grade B would be deluxe but universally available. Grade C food would be cheaper. Grade D would be available only to people over 40. Since mature bones do not incorporate as much calcium as younger ones, cancer would not develop for decades. Optimizing the slower absorption rate of old bones would suggest that most survivors "would die of other causes before they got cancer." Grade E food could be fodder for animals. Finally, assuming that Sr-90 binds to calcium in milk but lesser amounts lodge in animal tissues, he surmised that one could safely eat the meat of livestock which had grazed on contaminated pasture.[52]

Kahn added a further layer of mitigation. He suspected that his account of the relation between fission products and Sr-90 absorption was probably wrong, since it would take time before critical amounts of the isotope collected in the body. During this interval, postwar society could administer palliatives, "not to speak of the ones we still hope to discover." He proposed immediately instituting a research program for extracting Sr-90 from milk, adding calcium pills to the diet, and varying horticulture depending on the kind and amount of contamination in the soil. This heap of piecemeal remedies—exploiting slower rates of radiation absorption in middle-aged bones, grading and rationing contaminated food, adding calcium pills to the diet, sponsoring research in anti-radiation medicine and purification technologies, and careful horticulture—typifies Kahn's inventive response to a seemingly overwhelming problem.[53]

In order to "be as specific and quantitative as possible in discussing fallout effects," Kahn postulated two scenarios, the "early" and "late" attack on U.S. soil. The early attack hit 150 targets, expended 500 nuclear bombs, and yielded 1,500 megatons of fission products; the late attack hit 400 targets, expended 2,000 bombs, and yielded 20,000 megatons of fission products. These numbers measured nothing. They merely particularized the dynamic nature of the Soviet threat. "[What] might be valuable for the next few years may prove to be ridiculously inadequate somewhat later."[54]

Based solely on fission yield, even after an early attack, worldwide radiation would be three times greater than the maximum permissible amount. But Kahn confirmed his faith in weathering, uneven terrain, isotope decay, and the application of constantly improving decontamination technologies. "Calculations indicate" that this would decrease exposure levels to 1 percent of the first estimate. Even then, he insisted that "we would not accept the situation passively. We would [decontaminate and] . . . arrange our lives . . . to minimize exposure." People would garb themselves in protective suits when venturing outside, and otherwise live and work in shielded surroundings. An irradiated environment would not mean abandoning "our homes and factories, although we might have to give up some of their aesthetic appearance and convenience." (Perhaps the sand-bagged Quonset hut villages of wartime Los Angeles demonstrated to Kahn that people would accept cheerless dwellings.)[55]

Even after a heavy attack, the postwar environment would still be humanly tolerable. Highly contaminated areas would be accessible, and perhaps even habitable, "if we wished to accept a somewhat greater dose than our standards suggest, or be more aggressive in our anti-contamination." Folding one conditional into another, he admitted that mitigation would be impossible unless a multibillion-dollar civil defense program was initiated immediately. Otherwise the postwar environment would be too irradiated to allow improvised measures or short-term exposures. He stated grimly, "There are no conservation laws which state that we can survive this kind of war. Any such belief must rest on empirical knowledge and calculations and not on being able to 'rise to the occasion.'" Without intensive civil defense, American society might not survive. But by shielding living and working spaces and developing decontamination technologies, Americans would probably find long-term radioactivity bearable.[56]

Amazingly, Kahn conceded that his civil defense study did not look at the long-term effects of radioactive isotopes and gamma ray emissions. Since nuclear bombs created 200 isotopes, only on the basis of intensive study of the short- and long-term effects of each one could alleviating measures be invented. Fission products that had not been thoroughly explored might yet poison human, animal, and vegetative life. He admitted, "Some of them may have ecological effects that would sharply influence our preparations or expectations."[57]

Kahn's treatment of the postwar environment characteristically wended its way between the polarities of faith and insight. He flourished a broad assertion—in this instance, the worst-case scenario—softened it with mitigating activities, then, having thumped it into more encouraging shape, blurted out his misgivings. A dormant element may yet harm or destroy the world in spite of every precaution. Having thrown his argument into doubt, he reprised his confidence in hopeful outcomes. This performance could be bewildering, distinguished as it was by his compulsion to itemize the breadth of possible outcomes, his resourcefulness in problem solving, and his scruples to highlight the fabricated quality of his hypotheticals. While some people grasped his sustaining optimism, others, having followed his tortuous straggle through assertion, modification, reversal, concession, and conclusion, could not arrive at such happy finales. Some could not make out his meaning at all.

Modeling the Post-Attack World Picture

"Instead of asking 'What happened?' we asked 'What can we do about it?'" It was by virtue of making preparations, sponsoring R&D in decontamination techniques and anti-radiation medicine, designing habitable fallout shelters, instituting industrial defense, warehousing critical materials, distributing dosimeters, training cadres, and—equally importantly—considering the ways in which counterforce could blunt the intensity of an attack that Kahn fixed his wary optimism.[58]

Kahn's world picture was rooted in a faith in necessary inventions (that technical and scientific innovations evolved by necessity), in the perpetually new of the modern (that with each wave of technical innovation the defense avant garde had to be willing to think in a permanently new way), in human resiliency (that foresight erred by way of apocalyptic exaggeration; having staggered through near-millennial crises before, humankind would do so again), and in the absence of limits to growth (that the earth bore distinct properties, yet its riches and powers were illimitable; there would always be more for science to extract). Likewise, human ingenuity was infinitely adaptable. In its engineered stuff, human will propelled itself beyond the puny rotation of generation and corruption.

Kahn's scenarios of social and economic recuperation uncoiled from these fundamentals. He divided the country into an A part made up of the fifty to one hundred largest metropolitan districts of the

United States, and a B part of secondary towns and rural areas. If A was destroyed, B would have the resources to reconstruct "in about ten years." Belying those who objected that the economy was too interdependent to suffer the loss of its fifty or one hundred largest cities, he rejoined that a modern economy could smoothly adjust to these changes, and one shouldn't exaggerate the loss of resources, personnel, and equipment.[59]

Economically speaking, even if no special preparations were in place, he declared that the country could absorb the small attack and recover. Survivors would buckle down to reconstruction and ration essential stocks. Besides, he guessed that much of what had been destroyed was probably nonessential. B country possessed one quarter of the total industrial capacity of the nation. Assuming that many manufacturing plants operated at less than full capacity and that postwar industry would be devoted to basic needs (producing few consumer goods and no frills), even one-quarter plant capacity could retool the nation. Engineers would simply make do with critical shortages.

One simply couldn't ferry everyday mores into the postwar world picture. One had to adjust expectations of the economy and society. "People tend to do better in disasters and wartime situations than they expect. They 'make do.'" For example, rather than assume that damage to a factory took it out of operation, people would probably whip themselves to Herculean tasks with barely operational equipment. He stated serenely, "Both laymen and professionals tend to exceed their own and the experts' expectations, referring to the result as a 'miracle of production' or a 'miracle of ingenuity.' This kind of 'miracle' seems very common and is almost to be expected."[60]

A heavy attack required civil defense. The following should be held in readiness: "provisions for continuity of government, improvised post-attack radiation shelter at work and home, food supplies . . . manuals and instructions to aid adjustment to the new conditions of life, trained cadres, and radiation meters." In particular, he urged training a "permanent semi-military reserve" of between 100,000 and 250,000 cadres for immediate rescue, repair, and clean-up. They would be the core personnel of the postwar recovery effort, supplemented by masses of volunteers.[61]

Kahn had a special liking for pocket-sized radiation dosimeters. It was a perfect example of the social benefits that could be gotten from the universal availability of a cheap gadget. It solved the problem of how to rally survivors to work for immediate postwar recovery, when fear of radiation exposure might sap their will to join decontamination or reconstruction tasks. If one could reliably measure one's own exposure, most fears would be assuaged. Other radiological equipment would certainly be needed, but for its dramatic effect on morale, "a meter may well be the most essential."[62]

Kahn laid bare the "seven optimistic assumptions" on which he based his prognostications of postwar renewal. He presupposed that the United States had not lost the war, that it had not been occupied, and that able-bodied people, resources, and infrastructure survived. "The debris has been cleared up, minimum communications restored, the most urgent repairs made, credits and markets re-established, a basic transportation system provided, minimum utilities either set up or restored, the basic necessities of life made available, and so on."[63] In short, he eclipsed the ruin of war.

Of all the expectations underpinning his reconstruction ideas, the most cheering was that "bourgeois virtues survive." The survivors would not panic, languish, refuse to toil, rebel, or fall prey to brigands and chaos. None was especially likely if civil defense preparations were in place, if cadres were trained, manuals and dosimeters distributed, and stockpiles amassed. Folding one conditional into another (bourgeois virtues would survive if the pre-attack mobilization base had been assembled), he offered the words that would conciliate survivors to postwar arrangements. "In any situation calling for . . . mobilization or evacuation . . . we can expect some previous education of the people to the hard facts of life, and therefore a willingness to face up to the responsibilities . . . Desperate conditions demand desperate living. We did not choose this world, we just live in it."[64]

As for the mental health of the surviving population, he firmly believed that a short war would not instantly create a nation of shell-shocked numbskulls and zombies. While the agony of conventional war innervated society, "the habits of a lifetime" could not be swallowed up by the brief interval of nuclear war. Survivors would remain intact if their world altered suddenly.

Kahn believed that the survivors would be grateful and tractable if the government had anticipated war, had gathered reserves in protected facilities, trained cadres, published manuals of tolerable post-attack standards, and had a reconstruction plan ready to hand—especially "if the overall plan for recuperation looks sensible and practical." In fact, he predicted "a somewhat fanatic intensity" of reconstruction efforts among survivors. To the objection that "psychological, and political and social aspects might not be conducive to great postwar effort," he countered, "Assuming the program works no worse than calculations indicate, we can fairly hope for exactly the opposite effect." Unfaltering recovery from war and natural disaster repeatedly proved the point. Besides, "The government will be able to give an honest account of its reasons for going to war, one that will calm the ire of the populace. The nation has destroyed the enemy that had to be destroyed. It did so with fewer casualties than many expected. More important, the government has a feasible and credible plan for reconstruction. In short, all of our troubles were foreseen, evaluated, and found to be worth the cost." Should the reconstruction plan appear reasonable, "people will probably rally round and work for it."[65]

Interestingly and nobly, Kahn exposed the most presumptuous (and damning) of his postwar assumptions: that "neglected effects [are] unimportant." He admitted that he did not integrate all of the postwar problems into a single model. "We did not look at the interaction among effects we did study." While such research was tentative, he enjoyed "confidence in some partial conclusions" such as the feasibility of recovering from *each* of the problems resulting from a nuclear war, rectifying radioactivity, rubble, genetic injury, and radiation sicknesses separately. Countermeasures could be contrived for every dimension of the postwar world. The problem of radioactivity "if nothing else happened" could be mitigated; reconstruction "not complicated by social disorganization, loss of personnel, radioactivity" could be achieved; society could be reconstituted. And yet this was all provisional. "But if all these things happened together and all the other effects were added at the same time, one cannot help but have some doubts."[66]

He was guileless, acutely so. And bewildering. Just what was he confessing when he said: "Some of these interactions are researchable and should be studied even though we did not do so. However, I believe, though admittedly on the basis of inadequate evidence . . . that none of the problems encountered in the small attack would prove to be annihilating or even seriously crippling. No such judgment can be passed about the heavy attack without more research effort. Even then doubts may remain, depending on the quality of the preparations and the amount of research that has gone into the problem." Perhaps Kahn intended to prick American citizens, scientists, politicians, and soldiers into fearlessly examining post-attack survival. I have no doubt that he regarded candor as the very index of scientific integrity. And yet it was due to these kinds of disclosures that many people found his briefings horrific or unintelligible.[67]

He pressed on. "How much confidence did our researchers have in these recuperation calculations?" The RAND civil defense study imperfectly captured the totality of the post-attack situation. Because it didn't weave social, economic, and biological behavior into a seamless fabric, confidence in the research was minimal. Nevertheless, if weapons effects were contained, if only the A country was damaged, and if radioactivity did not exceed the levels proposed in the study, then arguments undermining his findings were "probably wrong." His summation displayed his characteristic faith and anxiety about the uncertainties confounding his optimism. More study was needed so that preparations could be readied for a calamity that might actually scourge America. "We may not be able to recuperate even with preparations, but we cannot today put our finger on why this should be so and I, for one, believe that with sufficient study we will be able to make a very convincing case for recuperation, if we survive the war, and, more important, that with sufficient preparation we actually will be able to survive and recuperate if deterrence fails."[68]

The Problem with Hypothetical Studies

The last lecture in *OTW* conjured up eight prototypes of world war—the two major wars that had already occurred in the twentieth century and six hypothetical ones. Kahn's scenarios of World Wars I–VIII illustrated the effect of technical innovation on strategy and tactics.[69]

World Wars I and II highlighted "the prevalence of unexpected (but, in retrospect, obvious) operational gaps." World Wars III and IV might have broken out in 1951 and 1956 respectively. The former began in Korea and could have been fought with atomic weapons. World War IV would have used thermonuclear weapons, introducing into history "the problem of the post-attack environment." World Wars V (1961), VI (1965), VII (1969), and VIII (1973) focused attention on strategic vulnerabilities arising from phasing in new weapons systems. World War V marked out present and near-future vulnerabilities. World War VI was sensitive to changes in current deployments. World War VII demonstrated the introduction of weapons systems in early stages of development. Finally, World War VIII extrapolated the arms race into the future.[70]

These wars illustrated the lag between the capabilities of a new weapon system and the conventional strategic concepts used by war planners. Since new systems succeeded one another willy-nilly, it was no longer possible to learn the capacities and defects of each through experience. The result was that strategic doctrine and the strategic reality could be "almost unrelated to each other." Presenting something close to the consensus view at RAND, Kahn argued that since the end of World War II there had arisen "a revolution in the art of war every four or five years." "Technological revolution" was hyperbole for the idea that atomic and thermonuclear explosives as well as their delivery systems (bombers, missiles, submarines) had speedily rattled into existence. The American atomic monopoly from 1945 to 1949, the attainment of Soviet atomic capabilities in 1949, the successful detonation of the U.S. hydrogen bomb in 1952 and the Soviet hydrogen bomb in 1953, and the introduction of missile technology necessitated different strategies for nuclear war-fighting.[71]

With the introduction of new weapons systems every five years, the forces-in-being were not instantly obsolete. Rather, multiple weapons systems overlapped. The time span from a feasibility study to initial operation could be ten or fifteen years, with a useful service of five or ten additional years. Consequently, the assortment of systems at any one time was mind-boggling. There was the legacy system soon to be retired; the more modern mainstay of the strategic forces; an improved system being phased in; and a new prototype. Within this interval, engineers, war planners, and systems analysts had to imagine a future system's use two to four "technological revolutions" ahead of present capabilities. As a result, "since it is impossible for fallible humans . . . to project two to four technological revolutions ahead," Kahn noted, "much of our preparation must be made in a partial fog."[72]

Uncertainty stalked the strategist at every point in this progression, beginning with the haste with which analysts and weapons designers were driven to present feasibility studies, well before a new idea had been thoroughly explored. "In a sense," he murmured, "you start your briefings before you know what the whole story is about." The multiple dimensions of uncertainty compounded by overlapping weapons systems opened up the *gap*, one of Kahn's favorite and most potent notions. The gap represented the unexpected and unknown possibilities, both strategic and operational, that emerged from the mix of new and old weapons systems in existence at any one time. The R&D gap exposed the vulnerabilities a new technology creates when "the other man knows more about some . . . hardware . . . or weapons effects than you do." The procurement gap described the additive competition of the arms race: "The enemy has . . . more of some weapons . . . than you have." The operational gap referred to the enemy's insight into the current strategic force. "An operational gap . . . arises out of a failure to react properly to a change in the situation . . . It is the operational gap that kills you. It is also the most subtle and hardest to recognize and guard against."[73]

In each of his world wars, gaps between Soviet and American capabilities were inconspicuous. "[They] may determine the course of events and are most likely to cause catastrophic failures of the system, but until one is faced with a disastrous failure, it is most difficult to take them seriously." This was Kahn's problem: how to invest hypothetical vulnerabilities, particularly unknown and undetectable ones, with urgency. Exhorting the "rigid thinkers, the budget-minded, . . . the loyal member of an operating organization, or the partisan advocate" to address airy possibilities was taxing and disheartening.[74]

The operational gap was detectable only in that unapproachable horizon, the post-attack situation. "The only way to find operational gaps is by intense observation of the whole system, reflection on unconventional possibilities, and paper . . . studies. This means that any gaps that are found will look hypothetical and unreal." The operational gap spanned the breach between rational planning and actual happening. It was the design complement to the abysmal infinitude of the strategist's uncertainties. "This problem of finding and correcting subtle (and hypothetical) weaknesses is, of course, compounded by the rapid rate of technological advance . . . The aggressor has to find one crucial weakness; the defender has to find all of them and in advance." Here we can pinpoint the impulse driving Kahn's utopia: the possibility of transcending every earthly limit through human ingenuity, resolve, and technical prowess. This yields the structure of the gap, the recognition of which rocks the analyst between confidence and doubt.[75]

Cold war visionaries pinned their hopes on the gigantic scope of the federal government. Kahn gloried in the colossal possibilities wrung from the administrative coordination of the nation's scientists, a cornucopia of experimental materials, and an inexhaustible pot of gold. "One of the most startling things that ever happened to me . . . [was when I] first came in contact with the philosophy which is willing to ask any question and tackle any problem. After study, people generally conclude that certain things are feasible but not practical because they cost a little bit too much. And I really mean just about 'any' proposal. Henry Kissinger [remarked] . . . that the fires of Prometheus had . . . been unleashed. This is an understatement of the things that are now technologically feasible but that 'cost . . . too much' . . . [like] melting ice caps and diverting ocean currents." What was technically feasible yearned to be realized. The only barrier to attaining extraordinary objectives was political support for R&D. Cost alone obstructed action, cost and not natural limits or ethical prohibition.[76]

Kahn embodied a recognizable strain of American optimism—brisk, liberal, masculine, and nonchalant. He believed that power was self-actuated, that man must mobilize his resolve to master history and nature, that science could be the instrument of political will, that stoicism was obligatory in the cold war, and that people who suffered too much had only themselves to blame. He shrugged, "While many people find it difficult to visualize the conduct of international relations in a nuclear-armed world, human society has adjusted to even larger changes than this in the past and may adjust again." Instead of shirking "inevitable future problems . . . [with] wishful thinking," Americans ought to "learn how to live with it."[77]

Affecting a lofty intolerance for timidity, he laid bare his reality principle. "In any question as complex as that under discussion, one must, in the long run, depend on informed judgment and intuition in addition to rigorous analysis." While he spurned disarmament as craven and illusory, he also wreathed sentimental wishes into his science of the unthinkable. One need only consider the miraculous advent of decontamination technologies, medical antidotes to radiation sickness, and the power of weathering to dilute irradiated terrain to recognize the manna inherent in his intuition.[78]

"What is physically possible," brooded Brodie months after Hiroshima, "must [now] be regarded as tactically feasible." The union of the possible and feasible opened the fantastic impulse within strategy. In a relay of strike and reprisal, strategic scenarios mirrored the extravagant worlds of espionage and science fiction stories. That actual nuclear war was impossible to picture in detail opened the way for the daisy chain of consequence worked out by reasonable men. Beyond artfulness, deterrence forced men to play with barbarism. Coolly promising avenging slaughter was expedient. For Kahn, deterrence was a gambling feint at madness. A *worldly* raving. Fire-eating. Watchful and unreal.[79]

Chapter 9

COMEDY OF THE UNSPEAKABLE

*Those Great, uncontrollable forces, natural and social,
which hover over the world of men are so terrifying in
their raw state that man has always had to humanize, to
personalize, to mythologize them that he might live sanely
with what he cannot control. Thus, for example, Mars,
Neptune, Cupid. Now we have a modern candidate for
this pantheon. His name is Herman Kahn . . . This contemporary man of myth, this enigmatic Cassandra and
20th century Dr. Jekyll and Mr. Hyde, is, most surprisingly, a real, live person.*

JAMES C. FLECK, S.J., 1961

Kahn didn't like right-wingers: "I wouldn't want to have dinner with
them and I wouldn't want my daughter to marry one." His friend
Robert Panero compared him to "one of those 1968 types, only this
was 1958. You know, 'This is a free country, damn it, and I can say
whatever the hell I want to say and you can't shut me up!' He was
very, very anti-establishment." But how could this be? I wondered.
Kahn wanted America's strategic forces to be equipped, trained, ready,
and resolved to strike first in an all-out nuclear war. Panero replied, "I
think of him as a real peacemaker. He took the issue to the public and
out of the hands of the elites." When Amitai Etzioni wrote "Kahn does
for nuclear arms what free-love advocates did for sex: he speaks candidly of acts about which others whisper behind closed doors," he captured the conundrum of Herman Kahn altogether. Kahn snagged the
public's attention not only because of *what* he said, but *how* he said it.[1]

His cronies relished his briefings. "If [*OTW*] reads the way he talks," scribbled a major general to the vice-president of RAND, "it is probably one of those books you just can't put down." "You have preserved much of the delightful style of [your] oral presentation," rejoiced the director of research of the Naval Warfare Analysis Group at MIT. "*On Thermonuclear War* consumed my weekend," gasped a writer from NBC News to Kahn, "and was the most fascinating thing I have read since *Lady Chatterley*."[2]

Of course other readers loathed the book. In his notorious review in *Scientific American,* James Newman fumed, "*On Thermonuclear War* is by turns waggish, pompous, chummy, coy, brutal, rude, man-to-man, Air Force crisp, energetic, tongue-tied, pretentious, ingenuous, spastic ironical, savage, malapropos, square-bashing and moralistic." Yammering, gurgling, *unruly* speech not only poured from Kahn but was shrewdly channeled to a titillated public. Magazines and book clubs hawked *On Thermonuclear War* as a sensation. The editors of *Popular Science* gushed, "You may disagree violently with its prescription (many experts do). You may be shocked by its blunt discussion of ghastly catastrophe. Yet its ideas are so brilliantly fresh, many of its conclusions so impressive, that [we] consider the following . . . one of the most important this magazine has ever published."[3]

The reception of *OTW* compounded political ideas and matters of taste. If you were conservative, if sick jokes, *Mad* magazine, and Lenny Bruce offended you, then you probably also objected to Kahn's approach to nuclear war. But for people at the political center and to the left, it was harder to sort out one's reactions. You could be morally offended by Kahn's argument: how could he *justify* a first-strike deterrence policy? You could be bewildered by his qualifications and reversals: how could he declare that scientific study had concluded "any picture of total world annihilation appears to be wrong" but later confess there were flaws in his models of the postwar environment? You could be offended by his attitude: how could he *joke* about nuclear war? You could be offended by his style: how *dare* he write so informally? Or perversely, you could regard him as an unlikely hipster and applaud him for discussing awful matters irreverently and frankly.[4]

While his jokes endeared him to the scores of visitors who nodded through week-long briefings and seminars at RAND, they infuriated his colleagues on occasion. For example, Bernard Brodie quietly circulated a memo he had written which was inspired by his own psychoanalysis. In it, he pointed out the affinities between an orgasm and SAC's war plan of massive retaliation, while RAND's recommendation of holding some strategic forces in reserve demonstrated the self-control of withdrawal before ejaculation. In a briefing to SAC officers, Kahn blurted out, "In a real sense you people don't have war plans, you've got *war-gasms*." He smirked, "It went *psssst* and everybody ducked." Brodie was mortified. He chided him, "So grim a subject does not exclude an appropriate kind of humor used very sparingly, but levity is never legitimate." Likening sex to nuclear war wasn't terribly shocking, but uttering "wargasm" to an assembly of strangers in a professional forum was a disgrace.[5]

Brodie's outrage nicely illustrates the pangs fetched by a grotesque anomaly. Kahn jumbled together ordinarily segregated kinds of speech into a mishmash of expressions high and low, exalted and vulgar, scientific and uncouth. If Brodie thought Kahn had been improper, it was because he considered his speech to be *grotesque.* "Something [was] illegitimately *in* something else . . . Things that should be kept apart [were] fused together." This is the essence of the grotesque. In it, there are no aesthetic standards and no separation of discourses; everything goes with everything.[6]

Stylistically, grotesque form tends to two extremes: too little meaning or too much. In the first instance, the refinements wreathing a topic compete for attention, glut the visual field, unfurl inexhaustibly, and stray so far from the center that the work collapses into utter meaninglessness. Or a work compresses a bundle of oddments into a single ambivalent symbol. The Rabelais scholar Mikhail Bakhtin called the second type, the condensed focal point, *a grotesque knot. OTW* exhibits both kinds of grotesque. Kahn's asides were amusing and unexpectedly hypnotic. "His barrage of wisecracks and bad jokes . . . awes and befuddles even the most hardened audience." His spectators were spellbound, if stupefied. His excursions, variations, reversals, and caprices seemed to swamp his argument entirely. "It is not unusual to hear someone say during the intermission, 'I don't understand a word he's saying, but he's terrific, isn't he?'" While his patter obscured his message at times—a case of the over-embellished grotesque—the real scandal of Herman Kahn was the unseemly join: jokes and nuclear war.[7]

We can think of *OTW* as a grotesque knot. This will let us pinpoint what was unsayable, what could be broached publicly, and how dread eventually broke into speech in the vulgar entertainments of the late 1950s. Only by throwing *OTW* up against other comic grotesques of the period can we guess how Americans might have heard and understood Herman Kahn in 1960.

The Restoration of Spring

Of the sundry threads snaking through *OTW*, let's tease out the bundle of Kahn's comic energies. "If we put one lion on the streets of New York City," he wrote in *OTW*, "every other mother [would be] paralyzed with fright. She just would not allow her children out on the streets." People would cower for a couple of days, but eventually they'd learn that lions don't eat very much. Most pedestrians could expect to live nice long lives. In fact, even if five or ten lions prowled the streets, people would still not stampede out of the city. "After all, five or ten lions might kill . . . as many people each year as [are] killed by automobiles." It mattered a great deal whether one, ten, or a hundred lions dined regularly on New Yorkers. He concluded smugly, "Ten lions will cause less than ten times as much trouble as one lion, but one hundred lions may make the city unacceptable for business or residence." "You've got to startle them," Kahn counseled Wiener, "so they pay attention." Appalled by passages like these, critics zeroed in on the "irrepressible shine" in *OTW* of *Schadenfreude*, brutality, paranoia, and "delight with the unlimited vistas opened by the nuclear age to the 'arts of war and blackmail.'"[8]

Sporting with forbidden subject matter is exhilarating. "These issues are fun to study," Kahn once said. You might interpret words calling attention to a speaker's daring exhibitionistic, but Bakhtin proposed a more gallant construction behind rude speech. A speaker's transgressions release his audience from ordinary proprieties and invite an answering candor. "Every age has its . . . words and expressions that are given as a signal to speak freely, to call things by their own names, without any mental restrictions and euphemisms." Kahn meant to be disarming in just this way. "You'll never get people to understand what's confusing unless you make it stark," he'd say. To another reporter, he explained, "Some of the things I say have shock value, but the reason for it is not to shock but to clarify. It wakes them up and makes them think that what I'm saying might be true."[9]

Romping with torture and dying makes for funny death. "The people play with terror and laugh at it; the awesome becomes a 'comic monster,'" observed Bakhtin. But the grotesque does not convey or induce an unmixed mood. It is ambivalent and volatile. "The grotesque is the feeling of anxiety aroused by the comic pushed to an extreme, [but also] the grotesque is the defeat, by means of the comic, of anxiety in the face of the inexplicable." We can easily spot the twinning of repulsion and mirth in the volcanic roar pealing in cinemas around the world when *Psycho* debuted in 1960. Hitchcock was simply dumbfounded by the near-hysteria of his audiences. "I don't think he was prepared for the amount and intensity of the on-the-spot laughs . . . he got," recalled his lead actor. His screenwriter was equally bewildered. "I saw people grabbing each other, howling, screaming, reacting like six-year-olds . . . I *never* thought it was a movie that would make people scream." Anxiety discharges in hilarity. This is critical for appreciating the grotesque. It is both liberating and excruciating.[10]

To no one's surprise, *Psycho* inspired boycotts, letters to the editor, and calls for suppression by clergy and psychiatrists. These civic measures characterize the moral panics that periodically erupt in response to novelty in popular culture. Decency crusades have surprisingly consistent features: they claim that young fans are harmed or threatened, they attack the personal decency of trendsetters, whose art is symptomatic of "imminent social breakdown," and they mobilize campaigns to censor or withdraw the offending object. *OTW* churned up much the same energies. Slurs against Kahn were found in nearly every hostile review of his book. Cursed as the devil in Scotland, at home a reviewer shuddered that he was ashamed to call Kahn a fellow American. The attack on Kahn was so insistent and personal that the director of Princeton University Press felt obliged to justify his decision to bring out the book. To a horrified friend at Simon & Schuster he responded gently, "I don't wonder that you were shocked by the book and by Newman's review of it, though I am sure that . . . you wouldn't want to have it suppressed." To another he rang out, "Kahn will have to defend his own statements and figures in detail, but . . . I firmly believe that the book was worth publishing."[11]

Repugnance attests to something essentially vulgar in *OTW.* Kahn was perfectly aware he galled many people. In fact, he called attention to this in a television broadcast. "If you knew a woman who had lost her only child. And you walked up to her and said, 'Madam, I know the world looks black to you. I know you can't envision a life in the future anymore. Nevertheless, in five years, you will have recovered from this loss. You will be laughing at jokes.' I mean, she won't forget about her child, but she will not grieve eternally in the sense that every day will be black. Everybody will be mad at you. They'll feel, 'What right do you have to walk up to her and say something like that! I mean, just what kind of a person are you???'"[12]

"Just what kind of a person are you?" neatly expresses the pique of offended Americans. Kahn attracted, and perhaps even welcomed, protesters. They heckled him at lectures; they flocked outside the Hudson Institute. Some even picketed his home in Chappaqua. It is hard to believe that "The Man Who Thinks About Atomic War" did not occasionally bait his public. "It is an unfortunate fact that on a lecture platform Herman Kahn looks like the mad scientist in an old horror movie," groaned a sympathetic observer. "Many people think he *is* a mad scientist."[13]

"There are all kinds of ways they look at me," Kahn shrugged, "'The idiot genius': he's a kind of genius, but he's also an idiot. 'The bizarre': thinking of 20 or 30 million dead at the office all day and then coming home and playing with the kids in the afternoon. I refuse to become paranoid about it." He became so used to controversy that in 1965 a reporter could blurt out, "Herman, why do so many people regard you as a monster?" To which he replied amiably, "There are a lot of reasons, none of which derive from my actually being a monster. One of the most important and obvious is the feeling that anybody who is interested in these kinds of problems *must* be a monster."[14]

While Kahn seemed to swagger with simple disinhibition, if we peer closer at the comic thread looping throughout *OTW*, we'll find other motifs that resonate with the historic traditions of vulgar comedy. Coupling death and vitality is a staple in Western comedy. From Greco-Roman festivals to the trial and execution of King Carnival in medieval European revels, violence is indispensable for reanimation and rebirth. Carnival's "screaming, frenzy, [and] savage brutality" is the medium for Spring. In the *buffo* tradition, ritual violence mimicked the weather: it was engulfing, potent, and wholly indifferent to its victims.[15]

The death of old Winter ushers in the Spring. What persists in the new season is elastic and provisional. We can find this idea in Kahn's prognostication of many possible postwar worlds. Woven throughout *OTW* is the suggestion of life irrepressibly bobbing through catastrophic vicissitudes. "Nations have taken shocks like this and survived." Life will carry on. "In such a postwar period you will have to readjust your life . . . It isn't quite the same as the prewar world . . . it's . . . another cost of the war. But not a cataclysmic cost." This surge into ever-new patterns of being is the essence of the comic spirit. Life is "always ready to exchange one form for another." To the idea of pure mutability, we add the crimp of Darwinian adaptation. "All creatures live by opportunities in a world fraught with disaster." The comic hero pits his cleverness and luck against an enigmatic foe. In comedy, the villain is the world.[16]

Kahn occasionally tried to coax his audience to consider the cold war under the sign of comic adventure. While explicitly warning that

America could not wish away the need for preparation. ("You can't rise to the occasion with a thousand hours of microcuries. You fall over . . . There is no conservation law which says that you can get through this next war.") Even so, like Figaro or Charlie Chaplin, he nearly always defied Great Peril with cheerful resourcefulness. Life would evolve new patterns in the postwar world. "People are just plain ingenious. Given a year or so the engineer always triumphs. It's a miracle of ingenuity, but he always does it. The answer to that is, let's see who makes the miracle this time." The post-attack world would be "just the change of the game."

> You cannot jeopardize civilization, as far as I can see, by genetic effects, and even if you could, you would then just change the form of civilization. If it really turned out that women were bearing more defective children than you could live with, you wouldn't go under. You would let the kids die in the delivery room . . . Great tragedy if you are hit, but it doesn't affect you if you are not hit. You know, just the change of the game. Even if the numbers were way off, things were ten times worse than we describe, you wouldn't be jeopardizing civilization . . . You would change your standards.[17]

The belief that society would adapt to an irradiated world has something perverse in it. In the teeth of appalling odds, comic personae are buoyant—gloriously, transcendently stupid. The connoisseur of *buffo*, Anthony Caputi, credited "stupid stubbornness" with "a toughness [that] . . . affirm[s] life regardless of what anything or anyone, even death, might say." We can see this in Kahn. His was the monomania of an incorrigible optimist. In a televised interview during the tense month of November 1961, when many Americans feared nuclear war might be touched off at any moment in Berlin, James Newman sneered that Kahn's ideas about post-attack recovery were a kind of "idiot arithmetic": "If human beings are not things, then you can't do that kind of arithmetic. That is, if you have a country with 200 million persons in it, and you kill 50 million, the kind of arithmetic that you do where you come out by saying, 'Then I have

150 million left' is a kind of idiot arithmetic that pays no attention to what is meant by the structure of a society—by its social . . . economic . . . and political structure . . . its moral configuration, and the feeling of community that people have with each other." For Newman, Kahn's argument was plainly stupid.[18]

Which brings us back to *buffo:* "Something about stupidity," Caputi continued, "resists the defeat of life . . . [Nature] will not yield, will not take the imprint of civilization; [it] . . . mindlessly resists everything but the impulse to be itself." Kahn's quantification of misery in *OTW* was not a sociological blunder but seemed rather to emanate a philosophy of life. Langer said it best, "What the buffoon really is: the indomitable living creature fending for itself, tumbling and stumbling . . . from one situation into another . . . with or without a thrashing. He is the personified *élan vital* . . . his whole improvised existence has the rhythm of . . . life coping with a world that is forever taking new uncalculated turns, frustrating but exciting."[19]

The symbolic traditions of comedy truly found an agreeable host in Herman Kahn. Even his fatness could stand for nature's swelling resistance to human ends. Obesity signifies "nature's unwillingness to conform to human expectations." A fat body "moves us to a happy knowledge" that life overflows the constraints of any particular arrangement. Whether Kahn willingly played the persona of a jolly fat man, most observers were eager to exploit it. They wrote he was "built like a prize-winning pear," that he was "a brilliant, good-humored, Santa Claus-shaped physicist." He was affable and disarming. "Herman Kahn . . . comes across better in person than in print . . . Face to face, it is hard to quarrel with this man. A lively sort with a Kris Kringle shape." Another was equally perplexed: "A soft spoken, good natured, Santa Claus-shaped physicist . . . with a keen sense of humor, he describes possible nuclear eventualities with millions of casualties with an air of hope for the future."[20]

He seemed not to mind drawing attention to his body. "When the lights have dimmed and the room has quieted, a figure goes to the lectern, a hulking shadow against the picture screen behind him. Across his body the slide projector writes: 'WORLD SEEMS SAFER

TODAY BECAUSE: . . .'" It was to his advantage to be as unthreatening as possible. Journalists tried out catchy metaphors suggested by Kahn's frisky behavior. Which would best describe him, a mind rattling along like a refrigerator-sized Pentagon computer, or a jabbering dynamo? Maybe Kahn was a computer. "His bulky figure, thick-lensed glasses, and staccato speech . . . sputters like the print-out on a high-speed computer." Maybe he was his book. "Into [*OTW*] Kahn has poured all of his personal qualities: a vast physical untidiness; a mind of overpowering force; powers of articulation so rapid as to be almost incomprehensible." By putting the accent on his body—the capering, huffing, *tearing* sight of him—Kahn cast himself as the clumsy intense boy who won the science fair, someone known to everybody, not an evil genius sequestered behind barbed-wire Government Secrets.[21]

Even his velocity could be folded into the comic tradition. Quickening action in farce and slapstick is a survival of the mounting uproar of ritual revels. Kahn couldn't keep still. Sweating freely, he'd peel off his jacket and lumber across the podium, "punctuating his points by pumping his thick right hand and pausing only to take a whale of a breath." He hurtled from topic to joke to scenario to an item in a table to a variation of the same point, to its inverse. He accelerated in a crescendo, urgently piling up ideas, vaulting over every impediment. His very speed attracted fascinated dismay. "Staccato words tumble over one another and his phrases march at an uneven pace . . . engulfing whole phrases, if not sentences, in a gushing sound." A British reporter could barely understand him. "This roly-poly genius is the fastest talker of any American I have ever met. And his mind races even faster than his tongue. He will leave a torrent of a sentence hanging in the air, uncompleted, with a chuckle."[22]

Vulgar comedy is restorative. Caputi observed, "There has probably always been a strain of hysteria in it because of the cheekiness of its affirmation. Superiority! Confidence! Sovereignty! Self-assurance! Mastery!" In the miraculous whirl of life-surviving, life-reproducing, life-adapting, life-enduring nuclear war, Kahn promised deliverance. How tonic, how bracing are the words: "Even though . . . human tragedy would be . . . increased in the postwar world, [it] . . . would not preclude normal and happy lives for the majority of survivors."[23]

Hard-boiled Detectives and Horror Shows

The vulgar motifs of brutality, irreverence, indifference to one's victims, comical torture, and death are unfailingly popular. In the 1930s and '40s Americans feasted on the exploits of gangsters, crime-fighters, and superheroes in pulps, tabloids, the Sunday funnies, radio shows, and movies. By the mid-1930s, over two hundred pulp magazines could be found at a metropolitan newsdealer. The most attractively modern of them featured FBI agents, detectives, and marvelous avengers. A lively, fanciful boy such as Kahn could not have been immune to the charms and shapes of life offered in Bronx's movie palaces, news kiosks, playgrounds, his school cafeteria, and the racks of his aunt's grocery store.

The private eye story debuted in May 1923. From the start, the main character was typically surly, sarcastic, and emotionally blunted. Detective story scribblers cooked up an exaggeratedly flippant, slangy argot for their heroes, which was intended to express the tormented outlook of the veterans of the Great War. During the 1930s, more than 150 different detective titles appeared monthly. In the hard-boiled world, life was mean-spirited and unfair. Heroes grimly justified their brutality, allowing no pity to soften their distaste for their victims. The genre's violence and repartee were imitable and irresistible. As soon as radio became widely available, its shows immediately duplicated pulp offerings. From the early 1930s to the late 1940s, crime radio programs could be heard every night of the week.[24]

The hard-boiled entertainments produced in the decade following World War II were angrier and thuggish. This was true in movies, radio shows, and the comic books and paperback novels that supplanted the pulps. After the war, observed a connoisseur of the genre, "comes the Great Fear . . . [The] wry grimace [was] replaced by abject terror, by a sense of ultimate impotence in a world suddenly full of danger, of nothing but danger." Even Disney animations were vicious. In 1947 the director John Houseman wondered at cartoons that featured "savage and remorseless creatures [who] pursue one another . . . rend, gouge, twist, tear, and mutilate each other with sadistic ferocity."[25]

Since Americans could never have enough of a good thing, following the withdrawal of the pulps a handful of publishers issued hardboiled fiction originals in paperback editions. Their covers typically depicted an alleyway, a bedroom in a flophouse, or a violated female corpse. In the works of Mickey Spillane and other paperback writers, sadism, gratuitous torture, and death abounded. By 1951—a year of McCarthy hearings, war in Korea, and tidings of World War III—lurid sex-and-death images appeared on paperback covers, most of which accentuated the erotic possibilities offered by a dead woman. By 1953 Spillane's novels had sold over 15 million copies.

While crime drama dominated popular culture, horror stories also toyed with death. As a hybrid of science fiction and melodrama, the "weird menace" genre debuted in October 1933. Instead of monsters and the undead, the villains in these tales were deranged scientists, psychotic cultists, and idolaters. By the end of the 1930s, depictions of sadism, necrophilia, gore, and sexual torture were its chief attractions. "Deformities, maimings, disembowelings [were] all presented in explicit, often loving detail." Politicians, reformers, and editorialists launched a decency campaign against the genre, and by 1941 weird menace titles disappeared from the market. But their sanitized cousins, the horror radio shows of the 1930s, struck many of the same notes and were greedily listened to by millions of adults (and pajamaed, tiptoeing children).[26]

The sibilant host of the radio program *Lights Out* opened each show at midnight with the greeting, "Lights out, everybody! This is the witching hour, the hour when dogs howl and evil is let loose on the sleeping world . . . Want to he-e-e-e-ear about it? . . . Then turn out your lights." Its writer, Arch Oboler, wallowed in bodily horrors. His first radio play was so repulsive that thousands of listeners complained to his broadcaster. His sound effects were sickeningly effective. To represent the sound of a man expiring on the electric chair, he fried bacon; for bones splintering, he crunched Life Savers between his teeth; for cannibal dining, he sucked up noodles with a plunger. Stephen King, the horror writer, recalled, "Part of Oboler's genius was that when [a famous *Lights Out* episode] ended, you felt like laughing and throwing up at the same time." Kahn must have listened to these programs in the 1930s. Most girls and boys did, in any sneaky way they could, in defiance of their parents' prohibition.[27]

It can be no surprise that we can root out these genre impulses in *OTW*. Look at the action thriller. A ghostwriter for a pulp title from the 1930s spelled out its driving idea: "The basic concept . . . was that he must save the United States from total destruction in every story, every month. When I was called in to start the series they already had a cover illustration . . . The White House being blown up." In the science fiction pulps, recalled one staff writer, "science seemed like a . . . wonderland that would . . . change the world and make things perfect." In a continuous thread from the genre motif of impending menace to humankind, to the suitcase bombs Leo Szilard fretted about in 1945, to the wily surprise attacks, decoys, "Soviet juvenile delinquent Eskimos," and other disguised raiders in *OTW*, one genre theme that migrated into Kahn's work was the solitary champion on whose resourceful shoulders rested the fate of the United States (the Free World, Planet Earth). Here and there in *OTW* we find wisps of the scientist-sleuth pulp hero. Kahn repeatedly reprised the valiant role played by a clever civilian, uniquely blessed with extraordinary powers of discernment and prognostication, who could smoke out the least visible clues of fatal vulnerabilities in the national defense.[28]

Hard-boiled stories offered an attitude of witty or stoic casualness to suffering that Kahn could emulate. We can hear echoes of this in such stern pronunciamentos as "Desperate conditions demand desperate living." Of course, this was not the only model of masculine daring for working-class boys to imitate, there were also athletes and inventors, Babe Ruth and Thomas Edison. Kahn doubtless would have been as enthralled with the derring-do of brainy rocketeers as he might have been with the austere line taken by unsparing and un-lovely G-men. Nevertheless, his unblushing "willingness to face up to the responsibilities" of engaging in thermonuclear war if necessary resonated deeply with conventional ideas of masculine competence and the popular acceptance of the instrumentality of violence.[29]

Finally, it is worth noting that while one might have supposed, in light of Auschwitz and Hiroshima, that jokes about medical tor-ture, maiming, and agonizing death were taboo in the 1950s, we should keep in mind that the weird menace pulps, horror radio shows and movies, and Charles Addams's cartoons elaborated a repertoire of macabre ideas with which adults in the 1950s and '60s would have been long familiar.[30]

The Postwar Anti-Comic Book Crusade

Five years after the Japanese surrendered, American GIs were fighting once again in Asia. The Korean War seemed like the open-ing round of World War III. Americans looked for scapegoats (which they found in leftists and union organizers) and an outlet for their anxiety (which they found in popular culture). It's worth taking a look at the efforts of decency crusaders to censor crime and horror comic books in the 1950s. Radio broadcasters and Hollywood were already regulated by obscenity laws and censorship boards, largely as a result of their crime and horror content. The comic book, a newcomer in the 1940s, was the only popular medium still free from legal oversight. The anti–comic book campaign paralleled the McCarthyite suppression of dissent. Whereas outspoken speech was effectively silenced in these years, lurid comic books commanded the overwrought attentions of decency crusaders. Powerless to stand against the riptides of the geopolitical cold war, adults stormed the flimsy ramparts of childhood. Children could be indoctrinated in atomic safety and survival, and children's amusements could be sani-tized and made innocent of brutality.

With the opening of the Korean War, Americans developed a bad case of atomic jitters. Children and adults alike were beset with official messages about surviving atomic war. At the height of the World War III scare, in January 1951, the federal civil defense agency distributed more than 20 million copies of its pamphlet *Survival under Atomic Attack*. NBC broadcast a series on atomic war survival seen by 12 million TV-owning households. With radio spots, billboards, newspaper columns, short films, posters, comic books, pamphlets, and traveling exhibits, the Alert America public relations campaign dunned into the collective mind the rudiments of civil defense protection. National evacuation exercises commenced just weeks into the Korean War.

Guided by federal and state recommendations, school districts around the country distributed "corrosion and heat-resisting" dogtags to their students. The duck and cover drills that millions of children (and hundreds of thousands of federal, state, municipal, and industrial workers) rehearsed throughout the decade began in the early 1950s. Teachers were encouraged to twine civil defense into their curricula. For example, a 1953 manual suggested that English teachers assign the following questions for discussion and composition, "Must destruction be our destiny? Will you be the lucky generation—or the last one? What moral problems does use of the A-bomb pose for humanity?" Science, health, home economics, math, gym, social studies, even trade and industrial classes could all incorporate civil defense lessons. Above all, teachers in the atomic age were reminded of their responsibility to build up the mental fitness of their charges. Proper emergency response to atomic attack, "made a fairly natural, commonplace experience," would ensure a psychically robust generation of survivors, should war come. All of this must have aroused panicky feelings. Since public alarm about escalation of the Korean War seemed to be foreclosed by mental hygiene prescriptions of unruffled calm, adults looked for a scapegoat. Comic books could stand in the place of unspeakable war hysteria.[31]

The anti–comic book campaign had all the hallmarks of a moral panic. Would-be censors alleged that comic books enticed children into insolent mischief and delinquency, contributed to "the breakdown of the moral fiber" of society, and were produced by debauched commercial interests that had been allowed to dominate the market without interference from the responsible public. While the reintegration of veterans into society was not explicitly thematized in their propaganda, nonspecific anxieties about family disharmony were slogans around which the reformers rallied.[32]

Ultimately the decency crusade boomeranged in the late 1950s and early '60s with a sharp, exultant reversal of taste. This was critical to the reception of *OTW*. One cannot fathom the explosive glee and disgust aroused by sick jokes without tying them to the struggle over the limits of acceptable speech articulated by moral reformers during the first half of the 1950s. This pulse of defiance and relief is something audiences would have heard in Kahn's briefing. Since other voices breaking into speech rang with the same note of satisfaction, it would have been hard not associate his performance with the sick jokes and sick comedians surfacing around the same time.

Vulgar entertainments were still going strong during the war and after it. In 1942 Philip Wylie blasted America's addiction to violence. "Lustfully, you consume the news . . . of ax murders, kidnappings, drug addiction, police beatings, lynchings, stonings, riots, revolutions, battles, tortures, [and] sodomies." While adults soaked up the sensations of crime and punishment, another critic observed in 1949 that virtually every American child experienced *as a daily imaginative practice* the sensation of torturing and murdering someone. Boys and girls who were six years old in 1938 had "by now absorbed an absolute minimum of eighteen thousand pictorial beatings, shootings, stranglings, blood-puddles, and torturings-to-death, from comic books alone, identifying . . . with the heroic beater, shooter, strangler, blood-letter, and/or torturer in every case." Whether or not violent comic books produced hordes of psychopaths was an open question, but surely they patterned the emotional and symbolic life of a generation. "Twenty million children [have] been brought up on violence, and sleep it, and eat it, and dream it, and love it to the marrow of their bones—and therefore can never love anything or anyone else."[33]

The comic book industry took off after the war. In 1948, 239 titles were released, twice as many as in 1946. By 1953, over 500 titles were offered for sale, with an average monthly circulation of 68 million copies. Patterned after newsreels, the all-crime comic book *Crime Does Not Pay* debuted in June 1942. Its host, Mr. Crime, breezily introduced each account of an actual murder with a comic flourish. By 1948, its sales had boosted to over a million copies per issue. Crime comics were as vile as the very worst of the hard-boiled films. They typically illustrated torture leading inexorably to murder. Always from the point of view of the killer, victims were objects of contempt or indifference. Rape, prostitution, the dope racket, violence against women, infanticide, and mutilation were its stock-in-trade. For example, in 1947 the first two pages of a story from *True Crime Comics* featured drug injections, machine-gun violence, burning bodies, and a hypodermic needle poised over a bound woman's eye.[34]

In 1950 William Gaines, publisher of EC comics, introduced a comic book version of the weird menace pulps. *Vault of Horror, Crypt of Terror,* and *Haunt of Fear* quickly become industry leaders. As children, both Gaines and his partner had adored the radio thrillers. When they adapted weird menace to comic book form, they kept the spooky host. The Crypt Keeper, the Vault Keeper, and the Old Witch—collectively called the GhouLunatics—presented the stories as playful sport, addressing readers with punning, silly commentary. For example, from *The Haunt of Fear* the Old Witch tittered, "Welcome to the Haunt of Fear! This is your Delirium-Dietician, the Old Witch, cooking up another revolting recipe! Ready? Got your drool cups fastened under your dribbling chins? Got your shrouds tied neatly around your necks? Then I'll begin dishing out the terror-tidbit I call . . . 'Horror We? How's Bayou?'" Gaines wanted laughs. Horror comics should be read out loud. He snatched each new story from the desk of his artists and performed them with great cacklings and chortles. "This was the fun part." A colleague recalled, "We always thought of our work as being theatrical . . . it had to read right."[35]

In the first year of EC's horror line, Gaines's business manager recalled, "Break even was 36 or 27%. Our magazines were coming in at 89% . . . 93% . . . even *Life* wasn't doing that well!" Other publishers scampered to add horror titles to their lists. By 1953, 150 horror comics were published monthly. Like the fans of the hard-boiled genre, adults pushed the craze for weird menace; 54 percent of the comic book market consisted of adults, which meant that more people were reading horror titles than *Reader's Digest* or *The Saturday Evening Post*.[36]

A decency crusade coalesced in 1948, when reformers hit upon the idea that comic books inspired juvenile crime. This displaced concern appeared at a moment when demobilized servicemen were being reintegrated into formerly female-headed households. Churches, women's and men's clubs, PTAs, and city councils mobilized crusades throughout the country. In September 1948 the Los Angeles County Board of Supervisors adopted an ordinance banning the sale of crime comics to children, punishable by a $500 fine or six months in prison. Within days the American Municipal Association announced that similar restrictions had passed in fifty cities. The Catholic National Organization for Decent Literature (NODL) and the Committee on the Evaluation of Comic Books drew up lists of offensive titles and lobbied newsdealers to withdraw them or face boycotts. From 1952 to 1954 civic, religious, and veterans' organizations agitated for comic book regulation. They testified before city or county councils and boards of supervisors. They organized boycotts, wrote letters, and distributed pamphlets to libraries, schools, and churches. At their annual assemblies, the American Legion, the General Federation of Women's Clubs, Amvets, the National Council of Juvenile Court Judges, and NODL all passed resolutions endorsing the suppression of crime and horror titles.[37]

On April 21, 22, and June 4, 1954, Senator Estes Kefauver presided over televised hearings investigating the comic book industry. One of the most prominent critics of comic books, the psychiatrist Frederic Wertham, testified that Superman induced "fantasies of sadistic joy" in normal children "in seeing other people punished over and over again while you yourself remain immune." He was seconded by the director of mental health services for the Domestic Court of New York City, who affirmed that the majority of children ordered to his clinic were comic book addicts.[38]

"Piffle!" sulked EC publisher Gaines, who also appeared before the committee. "I do not believe that anything that has ever been written can make a child hostile, over-aggressive, or delinquent . . . Delinquency is a product of the real environment in which a child lives—and not of the fiction he reads." Comic book pleasures were subjective, even non-arguable. He spluttered, "It would be just as difficult to explain the harmless thrill of a horror story to a Dr. Wertham as it would be to explain the sublimity of love to a frigid old maid. Pleasure is what we sell . . . Entertaining reading has never harmed anyone!" Rather than dwelling on the few boys who imitated comic-book hangings, theft, torture, and murder, he pointed to the masses of youngsters who devoured crime and horror stories every month. Had they *all* become monsters? The decency crusaders saw "dirty, twisted, sneaky, vicious, perverted little monsters who use the comics as blueprints for action." It was ridiculous to be afraid of boys and girls. "Do we think our children so evil, so vicious, so single-minded that it takes but a comic magazine story of murder to set them to murder?"

Gaines did not find a single friend on the committee. He was an outsider. Like Kahn, he was Jewish, fat, and vulgar. He was regarded as a deviant, little better than a pornographer.

> MR. BEASER: Is there any limit you can think of that you
> would not put in a magazine just because you thought a
> child should not see or read about it?
>
> MR. GAINES: No, I wouldn't say that there is any limit . . .
> My only limits are . . . what I consider good taste . . .
>
> SEN. KEFAUVER [HOLDING UP MAGAZINE]: Here is
> your May 22 issue [of *Crime SuspenStories.*] This seems
> to be a man with a bloody ax holding a woman's head up
> which has been severed from her body. Do you think that
> is in good taste?
>
> MR. GAINES: Yes, sir, I do. For the cover of a horror comic.
> A cover in bad taste . . . might be defined, as holding the
> head a little higher so that the neck could be seen drip-
> ping blood from it and moving the body over a little fur-

ther so that the neck of the body could be seen to be
bloody.

SEN. KEFAUVER: You have blood coming out her mouth.

MR. GAINES: A little.

SEN. KEFAUVER: . . . I think most adults are shocked by
that. Here is the July issue [of *Crime SuspenStories*]. It
seems to be a man with a woman in a boat and he is
choking her to death here with a crowbar. Is that in good
taste?

MR. GAINES: I think so.

MR. HANNOCH: How could it be worse?

"I sat there," groaned Gaines, "like a punch-drunk fighter, getting
pummeled." It was great copy. It made front-page news. Civil liberties could not compete with the welfare of the nation's children.[39]

Realizing that he stood to lose his company, Gaines proposed that
the industry band together into a trade association. Representatives
of eight publishing houses attended his meeting. Tossing a bone to
Congress, they quickly agreed to withdraw the bloodiest of their
crime and horror titles. Gaines was stunned. "I was the guy who
started the damn association," he gasped, "and . . . the first thing they
did was ban the words 'weird,' 'horror' and 'terror' . . . Those were
my three big words!" The Comics Code of the new Comics Magazine Association of America proscribed "scenes of horror, excessive
bloodshed, gory or gruesome crimes, depravity, lust, sadism and
masochism . . . the walking dead, torture, vampires, ghouls, cannibalism and werewolfism." Gaines capitulated. EC retired its horror and
crime lines.[40]

By January 1956 the General Federation of Women's Clubs declared the campaign a great success. Thirteen states had passed laws
to restrict or ban crime comics, and monthly sales for all comic books
had dropped from 80 million several years before to 40 million. By
1962 comic book sales dwindled to 350,000 copies sold *per year*.[41]

Within a few years, comic art swept back into vogue, and by the
mid 1960s it was ubiquitous. Not only did every kind of advertising

medium shower the public with comic strips, but everything else gamboled in four-color dumb-show: billboards, book jackets, films, TV shows, dolls, bubble bath, curtains, wallpaper, jigsaw puzzles, pajamas, lipstick, and hostess aprons. For one awful moment in 1966, it looked as though every possible thing had assumed the shape and style of comic book art.[42]

Mad Magazine and Other Sick Jokes

In 1956 the author of a *Reader's Digest* article crowed with satisfaction over the newly decent fare offered by comic books, thanks to the sober strength of parents who had joined together to force reform upon a reluctant industry. But it was only "an uneasy truce in the campaign against moral debauchery," he warned. "To maintain it, we must continue to exercise constant vigilance." The way forward was an energetic redirection of young people's taste toward more wholesome amusement. *Mad* magazine was hardly what he had in mind. One of the best-selling magazines of the second half of the 1950s began as a sideline to Bill Gaines's crime and horror comic book empire. In the summer of 1952 one of his artists, Harvey Kurtzman, threw the premiere issue of *Mad* magazine together as a parody of horror comics. The first three issues sold poorly, but Gaines decided to continue *Mad*, using the profits of his other EC series, just as he published *Weird Science* and *Weird Fantasy* at a loss. "We just did what we liked to do—things that amused us. And we were sure kids would respond to it."[43]

Within a year, *Crazy, Insane, Whack, Nuts, Riot, Flip, Get Lost, Bug House, Mad House,* and *Eh!* jostled *Mad* on kiosk shelves. When Gaines folded his horror and crime titles in 1954, he continued publishing *Mad, Panic* (a *Mad* spin-off), *Weird Science-Fantasy,* and *Two-Fisted Tales.* The only title that sold consistently well was *Mad.* In July 1955 Gaines rid himself of CMMA censorship by reformatting *Mad* as a satirical magazine. But Hugh Hefner, the publisher of *Playboy,* planning to publish his own comic monthly to compete with *Mad,* lured Kurtzman and several others away from EC. The new staff now assembled for *Mad* were artists who had worked on Gaines's old horror titles.

The conjunction of *Playboy* and *Mad* in 1956 is fortuitous. They were lumped together in one of the first notices of *Playboy*. By 1968 *Mad* and *Playboy* were recognized as the "smash-hit phenomena of the postwar magazine business." Just as *Playboy* flaunted irreverence toward the oversold merits of marriage, church, and children, *Mad* was just as brazen. It sneered at politicians, celebrities, parents, advertising, movies, television, and, on occasion (but not regularly and not particularly deftly), the cold war. In almost every issue, *Mad* mocked the chirps and blather of advertising rhetoric. In one piece, it restyled the cold war as a public relations campaign.

> Do you feel left out of things? Is the fast-moving Arab world passing you by? Then why not do what so many Middle Eastern nations are doing and join NASSER'S FRIENDSHIP CLUB. You'll be surrounded with friends who will fill your life with excitement and intrigue! You'll be swept off your feet by the rising tide of Arab Nationalism! No longer will you feel isolated from your neighbors. Everyone's joining. Why not you? Nasser's Friendship Club. Cairo, Egypt. Branch Offices in Damascus and Baghdad.
>
> A Rugged Outdoor Life is Yours! At Fidel Castro's Cuban Health Camp. Are you 18 to 35 years of age, and tired of your stuffy life in the city? Does a holiday in the open appeal to you? If your answer is "yes," then join the thousands of happy rebels at Castro's Health Camp! Tent out under the stars overlooking gay, glamorous Havana! Commune with nature! Explore the countryside! Discover the excitement of foraging for food, raiding arsenals for ammunition, kidnapping hostages! The perfect place to get away from it all! Nobody (even including yourself) will know exactly where you are![44]

Mad energetically taunted the decency crusaders, but only rarely yoked them with cold war themes. Its parody of *Pravda*, the Soviet newspaper, attacked the magazine's mascot, Alfred E. Neuman, for being "responsible for deceiving millions of unsuspecting US readers": "Our unsavory American for today is Alfred E. Neuman . . .

[He] is the 'brains' behind one of America's most insidious publications, which cunningly distracts its exploited readers from the misery and deprivation around them by filling their minds with propaganda-filled nonsense under the guise of humor."[45]

Mad was a hit. Without carrying any advertising, by the end of the decade it sold well over a million copies per issue. Its core audience was teenagers and college students. *Time* magazine, both respectable and a respecter of business success, gushed that "*Mad* is a refreshingly impudent reaction against . . . 20th century hucksterism, its hopped-up sensationalism, its visible and hidden persuaders." Happily awed by yet another reversal of fortune at EC, Gaines chuckled, "All I can say to explain it is something glib like, 'Everyone is under a strain, and some sort of comic relief is a good thing.' If we knew exactly what we were doing right, we'd do more of it." By 1960 "Alfred E. Neuman for President" posters bobbed up at a Goldwater rally at the Republican National Convention.[46]

Inevitably, observers pondered the magazine's social significance. The critic Dwight Macdonald was disappointed that *Mad* pandered to adolescent cynicism. For the sarcastic young, the adult world was "full of hypocrisy and pretense, so governed by formulas." Its comedy was unrelievedly vulgar. "It speaks the same language, aesthetically and morally, as the media it satirizes; it is as tasteless as they are, and even more violent." No, no, *Mad* was good news, howled another. It meant that "the organization-man, conformist-man wave is not engulfing the younger generation." This last was too much for yet another observer, who protested that *Mad* only affected an attitude of scurrilous worldliness. Its smirk conveyed "a sense of defeat so total" that the very smile betokened surrender. *Mad*'s grin "was, in the precise meaning of that all-American phrase, a 'shit-eating smile,' borne by the combat-fatigued veteran of Dad's ad culture."[47]

Analyzing the data from a survey of readers, a psychologist observed that his respondents did not include "major social issues of our time, like desegregation and atomic war," as topics for satire. He wondered whether "teenagers may be so fatalistic about nuclear war that they could not face even a satirical treatment of the subject."

Perhaps their "sensitivity . . . to the near-intolerable" was the reason for their sick humor. The absence of social criticism in *Mad* could be construed as evidence that by the late 1950s the atomic age had made everything but itself vulnerable to ridicule. Concerning nuclear war, words formulating its possibility or challenging deterrence were unsayable for all but the most audacious or politically marginal of Americans.[48]

At the same time that *Mad* was making a hit, a fashion in joke-telling also flowered. It was called "the sick joke," and it was a sign of the times. "On college campuses and grade-school playgrounds, youngsters—and many of their elders—are laughing at a new kind of joke that has spread across the nation with appalling thoroughness," reported *Time* magazine in 1957. Sick jokes went like this:

MOMMY, I HATE MY SISTER'S GUTS.
SHUT UP AND EAT WHAT'S PUT IN FRONT OF YOU.

MOMMY, MOMMY, DADDY JUST POISONED MY
    KITTY.
DON'T CRY DEAR. MAYBE HE HAD TO DO IT.
NO HE DIDN'T. HE PROMISED ME I COULD!

MRS. BROWN, CAN SHELDON COME OUT AND PLAY?
NOW, YOU CHILDREN KNOW HE HAS LEPROSY.
THEN CAN WE COME IN AND WATCH HIM ROT?[49]

Time adopted a benign attitude toward jokes fixated on amputation, disease, cannibalism, sadism, and death. They were no worse than the Little Willie and Little Audrey jokes before them, and no doubt the forerunner of humor that would amuse future children. But they did represent cold war sensibilities. "They strike a responsive chord in our tense, violence racked age." Turning to the cultural authorities of the day, *Time* consulted a child psychiatrist and a popular author for clues to their larger meaning. Dr. Martha Wolfenstein obliged with the idea that these jokes flouted the injunction to "constantly . . . sympathize with human misery in a century that has had more than its share." Philip Wylie, the scorching editorialist, added, "We use the sick jokes to wipe away a little of the burden of terror put on us by living in this age."[50]

Between September and December of 1958 the folklorist Brian Sutton-Smith collected 155 sick jokes from young people. They frolicked with ideas of murdering relatives and friends, mutilation, corpses, beasts, excrement, indifference to the young, degenerate parents, afflictions, disease, religion, and famous people.[51] The editor of a wildly popular series of sick joke anthologies underscored its therapeutic benefit: "Laugh at it, no matter how sad . . . and you'll feel less worried and better able to handle trouble . . . So don't run to a psychiatrist if you find yourself laughing at the sickest of the sick. It just means that there's something wrong with you—the same thing that's wrong with all of us!"[52]

Folklorists Alta Jablow and Carl Withers compared children's jokes and riddles they recorded in 1962 to those they had gathered twenty-five years earlier. They were struck by the changes in children's wordplay. Their stories were now pointedly meaningless. "The stress today . . . seems to be on an enormous and rapidly accelerating elaboration of verbal nonsense." Circular and endless jokes were popular, such as "That's life! What's life? A magazine. How much. Ten cents. I've only got a nickel. That's life . . . " Jablow and Withers observed that these jokes "are parodies of narrative art, substituting . . . boredom for narrative interest, and hoax for point." Children also delighted in absurd riddles:

WHAT DO A DOG AND RATTLESNAKE HAVE IN
    COMMON?
THEY BOTH DON'T PLAY THE SAXOPHONE.

HOW IS A HOUSE LIKE A MOUSE?
THEY BOTH DON'T RIDE BICYCLES.

The folklorists interpreted these as fantasies of an enigmatic world lashing witless humanity. The commonest item they heard on the playgrounds of New York in 1962 was a heartbreaking sample of the atomic unsayable called the World War III joke:

KNOCK, KNOCK.
WHO'S THERE?
THERE IS NO ANSWER.[53]

The Sickniks

By 1957 and '58 American teens and young adults greedily snatched *Mad* (and *Playboy*) off the racks of newsdealers. The frontiers of permissible public culture had begun to shift. But the campaign to censor vulgar comic books in the early 1950s must be bundled with the McCarthyite suppression of political dissent. Only by remembering what it meant to hear comic and political voices defy proscription can we grasp the sensibilities of Herman Kahn's wrathful, snuffling, cheering publics.

In January 1952 Supreme Court Justice William Douglas accused McCarthy and his minions of having "magnified and exalted" the threat of domestic Communism "far beyond its realities." His tribunals had sapped democracy of its meaning, smothered debate, goaded "thoughtful people to despair," and quashed the skepticism natural to every rising generation. It was youth's glory to "cast doubts on our politics, challenge our inarticulate major premises, put the light on our prejudices, and expose our inconsistencies." But America's youngsters had been cowed; they were "largely holding [their] tongue."[54]

In 1951 it seemed that there were no young comedians on the scene. At the height of the World War III scare, people were so wound up that playfulness seemed improper. "No man wants to be accused of laughing . . . during a wake." Indulgence in comedy was boorish; it looked like fiddling while Rome burned. And yet society could not do without laughter. "Where are these younger humorists?" one writer cried out forlornly. "Come out, come out, wherever you are."[55]

One of the few voices that did pipe up was a mathematics graduate student named Tom Lehrer. As an undergraduate at Harvard, he had performed topical satirical songs at parties to such acclaim that he eventually appeared in Boston cafes and nightclubs. "When [Lehrer] finished, the audience happily howled for more." *Newsweek* applauded the spectacle of Lehrer "chanting and thumping his way through a repertory which offers something for every depraved taste." His was a college wit: shrewd, puckish, but not scalding.[56]

By the mid-1950s McCarthy was vanquished, *Mad* and *Playboy* were unmolested by posses of decency crusaders, and sick jokes were traded among clutches of youngsters in schoolyards and college dormitories. What was missing was satire about segregation. Civil rights agitation had begun to unsettle white public culture, and Jim Crow was as taboo for comedy as atomic annihilation. By 1961 young people considered jokes about race and the bomb unsayable to strangers and adults.[57]

Only Lenny Bruce, Dick Gregory, and Jules Feiffer dared to joke about civil rights. In a cartoon published in 1959, Feiffer lumped together civil rights agitation with atomic anxiety:

> When my husband began to build our shelter, he was going to build two of them. One for the family and one for our hired girl. Same dimensions. Same material exactly like ours in every detail . . . Well you should have heard that girl talk when I told her the news. I don't know where she picked up some of the ideas she has. She's been with us ten years and never had them before . . . Well you can't argue with a stubborn mind so we gave in. Good girls are too hard to get these days. So I told her that . . . during the next alert she could join us in our shelter . . . And suddenly . . . [she] changed her mind. She would not share our imperialist air raid shelter! She was now a neutralist and wanted a separate air raid shelter . . . We lectured

her about democracy and quoted Abraham Lincoln but in the end we had to build a shelter for us and a shelter for her. Good girls are too hard to find these days.[58]

Dick Gregory also joined the two unsayables:

I love that expression "survival kit." Up till recently, we used to have survival kits in Mississippi. Ten "Yassuh, bosses" and a shuffle.

This international situation raises some interesting ethical problems. Like, if [Governor Orville] Faubus is driving through one of our neighborhoods when they drop the bomb, would he go into a colored shelter? . . . And if he did—should we let him in? . . . "Orville, stop pounding on that door! Don't you know it's three o'clock in the morning?"

They always talk about Russia dropping *the* bomb. I got news. If it happens, it's gonna be more like the *10,000 bombs*. There'll be a 100-megaton bomb for New York, a 50-megaton one for Chicago, a 30-megaton for Cleveland—and a quarter-megaton job for Grosse Point . . . I figure a quarter-megaton 'cause it doesn't take much for those people to go to pieces . . . Like one of us looking at a For Sale sign.[59]

In the spring of 1957 a mass of articles appeared diagnosing the crisis in comedy. "Good laughs—rich, full-bellied yoks and boffs— are . . . hard to find," mourned *Life*. Everybody in the television business agreed that the jokes weren't funny and people weren't in the mood to be amused. "Audiences lack . . . a genuine interest in any comedy," the comedian Sid Caesar complained. "We need a new breed of writers to supply the jokes, and a new breed of people to enjoy them."[60]

The poet Kenneth Rexroth thundered that the crisis in comedy was symptomatic of the hypocrisy of capitalist public culture: "The accepted, official version of anything is most likely false and . . . all authority is based on fraud." People were groggy and timid. Comedy in such a society would have to be insipid. "Like the movies, nothing ever happens that would offend any conceivable group . . . or in any way interfere with the sale of any commodity whatsoever. Nothing important must happen—it would be bad for business."[61]

Many others agreed. "These days we seem to be so insecure that we can't bear to be laughed at," frowned another observer, Jerome Beatty, Jr. "Our desperate materialism and strange values . . . leave no room . . . for a joke which might release our tensions for a moment and let us see ourselves as we are." He blamed censorship intended to forestall letters of complaint. The consequence was, in the case of editorial cartoons, "an elaborate system of institutionalized taboos that have destroyed . . . cartoon's power to make any kind of realistic . . . or funny comment on our society." Political humor was especially forbidden since it was "open to too many interpretations." And like Rexroth, Beatty attributed the mawkishness of mass culture to the media's dependence "on the sensitivities of [its] advertisers."[62]

The exception was *The Washington Post*, whose editors allowed the cartoonist Herbert Block to persecute whatever he pleased. He mocked atomic, scientific, military, and foreign relations secrecy; arms control talks; the Atomic Energy Commission's preposterous propaganda about the "clean" bomb; President Eisenhower's televised address regarding the leaked Gaither Report; *Sputnik* and the state of science education in American schools. His colleagues celebrated Block's fearlessness. In 1957 they elected him cartoonist of the year. In 1958 they voted him best editorial cartoonist. But as much as they admired Block, very few cartoonists emulated him.[63]

When the annual Gridiron party wheeled around in 1958, it was a big deal. "Though this happens once a year," James Reston whooped in *The New York Times*, "laughter in Washington is still news." Washington was otherwise unbearable. "Our . . . magistrates are a flat and cheerless lot." Yes, it was true that Eisenhower smiled, yes, public servants tended to be "militantly" optimistic, and yes there were a few good jokes at the Gridiron. But politicians "do not really have much fun." How could good government survive without merriment? (Lenny Bruce later muttered, "Up till now, Presidents have never seemed like real people to me. I could never visualize Eisenhower even kissing his wife. Not on the mouth anyway. He didn't even go to the toilet either, he just stood there. He didn't even go to bed, he just sat up all night with his clothes on, worrying.")[64]

Americans, one cartoonist observed, "try to please everyone . . . and try not to hurt anyone's feelings." John Sisk suggested that the absence of satire in the cold war was due to "the sectarian touchiness of the pluralist society." Civic discourse in a democracy could be maintained only by wary politeness. Contrary to subsequent clichés about the consensus society of the 1950s, Sisk described his present—March 1958—as a moment "when there is little community of moral and religious values." Social harmony was achieved by exaggerated fastidiousness. "The vociferous minorities protect not only themselves but one another . . . out of a common awareness of the importance of co-existence: which is also a shared fear of the dissension and chaos that is always in potential." Satire, critique, frank disagreement had to be sacrificed to social cohesion.[65]

The problem wasn't pluralism, observed the writer Frank O'Connor, but coercive emotionalism. It steered understanding into the honeypot of smothering empathy and away from conflict: "American thought is drenched in a syrupy liberalism. Who could be more liberal than . . . psychologists who . . . warn us to understand rather than condemn?" Maudlin kindliness in public speech was reinforced by ad campaigns in the same style. Since radio, TV, and film production was so expensive, "no poor writer could get near it" with material "liable to offend anybody."[66]

This was the new American orthodoxy. The political culture imposed "a tolerance so profound that it is not . . . entirely unlike terror," chimed in Gore Vidal. "One dares not raise one's voice against any religion, idea or even delinquency if it is explicable by a therapist." He wondered if the "stern tolerance" of society had prepared the ground for an American dictator. Who would dare to criticize him? You wouldn't see one on television. "Sorry, the fellow has a lot of admirers; yes, we know he's bad news but you can't hurt people's feelings, you know. And . . . well, he could be right; after all a lot of people seem to agree with him."[67]

Harold Clurman, the theater director, suggested that anticommunist politics had driven attention inward "as if to say 'please mind your own business and let me mind mine.'" If people were listless, it wasn't because they were subdued by a threat with real teeth, "now that McCarthy has passed away," it was because their energies were "transfixed, stuck, spiritually immobilized."[68]

Jules Feiffer made this spiritual immobilization the foundation of his art. Psychoanalytic introspection was the butt of much of his scorn. It robbed people of their good sense. "Answers come more easily now," he wrote in a squib in 1958. "All the old problems become familiar and time-worn . . . Neighbors drop by to confess. No one feels guilty any longer because who in this crazy . . . H-bomb world can be blamed for having problems? The idea is to look into one's self. The whole idea is to dig." While most of Feiffer's cartoons explored the doomed scramble for romance, he also mocked the cold war.

> The item on the agenda, gentlemen, is the fallout bit. Our client isn't happy with our campaign. The public is negative fallout conscious . . . I have here the outline of a "Fallout is Good For You" saturation campaign. It includes such items as "I like Fallout" buttons, decals inscribed with "Your Government Knows Best"—a TV spec called "I Fell for Fallout." And as a capper—a "Mr. and Mrs. Mutation" contest—designed to change the concept of beauty in the American mind.
>
> But what about the scientists, chief?
>
> No problem. We'll say they're "organized" and have them all subpoenaed. It's one of our most successful sales devices.[69]

Feiffer was especially attuned to the currents of contempt, longing, solitude, and dread coursing through daily life. With the exceptions of Charles Addams's cartoons in *The New Yorker* and Charles

Schulz's angst-ridden children in *Peanuts,* this had rarely been a subject for cartoonists. Feiffer was closer to the great nineteenth-century European caricaturists than American humorists. *Time's* appreciation faltered: "Many of Feiffer's best cartoons are not funny at all, instead sting with bitterness and poignancy." He concentrated steadily on the savagery of the civil rights struggle, on world affairs, and the possibility of nuclear war. In 1961 he remarked, "Lately I've tried to satirize self-hypocrisy at its most serious level—the level of authority . . . when it's someone lying in a position of power, then it becomes more serious and frightening."[70]

Toward the end of 1957 Mort Sahl stepped into the tiny spotlight of a hipster club in North Beach, the hungry i. Clutching a newspaper, free-associating in a potpourri of erudite allusions, current affairs, and slang, Sahl was something new. "I'm an intellectual in this field by default," he explained. "This is an era of . . . apathy, even among much of the Left." His material was political. "For a while, every time the Russians threw an American in jail, the Un-American Activities Committee would retaliate by throwing an American in jail too." "[Hitler's] painting now and wants to be judged solely on the basis of his art . . . I don't want you to think these college people were impressed with him just because he was Hitler. It was more the fact that he's from Europe." "I'm not a comedian," he insisted. "I don't build jokes around myself. There's too much to say about everything else, and nobody is saying it." He always closed with the taunt, "Are there any groups we haven't offended yet?" Sahl did, in fact, fluster television executives. He had signed contracts with CBS and NBC, but not only did he not appear on TV, he didn't make it past the censors to the rehearsal stage. He scoffed at the whole affair. "They're afraid, and unfocused fear is insane. I told one guy at an agency, 'You can't be afraid of everything.' 'But we are!' he said." "The ultimate taboo," according to Sahl, "is not against racial jokes or off-color jokes but against intellectual content."[71]

In his heyday, Sahl was elevated to major significance. A *New Yorker* profile opened with the opinion that "Mort Sahl is almost certainly the most widely acclaimed and best-paid nihilist ever produced by Western civilization." He preened himself on being an iconoclast and truth-teller. His producer declared excitedly: "He is the voice of mankind in the atomic age. When he says he doesn't know whether the approaching unidentified aircraft is going to drop a hydrogen bomb or spell out Pepsi-Cola in skywriting, he speaks for all of us!"[72]

The persona of Lenny Bruce was far less wholesome. He styled himself as a dissolute jazz artist, concocting parodies of celebrities, movie characters, and politicians, sloshing together Yiddish with drug-culture dialect, all spasmodically delivered in blocks of an urgent New York drawl. Comparing the two, the critic Nat Hentoff reflected, "Unlike Mort Sahl, whose heaviest ammunition is aimed at the Republicans, Lenny Bruce . . . cuts beneath politics into the daily evasions of what he terms 'first-plateau liberals.'" Bruce skewered adoring middle-class liberals as well as conservative politicians, southern bigots, and anticommunists. "All my humor is based upon destruction and despair," Bruce assured *Newsweek.* His material was more caustic than Sahl's. "I've been accused of bad taste," he shrugged, "and I'll go down to my grave accused of it and always by the same people." In his autobiography, Bruce spoofed the emcees who nervously introduced his act in the 1950s:

> The owner decides to cushion me with his introduction: "Ladies and gentlemen, the star of our show, Lenny Bruce, who, incidentally, is an ex-GI and, uh, a hell of a good performer, folks, and a great kidder, know what I mean? It's all a bunch of silliness up here and he doesn't mean what he says. He kids about the Pope and about the Jewish religion, too, and the colored people and the white people—it's all a silly, make-believe world. And he's a hell of a nice guy, folks. He was at the Veterans Hospital today doing a show for the boys. And here he is—his mom's out here tonight, too, she hasn't seen him in a couple of years—she lives here in town . . . Now, a joke is a joke, right, folks? What the hell. I wish that you'd try to

cooperate. And whoever has been sticking ice picks in the
tires outside, he's not funny. Now Lenny may kid about narcotics, homosexuality, and things like that . . ." And *he* gets
walkouts.[73]

In 1960 Bruce acknowledged, "I try to say as much as I can get
away with and still make the audience laugh." With increasing notoriety he grew bolder. By 1962 a journalist marveled, "No attitude
seemed too sacred for Bruce to lampoon, no word too improper for
him to utter; he seemed perfectly willing to say absolutely anything."
The censorship issues that hovered around Bruce were always more
serious than Sahl's skirmishes with TV. Bruce occasionally swatted at
the cold war: "The bomb, the bomb—oh, thank God for the bomb.
The final threat is: 'I'll get my brother—the bomb.' Out of all the
teaching and bullshitting, that's the only answer we have." But his
chief topics were sex, narcotics, white bigotry, anti-Semitism, desire
across the color line, homosexuality, incest, and pedophilia. Needless
to say, Bruce was arrested repeatedly on obscenity charges.[74]

It looked like "the last days of Rome—all this horror and mayhem
in humor." The sicknik mixture of "jolly ghoulishness and . . . a personal and highly disturbing hostility toward all the world" skated so
close to atrocity "that audiences wince even as they laugh." Were the
sicknik comics really social critics? While their publicity hailed these
"stinging social satirists who were plunging hungrily into dissections
of the delusions and evasions of us all," for Nat Hentoff most of it did
not add up to political satire. He roundly seconded Feiffer's dismissal
of the newly defiant style. Feiffer had observed, "Our society, even
with all of its obvious freedom, is so rigidly structured today that it's
easy for an artist to feel daring and nonconformist and still stand for
nothing." Only Lenny Bruce did not pander to the fashion for saucy
bravado. His future biographer remarked that "Bruce seems immune
from that permissiveness that is in the end perhaps more subversive
of true protest than censorship."[75]

In a thoughtful essay, Benjamin DeMott added his suspicions

that sicknik comedy barely attained the political force of real dissent. Its fans marked themselves off as appreciative insiders by excluding the groundlings "who understand nothing but the . . . dictionary definitions of the words said." But undifferentiated irony wasn't critique, he objected; it was vastly flimsier. The mistake was to think it a sharp instrument, when in fact it blunted the degrees of badness of its targets. Sick comedians blurred historical particulars into a murky continuum. The result was a fugitive rejection of everything. While seeming to throw down a challenge to the status quo (and flattering an audience who eagerly exchanged ticket money for the privilege of belonging to the naysayers), sick ridicule offered little more than the pose of mastery; it evaded the psychic burden of the atomic age, "the desire to know and act, and the disabling fear that it is too late to know and act." But at least sick comedy wasn't feeble. Its guffaws invested its audience in the rugged identity of "Patriot as Laughing Man." No strains of self-pity quavered in this American laughter.[76]

By 1963 sick humor had quickened into a fad. The sickniks had scores of imitators. "By now, so completely have the so-called 'sick' comics caught on," began an appreciation of Bruce, that "it no longer requires daring, originality, or courage to attack sacred cows . . . Such things are done . . . in diluted form virtually on every network."[77]

Political Humor

In 1961 some improvisational actors performed a sketch of an idle soldier who begins to play with a missile control panel. He closes his eyes, pokes out a finger, and begins pressing buttons. It was "simultaneously hilarious and terrifying," Nat Hentoff shuddered. "One is forced into a nightmarish realization of how impotent we are to save ourselves." The crisis in comedy had surely passed. Attending a convention of newspaper editors, James Reston rejoiced in his colleagues' mirth. Only months after the resolution of the Berlin Crisis, "Somehow they don't quite believe the world is coming to an end on Monday, so they've come away here to relax and get a little perspective.

Jokes that would have split the editors in the McCarthy period now get a big laugh across the entire political spectrum."[78]

Little more than two months after the denouement of the Cuban Missile Crisis in October 1962, Russell Baker echoed the idea. "One of the Kennedy Administration's brighter achievements in 1962 has been its restoration of the sound of laughter to the American scene . . . All the evidence suggests a country almost eager for any excuse to laugh." Political satire was fashionable. "Night club satirists are tilting at everything from John Birch to Nikita Khrushchev." Whereas Reston suggested that Americans were entitled to a spell of relief, Baker interpreted the mood as gallows humor: "Ten years ago Americans feared their neighbors. Nowadays they are more worried about more cosmic ménages, and the jest usually comes easier when the odds are fearful."[79]

Whatever the reason, political satire had become tolerable. Even nuclear humor—still taboo for the young readers of *Mad*—had become sayable. In 1957 two Yale students, Victor Navasky at the Law School (and future editor of *The Nation*) and Jacob Needleman, a philosophy grad student, founded *The Monocle*, a "Leisurely Quarterly of Political Satire." Its first issue of 500 copies was gobbled up— nice enough figures for the equivalent of a college humor magazine. Appearing quarterly, the magazine reached a circulation of 15,000 to 20,000 copies. With 5,000 subscribers and wide representation in bookstores, *The Monocle* developed "an underground following all over the country." It attracted all kinds of contributors: the art editor for *Mad* drew something occasionally, a foreign service officer dashed off stories about a State Department nudnik, the managing editor of *American Heritage* magazine parodied Eisenhower stumbling through the Gettysburg Address. Some notable authors also appeared in its pages: Kurt Vonnegut, Jr., Nora Ephron, Neil Postman, Calvin Trillin, David Levine, even William F. Buckley, Jr. Navasky recalled, "Unofficially we were mostly left-liberal Democrats with anarcho-syndicalist pretensions." As proof of the magazine's cult popularity, when Navasky arrived in Chicago in 1968 to cover the Democratic Convention, his cabby asked him his name, curious to know whether his fare was a celebrity. Navasky told him, muttering, "You would never have heard of me." "Navasky? *The Monocle,* right?" shot back his driver, to the everlasting satisfaction of his passenger.[80]

Herman Kahn was mocked in *The Monocle.* In a satiric interview with the Kissingeresque Heinz Grubble, director of the Boston Institute for Advanced Studies (BIAS), Kahn's ideas were folded into "The Ultimate Solution" for the world's troublespots:

> What are the major danger areas in the world? . . . Four. Vietnam, Berlin, Congo, Cuba. In each case, the problem is insoluble by traditional diplomacy or political maneuvers, but the newly developed tactical atomic weapons make these things perfectly simple. Obliteration is the solution. If they simply ceased to exist, who would miss them? . . . And as for the hysterical myth that war would mean universal death, there's simply no statistical evidence for it whatsoever. You've read Kahn, I assume, and Kissinger, and the others—all influenced by me, of course—brilliant fellows. Naturally, there would be casualties—20, 30, 40 million, depending on our state of preparedness—you can check the presumptive casualties in a paper one of my assistants wrote in the Statistical Quarterly. But is that so terrible in view of all the problems that would automatically be solved?[81]

Navasky and another friend, Richard Lingeman, also put out a satirical paper called *The Outsider's Newsletter.* Its premiere issue claimed that "just about anybody can get the 'inside' story by reading . . . *Time* and *I.F. Stone's Weekly.* But it takes persistence, courage, and intelligent ignorance to get the outside story—the story of what is *not* going on."

> DEAR COL. CHESTNUT: I read that a symposium of scientists in Philadelphia concluded that we Americans are not thinking about the threat of nuclear obliteration. We know it is real, but we just refuse to think about it. I am

chairwoman of the program committee for the next
meeting of our women's club and thought it might be a
good idea if we devoted our time to thinking about nuclear oblivion. Can you advise us how to go about it—
reading lists, audio-visual aids, etc? Dolores Hazen
Humbert

DEAR MRS. HUMBERT: Thinking the unthinkable is one of
the primary duties of the American citizen. Just that
phrase was used as the title of a book by the well-known
American philosopher, Herman Kahn . . . As for your
club meeting, I recommend a perusal of Herman Kahn's
works. Also, the movie *Hiroshima Mon Amour,* otherwise
leftist-leaning, has some good shots of survivors emerging from the rubble after an atomic attack. CCC

DEAR COL. CHESTNUT: [Recently] . . . some dame at a
PTA meeting quotes a California psychiatrist as saying
that shelters and defense drills "raise questions in the
minds of school children about the adequacy of such
measures and, in turn, about the adequacy of the officials
who offer them" . . . It's people like him who are opposed
to shelters that undermine authority and cause juvenile
delinquency. If any of my kids started bellyaching about
one of my civil defense drills . . . I'd take a monkey
wrench to him and that would be that. Instead of cod-
dling these kids' feelings, we should be laying down the
law to them. What do you say, Col.? "Grease Monkey
Gus"

DEAR "GREASE MONKEY GUS": . . . Fear of nuclear war is
very real to children . . . It is up to their parents to reas-
sure them. Parents should emphasize the positive aspects
of a nuclear war—i.e., freedom vs. slavery, our superior
missile strength, the effectiveness of fallout shelters, the
chances of survival . . . Schools should teach Nuclear
War, just as they teach reading, writing, anti-Commu-
nism . . . If the facts about nuclear war—and thanks to

the efforts of such groups as the Rand Corporation and Herman Kahn's Hudson Foundation we have a lot of good solid knowledge in this area—were presented to the kids dispassionately and objectively, their irrational fears would thus be dispelled. C.C.C.[82]

The Outsider Newsletter even had a comic strip drawn by Ed Koren called *SuperKahn, Government Contractor.* Its debut panel heralded the new super-hero: "Equipped by a bountiful nature with superhuman, extra human and inhuman capabilities, SuperKahn roams the world, thinking about the unthinkable and protecting the United States, her citizens and her allies from evil deeds."[83]

Dr. Strangelove

Herman Kahn wasn't the only playful man in America who studied nuclear deterrence. The men at RAND teased and mocked one another in seminars, memoranda, and especially during presentations of new research, which were unofficially called "murder boards." RAND murder boards ritually pounded the authors of a new study with a volley of spitballs, spoofs, and insults. It's easy to imagine that people bandied sick jokes in these gatherings. But nobody other than Kahn dared to crack sick jokes in formal briefings where visitors and outsiders were present. Still, he wasn't the only cheeky performer in his world. During the interval in which he delivered his "On Thermonuclear War" briefing to professional audiences around the country, vulgar comedy was seeping back into mainstream public culture. Children amused their parents with the latest sick jokes, parents repeated them at cocktail parties, and comedians reeled them off on TV. But by 1963 sick humor was overexposed; its sting had mostly dissipated. Fans of Lenny Bruce complained, "The authentic radical satire of a few years ago [has] been rendered innocuous by sheer acceptance and then imitation. It no longer requires daring, originality, or courage to attack sacred cows like integration, Mother's Day, the

Flag. Such things are done, albeit in diluted form, virtually on every network."[84]

In 1964 Stanley Kubrick released a film about nuclear war that revived the insurgent energies of the best sick comedians. *Dr. Strangelove* was a genuine provocation. In it, the incompetence of the President and senior military officials, all of them boobs and lunatics, resulted in nuclear Armageddon. "*Dr. Strangelove* is beyond any question the most shattering sick joke I've ever come across," spluttered a critic in *The New York Times*. "And I say that with full recollection of some of the grim ones I've heard from Mort Sahl, some of the cartoons I've seen by Charles Addams and some of the stuff I've read in *Mad Magazine*." *Dr. Strangelove* afforded its audience an opportunity to stake their claims in the cultural struggle over acceptable speech. Nearly every critic framed his or her review of the film as an entry in the public etiquette of the cold war. Was *Dr. Strangelove* funny? Was it immoral and improper? Just what was the right response to the nuclear grotesque? [85]

Herman Kahn played a part in this. While he didn't originate the plot—Peter George did that in *Red Alert*—and he didn't write the screenplay (although Kubrick, George, and Terry Southern slipped excerpts from *OTW* into the film), *Dr. Strangelove*'s grotesque derives from Kahn. Kubrick had originally intended to make a serious movie about nuclear war. His working title borrowed from Albert Wohlsetter's famous *Foreign Affairs* article. It was called *The Delicate Balance of Terror*. But in due course, Herman Kahn sat down with Kubrick, shared a meal, and talked about nuclear war. They both believed that sick humor loosened public inhibitions. Listen to Kahn: "One does not do research in a cathedral. Awe is fine for those who come to worship or admire, but for those who come to analyze, to tamper, to change, to criticize . . . sometimes a colorful approach is to be preferred." "One wishes to relieve the grimness of the subject matter. People in a state of horror are not good analysts or detached and objective listeners." And here is Kubrick: "Why should the bomb be approached with reverence? Reverence can be a paralyzing state of mind." It's hard to believe that over the course of several meals Kahn did not regale his dinner companion with some of his best briefing jokes. Every time he sat down to write a scene for *Dr. Strangelove*, Kubrick later told *Newsweek*, "it came up funny."[86]

The strategist Thomas Schelling was the intermediary between Peter George, the author of *Red Alert*, and Kubrick. Schelling had written an article about accidental war with a discussion of three recent novels. He praised George for having done a better job of projecting how a nuclear war might start than any professional analyst he knew. The piece was published in the *Bulletin of the Atomic Scientists* and picked up by the *Observer* in London. Kubrick, then living in London, tracked down George and asked him to accompany him to the United States and help him write a screenplay.[87]

Kubrick and George visited Schelling at Harvard. They were having problems with the crisis scenario. When *Red Alert* had been published in 1958, nuclear weapons were ferried about by bombers. In the George novel, a rogue general launches a wing of SAC bombers against Russian targets under the provisions of a policy that authorized a base commander to launch his forces in the event that Washington and SAC headquarters had been eliminated in an enemy strike. The general planned to coerce the President to order a preventive war. The chairman of the joint chiefs of staff urges the President to support the initial attack. Since the bombers are flying under radio silence, they couldn't be recalled. "There is an absolute military necessity to follow up their attack as hard and as fast as we can. Any other course of action will . . . [mean] we lose cities, and take casualties . . . Mr. President, the Joint Chiefs unanimously recommend that a full scale attack on Soviet Russia be launched immediately."[88]

George's scenario was already obsolete by the time Kubrick began thinking about his movie. The bomber force had been augmented with Minuteman ICBMs and Polaris submarine-launched missiles. Schelling recalled, "There was no way that you could launch [missiles] and then call the President and tell him the strike is on the way, you'd better launch the whole outfit. The question was how could a brigadier general somewhere get the war started?" He, Kubrick, and

George spent an afternoon fiddling with one scenario after another. "We wanted to show that getting a war started was going to be very very hard, but not impossible. By the time we broke up, we decided that there wasn't a very plausible way to get this unintended war started." Recognizing they were at an impasse, Kubrick and George decided to make *Dr. Strangelove* a comedy. [89]

In the *Strangelove* plot, after the unauthorized launch of a bomber squadron to Soviet targets, the American president telephones the Soviet premier to brief him on the accident. The premier informs the president that should a single bomb detonate over Russia, a Doomsday Machine would automatically and irrevocably retaliate against so many targets in the West that life would end on the planet. The president successfully retrieves all but one of the bombers. In the final scenes SAC gives its Soviet counterpart detailed operational information, including general patterns of evasive tactics the pilot of the remaining bomber would probably employ, in a last-ditch effort to help the Soviets shoot the plane down before it releases its payload. The last moments of the film are an agony as the bomber evades area defenses. The final scene shows a Texan captain bronco-busting a falling bomb, ten-gallon hat in hand. The credits roll as the screen fills with a mushroom cloud to the strains of the lilting "We'll Meet Again Some Sunny Day."[90]

On January 29, 1964, *Dr. Strangelove, or How I Learned to Stop Worrying and Love the Bomb* debuted in New York. To no one's surprise, Kubrick's "contempt for our whole defense establishment, up to and even including the hypothetical Commander in Chief," shocked many people. If every authority was a nincompoop or worse, what could be the ultimate message of *Dr Strangelove?* "I want to know what this picture proves," demanded the reviewer for *The New York Times*. Its denouement was simply heartless. "Somehow it isn't funny," he grieved. "It is malefic and sick."[91]

That *Dr. Strangelove* triggered moral outrage is to be expected, as were the various attempts to present it to American audiences as a laffarama. *Newsweek*'s critic breezily elucidated its message—society cannot "afford such dangerous toys as hydrogen bombs"—cozily tucking it into place as a pill anyone could swallow, popular and edifying. *Time* also assumed an air of companionable urbanity, assuring its readers that nuclear humor was a bracing but pleasant tonic. "The film is an outrageously brilliant satire . . . and at the same time a supersonic thriller that should have audiences chomping their fingernails right down to the funny bone."[92]

In 1961 and '62 thoughtful observers noticed that fans of Mort Sahl and Lenny Bruce coyly congratulated themselves on their sophisticated taste. In many telling ways, they marked themselves as appreciative insiders by taunting the clods "who understand nothing but the public, dictionary definitions of the words said." While the publicity for their many imitators described them as "stinging social satirists who were plunging hungrily into dissections of the delusions and evasions of us all," in most cases what was performed was a kind of preening braggadocio, not real critique. Setting aside outrage and attempts to bowdlerize its message, the most interesting response to Kubrick's movie is this slip of attention. Since the actual possibility of nuclear war was hard to take, it was easier to focus on one's feelings. *Dr. Strangelove* inspired flurries of just this kind of vamping. While the film was strong stuff, admirers covertly boasted that they were equal to the demand to tolerate it sportingly.[93]

One review said it point-blank, "If you can stomach all this nuclear horror as subject matter for a satirical comedy, you may have a good time at 'Strangelove.'" Sicknik insiders exercised their wits on the dividing line between those who enjoyed the film and the yokels who could not control their nerves half so well. For example, the reviewer for *Life* magazine confided, "I found myself at the edge of tears as I watched a series of nuclear explosions fill the screen . . . Was I sad that the movie's world was ending? Was I having an attack of hysterics? Or had I suddenly arrived after prolonged laughter at a glimpse of some awful truth?" *Strangelove*'s meaning was undeniable, but not everyone could see it. The prigs who rebuked Kubrick for defeatism couldn't hope to understand contemporary sensibilities. "Their outrage underlines . . . [the] truth that the half-life of Not Getting the Point is forever." Americans probably wouldn't get the point, sighed the reviewer for a Catholic weekly. A society nourished on pablum could scarcely grasp *Dr Strangelove*'s message, "let alone be swayed by it." She predicted that most Americans would "attach as little significance to it as [they do] to a Jerry Lewis movie."[94]

Detailed scenarios of nuclear war invariably arouse panicky feelings. You could suppress anxiety with forgetting, you could minimize it, go completely limp, find a scapegoat, or channel your energies into peace marches or civil defense exercises. Kahn very rarely discussed hysteria in his briefings, but in one passage he dramatized the collision between the tender subjectivities of a survivor and a resolute foreman.

> The radiation from fallout has curious and frightening effects. Most people already know . . . that if you get a fatal dose of radiation the sequence of events is . . . like this: first you become nauseated, then sick; you seem to recover; then in two or three weeks you really get sick and die.
>
> Now just imagine yourself in the postwar situation. Everybody will have been subjected to extremes of anxiety, unfamiliar environment, strange foods, minimum toilet facilities, inadequate shelters, and the like. Under these conditions some high percentage of the population is going to become nauseated, and nausea is very catching. If one man vomits, everybody vomits. Almost everyone is likely to think he has received too much radiation. Morale may be so affected that many survivors may refuse to participate in constructive activities, but would content themselves with sitting down and waiting to die—some may even become violent and destructive.
>
> However, the situation would be quite different if radiation meters were distributed. Assume now that a man gets sick from a cause other than radiation. Not believing this, his morale begins to drop. You look at his meter and say, "You have received only ten roentgens, why are you vomiting? Pull yourself together and get to work."

Thinking he's stricken from radiation sickness, the cadre vomits, but he's only suffering from shaky nerves. That the body imperatively interrupts human purposes is the stock-in-trade of physical comedy. Kahn's scenarios of nuclear war-fighting and the postwar world were typically bloodless, fleshless, and sexless. But here he pictures the body's loss of control. If radiation sickness is tragic, hysterical vomiting is funny. "If one man vomits, everybody vomits" is a joke, or at least resembles a joke. Picturing survivors vomiting in a postwar world is plainly impudent, straying well beyond the proprieties of the scientific advisory culture. Kahn mocked the military and the public with his scenarios and his burlesques, his gadgets and his predictions, and his unseemly dialogue between the earthly and the cerebral, the high and the low, the vomiter and the scientist.[95]

Chapter 10

MASS MURDER OR THE SPIRIT OF HUMANISM?

Ideal for Christmas . . . Your chances for survival are . . .
surprisingly greater than you dared hope . . . Far from
making anyone's Christmas morbid, this book will bring
you hope in keeping with the season's spirit. For the person
on your gift list interested in science's impact on world af-
fairs.

SPACE WORLD, 1961

"These issues are fun to study," Kahn once said. "There are qualities of paradox and absurdity that appeal to analysts and other non-serious people." Nietzsche's sly description of Machiavelli's *Prince* would have been a fitting epigraph for *OTW:* "[He] cannot help presenting the most serious affairs in a boisterous *allegrissimo:* not perhaps without a malicious artist's sense of the contrast he is risking—thoughts protracted, difficult, hard, dangerous and the tempo of the gallop and the most wanton good humor."[1]

Kahn knew his book would be controversial. In 1959 he circulated drafts to as many people as could be wheedled into reading them. An astute if unflattering ally in this process was the Berkeley psychoanalyst Walter Marseille. He wrote to Kahn that the manuscript he read would "antagonize most readers by the tone it is written." He realized Kahn probably couldn't improve his writing: "How else could I explain the way your treat the English language, committing three to eight atrocities per page against logic, grammar, and style?" These remarks were a foretaste of James Newman's gleeful ridicule of Kahn's "solecisms, pleonasms, jargon, clichés, fused participles, and cannibalized words" in his *Scientific American* review. Marseille closed his letter primly. "If we are to withstand" the deterrence ordeal, people needed to know that nuclear war "need not mean the end of everything." He sighed, "You *could* make an important contribution," but given the book's stylistic barbarisms, "I am disappointed to see that this is not what will happen."[2]

Kahn apologized for the clumsiness of his prose and beseeched his readers for forbearance and editorial assistance. In the preface to the transcript of his briefing at Lawrence Radiation Laboratory, he begged for help. "The publishing schedule is such that I may be able to make changes for the next couple of months or so. I would be grateful for any helpful suggestions received before then." Acknowledging the crudeness of his work, he admitted that "I publish [this] with some hesitation." While feeling "no qualms" about delivering briefings ripe with conjecture, his ideas looked "much more shaky when put into cold print." Nevertheless, rather than defer publication "until all the ideas could be thought out," which might take years, he offered his ideas "in the form I gave them." He went so far as to suggest that he would gladly retract his arguments in light of fresher data or ideas. "[In] five or ten years from now, I will not be too disappointed if the passage of time and thought causes me or others to revise most of these remarks."[3]

In addition to stumbling over his graceless diction, Kahn's readers would probably recoil from systems analysis, he realized. "It sometimes gives an impression of almost incredible callousness." It didn't mean that he "approve[d] of the subject being analyzed—only that . . . [it was] important to understand it." Readers would doubtless shrink from "the frankness with which . . . military problems are discussed." He added artlessly, "They may have a point."[4]

In the preface to the Livermore version of *OTW*, he invited his readers to jump into the nuclear debate. One man who spoke up was Marshall Windmiller, a professor at San Francisco State College. He rebuked Kahn in a diatribe broadcast by the public radio stations KPFA in Berkeley and KPFK in Los Angeles in March 1960. Windmiller had been invited to a two-day Kahn briefing sponsored by the World Affairs Council of Northern California. His commentary, a transcript of which was disseminated to peace groups in the Bay Area, denounced Kahn for cooking up propaganda to advance the arms race, and for being immoral and stupid. "While professing a hard-headed realism," he thundered, Kahn was "naïve about politics. In the final analysis, our problems with the Russians are primarily political, not just military."[5]

Walter Marseille, who also broadcast on KPFA, pounced on Windmiller, firing back with his own radio commentary. "Hardly anything could show the need for Herman Kahn's 'Lectures on Thermonuclear War' more drastically" than Windmiller's tirade, which flinched from the very subject of nuclear war and had virtually nothing to offer against Kahn's arguments. "If someone believes he has the facts to refute [Kahn], we might get a genuine controversy. But a critique that evades this point lays itself open to the suspicion that its author has . . . misunderstood what it is all about." Marseille's remarks typified the personal attacks with which the pro- and anti-Kahn camps pelted each other: "Windmiller exhibits a more perfect combination of insensitivity toward the actual danger of nuclear war with squeamishness toward any realistic discussion of that danger." Such smug high-mindedness was plainly foolish. He commented acidly, "When insensitivity and squeamishness [are] compounded by a self-righteousness . . . quick to brand all opponents as immoral and frivolous, one loses the incentive to regard it as excusable."[6]

Certain that the book would ignite this kind of quarrel, Kahn arranged for Senator Hubert Humphrey to enter an abridged version of *OTW* into the Congressional Record as a Senate Document. Humphrey was chairman of the Subcommittee on Disarmament of the Committee on Foreign Relations. The senator threw his weight behind Kahn's ideas. "I consider it an honor to present [the pamphlet] because it embodies the intellectual honesty and rigor so much needed in discussing the problems of our survival . . . Dr. Kahn examines without fear or favor many controversial problems. His views . . . merit serious consideration by serious people."[7]

Princeton University Press contracted with the History Book of the Month Club to offer *OTW* as its main selection for January 1961. In its promotional literature, the book club editors wrote that Kahn's book was "of such importance that we are taking the extraordinary action of recommending that our members not exercise their privilege of rejection . . . His thesis . . . is frightening and repugnant, but just for these reasons one which must be given the most sober attention." The accompanying pamphlet predicted the book would become notorious. "For that reason if for no other . . . the Kahn gospel demands serious attention. To many it will seem repulsive and to some fantastic, but no one can afford simply to shrug it off." While Kahn and his editor pitched their marketing campaign to this possibility, they were wholly unprepared for the ballyhoo touched off by an early review of *OTW*'s unthinkable thoughts.[8]

The Newman Affair

As a young lawyer, James Newman had devoted himself to atomic energy. One of his chief accomplishments was authoring an early draft of the Atomic Energy Act of 1945. When Gerard Piel launched *Scientific American* magazine in May 1948, he hired Newman to run the book review department. While it wasn't a public affairs journal, each issue featured a lead article and book reviews about the political and social consequences of scientific advances. Piel had a longstanding interest in the atomic bomb, and advocated the Acheson-Lilienthal proposal to internationalize atomic science. In the spring of 1950, defying the FBI, he dared to publish a series of articles on the ramifications of the hydrogen weapon at a time when the Truman administration sought to stifle public discussion of the matter. Piel was pleased with Newman's treatment of *On Thermonuclear War*. "When he had the Kahn book," he exulted, "he was inspired."[9]

Newman opened his review with a sarcastic flourish, excerpts of which were subsequently quoted in nearly every book review and profile about Kahn.

> Is there really a Herman Kahn? It is hard to believe. Doubts cross one's mind almost from the first page of this deplorable

book: no one could write like this; no one could think like this. Perhaps the whole thing is a staff hoax in bad taste.

The evidence as to Kahn's existence is meager. The biographical note states that . . . he was trained as a physicist and a mathematician. This explains, he says, why he finds it "both satisfying and illuminating to distinguish the three kinds of deterrence by I, II, and III, [despite the fact that] many people have been distressed with the nonsuggestive nature of the ordinal numbers." I find this passionate attachment to the ordinal numbers implausible.

One more personal note. In his preface Kahn says he carried the manuscript around for a year "on airplanes and railroads." This has the ring of truth . . . At times it almost seems as though the author is suffering from motion sickness.

Kahn may be the RAND Corporation's General Bourbaki, the imaginary individual used by a school of French mathematicians to test outrageous ideas. The style of the book certainly suggests teamwork. It is by turns waggish, pompous, chummy, coy, brutal, arch, rude, man-to-man, Air Force crisp, energetic, tongue-tied, pretentious, ingenuous, spastic ironical, savage, malapropos, square-bashing and moralistic. Solecisms, pleonasms and jargon abound; the clichés and fused participles are spectacular; there are many sad examples of what Fowler calls cannibalism—words devouring their own kind. How could a single person produce such a caricature?

No less remarkable is the substance of the book. An ecstatic foreword by Klaus Knorr of Princeton University's Center of International Studies states that this is "not a book about the moral aspects of military problems." The disclaimer is much to the point; it is exactly wrong. This is a moral tract on mass murder: how to plan it, how to commit it, how to get away with it, how to justify it.

He concluded his "portrait of the mind of Herman Kahn" with the words: "Herman Kahn, we are told [by Klaus Knorr], is 'one of the very few who have managed to avoid the "mental block" so characteristic of writers on nuclear warfare.' The mental block consists, if I am not mistaken, of a scruple for life. This evil and tenebrous book, with its loose-lipped pieties and its hayfoot-strawfoot logic, is permeated with a bloodthirsty irrationality such as I have not seen in my years of reading."[10]

While Newman's was not, strictly speaking, the first review, it was among the first, and it set the agenda for the debate about *OTW*, including the defamation of Kahn's character. "We were horrified that the *New York Times* had solemnly reviewed the . . . book as though it was a subject for civilized discourse," Piel recalled. He made only one editorial correction to Newman's copy. "He had a wonderful line" comparing Kahn's distinctions among numbers of dead to SS deliberations to the effect that "if lampshades will be made of Jewish skin, it should be done with good taste. We decided that we didn't quite need that one." Piel didn't expect an outcry, but he didn't particularly mind when the magazine received scores of approving letters. "We just thought it was a swell review and that took care of that one, and let's get on with the next subject . . . We went to press. We were happy to see it make a rumpus when it did get published, because I was appalled by the way people were talking."[11]

Newman's review was excerpted in *The Washington Post* in late February. The March issue of *Scientific American* had already appeared, and the *Post*'s readers immediately registered their responses. Their letters to the editor offer a snapshot of the moral seriousness with which letter-writing people understood their present moment. One man defended Kahn's uprightness: "Only a butcher, or a fiction, [Newman] shrieks, could even suggest" the possibility of nuclear war. "Newman, alas, is no fiction, but is only too typical of our generation. He entirely ignores the fact that our Nation is preparing and must prepare for dreadful possibilities. Is it immoral to ask us to reflect harder on what these possibilities really may be?" Another reader trumpeted Newman's review as "a magnificent statement which should be reprinted as a pamphlet and given wide circulation." Kahn's book was a product of RAND, the nation's foremost think tank, which had substituted "the brain-power of computers . . . for the critical and creative activities of men." It was only in light of the "coming world of computers" where "man is . . . little more than a biological nuisance" that it was "possible to be blasé about 50 million casualties," as Kahn had been.[12]

Kahn was wounded and surprised by Newman's slurs and the letters it inspired. He wrote privately, "Most of it is, of course, just abusive. Much of the rest is just the worst kind of anti-militarism . . . Does he really think it is wrong to make distinctions, not to do the best one can if war comes, not keep our conceptual, doctrinal, and linguistic framework up to date?" He drafted a rejoinder that his editor at Princeton University Press could send to *The Washington Post*. In his cover letter he explained, "My efforts were touched off by the visit of some friends from Washington, who told me that everyone who knows me or has even heard of me is talking about the Newman review and that therefore, either to capitalize on the excitement or just to defend myself, I ought to have an answer published in the *Post*." His suggested letter asked: "Is OTW a 'Moral Tract on Mass Murder?' 'Yes,' says James R. Newman. In his lengthy review of Herman Kahn's book, Mr. Newman could not find a single item of merit. He attacked the author's syntax, sanity, diction, digestion, morality, grammar, humanity, organization, rationality, competence, and even cast doubt on his existence. We were awed. As publishers we do not take sides on such substantive issues. However, we are proud to have published this book." This was followed with a handful of excerpts from laudatory reviews. Kahn closed with the pitch:

> We do not mean to imply by the above that all the people cited support Mr. Kahn. Far from it. Many disagree violently and probably only Kahn agrees with all of Kahn. We do mean to assert that *OTW* is an important book which all who are interested in National Security and the Arms Race should read; that even if you disagree with Mr. Kahn you are likely to be instructed and stimulated . . . and that if you would like to make up your own mind about this controversial book, why

then as publishers we are delighted to suggest that you go out
and buy a copy. At all bookstores for $10.00.

Princeton University Press published Kahn's riposte in *The Reporter,*
The New York Times, The New York Times Book Review, The Washing-
ton Post, The Times Herald, The Nation, The New Leader, The New Re-
public, and *The Progressive.*[13]

While he was pleased to receive acclaim from a spectrum of public
figures, Kahn could not coax *Scientific American* to publish a rebuttal.
On March 6, 1961, he wrote the first of a string of letters to the magazine's editor. "Dear Mr. Flanagan, I have just read Mr. Newman's
review . . . and can only say that it should not have appeared in a
magazine called the *Scientific American.*" The problem with the review was that Newman had shrugged off the necessity of engaging
any of *OTW*'s major arguments. He simply wreathed excerpts with
moral censure. "If you are interested in a serious discussion of the
difficulties and techniques which specialists have in coming to grips
with this unpleasant problem, I would be delighted to prepare one
for you." He offered to write an article called "Thinking about the
Unthinkable," which would consider "the methodological, psychological, and moral problems that anyone attempting a serious analysis
of national security must face."[14]

Flanagan responded curtly that the title of Kahn's proposed essay
"precisely expresses my personal view of the matter in reverse." Since
there wasn't "much point" in this kind of thinking, "I should prefer to
devote my thoughts to how nuclear war can be prevented. It is for
this reason that we must decline your offer to give us your article."[15]

Kahn was baffled. He tried again. He registered his surprise that
Flanagan had interpreted his comments as simple huffing indignation against Newman's invective. On the contrary, the matter was political and impersonal: "Nuclear war may be unthinkable but it is not
impossible." Unless Flanagan believed that unilateral disarmament
was the only possible future for humanity, "I fail to see how you can
devote your thoughts to how nuclear war can be prevented without
thinking about nuclear war itself." Kahn offered to discuss the problem with him in person. Flanagan declined and moved to close off

their correspondence. While "it is good of you to make yourself available . . . I do not think that any purpose would be served by such a meeting. We know your views, and I believe you know ours. Perhaps . . . we should simply agree to disagree."[16]

Unwilling to let the matter drop, Kahn pressed Flanagan a third time. If *Scientific American* rejected immediate unilateral disarmament, then it affirmed some kind of deterrence, which could not be addressed by *not* thinking about it. "You seem . . . unwilling to ask 'What would happen if this establishment were used or if the Soviets challenged us?' I now conjecture, I hope incorrectly, that you are willing to put complete, if temporary, faith in deterrence and therefore find it unnecessary to analyze these notions more carefully." But should these ideas be kept out of the pages of his magazine? If his article "Thinking about the Unthinkable" was not wanted, would Flanagan agree to publish something from Kahn in the Letters section?[17]

Herbert Bailey, Jr., director of Princeton University Press, stepped in with a plea to Flanagan to meet Kahn. "I hope that at least the two of you will be able to agree on the meaning of 'unthinkable'—something too horrible to think of, or something beyond the possibility of thought. Whether you can agree on anything else is a question that ought to be explored." Bailey seconded Kahn that Newman had sniped at Kahn himself, not the ideas in his book. "Newman did not really review the book; he simply objected to its existence . . . to the whole idea of thinking about the possibility of thermonuclear war."[18]

In a terse reply, Flanagan agreed to consider a letter to the editor. Incensed by Flanagan's condescension, Kahn batted back one last letter expressing disgust with the whole affair. "Well-wishing friends" and "gossips" had reported to him that Newman and Piel were immensely proud of the review and had sent reprints to everyone they knew. "I am also told that Mr. Newman habitually discusses me in semi-public and private meetings in four-letter words but has declined the opportunity to confront me in any sort of public debate." Apparently Newman loudly approved Flanagan's and Piel's decision to forbid Kahn a platform to "propagate my 'obscene' views." This was too much: "Altogether I get a picture of such emotional bias and uncritical self-righteousness that it makes me believe you would not do the reasonable thing even out of motives of prudence and self-protection, much less fairness and objectivity."[19]

Since Flanagan refused to meet him in person, Kahn was obliged to enumerate Newman's errors by letter. He stated firmly, "I do wish to make clear that [his] inaccuracies . . . are not my major objection . . . It is the level of the discussion, the proud and self-satisfied unwillingness to 'think about the unthinkable,' and the implication . . . that anybody who takes the details of defense problems seriously is either a knave or a fool." While Newman was free to revile the subject, "it seems rather absurd to have as a reviewer of books on defense a man who objects to writing or thinking about any details of the subject." In closing, Kahn once again offered to submit a letter of rebuttal to *Scientific American* provided Flanagan publish it in its entirety.[20]

Piel recalled that he thought it was "a deplorable nuisance that people were so misled as to take indignation at the review we published." He was unmoved by Kahn's and Bailey's appeals to fair play. "We weren't interested in publishing Herman Kahn in the *Scientific American.* So far as we were concerned, we attempted to represent in our moral and political and social attitude the consensus of the scientific community. The rest of the spectrum of opinion was well covered in other parts of the press. Those were open to Herman Kahn. Let him use them. We certainly weren't going to give him house room."[21]

Piel explained that he was ideologically opposed to the professional interests of the civilian defense intellectuals at RAND and elsewhere. "That's something that we hire the military for and put them in uniforms to conduct this monstrous, inhuman enterprise of warfare." But credentialed scientists working for the military were "moochers on the work of their betters." "That whole RAND Corporation nest" was peopled by mediocrities poaching on the labors of academic scientists. "RAND analysts were like jackals around the lions picking up after them."[22]

Kahn's friends at RAND scrawled indignant letters to Flanagan and Piel. John Williams protested, "I do not believe that those of us so engaged are evil, though some do . . . The organization to which Kahn and I belong is characterized in one Russian journal as the Academy of Death and Destruction, and another expresses the view that our scientists should be beheaded. I trust that Mr. Newman will not echo these [ideas] in the *Scientific American*." Another letter defended Kahn's notorious distinction among numbers of dead. "Does Mr. Newman really value human life? . . . We would all prefer that no one . . . die from any cause; but if some must die, then surely a scruple for human life values a 2-to-1 cut in the death rate! Surely it takes a strange valuation of human life to reject, out of hand, consideration of non-provocative measures that might save tens of millions of lives in and after a nuclear attack."[23]

In his note to his friend William Clifford, an editor at Simon and Schuster, Bailey demanded, "Do you object to publication . . . by Princeton University Press, or do you feel simply that it should not have been published at all by anybody?" If Kahn directed unwilling attention to "grim realities," then wasn't that a good thing? In fact, it was one of the book's merits "that it can provoke even such hysterical diatribes as Newman's review." In his reply to the RAND mathematician Richard Bellman, who sent angry letters protesting *OTW* to twelve periodicals as well as to Princeton University Press, he applauded Kahn's civic courage in assigning "numbers to . . . catastrophes that are virtually beyond imagination." Of course the numbers were provisional. But "I firmly believe that the book . . . is doing a lot of good in the world . . . [in] forcing people to look at the numbers and if possible to try to find better ones."[24]

OTW had sold so well in its first three months (14,204 copies) that Princeton University Press had planned a series of follow-up ads well before the Newman review appeared. PUP expanded this round of advertising "to help combat the effects of [Newman's] review," according to the Press's marketing director. "If anything, [it] adds to our wish to do everything possible . . . to see the book more widely promoted and distributed." With great satisfaction Bailey reported to Kahn that he had decided to use his proposed rejoinder for a large-format ad in *The Washington Post.* The marketing campaign, combined with Kahn's exasperated efforts to disseminate his ideas, sustained the issue as a public scandal for several years. For a book on nuclear strategy over 650 pages long, *OTW* did very well indeed. It sold 23,847 copies in its first eighteen months.[25]

But Do We Live in Kahn's World?

The critical reception of *OTW* offers a tableau of people's preoccupations in 1961: anxiety about the impact of computerized weapons systems on the nation's defense, the influence of systems analysts on policy, repugnance for Kahn's grotesque style, and expressions of despair, bitterness, fear, and regret.

In a review for *The Bulletin of the Atomic Scientists* designed to preempt criticism of Kahn's comic style, Walter Marseille observed, "Funeral directors are not supposed to gambol or frolic in public. Kahn does not violate these taboos, but his . . . prose deals so enthusiastically with the grimmest problems that the reader cannot help expecting him to do so at any time." Other reviewers were not so generous. "Geminus," the author of a column in *The New Scientist,* voiced his "profound objection" to Kahn's "grisly jokes like megadeath." Such tomfoolery disgraced the vocation of science. "Rightly or wrongly the RAND Corporation is regarded the world over as a scientific organization. Mr. Kahn's little fun is one important way in which people in general come to believe that scientists have merely an irresponsible attitude towards the problems of our times." A reviewer for a journal on religion and public affairs also chided Kahn for his "curiously chatty . . . digressing . . . jazzy style": "A certain awe—to put it mildly—should surround our contemplation of [nuclear war] . . . It should not . . . be set forth in jazz-talk." Irked, Kahn reproached him for fearing moral pollution in a letter to the journal's editor. "It is indispensable that some people at some time for some purposes suspend their awe long enough to find out just exactly what it is we are talking about."[26]

The historian Gabriel Kolko blasted *The New York Times* book reviewer, Jerome Spingarn, for certifying Kahn's benignity. Spingarn had coyly offered the usual portrait: "It should be stated that Kahn is a cheery and gregarious Californian without a trace of bitterness, and a zestful gourmet who certainly cannot feel detached about the prospect of decades of poisoned crops." Kolko fumed, "It is significant that Mr. Spingarn pauses to attempt to show that a man who proposes basing political strategy on the assumption of 40 million deaths also loves life." He was horrified by Kahn's "abjectly dehumanized" view of postwar prospects. Not only does he "destroy all possibilities for sanity and democracy," but "in the name of defending 'freedom,' the Kahns of America would create mountains of corpses and an authoritarian and irrational society." Spingarn, in turn, confirmed his man's rectitude. "Mr. Kahn's integrity and intellectual honesty and those of his book's sponsor, Princeton's Center of International Studies, need no defense from me." Like Marseille and Bailey, like Strachey, like all of Kahn's defenders, Spingarn retorted that it was easier to malign the man than fix one's attention on the implications of cold war peace through deterrence. Surely *OTW* ought "to be . . . analyzed on its merits."[27]

Whether or not the book's arguments could be creditably addressed at all was an open question. The philosopher Irving Louis Horowitz diagnosed among the "new civilian strategists" a confusion from which they could not extricate themselves. The concept of deterrence was dangerously unstable. The defense intellectuals talked of disarmament when they meant arms control; they talked of arms control when they meant the perpetual modernization of the strategic arsenal; they talked of deterrence when they meant the capability to fight a nuclear war. Deterrence could swell to include war-fighting or swerve to the niceties of arms control and inspection. Horowitz warned that "until the logical status of this concept is made plain," nuclear strategy "will obfuscate and disguise policy considerations, and, worse, . . . cast serious doubt on . . . disarmament negotiations."[28]

More damningly, Horowitz charged Kahn's vaunted scientific approach as a debauched rationality wholly divorced from early modern ethical reason. What long ago had been science's stately, well-earned independence from state and church doctrinal authority had by now jettisoned morality. It assumed that "indifference to valuational issues, if not stupidity in the face of them, is the best possible pose for the true scientific mind." Solemnly, dolefully, Horowitz concluded that systems analysis had lured American scientific creativity into a blind alley. Its abstractions could not possibly penetrate "the actual conflict of interests that exists." The result was that the new civilian militarists wobbled between haughtiness and indifference, forsaking the heritage of science's historic alliance "with the deepest causes of human survival and growth."[29]

Whereas Horowitz regarded Kahn's approach to nuclear war as an adulterated form of means–ends rationality from which social and ethical content had been expunged, the mathematician Anatol Rapoport objected to the *social* content in the work of the defense intellectuals. His book *Strategy and Conscience* was an ideological exposé—unmasking allegedly neutral categories as harbors for societally specific values. In fact, he wrote it in white-hot response to *OTW*. "The starting point was my 'gut reaction' to the writings and lectures of Mr. Kahn, who is the arch villain . . . I have cast him in the role of arch villain, because he showed himself to be way ahead of the traditionalists—a living demonstration of where strategic thinking is taking us."[30]

Rapoport refused to accept the validity of the science or sentiment dilemma. Kahn had metamorphosed political conflict into mathematical jargon. By doing so he shielded decision makers from "the awareness of the implications of their . . . policies." While "those who know him tell me that he is a kind and perceptive person," Kahn's affability did not obviate the fact that institutions like RAND filtered out the social, political, and historical significance of their recommendations.[31]

Mark Hedden accepted *OTW*'s stoical dogma—"We did not

choose this world; we just live in it"—as Kahn's unimpeachable rationale. "But," he demanded, "do we live in Kahn's world?" He challenged
the assumption that America's enemies were "bright, knowledgeable,
and malevolent." Kahn had made no attempt to demonstrate that such
an enemy actually imperiled the United States. Hedden concluded
that *OTW* was more properly a work of propaganda rather than a
scientific study so much did Kahn "weight his data."[32]

Kahn's pose of scientific detachment became the focus of liberal
anxiety. Had his impassivity triggered "the hysteria of Mr. Newman,
et al.?" John Strachey of the London Institute of Strategic Studies
wondered whether the ideals of cultured humanism were compatible
with the cold war imperatives that shaped national security and the
NATO alliance. Would humanism be vanquished in the thermonuclear age? He argued that Kahn had surpassed the works of the peace
movement in filling out the grisly realities of the post-attack world.
Having "out-described" the peace activists, he outlined policies such
as active and civil defense that offered a better chance of preventing
war than unilateral disarmament. Since the Soviets had forced upon
the West the grinding choice between appeasement or defiance, he
concluded that Kahn's counterforce arguments honorably straddled
anticommunism and humanism.[33]

An anonymous essayist in the *Times Literary Supplement* suspected
that the systems analysts' formative training omitted political and
historical study, which would explain their failure to penetrate the
meaning of their own work. "At times one seriously wonders whether
the authors have any real comprehension of those western values . . .
which they claim so staunchly to defend." From the "infinite complexities of reality," the analysts plucked and simplified a handful of
factors. "There is more to every problem, military or political, than
can ever be quantified and fed into a computer, and every situation
which confronts the statesman will be unforeseeably complicated and
entirely unique." Their models and scenarios were oddly apolitical.
The span between their scenarios and reality was "as great as that between an electronic computer and a fully developed human brain."[34]

Evidence from *OTW* suggested that Kahn believed the USSR was ravenous for world domination. What he overlooked were the multiple interests that conditioned and nuanced Soviet policy, "ideology . . . [being] only one factor among many." The whole pack of strategists invited scorn for assuming Russia's "deluded or terrorized mass of automata" were governed by "fanatics." Given the crudeness of their political understanding, the *TLS* essayist suggested that it would be best for all if they cultivated an attitude of "skeptical and self-doubting humility" and restricted themselves to charting the range of action open to more qualified persons. "Their skills do not qualify them to take either political or military decisions."[35]

A critic for *The National Review* rebuked Kahn for not being properly dedicated to the struggle against communism. "The multifarious levels of the Communist attack upon the West . . . the aims and ends of our struggle as they operatively affect our actions—all these are missing from the world in which Herman Kahn's mind moves back and forth over the data like a flashing computer endowed with an adventurous imagination." *OTW* was altogether too formal for his liking. "It would be only a slight exaggeration to say that in this book any great power X could be substituted for the concrete Soviet enemy, and any great power Y substituted for the United States, without requiring serious emendation of the text." Genuinely committed cold warriors should therefore read *OTW* mindful of its "distortion of understanding."[36]

While Kahn made sparing use of game theory, critics wrongly elided systems analysis with Von Neumann and Morgenstern's mathematics of game theory. For example, in *The New Republic* Robert Paul Wolff, a Harvard philosopher, objected to Kahn's use of game theory with the argument that "in the first place, Game Theory assumes a simplified, closed-off, calculable situation in which the contestants act on 'rational' motives." Just as classical economic theory interpreted market behavior in light of the figment *Homo economicus*, so Kahn postulated *Thermonuclear Man*, "an enemy bent simply on military domination." The result was an inane exercise in threats among robotic belligerents. Kahn's fabrications were maddening.

"The reader may search the book for the slightest hint as to the origins of [his data]. He will find no citations of studies by economists, nor even a cryptic reference to classified documents. The whole is an essay in imagination."[37]

The essayists Walter Goldstein and S. M. Miller borrowed the expression "crackpot realism" from C. Wright Mills to characterize the rugged *realpolitik* that justified Kahn's approach to nuclear warfighting. In their portrait of Kahn as "military ideologist," they declared, "Each of his premises is based not upon empirical evidence but upon abstracted inferences." The problem was that "in his effort to explore new hypotheses, Kahn often distorts his perspective so greatly that his strategic scenarios become further and further removed from reality." By focusing wholly on technical considerations such as the "rationality of conflict, the extension of communications, and the perfection of nuclear gadgets," the worldview of *OTW* exhibited a peculiar "quality of fantasy plus realistic analysis," rendering it "more bizarre and sensitive to common sense objections." Alastair Buchan made much the same point, objecting to Kahn's tendency to generalize from hypothetical scenarios so broadly and so often that much of *OTW* amounted to "political nonsense." "He says elsewhere, 'We cannot afford to eliminate completely our ability to go to war if provoked in some extreme fashion.' But will the Soviet Union, knowing the stakes, ever offer an extreme provocation? What does 'extreme' mean in so dire a context?"[38]

To his critics, the objects, methods, and values belonging to speculative literature, public policy, and the sciences were incommensurable. On these grounds, they complained that Kahn's book should have been marketed as something other than a scientific work. In his "Critique of Some Contemporary Defence Thinking," P. M. S. Blackett suggested that Kahn's postwar world picture had abandoned the demonstrable rationality of operations research. "When a highly simplified model has to be used, any prediction . . . is likely to be so uncertain that it is essential to check it against the conclusions reached in a more intuitive manner by attempting to envisage the situation as a whole." Given the model's uncertainty, Blackett, unlike the men at RAND, admonished, "Never should [an operations research group] fall into the trap of decking out what is essentially only a hunch with a pseudo-scientific backing."[39]

The strategist John Polanyi was also troubled by Kahn's quantification of the geo-political universe. Whereas the actual world exhibited "staggering complexity," Kahn's model was simple enough to permit numerical manipulation. But he doubted whether anything useful could be extracted from these transactions, "if we are forced, ultimately, to rely on an intuitive assessment of the reasonableness of [its] conclusions . . . It will be enough to note that the intuitive assessment is not made *in vacuo* but will undoubtedly be influenced by the calculation it is meant to assess."[40]

What Blackett called the "verbal and scholastic bias" of systems analysis, Paul Johnson of *The New Statesman* regarded as purest demagoguery. Casting Kahn as the very epitome of RAND, Johnson condemned systems analysis for grossly misrepresenting itself as authoritative science. "I call the work of the Corporation a pseudoscience for the simple reason that its exponents have no means of verifying their conclusions by experiment . . . These studies are essentially works of science fiction." Because the simulationists unfolded their speculations within the circuit of a dogma rather than pressing ahead in an open-ended process, he likened them to medieval scholastics. "The schoolmen believed that the world would soon be destroyed by God; their problem was to discover a system of belief and a code of morals which would permit the human race to survive this catastrophe and pass safely to the other side." Accordingly, they stuffed the encyclopedic universe into their cosmological design. The problem was that their founding assumption "could not be proved; it could only be believed." Whether tricked out in precedent or economic and physics jargon, intuition and wisdom would still guide the military in the thermonuclear age.[41]

The snare in systems analysis was its attractively implacable brutality. "Ambitious young politicians who have yet to experience the sobering reality of taking life-and-death decisions could be—and, I believe, have been—corrupted by such books. They possess an intellectual ruthlessness which appeals strongly to men learning—or yearning—to wield the levers of power." Such books wielded an unwholesome influence over officers "whose moral reflexes have been blunted by the exigencies of the Cold War." Without grounding in philosophy, history, and political theory, scientifically oriented young officers could not recognize the "evil dogma" communicated by futurology's scientific veneer. Johnson concluded in the strongest possible terms: "Books like these should be treated as pornography within the meaning of the act; otherwise we may all be factored into oblivion."

In the teeth of these arguments, Marseille countered that *OTW* was defensible in spite of its unproven models. Kahn "freely admits the incomplete, tentative and speculative character of the group research which led to his conclusions." But in spite of the impossibility of evaluating his conjectures about a post-attack world, Marseille argued that Kahn's deterrence arguments were well-founded. After all, how could one be sure that the Soviets had ruled out a first strike? Perhaps they would not, in which case, like it or not, Americans must face up to the possibility of suffering a nuclear strike against their cities. He found this line of thought persuasive. "If this factor is taken into account, the question is not . . . [whether] nuclear defense can be proved. It is only necessary to show that at the present time nobody can prove the impossibility of nuclear defense—and all of Kahn's major conclusions follow." No sensible man would haplessly rely on the promises of his mortal enemy *not* to exploit his vulnerabilities. Wasn't self-defense, procuring protection against enemy assault, a better safeguard? "This is so obvious that our almost complete neglect of civil defense appears incomprehensible."[42]

Marseille invoked the failed reality principle to explain why disarmers did not yield to the good sense of civil defense. The peace movement had mesmerized itself with the wish that because nuclear war was "insanely horrible," it will never happen. Marseille's notion of political and psychological realism was as hard to swallow as Kahn's. His remarks prompted letters to the *Bulletin* disparaging Kahn and civil defense. One woman cried, "Unless we come to grips with basic issues of the nuclear threat and refute the barbarous illogic of such men as Air-Force-Rand-subsidized Kahn, then we may expect even less meaningful exploration of the infinitely complex international conflicts."[43]

Marseille was unmoved. In response, he interpreted disarmament as a "deep-seated emotional resistance against the possibility of nuclear war. Mrs. Petrick's letter exhibits a strong dislike of nuclear war—an emotion which is healthy, but hardly noteworthy, since it is shared by three billion other human beings." She missed the point altogether by accusing Kahn of war-mongering. The problem was not that Kahn proposed the numbers of casualties America could absorb and still recover; the problem was that the enemy has actually accepted catastrophic losses *already*—could, has, and might again in the future. He asked bluntly, if belittlingly, "What guarantee can Mrs. Petrick give us that Khrushchev's and Mao's calculations will always be less 'monstrous,' 'barbarous,' and illogical than those of Herman Kahn? Does she want us to ignore the fact that the Communists actually have accepted many millions of casualties, more than once, in the pursuit of their peacetime collectivization programs?"[44]

Some people in the peace movement praised Kahn for his unflinching realism. The disarmament activist H. Stuart Hughes wailed that "the arguments of most 'peace' people seem vacuous and sentimental" compared to those of the defense intellectuals. Unless the peace community could "meet and answer the magisterial authority of a Herman Kahn," they would remain marginal to the national debate. At the center of the cold war dilemma was the question whether "the matters at issue between us and the Communist world [are] worth such a sacrifice?"[45]

Though skeptical of the necessity of readying the country for nuclear war-fighting, Hughes noted that "it would be easy—all too easy—to dismiss the Kissingers and the Kahns and the Schellings as bloodthirsty men who have computing machines where their hearts should be." Yet he affirmed the probity of all three men. In spite of having assumed belligerent positions on deterrence, they were not immoral. "Faced with the frightful dilemmas of peace and war today, the best any man can do is . . . make his . . . choice in the agony of his conscience," he reflected, "convinced that whatever he does will be in some sense wrong, that, like Pascal, he is making a desperate wager in the dark, and that no one will forgive him if he proves to have been in error."[46]

From a mainstream Christian perspective, John Fry of *Presbyterian Life* pondered the role of the Church in the thermonuclear age. He implored his brethren to fix their hearts and minds on the possibility of nuclear war in the hopes that they may "have the most imperative and creative word to say." Straining against American apathy, he urged the Church to advocate arms control among its parishioners. "People who want to stay alive, who enjoy human prospects, might begin acting as if arms control were pertinent to continued human community." It was therefore important to learn from experts like Kahn so that Christians could pore over their studies "line by line, then begin looking for holes, shortcomings, omissions, obscurities, unnecessary pessimism, unwarranted optimism. We must not ever be convinced that foreign policy experts, nuclear physicists and program analysts automatically have the last or the true word on survival." Failing that, Fry pressed his readers to confront the worst possible outcome, nuclear war, with wisdom and grace. "Surely the Church can begin talking to people about the possibility of mass death," he cried plaintively, "in a way that does not invoke despair or hysteria. Christians above all should be able to know how to die."[47]

Kahn's civil defense proposals were a sticking point. Donald Michael, a policy analyst at the Brookings Institution, considered them distastefully authoritarian. In his review for *Science*, he noted that there was nothing in *OTW* to suggest that postwar reconstruction could unfold within a democratic political order. "It seems clear . . . that the required degree of peacetime integration and control of economic, political, institutional, and personal activities would very likely conflict with traditional concepts of the private and public rights and privileges of Americans." On these grounds alone, Kahn's recommendations should be rejected out of hand.[48]

Another critic, John Bennett, directed attention to Kahn's impoverished cultural imagination. Kahn had glossed over associational life in his projections of the postwar world. "What will happen to the emotional health or morale of the people, to the structures of community, to the quality of life, to the institutions of freedom?" Kahn's engagement with these matters was perfunctory at best. Establishing civil defense in peacetime would suppress popular "moral revulsion" against such precautions.[49]

The geographer Roy Wolfe was worried by Kahn's either-or: "Without nuclear war, a garrison state would be morally indefensible, with nuclear war it would be . . . indispensable, or else chaos would result." Wolfe was especially attuned to the social complexity of the built environment. "Here is a book on war in which *all* the old geographic factors have disappeared. Forgotten are terrain, frontiers, rivers, oceans." There was no geopolitics, no heartland and frontier; Kahn annihilated the distance between places. "The earth has become a featureless sphere, inhabited by featureless populations, and moves and countermoves pour out from the featureless computers." Cherished metropolitan institutions such as universities, libraries, museums, zoos, public gardens, art galleries, opera houses, and concert halls were largely located in the target zone. "Not once in this large book is the existence of any of these recognized," he wrote wonderingly. "The repositories of knowledge and art in our great [cities] are the indispensable cultural link between past and future. To Kahn, it would seem, man is economic man, and nothing more."[50]

Getting down to particulars, Wolfe faulted Kahn for his utterly abstract notion of a nation's activity. The hinterland of America, on which Kahn's projections for postwar recuperation rested, could not plausibly be deracinated from target areas. "One of the chief characteristics of a highly developed society is its nodality, with clusters of intense, concentrated activity being connected to their supporting hinterlands and to other clusters by a network of links." If the nexus that honeycombed the target areas with its outlying interspaces was damaged, it was doubtful that whatever survived could reconstitute the economy.[51]

It wasn't good science, it wasn't good geography, it wasn't good policy. David Lilienthal complained that the simulations of the RAND avant-garde "epitomize how ill-adapted . . . the scientific method [was] to deal with the conflicts that . . . shake the world of men." These "exercises and stream-of-consciousness cerebration" pursued "with such zest and confidence" besmirched "the good name of science." The scenarios, war games, and the rest of the intuitive rigmarole of the simulationists were shuffled out of the purview of the public accountability that was required for good government and good science alike.[52]

On these grounds, Marcus Raskin, a onetime member of the Kennedy administration's National Security Council staff, argued that *ad hominem* attacks were perfectly germane to the scrutiny of contemporary strategists. "Who paid whom to say what and why?" he demanded. Having combed through the works of all of the major strategists sponsored by the government, think tanks, and universities, he concluded that nuclear policy was "essentially metaphysical, with no reference at all to numbers of weapons, the size of the budget, or the power of the military establishment itself." One could only surmise that the business of the defense intellectuals was propaganda designed to "justify and extend the existence of their employers."[53]

Norman Thomas, the evergreen Socialist Party presidential nominee, embraced Kahn's book in the service of his crusade against the tyranny of nation-states. In *The Saturday Review* he wrote, "Mr. Kahn deserves . . . attention from those of us who believe that universal disarmament down to a police level under a strengthened UN is our sole valid hope of a decent existence for our race." Was national security and the sanctity of the nation-state worth defending no matter what the human cost? Why should humankind "deserve to survive" World War III? Only to renew ourselves for "new slaughter in the strife of garrison states worshipping at the altars of National Power." Although Thomas's campaign for world government had become risible by 1961, he still commanded attention in the public arena. His perverse commendation of *OTW* was oddly florid and seemed stately enough to merit inclusion in a Princeton University

Press advertisement. He promptly begged them to remove it (which they did). "I abhor the book," he wrote, "sharing quite largely the opinion so vigorously expressed by Dr. James Newman."[54]

The systems analysts' worldview commanded much attention. William Lee Miller spoke for many observers when he noted "the language and method and assumptions needed for 'analytical' and mathematical work often bootleg in an ethic and a metaphysic of a dubious sort." Indeed, a number of reviewers proposed glosses of the metaphysics underlying Kahn's proposals. One man, Sumner Rosen, regarded *OTW* as the product of "a new breed of utopian writers . . . spawned by the atomic age." He argued that Kahn's book was flagrantly utopian by virtue of its representation of the world picture of nuclear war in the past, present, and future. In *OTW* Kahn implicitly supposed that social harmony could be achieved through the application of techniques used for natural investigation. "This book accepts . . . the threat of nuclear weapons . . . as part of the innate design of the world, and proceeds to teach us how to use our brains to control them, as we do to outsmart microbes and tame the rivers." Rosen emphatically rejected Kahn's segregation of war-fighting matters from diplomatic and social concerns. Without an enveloping "political and social context," he declared, "they are, in the deepest sense, meaningless."[55]

While Rosen considered *OTW* to be an unsavory utopia because of its thesis that human reason could master the catastrophe of nuclear war, Midge Decter read the same book and saw politically useful satire. In her review of Kubrick's *Dr. Strangelove* some years later, she observed, "Where *Dr. Strangelove* is at its best, it most resembles Kahn in the way it rubs the hypothetical up against the real." In fact, she continued, "the movie could very easily have been written by Herman Kahn himself; he outlines just such plots in his books." *OTW* had been stuffed with Strangelovian scenarios, but not because Kahn suffered from social idiocy. On the contrary. He was exquisitely sensitive to the radically near, horrific possibility for chaos the present moment enjoined. Herman Kahn, she announced, "was perhaps the most thoroughgoing negative utopian of our time. It may well be the most powerful dystopia of all times. Not even a George Orwell could be expected to bring the point home to us with more dramatic force."[56]

While Rubinoff's remarks appeared in *Philosophy Forum* on the occasion of the publication of the paperback version of the second edition of *OTW* in 1969, his earnest, sad mood typified the tone of many reviews probing Kahn's metaphysics. Rubinoff was distressed by Kahn's nihilistic assumption that survival was the sole objective of humankind, next to which the ethical question "What ought I to do?" lost its pertinence. Civilization's survival hardly counted as an ethical principle, since no one disputed the merits of existence. "While nihilism is the negation of values, it is at the same time an affirmation of the negator." Since nihilism was, strictly speaking, self-transcendent, Rubinoff pondered the sort of human being projected by this method: *l'homme machine*. "To adopt this attitude uncritically runs the risk of confusing the power of apocalyptic destruction with the capacity to protect."[57]

Rubinoff did not vilify Kahn but instead extended his sympathy to the occupation of military analyst. "It is not Mr. Kahn but the world which is at fault . . . We can hardly blame him for refusing to be a theologian and metaphysician before assuming the responsibilities of a tactician." While metaphysics was not the chief concern of the nuclear strategist, necessity made it the predicament of the rest of humanity.[58]

Most astonishingly, Rubinoff suggested that *OTW* could be the doorway to "a new critique of consciousness, a new phenomenology of mind." It could be a catalytic means for investigating the evil reposing in industrialized civilization. In the therapeutic experience of reading Kahn's book, the "nihilism of *l'homme machine*" could be overcome by "imaginatively liv[ing] through, in order to transcend, the human capacity for evil." Once evil had been confronted "as desire," it could be neutralized. Rubinoff counseled his readers not to consider nuclear war-fighting as the worst possible nightmare but to address it whole-heartedly as the most intensely desired wish of contemporary life. Kahn's book had a critical role to play in this. "It is only through such a Faustian immersion into the purgatory of the human condition that we can cleanse ourselves of the illusions which have given rise to the predicament in which we find ourselves. If read with the proper imagination, Mr. Kahn's book is a step in the direction of such a Faustian immersion." Having done so, Americans would be braced to take the necessary steps required to de-escalate the cold war and disarm.[59]

While Kahn often succeeded in charming his audiences, he was too busy establishing the Hudson Institute, and frankly too self-assured, to manage the reception of his book by responding to every slur. Every once in a while he would be moved to write letters to journals or newspapers to correct some egregious exaggeration of his views. He once chided the author of a series of articles published in *The San Francisco Chronicle* for distorting his views. "Of course, people are entitled to criticize my ideas, and maybe even my character, but it would seem more reasonable to do so on the basis of what my ideas really are." To set the record straight, he laid down three propositions which he implored the readers of the paper to associate with his name forever after:

> (1) I do not prefer war to peace. I think we can try, and may succeed in avoiding war. If we fight a war, I think it should, if possible, be fought without nuclear weapons.
> (2) I do not regard with equanimity the death of any number of Americans—or Russians—no matter how small. On the contrary, I am actively concerned with saving lives in all contingencies.
> (3) I believe that our country is worth taking risks to defend, and that, although the Russians are not malevolent monsters waiting to attack us as soon as they have a chance, it is necessary and practical for us to be prepared to defend it.[60]

Some months later, Kahn synthesized the strands of his responses to the reception of *OTW* into an article for *The Saturday Evening Post* entitled "We're Too Scared to Think." He opened with the complaint, "Few people have criticized my search for means of avoiding thermonuclear war—but I have been criticized severely for spending any time at all on the problems of fighting, surviving and ending such wars. To many, this is an unthinkable subject; any attempt to think about it is either evil or insane." The attack wasn't personal, he was sure; it was a reflection of the national mood. Americans were will-fully deluded about the actual dangers in the present moment. "We may come face to face with a blunt choice between surrender or war. And we must face this possibility," he declared. "We cannot wish it away." While he could easily sympathize with the fears and wishes motivating disarmament, it was even more improbable than war. He pointed out, "I know of no occasion in history in which negotiators from two opposing nations . . . sat around a table and said, 'We're enemies. Let's be friends.'" Just as it was folly to suppose that war was impossible, it was just as irresponsible to consign this ultimate fact of life to the President alone. "Plans cannot exist unless we face the hard realities of the situation. We cannot do it by . . . thinking that in Washington there is some . . . expert or . . . father figure doing all of our thinking for us."[61]

What was unthinkable to Kahn was that his fellow citizens could not be roused from their stupor to acknowledge the intangible but not improbable danger of war. "I am . . . troubled that so many Americans today seem so unconcerned . . . And if a cataclysm should occur, a historian from Mars would never believe that while there was still time to think, to discuss, to plan, we failed to act because we had our heads in the sand"—that when actually menaced by the possibility of nuclear war, Americans lolled.[62]

The Hudson Institute

By 1959 tension between RAND management and its strategists had reached the breaking point. As a professional group, they yearned for a wider sphere of influence. Alain Enthoven later complained, "We were doing very important studies on very important matters, on which we had conclusions that really should be listened to and acted on and were being received politely and filed away. I became . . . fed up." He resigned in April 1960 and emigrated to the office of the director of defense for research and engineering at the Pentagon. In February 1960 Albert Wohlstetter submitted a 69-page memorandum to senior management airing his grievances. While outlining his thoughts, he conferred with a knot of resentful men, including Henry Rowen, Andrew Marshall, Burton Klein, Armen Alchian, Edward Barlow, James Digby, Charles Hitch, John Williams, Olaf Helmer, and Herman Kahn.[63]

By the time *OTW* appeared in print, RAND's president, Frank Collbohm, had announced a plan to restructure research procedures and administration. Like his colleagues, Kahn felt smothered by the newly prohibitive clearance procedures. Collbohm's hostility to civil defense added to his growing disenchantment with RAND.

As a supplement to a major study of strategic air power, in 1956 Kahn and a colleague had proposed a research agenda in civil and passive defense. His analysis subsequently ballooned into a substantial study, which appeared in several RAND publications. Senior management and the air force were mortified. Civil defense was anathema to the philosophy of air power. Kahn had anticipated objections from the air force advisory board, but he had not expected Collbohm to try to choke off independent research. Kahn coaxed a senior vice-president to approve his civil defense study. "People said . . . this would probably be the end since the president wouldn't stand for it. Then I got into a series of fights with the president and . . . I got pretty nasty." He accused Collbohm of cravenly submitting to the air force. Collbohm countered that civil defense deflected attention away from air power, and that what had been intended as an annex to a report would soon swamp the original study. "Basically I said that the study would be dull and uninteresting. It got very interesting and Collbohm thought I promised to keep it dull." Collbohm also complained about Kahn's scamper around the country with his *OTW* briefing. "It ended up with the president telling me that if I stayed at home at RAND and worked on what I was supposed to work on, then things would be fine." Kahn bridled. "I just didn't want to work under their restrictions, and then I decided to start something of my own invention. I just can't work around silly restrictions. I quit."[64]

When Kahn returned to Santa Monica after his fellowship at Princeton, he and Max Singer toyed with the idea of creating a wholly autonomous unit within RAND. But in the wake of tensions with his boss, constrictions on researchers' autonomy, and Kahn's unexpected fame, his friends urged him to create his own institute. By spring 1961, Kahn had decided to leave.

Financing for Kahn's new organization, the Hudson Institute, came from a donor associated with Nelson Rockefeller's circle of advisers, as well as advances for contracted studies. IBM's Federal Systems Division, the Martin Company, the MITRE Corporation, and the Stanford Research Institute gave Hudson its first commissions.[65]

In September 1962 the staff of the new think tank settled into seven buildings on a twenty-one-acre wooded campus in Harmon-on-Hudson. Unlike RAND, Hudson was resolutely independent from proprietary sponsorship. At its opening ceremony, Kahn explained to reporters, "The difference between RAND and Hudson is that RAND is the loyal opposition, and Hudson is not necessarily even loyal. We will have people with security clearance, without it, people who don't want it and people who couldn't get clearance if they tried." Undoubtedly, some of his staff would champion controversial ideas. He added wryly, "I expect some minor scandals, but I am almost immune to attack."[66]

EPILOGUE: A COMIC PHILOSOPHY

What . . . could be more splendidly sincere than the impulse to play in real life, to rise on the rising wave of every feeling and let it burst . . . into the foam of exaggeration? Life is not a means, the mind is not a slave nor a photograph: it has a right to enact a pose, to assume a panache and to create what prodigious allegories it will for the mere sport and glory of it.

GEORGE SANTAYANA, 1924

Parallel worlds, fateful coincidences, panaceas, sneaky ploys, Doomsday, the doubling of America in secret caverns underground—pregnant with marvelous doings, Kahn's scenarios might easily have been fairytales. While his performances were shot through with hilarity, he enfolded his wonders in the parsimonious idiom of systems analysis. The simulation aesthetic choked off the arousals of epic imagining. Only resolve, that grinding exertion of will, was permissible.

The marrow of *On Thermonuclear War* was Kahn's faith in the titanic power of the futurological method. We can see this in the question-and-answer exchanges he reproduced in the appendix to his book. For example, briefing audiences grimly challenged his prophecy of postwar reconstruction. Even if material resources were available, wouldn't the survivors be paralyzed with shock? Could they rally the psychological, political, and social wherewithal to rebuild? Wasn't it more realistic to expect chaos and rebellion? Kahn braved their skepticism with an obtusely hopeful homily.

Assuming the program works no worse than calculations indicate, we can . . . hope for . . . a trend toward conservatism and an over-riding drive to rebuild all that has been destroyed. The government will be able to give an honest account of its reasons for going to war, one that will calm the ire of the populace. The nation has destroyed the enemy that had to be destroyed. It did so with fewer casualties than many expected. More important, the government has a feasible and credible plan for reconstruction. In short, all of our troubles were foreseen, evaluated, and found to be worth the cost.

Given that a reasonable program is presented, the people will probably rally around and work for it . . . Nonetheless, there might be serious long-term effects on our political and economic institutions . . . But, equally well, we can imagine a renewed vigor among the population with a zealous, almost religious dedication to reconstruction . . . Clearly, the question of what kind of political and economic institutions we could have in the postwar period is not independent of the planning that has been done—which is another pressing argument for better planning.[1]

One can hardly picture the events suggested by Kahn's handful of slogans. While he suppressed the social milieu within which nameless office-holders act and react in situations of world-historical consequence, one can *see through* systems analysis to a livelier world picture. I call it comic: buoyant, sustaining, inviolate, dynamic.

Hegel once defined the comic hero as a man who enjoyed "an inherently firm personality . . . raised . . . above the downfall of the whole [world] and is happy and assured in itself . . . Comedy has for its . . . starting-point what tragedy may end with, namely an absolutely reconciled and cheerful heart." The hero's complacency means he will never stake his will wholeheartedly in any single enterprise and therefore can never be deflated. "It is to this absolute freedom of spirit which is utterly consoled in advance of every human undertaking, to this world of private serenity, that [comedy] conducts us."

Hegel wrote wonderingly, "You can scarcely realize how men can take things so easily." In the comic world, actual limits to action dissolve. This is the crux of its magic: objective limits to human action are abandoned. The comic spirit assumes a world in which human cleverness is not checked by any terminus.[2]

Comic *reason* is the power to modify social and natural limits into transient ones with the wit that exploits every contingency. It describes that happy conjunction of rationality, resolve, and mettle in which war-fighting scenarios align with the war-fighting calculations of briefing tables and graphs. It attains an astoundingly neat conformation of plan with happenstance, as in Kahn's assurances that "the government has a feasible and credible plan for reconstruction. In short, all of our troubles were foreseen, evaluated, and found to be worth the cost." Comic reason denotes the faculties of will, intellect, and imagination that turn every fortuity to good purpose. Kahn's feint of anticipating every possible future springs from this deathless conception of human and earthly nature. Under the sign of comic reason, every obstacle is a temporary hindrance, to be contested and always felicitously vanquished by ingenuity, given enough time, money, and resolve.[3]

Thinking about the unthinkable outrides social pieties. But, alas, human will is not the author of the universe that nuclear war would assault. The living world is no modular tool or resource for extraction. The error is just here. Kahn magnified humankind's mastery over nonhuman being and processes, known and unknown. The nonhuman world, that alarmingly uncivil reality, is not molded by wishes, may yet be uncoercible, may yet stand fast against resolve. Slighting this, Kahn lunged into a body of fog, winning victory from no resistance at all. This is kitsch, a stroke against nothing.

Humankind can adapt, exhorted Kahn, devise solutions to problems, and alter habits. Humanity was not inert. Kahn's comic reason wished for decontamination technology and an anti-radiation cure-all. It held out the possibility "that drugs can be developed which, if taken in advance, will increase our ability to accept large radiation doses." He was not alone in this wish. Scores of people both high and low busied themselves in labs. In 1957 scientists at the Air Force Laboratory at the University of Chicago began testing 10,000 different compounds for their efficacy in protecting living tissue from radiation injury. By spring 1961 they had identified four substances that promised anti-radiation protection.[4]

In one experiment, they administered serotonin to laboratory mice before irradiating them. The substance elevated a lethal dosage from 542 roentgens to 880 roentgens. In another experiment, AET gave some protection to monkeys. Whereas a lethal dose was ordinarily 500 roentgens, with AET 80 to 90 percent of a monkey population survived exposure to 700 roentgens, and 50 percent survived exposure to 900 roentgens. Sulfur and even the nerve gas DFP were reported to offer protection.[5]

Just as foolish as prescribing nerve gas as an antidote for fallout, but heartbreakingly whimsical, was the experiment of a British pathologist who valiantly turned out lollipops in his kitchen. His sugar syrup contained iodine, strontium, and potassium, on the theory that if his children sucked the candy, their bodies would store these chemicals and be too saturated to absorb chemically similar radioactive isotopes.[6]

For comic reason, the earth itself is plastic. Just think of Kahn's excited remark, "Relatively thin margins of cost prevent us from doing such extraordinary projects as melting ice caps and diverting ocean currents." Tampering with the climate and geography of the planet was not a cranky idea; like the radiation pill, weather warfare inspired experiments. John von Neumann was also intrigued by the prospect of weather modification. In 1955 he observed that it would take a social investment equivalent to building the railroads to attain control of the climate. "There is little doubt that one *could* carry out analyses needed to predict results, intervene on any desired scale, and ultimately achieve rather fantastic effects. The climate of specific regions and levels of precipitation might be altered."[7]

Flourishing the climactic gesture inclusive of the Western inheritance, Kahn put Reasoning Man at the pivot of the cosmos. As comic as the romantically willful cry, "Open the Age of Reason—

Colonize Space!" his science of postwar survival slighted the mortal fragility of life. He wished away the nonsocial elements of our humanity, the terrestrial and the humbly biological. Unarmored humanity is swaddled in the very earth, air, fire, water of Being—Kahn shook off this dependency. In the 1970s he pushed humankind off the great globe in his predictions of future history. While his book *The Next 200 Years* focused on market activities on planet Earth, Kahn and his co-authors confessed they were "somewhat more inclined" to a "space-centered" prospect. There were no limits to growth. "If . . . limits set by a 'finite earth' really exist, they can be offset by the vast extra-terrestrial resources . . . that will become available soon."[8]

Did Kahn really believe that the earth's panting dwellers could adapt to a world in which "every now and then a city or town is destroyed or damaged as a result of blackmail, unauthorized behavior, or an accident"? In 1959 he was ready to persuade the American President that it would be safe to initiate thermonuclear war under certain conditions on the strength of estimates assessing the survival of the nation. Several years later he described these as cast-off beliefs. In an interview in the mid-1960s, he shrugged, "The truth is I'm bored with nuclear war as a subject. Not repelled, you understand. Just bored. Like the people in Washington, like most people, like you, I don't really believe in it."[9]

In 1950 Norbert Weiner dramatized the unstable dynamism of the postwar world with a parable of the woebegone inventor: "We are in the position of the man who has only two ambitions in life. One is to invent the universal solvent which will dissolve any solid substance, and the second is to invent the universal container which will hold any liquid. Whatever this inventor does, he will be frustrated." Like Weiner's hapless scientist-engineer, the men who drew up the nation's plans to fight and survive thermonuclear war fumbled with contradictory aims. No matter how artificial and poor were their simulations of nuclear combat, strategists still had to trust them, if they wanted to draw up plans for the next war. And yet in order to satisfy their consciences, they felt compelled to dispute the various idealizations invested in their models. In short, whatever the analyst does, he will be frustrated.[10]

Even though Kahn pressed his audiences to accept the necessity of nuclear war-fighting and civil defense with bravura maxims of self-reliance, he was inescapably anxious. In his briefing about pitfalls in modeling, he murmured, "A judicious mixture of faith and caution seem to be needed; faith that seeming difficulties will yield to research and development, caution because they may not." This neatly captures the contest between faith and insight that bedeviled strategists in the 1950s and 1960s. Hypothetical simulations of nuclear war depended for their cogency on the wager of faith. The problem was simple and dramatic. Either the model grasped life-sustaining phenomena well enough to support projections of the postworld or it erred catastrophically. There were no decisive means to settle the issue.[11]

The dilemma confronting Kahn and the defense intellectuals could easily be transposed into Pascal's wager. "Infinite Chaos separates us. At the far end of this infinite distance a coin is being spun which will come down heads or tails. How will you wager? Reason cannot make you choose either, reason cannot prove either wrong." The wager is duplicitous and grounded in doubt. It forces one to stake a claim, yet promises no definitive outcome. And yet one must affirm some position; it is not possible to be agnostic on the matter. The men invested with the responsibility of contemplating a nuclear encounter could not refrain from unthinkable thoughts.[12]

Ultimately, I found myself reading Herman Kahn's book in the forlorn light of presumption and dismay. The best reason for doing so was that the strategists themselves regarded their activities in these anxious terms. The wager unfolded in an atmosphere of dread and confidence. In *OTW* Kahn remarked, "I find it hard to believe that we have uncovered all of the problems from which our systems may suffer. Extreme dependence on such theoretical investigations as substitute for (unobtainable) experience can be dangerous." Survival itself was profoundly unknown. "It is not at all clear that we will be able to predict the post-attack environment in enough detail to be able to take into account adequately all the phenomena that will occur . . . The only question is how important will they be." Given the uncertainties in plotting weapons effects, battle scenarios, social response, and mobilization, it was impossible to determine any major perimeter of a war. Analysts could only gamble that the modes of simulation encompassed the problem, however imperfectly.[13]

In a few short years after the publication of *On Thermonuclear War*, Kahn had grown easy that the world was not in immediate danger. But the wager of deterrence was unaltered. Let's hear again the words of the operations researcher who admitted he could only hope that the findings from simulations of nuclear war were true, since there was no way to check them: "We know that these tests are carried out under controlled conditions. And we know that these conditions will influence the outcome. We also think we know, given information from the test center, what these effects are likely to be. But we can never *really* know. The thing that troubles us is that we don't even *know* if our results are erroneous. We may think they're good. We try to evaluate everything that can affect them . . . All we can hope is that on balance it works out in action as it works out on exercises."[14]

Since there was no basis for certitude, Kahn and the other simulationists painstakingly and repeatedly pointed out the fabrications of their enterprise. Yet they justified its legitimacy with the protest that one couldn't be sure the science was right, only that the science *might* be right, and that it was the only possible approach at the moment. In the teeth of charges of arrogance and omniscience, they put the simulations, scenarios, and games of nuclear war in the place of Nothing and proffered uneasy faith.[15]

Abbreviations

AF	*Aircraft Flash*
Burch	Stanley Burch, "The real Dr. Strangelove," *The Daily Mail* (U.K.), 6/21/65.
Chappaqua	Kahn's private papers in his home in Chappaqua, New York.
Collins	Martin Collins, Planning for Modern War: RAND and the Air Force, 1945–1950 (Ph.D. diss., University of Maryland at College Park, History Department, 1998).
Counsels	Gregg Herken, *Counsels of War* (Alfred Knopf, 1985).
FBI (A)	FBA File no. 116-103292.
FBI (B)	FBA File no. 140-21969.
FBI (C)	FBI File no. 116-11440.
Jardini	David Jardini, Out of the Blue Yonder: The Rand Corporation's Diversification into Social Welfare Research, 1946–1968 (Ph.D. diss., History Department, Carnegie Mellon University, 1996).
Kahn, Mann (A)	Herman Kahn and Irwin Mann, *Techniques of Systems Analysis* (RAND, 12/3/56, revised 6/57).
Kahn, Mann (B)	Herman Kahn and Irwin Mann, *Ten Common Pitfalls* (RAND, 7/17/57).
Kahn, Mann (C)	Herman Kahn and Irwin Mann, *Game Theory* (RAND, 7/30/57).
Kahn, Mann (D)	Herman Kahn and Irwin Mann, *Monte Carlo* (RAND, 7/30/57).
Kahn, Mann (E)	Herman Kahn and Irwin Mann, *War Gaming* (RAND, 7/30/57).
MAG	Herman Kahn, *Briefing on Ten Common Pitfalls to Military Advisory Group of Air Force* (RAND briefing, 3/22/55). Transcribed by Irwin Mann.

MITRE	Herman Kahn, Strategic Postures for the U.S. and Soviet Union (MITRE briefing, 12/16/59). Unpublished transcript, MITRE Corporate Archives.
Newman	James Newman, "Two Discussions of Thermonuclear War," *Scientific American*, 3/61.
NDU	Herman Kahn/Hudson Institute archive in the National Defense University library.
Obscure	William McWhirter, "'I Am One of the 10 Most Famous Obscure Americans,'" *Life*, 12/6/68.
One Man	Richard Kostelanetz, "One-Man Think Tank," *New York Times Sunday Magazine*, 12/1/68.
OTW	Herman Kahn, *On Thermonuclear War* (Princeton University Press, 1960).
Princeton	Herman Kahn, Lectures on Thermonuclear War in the 1960–1970 Period (Princeton University briefing, 3/13–14/59). Unpublished transcript, Chappaqua.
PUP	Princeton University Press archive
SAB	Herman Kahn, Briefing to Science Advisory Board of the Air Force, (RAND briefing, 3/25/55). Transcribed by Irwin Mann.
TAU	Herman Kahn, *Thinking about the Unthinkable* (Horizon Press, Avon Books, 1962; Discus Edition, 1971). Pagination is for 1971 edition.
Wizards	Fred Kaplan, *The Wizards of Armageddon* (Simon and Schuster, 1983).

Notes

PROLOGUE: A MATTER OF FAITH

1. US DoD News Transcript, 6/6/02. Rumsfeld made the same remark four months earlier. See US DoD News Transcript, 2/12/02. www.defenselink.mil/transcripts/2002.

2. In early 1959 the Air Force Council noted, "Soviet security measures will permit the development of forces under concealment, capable of neutralizing the effect of our programmed deterrence force." Wizards, 406. In 1961 a national intelligence estimate stated, "The high sides takes into account the limitations of our coverage and allows for the existence of a few other complexes . . . now operational but undetected." NIE 11-8/1-61, in Kevin Ruffner, ed., *CORONA, America's first satellite program* (Central Intelligence Agency, 1995), 141. John Prados, *The Soviet estimate, U.S. intelligence analysis and Russian military strength* (Dial, 1982), 119. Donald Steury, ed., *Intentions and capabilities, estimates on Soviet strategic forces, 1950–1983* (Central Intelligence Agency, 1996), 57.

3. OTW, 534, 326. US DoD News Transcript, 6/6/02. www.defenselink.mil/transcripts/2002.

4. OTW, 368. Robert Panero interview, 8/2/91.

5. Newman, 197. A. M. Stone, Applied Physics Laboratory, letter to Kahn, 12/12/60, NDU. Alexander Cockburn and James Ridgeway, "Pitchman for the apocalypse: the horrible legacy of Herman Kahn," *Village Voice*, 7/19/83, 15. Marvin Feldman, "Thinking about the unthinkable," *Humanist Newsletter* (New York), 3/63, 2, Chappaqua.

6. OTW, 22.

7. Ibid., 54. MITRE, 64–65. See OTW, 156–157, for a more demure formulation of the same idea.

8. OTW, 20.

9. Ibid., 514–515.

10. Fred Kaplan, "JFK's first-strike plan," *Atlantic Monthly*, 10/01, 84. Andrew Wilson, *The bomb and the computer: wargaming from ancient Chinese mapboard to atomic computer* (Delacorte, 1968), 129.

1. HOW MANY KAHNS CAN THERE BE?

1. SAB, 7–8. Please note: I have pieced together this imaginary briefing from snippets of actual transcripts and published documents in order to give the reader a feeling for Kahn's timing, asides, and jokes. Throughout the book, where I offer quotes from Kahn's briefing transcripts, in order to transpose his comic delivery onto the page, I have omitted ellipses. While condensed, the transcript quotes do not change the meaning of his original utterance.
2. SAB, 5–6.
3. SAB, 9.
4. SAB, 176. Kahn, Mann (B), 17, 19.
5. SAB, 72.
6. MAG, 6.
7. Princeton, 73–74.
8. MAG, 12.
9. Kahn, Mann (B), 1–2.
10. MAG, 40.
11. MITRE, 159.
12. MITRE, 152–153. Arthur Herzog (A), "A visit with Herman Kahn," *Think*, 10/63, 14.
13. Letter, Barbara Blumenfeld to Kahn, no date, Folder, Saturday Evening Post 1961, NDU.
14. Letter, Cathy Chisholm to Kahn, 9/24/61, Folder, Saturday Evening Post 1961, NDU.
15. Letter, Hamilton Dixon to Kahn, 9/12/61, Folder, Saturday Evening Post 1961, NDU.
16. Letter, John Holt to Kahn, 4/2/61, Folder, Correspondence 1961, NDU. OTW, 21. Letter, John Holt to Kahn, 11/19/61, NDU.
17. Bradford Lyttle interview, 9/22/00. Bradford Lyttle, *We come with naked hands: the story of the San Francisco to Moscow walk for peace* (Greenleaf Books, 1966), 29. Lyttle interview.
18. Jules Feiffer, *Hold me!* (New American Library, 1964). Susan Sontag, "The imagination of disaster," *Commentary*, 10/65, 42. Lawrence Freedman, "Escalators and quagmires, expectations and the use of force," *International Affairs*, 67(1) (1991), 25. Obscure, 110.
19. Eliot Fremont-Smith, "The last word and other illusions," *Village Voice*, 5/24/62, 12.
20. Roscoe Giffin, "Encounter with Herman Kahn," *Friends Journal*, 4/15/61, 158.
21. Letters confirming this can be found in Folder, Correspondence 1961, NDU, and Chappaqua.
22. John Strachey, "On thermonuclear war," *Survival* (UK), 5–6/61, 147. Newman, 197. Science Correspondent, "Nuclear warfare and after," *Glasgow Herald* (UK) 4/27/61, Chappaqua. Walter Marseille, Letters column, *Bulletin of the Atomic Scientists*, 9/61, 294.

23. Congratulatory letters greeting advance copies of the book were sent from George Ball, 11/28/60, McGeorge Bundy, 2/10/61, Leo Hough, director, Office of Civil and Defense Mobilization, 12/1/60, Secretary of Defense Robert McNamara, 1/17/61, Secretary of the Air Force Dudley Sharp, 11/28/60, Assistant Secretary of State Gerard Smith, 11/30/60, Director of Defense Research and Engineering, Herbert York, 12/20/60, Secretary of the Air Force Eugene Zuckert, 12/30/61. Chappaqua. Letter, Alain Enthoven to Kahn, 12/22/60, Chappaqua. Herzog (A), 12. Yarmolinsky attended the open house ceremony of the Hudson Institute on 9/21/62 as reported in the *New York Times* the following day. Thereafter, he was known to attend Hudson Institute events.

24. Kahn and the vice-president of RAND, Lawrence Henderson, received scores of congratulatory letters from such high-ranking officers as Dr. Alexander Flax, chief scientist, United States Air Force (USAF), 12/9/60, Gen. Laurence Kuter, USAF, commander in chief, North American Air Defense Command, 1/4/61, Admiral L. L. Lemnitzer, Joint Chiefs of Staff, 12/1/60, Gen. Curtis LeMay, USAF, vice chief of staff, 11/28/60, Gen. Lauris Norstad, supreme commander, Allied Powers, Europe, 12/28/60, Gen. Thomas Power, USAF, commander in chief, Strategic Air Command, 11/30/60, Gen. Thomas White, USAF, chief of staff, 11/28/60, Chappaqua. *Air Force Magazine*, 2/61. *Topics*, Office of Information, HQ NORAD, 1/15/61, 2. Similarly, the air force *Information Policy Letter for Commanders* noted that OTW was "one of the most important current books." *Air Force Information Policy Letter for Commanders*, 2/1/61, no page. Also see *USAF Information Program Bulletin* 12/15/60, 4, which alerted readers to "a new book on Thermonuclear War."

25. Professor Bernard Cohen, University of Wisconsin, to Kahn, 12/24/60. Dan Seligman, Editor, *Fortune*, to Kahn, 1/4/61. H. Field Haviland, Jr., letter to Kahn, 12/1/60. A. M. Stone, Applied Physics Laboratory, Johns Hopkins University, to Kahn, 12/19/60. Chappaqua.

26. On the strength of the reception of OTW, in 1961 Kahn persuaded A. J. Muste to sit on the advisory committee of his Hudson Institute. As to why he had associated himself with nuclear war-fighters, Muste replied mildly, "I don't think Kahn and the others are devils—they are trying to find a way." Arthur Herzog (B), "Report on a 'think factory,'" *New York Times Magazine*, 11/10/63, 30. H. Stuart Hughes, "The strategy of deterrence," *Commentary*, 3/61, 186. Bertrand Russell, "The case for British nuclear disarmament," *Bulletin of the Atomic Scientists*, 3/62, 6, 7.

27. Etzioni, 4. Letter, Chester S. Williams, assistant to the director, Hudson Institute, to John Fletcher, Harper & Bros., 3/30/61, 1, NDU. Kahn eventually penned an article in response to the reception of OTW. Herman Kahn, "We're too scared to think," *Saturday Evening Post*, 9/16/61.

28. Letter, Hedley Bull, the London School of Economics, to Kahn, 5/15/61, Chappaqua.

29. "Throng sets arena record—Nixon is platform guest," *New York Times*, 7/21/57, 1; 2,149,700 people attended the New York Crusade. "Graham crusade termed a record," *New York Times*, 8/30/57, 21. "Graham to hold week of rallies," *New York Times*, 9/21/57, 20. "Three assail crusade," *New York Times*, 6/10/57, 35.

30. "Graham's farewell packs Broadway," *New York Times*, 9/2/57, 9. "Prayerful mood felt in midtown," *New York Times*, 9/2/57, 9.

31. "Virginians sing way to crusade," *New York Times*, 5/16/57, 68. "Graham is honored for crusade here," *New York Times*, 10/29/57, 25.

32. "Graham exhorts Wall St. throng," *New York Times*, 7/11/57, 27.

33. George Burnham and Lee Fisher, *Billy Graham and the New York crusade* (Zondervan, 1957), 59, 61. "Graham cites drug use," *New York Times*, 7/12/57, 46. Graham favored an American test suspension. "Graham proposes Russian crusade," *New York Times*, 6/20/57, 35.

34. "Graham points to sin," *New York Times*, 6/28/57, 47. "Graham tells way to better sermons," *New York Time*, 8/25/57, 56. "Graham in warning on atomic disaster," *New York Times*, 7/8/57, 26. "Graham foresees peril," *New York Times*, 7/4/57, 37. "Graham outdrew past evangelists," *New York Times*, 9/3/57, 29.

35. David Segal, "Feiffer, Steinberg, and others," *Commentary*, 11/61, 435.

36. Paul Hutchinson, "Have we a 'new' religion?" *Life*, 4/11/55, 143. Gore Vidal, "The unrocked boat," *Nation*, 4/26/58, 371. Robert Osborn, "The emasculation of American humor," *Saturday Review*, 11/23/57, 17.

37. Henry Lee, "This age of fear," *American Mercury*, 5/57, 52–53. Archibald MacLeish, "The American state of mind," *American Scholar*, Autumn 1950, 401.

38. Raymond Fosdick, "Acts of faith for a time of peril," *New York Times Magazine*, 4/8/51, 9. Bertrand Russell, "No funk, no frivolity, no fanaticism," *New York Times Magazine*, 5/6/51, 7.

39. Louis Kronenberger, "The spirit of the age," *American Scholar*, 1/52, 10. John Wright, "After the brave new world," *Commonweal*, 9/18/53, 579.

40. Lester Markel, "Report from 'Foggy Bottom,'" *New York Times Magazine*, 3/28/54, 3. Robert Fitch, "The fears of the intelligentsia," *Commentary*, 10/54, 328–329. Hutchinson, 143. Lee, 51.

41. Allan Seager, "Our dream of comfort," *Nation*, 12/12/53, 519. Jerome Frank, MD, "Are you a guilty parent?" *Harpers*, 4/57, 58. Editorial, "Domestic tranquility," *New Republic*, 6/24/57, 6. Seward Hiltner, "Atomic fears and Christian courage," *Christian Century*, 3/19/58, 337.

42. "Soft," *Nation*, 11/21/59, 370–371. Eric Goldman, "Good-by to the fifties—and good riddance," *Harpers*, 1/60, 27, 29.

43. George Stevenson, "The antidote for atomic jitters," *New York Times Magazine*, 5/13/51, 55: John Spiegel, "Cry wolf, cry havoc!" *Bulletin of the Atomic Scientists*, 4/54, 144.

44. Fosdick, 66. Russell 1951, 7. Lee, 57. Hiltner, 337.

45. Fosdick, 68. Russell, 23.

46. Hutchinson, 140, 144. Goldman, 28.

47. Fitch, 334, 335. "Psychiatry and being," *Time*, 12/29/58, 27.

48. Kronenberger, 14. Ernest Havemann, "The age of psychology in the U.S.," *Life*, 1/7/57, 72, 79.

49. Francis Bello, "The tranquilizer question," *Fortune*, 5/57, 162, 164.

50. Kronenberger, 12. Gerald Walker, "Psychoanalysis of the couch," *New York Times Magazine*, 4/13/58, 20. Ralph Schoenstein, "Merrily we probe along," *Saturday Evening Post*, 9/25/62, 10.

51. "Mind over machine," *Newsweek*, 9/9/57, 52.

52. "A new American poet speaks: the works of A. B.," *Horizon*, 5/62, 97. It was reported that the *cri de coeur* "Ah, I am not a machine!" was especially well received. "The machines are taking over," *Life*, 3/3/61, 118. Worthy directed the Auto-Poet project at the Librascope Laboratory for Automata Research in Glendale, CA. See R. M. Worthy, "How A.B.'s poems are written," *Horizon*, 5/62, 98–99.

53. Gilbert Burck, "The boundless age of the computer," *Fortune*, 3/64, 108. "Machines are this smart," *Newsweek*, 10/24/60. "Thinking machines take over!" *Science*, 3/61. Burck, 107.

54. See Francis Bello, "How to cope with information," *Fortune*, 9/60. John Pfeiffer, "Machines that man can talk with," *Fortune*, 5/64, 198. Burck, 104. John Kemeny, "Games of life and death," *Nation*, 1/21/61, 48–49.

55. Lester Velie, "Automation—friend or foe?" *Reader's Digest*, 10/62, 102. "Machines are taking over," *Life*, 3/3/61. "Computers start to run the plants," *Business Week*, 11/5/60. "You can be replaced," *Newsweek*, 5/4/64. John Diebold as told to Patricia Lovelady Cahn, "When will your husband be obsolete?" *McCall's*, 7/63, 64. From a February 1962 press conference in Henry Hazlitt, "Automation makes jobs," *Newsweek*, 3/5/62, 70.

56. Gerard Piel, "End of toil" *Nation*, 6/17/61, 519. Norbert Wiener, "Some moral and technical consequences of automation," *Science*, 5/6/60, 1357. Harrison Brown, "Point of no survival," *Saturday Review*, 12/27/58, 18.

57. The opening of the Geneva arms control talks sharpened public concerns about mechanical accident in the increasingly rapid responses of the strategic weapons complex. The Surprise Attack Conference (11/10/58–12/18/58) focused on narrowly technical dimensions of establishing a global on-site inspection regime as an impediment to surprise attack. "A-war by accident?" *Newsweek*, 3/24/58, 62.

58. Carl Dreher, "War by accident," *Nation*, 9/6/58, 107, 108.

59. The phrase "new civilian militarists" comes from Irving Louis Horowitz's critique of OTW in "Arms, policies, and games," *American Scholar*, Winter 1961–62. Letter, Muriel Short to Kahn, 11/1961, Folder, 1961 Correspondence, NDU.

60. Letter, Andrew McGaughey, the Menninger Clinic, to Kahn, 9/16/61, Folder, Saturday Evening Post, NDU.

61. Hilbert Schenck, Jr., "Computing 'ad absurdum,'" *Nation,* 6/15/63, 505–507.

62. Letter, Stewart Meacham, Peace Education Secretary, American Friends Service Committee, to Kahn, 5/5/61, 2, Chappaqua.

63. Herzog (A), 15.

64. Stephanie Gervis, "Kahn vs. Etzioni, how much stability is there in the balance of terror?" *Village Voice,* 1/17/63, 8. Jessica Smith, "Unthinkable thinking," *New World Review,* 1/63, 46. Strachey, 147.

65. Burch, 11.

66. Gervis, 8. Herzog (A), 13. Norman Moss, *Men who play God: the story of the hydrogen bomb* (Victor Gollancz, 1968), 243. "Face to face," *New York Herald Tribune,* Sunday Magazine, 11/26/61, 1. One Man, 58. Burch, 11.

67. To one friend who had spent much of his life abroad, Kahn's dress was inexcusably casual. Panero chuckled, "The only effect I ever had on Herman was, I told him, 'I don't think you can talk about thermonuclear war unless you wear a tie.'" From then on, at least for several years, Kahn sported a tie whenever he spoke about all-out war. Robert Panero interview, 8/2/91. Wizards, 119, 96. Kahn wrote that in the postwar world, "[We would limit] exposure to the unshielded environment. The rest of the time we would have to live in protected areas. This would not mean that we should have give up our homes and factories, although we might have to give up some of their aesthetic appearance and convenience." OTW, 61. Paul Vangelisti, ed., *LA exiles: a guide to Los Angeles writing, 1932–1998* (Marsilio Publishers, 1999), 318.

68. Frances FitzGerald, "Herman Kahn, metaphors and scenarios," *New York Herald Tribune Sunday Magazine,* 7/4/65, 3.

69. Obscure, 119.

70. One Man, 82, 59, 82.

71. Herzog (A), 14. Obscure, 119.

72. OTW, 29, 40, 157, 42.

73. OTW, 145.

74. Christopher Hollis, "Dr. Strangelove and Dr. Kahn," *Spectator,* 2/28/64, 275. *Sunday Times* (UK), 2/9/65. The paper soon after published a protest from Peter George, one of the screenwriters of *Dr. Strangelove,* explicitly denying this. Letter, Thomas Schelling to author, 10/12/98. Burch, 11. Obscure, 114.

75. "On Herman Kahn," *Newsweek,* 5/7/65, 54. Obscure, 94. See pp. 49, 97, 98, 115, 123, 142, 143 in Peter George, *Dr. Strangelove, or, how I learned to stop worrying and love the bomb* (Bantam Books, 1964), for direct quotations or close paraphrases of passages from OTW.

76. Midge Decter, "The strangely polite 'Dr Strangelove,'" *Commentary,* 5/64, 76. Arthur Herzog (B), "Report on a 'think factory,'" *New York Times Magazine,* 11/10/63, 42.

77. TAU, 26.
78. Ibid., 26, 40.
79. Ibid., 38, 26, 283.
80. Joseph Kraft, "RAND, arsenal for ideas," *Harpers,* 7/60, 75. It was probably Kahn's. The joke appears *verbatim* at the conclusion of his paper *Why go deep underground?* (RAND, 2/6/59), 37.
81. He added, "There are of course, special situations in which one should meticulously observe formalities . . . Thus, for various reasons, 'thermonuclear humor' might be inappropriate or in bad taste in a talk by an American in Asia or even Africa and Latin America, and I tend not to use it in such talks—even to professional or official audiences." TAU, 282. Eunice Armstrong, letter, *Progressive,* 2/61, 43. One Man, 82.
82. Benjamin DeMott, "The new irony, sickniks and others," *American Scholar,* Winter 1961–62, 109, 110, 118.
83. TAU, 282.

2. THE COLD WAR AVANT-GARDE AT RAND

1. P. M. S. Blackett, "Operational research: recollections of problems studies," H. G. Thursfield, ed., *Brassey's Annual: the armed forces year-book* (Macmillan, 1953), 106. John Slessor, *The central blue* (Cassell, 1956), 487.
2. Slessor, 524, 525.
3. For more on RAND and the Kennedy administration, see Wizards, 248–257; Counsels, 148–162; Jardini, 190–228.
4. RAND strategists advocated accelerating the navy's Polaris program (i.e., submarine-launched ballistic missile capability), limited war, civil defense, train-mobile ICBMs, and the phasing-out of manned strategic bombers, all of which defied air force doctrine and plans. The air force complained, "RAND employees were publishing papers and books that were often in opposition to Air Force policy, or contained statements that the Air Force would rather not have had published." Laurence Henderson, *RAND and the air force: the context of the problem,* 11/14/61, in Jardini, 237. When RAND recommended phasing out SAC's manned bomber program, SAC responded by periodically and abruptly terminating contact with RAND between 1957 and 1961. The air force objected, "RAND scientists tended to become cynical and arrogant, particularly toward Air Force officers and . . . decision makers when RAND ideas and recommendations were not accepted by the Air Force." Henderson in Jardini, 237. Wizards, 256. General Thomas White, "Strategy and the defense intellectuals," *Saturday Evening Post,* 5/4/63, 12.
5. Kahn, Mann (A), 2
6. Ibid., 3. "Planners for the Pentagon," *Business Week,* 7/13/63, 10.
7. White, 10.
8. Anthony Wiener interview, 8/1/91.

9. "The 36-hour war," *Life*, 11/19/45, 28, 29, 30.

10. Joseph and Stewart Alsop, "Are we ready for a push-button war?" *Saturday Evening Post*, 9/6/47, 13. *Atom-Age Combat* (St. John Publishing, 2/58), 1–3.

11. Vaughn Bornet, *John Williams: a personal reminiscence* (RAND, 8/12/69), 1.

12. Memo paraphrasing Arnold's talk from Brigadier General Thomas Rives to Gen. McClelland, 1/14/45, 2, in Collins, 30–33.

13. Wizards, 59. Frank Collbohm interview, 7/28/87, 18. RAND Oral History Project, National Air and Space Museum, Smithsonian Institution.

14. Bornet, 18–19. Memorandum, Williams to Collbohm, 6/6/46, in Collins, 239.

15. Bornet, 24–25.

16. James Digby, *The development of strategic thinking at the RAND Corporation, 1948–1963, an electrical engineer's view: interview with E. J. Barlow* (RAND, 8/12/86), 8, 12. Williams initially hired mathematicians, engineers, statisticians, and physicists. By late 1947 a social science division was established, adding economists, political scientists, social psychologists, sociologists, and historians to the staff.

17. An air force policy statement written in the summer of 1948 makes this clear. "Project RAND represents an investment by the AF in objective research and analysis. To preserve this objectivity, the RAND management is given maximum freedom in planning the Project RAND research program." Letter 7/21/48, Jardini, 119. Sidney Winter, Jr., interview, 8/23/91.

18. James Digby, *The development of strategic thinking at the RAND Corporation, 1948–1963, a physicist's view: an interview with Albert Latter* (RAND, 9/9/85), 1.

19. Memo, Joseph Goldsen to Social Science Department, "20 Years at RAND," 5/23/68 in Wizards, 62. Hans Speier interview, 7/28/87, 46. RAND Oral History Project, National Air and Space Museum, Smithsonian Institution. Olaf Helmer interview, 6/3/94, 7. RAND Oral History Project, National Air and Space Museum, Smithsonian Institution. James Digby, *The development of strategic thinking at the RAND Corporation, 1948–1963, an aeronautical engineer's view: an interview with Bruno Augenstein* (RAND, 5/22/86), 5. For more reminiscences of RAND in its early days, see the RAND Oral History Project collection, National Air and Space Museum, Smithsonian Institution.

20. John McDonald, "The war of wits," *Fortune*, 3/51, 144, 99.

21. Ibid., 158, 152.

22. *Scientific American*, 5/57, 38

23. *Scientific American*, 7/57, 40.

24. Gene Martin, "Think factory de luxe," *Nation*, 2/14/59, 133.

25. "Valuable batch of brains," *Life*, 5/11/59, 101.

26. "Manufactures nothing" from "Games of survival," *Newsweek*, 5/18/53, 75.
27. James King, Jr., "Strategic surrender: the senate debate and the book," *World Politics*, 5/59, 420, 421. "No part of the funds appropriated in this (or any other Act) shall be used to pay . . . any person, firm or corporation . . . to conduct a study or to plan when and how or in what circumstances the Government of the United States should surrender this country and its people to any foreign power" (passed on 8/27/58, Section 1602, Public Law 85766, 72 Stat. 864: H.R. 13450, "Supplemental Appropriations").
28. "Text of Eisenhower's farewell address," *New York Times*, 1/18/61, 22.
29. For the fullest public disclosure of the activities of the nonprofit corporations since their founding, see *Systems development and management*, Hearings before a Subcommittee of the Committee on Government Operations, House of Representatives, 87th Congress, 2nd Session, parts 1–5, 1962.
30. David Lilienthal, "Skeptical look at 'scientific experts,'" *New York Times Magazine*, 9/29/63, 82, 23, 80, 82.
31. OTW, 162.
32. Frank Collbohm, *Scientific aids to decision-making—a perspective* (RAND, 1/31/57), 3.
33. Wesley Marx, "Hired brains for the brass," *Nation*, 12/2/61, 451.

3. THE REAL DR. STRANGELOVE

1. Max Singer interview, 7/17/91. Henry Rowen interview, 8/10/95.
2. FBI (A), Report, 3/14/60, 3. FBI (B).
3. Sam Cohen interview, 8/7/95. Also see Sam Cohen, "Smartest guy in the army," *Army*, 1/84.
4. Cohen interview, 8/7/95.
5. Cohen interview. FBI (B), AirTel, 3/10/60. Andrew Marshall interview, 8/16/04.
6. FBI (C), Report, 8/27/48. FBI (A), Letter, 9/2/48. FBI (B), Security investigation data for sensitive position, 2/26/60. Wiener interview, 8/1/91. Kahn's history of security clearances are documented in FBI (B), Report, 3/21/60, 2.
7. Letter, M. C. Leverett, technical director, NEPA Division, Fairchild Engine and Airplane Corporation, Oak Ridge, TN, to Kahn, 2/6/50, Folder, Correspondence, 1949–50, NDU. Also see Jardini, 78–81. Carolyn James, "The politics of extravagance, the aircraft nuclear propulsion project, *Naval War College Review*, Spring 2000.
8. Singer interview, 7/17/91. Wiener interview, 9/18/04.
9. Wiener interview, 9/18/04. Cohen interview, 8/7/95.
10. One Man, 93. This is odd, since his work had been underwritten by the Atomic Energy Commission and RAND.
11. Jane Kahn interview, 8/31/89.
12. FBI (A), Report, 10/14/53, 1, 2.

13. Marshall interview, 9/3/91.
14. Ibid. See Herman Kahn and Andrew Marshall, *A simplified study of reconnaissance in strategic bombing campaigns* (RAND, 3/6/52). Herman Kahn and Andrew Marshall, *Methods of reducing sample size in Monte Carlo computations* (RAND, 8/18/53).
15. FBI (A), Letter, Reinvestigation of Kahn, 7/27/53. There were other security investigations at RAND. For example, J. C. C. McKinsey, a mathematician and author of five memoranda on game theory in the early 1950s, was openly gay. He was subsequently fired from RAND on the grounds of "fear of blackmail and emotional instability." Roberta Wohlstetter recalled, "He was really indignant. He said, 'Good God, I've lived with this man for fifteen years. What's irregular about that?'" Roberta Wohlstetter interview, 8/6/89. Also see FBI (A), Telegram, 8/3/53. FBI (C), Report, 9/18/53.
16. Letter, Francis Hammack, chief, Personnel Security Branch, AEC, to J. Edgar Hoover, director, FBI, 8/31/54, 2. Department of Energy, FBI File, 390990–001. FBI (A), Report, 9/22/54, 2. U.S. Civil Service Commission, File #140-21969-15, 2–4.
17. Marshall interview, 8/16/04.
18. Marshall interview, 8/16/04. His remarks became the basis for Kahn, Mann (A) and (B). Marshall interview, 3/24/99.
19. Marshall interview, 3/24/99.
20. Marshall interview, 9/3/91. Digby and Goldhamer, *Interview with Albert Latter*, 5.
21. Roberta Wohlstetter interview, 8/6/95.
22. Gustave Shubert interview, 1/20/01.
23. Wiener interview, 8/1/91. Obscure, 124, 110B.
24. Jane Kahn interview, 8/31/89.
25. Obscure, 116. Wiener interview, 8/1/91.
26. Everett Mendelsohn interview, 11/20/00.
27. Lyttle interview, 9/22/00. Lyttle, *Naked hands*, 28, 29.
28. Lyttle interview, 9/22/00.
29. Lyttle, *Naked hands*, 30.
30. Letter, Kahn to Robert Pickus, 4/11/62, NDU.
31. Letter, Roger Hagan to Kahn, 5/12/61. Letter, Kahn to Hagan, 6/20/62, NDU.
32. Letter, Kahn to Hagan, 6/25/62. Hagan replied, "While there is a certain risk of mutual contamination in this, there is not much likelihood of . . . you marching around with signs . . . I've always been sympathetic to your desire to maintain contact, no matter what your purposes were." He closed, "I nowhere liked you better or the *Scientific American* worse than where you offered to meet and talk with them and they refused." Letter, Hagan to Kahn, 6/28/62, NDU.
33. Air Force Inspector General, Office of Special investigations, Report of

Investigations, 8/13/62, Department of the Air Force, Air Force Office of Special Investigations, File no. 1028.

34. Wiener interview, 8/1/91.

35. Obscure, 124. Letter to William McGlothlin, 10/15/62, HK Correspondence, NDU. Also see Letter, Kahn to Dr. Sidney Cohen, Veterans Administration Hospital, 10/8/62, NDU. Not surprisingly, given Kahn's public admission that he had taken acid, the FBI investigated the LSD experiences. On 9/29/72 an agent interviewed Cohen, one of the co-directors of the study. Consulting his notes from the experiment, Cohen reported that he had conducted an interview with Kahn in order to assess his emotional stability for the experiment. He subsequently administered to him a dose of one hundred micrograms of acid. Kahn's experience was "normal in that he had no difficulty and no complications." Cohen interviewed Kahn once more and determined that he had not suffered any untoward aftereffects. FBI (B), Teletype 10/3/72. Also see Steven Novak, "LSD before Leary: Sidney Cohen's critique of 1950s psychedelic drug research," *Isis*, 3/97.

36. Wiener interview, 8/1/91.

37. Jane Kahn interview, 7/10/91.

38. Wiener interview, 8/1/91.

39. Ibid. Kahn contrasted the recent past with exemplars from world history, including myth. For example, he presented a table of "historical prototypes" of crises that included Armageddon and Camlan, the field of King Arthur's last battle, as well as Berlin, Korea, and Pearl Harbor. OTW, 525.

40. Panero interview, 8/2/91. Wiener interview, 8/1/91.

41. Wiener interview, 8/1/91.

42. Panero, interview, 8/2/91.

43. Winter interview, 8/23/91.

44. Panero interview, 8/2/91.

45. Irwin Mann interview, 7/10/91.

46. Ibid.

47. Panero interview, 8/2/91.

48. Wiener interview, 8/7/91.

49. Ibid.

50. Ibid.

51. Ibid. Winter interview, 8/23/91. Singer interview, 7/17/91.

52. Wiener interview, 8/1/91. Marshall interview, 9/3/91.

53. Steuart Pittman interview, 8/22/91.

54. Cohen interview, 8/7/95.

55. MAG, 52.

4. AN OPERATIONAL BUT UNDETECTED CAPABILITY

1. MITRE, 175–176. OTW, 163, 286, 326.

2. OTW, 347.

3. Sigmund Freud, "The uncanny," *Studies in parapsychology*, ed. Philip Rieff (Collier, 1963), 41, 47.

4. See Gallup Poll #517 (7/53) and #627 (4/60), Princeton, New Jersey.

5. Spurgeon Keeny interview, 1/30/01.

6. Spurgeon Keeny interview, 1/30/01, 9/25/04.

7. On 8/19/50, 57 percent polled believed that World War III had already begun; by December 6, 55 percent still believed that atomic war was imminent. George Gallup, *The Gallup Poll: public opinion, 1935–1971*, vol. 2 (Random House, 1972), 933, 951. John Popham, "Bradley denounces slogans of war as tricky, perilous risks to U.S.," *New York Times*, 2/23/53, 1, 2.

8. Gallup, 1435. "Russian warning given on mideast," *New York Times*, 7/2/56, 7. See John Lewis Gaddis, Philip Gordon, Ernest May, and Jonathan Rosenberg, eds., *Cold war statesmen confront the bomb: nuclear diplomacy since 1945* (Oxford, 1998).

9. For the deployment of nuclear weapons to American bases overseas, see Robert Norris, William Arkin, and William Burr, "Where they were," Appendix B, "Deployments by country, 1951–1977," *Bulletin of the Atomic Scientists*, 11–12/99.

10. Dwight D. Eisenhower, *The White House years: waging peace, 1956–1961* (Doubleday, 1965), 89.

11. "Ambassadors walk out: protest at speech by Mr. Khrushchev," *Times* (UK), 11/19/56, 8. Also see Welles Hangen, "Thirteen envoys walk out on Khrushchev talk," *New York Times*, 11/18/56, 1, 35.

12. "Texts of Soviet statement on disarmament proposals and of Bulganin's letter," *New York Times*, 11/18/56, 33. "Soviet discloses a nuclear blast," *New York Times*, 11/18/56, 33.

13. "Khrushchev tirade again irks envoys," *New York Times*, 11/19/56, 12.

14. "Khrushchev bids Reds copy Stalin," *New York Times*, 1/18/57, 8.

15. Seymour Topping, "Premier shows proverbial wit," *New York Times*, 9/24/59, 23.

16. Harrison Salisbury, "Khrushchev calls speech by president conciliatory," *New York Times*, 9/23/60, 13.

17. "And now a message from a Soviet sponsor," *New York Times*, 9/24/60, 6.

18. Thomas Hamilton, "Chairman acts after colonialism debate causes an uproar," *New York Times*, 10/13/60, 14.

19. Benjamin Welles, "Khrushchev bangs his shoe on desk," *New York Times*, 10/13/60, 1.

20. Ibid., 14.

21. Thomas Hamilton, "Khrushchev goes home after a threat in UN to boycott arms talks," *New York Times*, 10/14/60, 2.

22. Frank Collbohm, *Scientific aids to decision-making* (RAND, 1/31/57), 3.

23. OTW, 98. Singer interview, 7/20/91.

24. Tzvetan Todorov stipulated, "The fantastic occupies the duration of

this uncertainty." Todorov, *The fantastic—a structural approach to a literary genre* (Cornell, 1975), 25.

25. OTW, 558, 553.

26. Karl Jaspers, *The atom bomb and the future of man* (University of Chicago, 1961), 187. Born quote in ibid., 201.

27. "[Fermi] suddenly offered to take wagers from his fellow scientists on whether or not the bomb would ignite the atmosphere, and if so, whether it would merely destroy New Mexico or destroy the world." Leslie Groves, *Now it can be told* (Harper & Row, 1962), 296. Senator Kefauver set forth this startling fact on 10/17/57. For the flurry of response, see 10/17, 10/18, and 10/27 reports in the *New York Times*. For other observers, A-bombs did not differ significantly from conventional explosives and therefore did not emanate a transcendental aura. Curtis LeMay, the commanding general of the air campaign over Japan comes to mind as representative of those who dismissed the exceptional nature of the atomic bomb. In the course of addressing the morality of obliterating Hiroshima and Nagasaki in his memoirs, he commented, "I can recognize no more depravity in dropping a nuclear weapon than in having a V-2 rocket equipped with an orthodox warhead, and shooting it vaguely in the general direction of London, as the Germans did. No difference whatever." Even while minimizing the special status attached to atomic weapons, he acknowledged popular feelings of awestruck dread. "These bombs brought a strange pervading fear which does not seem to have affected mankind previously from any other source. Nothing new about death, nothing new about deaths caused militarily. We scorched and boiled and baked to death more people in Tokyo on the night of March 9–10 than went up in vapor at Hiroshima and Nagasaki combined." Curtis LeMay with MacKinlay Kantor, *Mission with LeMay* (Doubleday, 1965), 383, 387.

28. "The younger generation," *Time*, 11/5/51, 46, 47, 48, 50, 52.

29. Ibid., 52.

30. Denys Volan, *The history of the Ground Observer Corps* (Aerospace Defense Command Historical Study No. 36, 1968), 152. Also see the pages of *Aircraft Flash* for corroborative details of these activities.

31. World War I veteran, AF, 1/54, 6. Boys on observation posts, AF, 11/53, 7. Colorado blizzard, AF, 2/56, 9.

32. South Dakota, AF, 11/55, 10. Indoor loudspeaker, AF, 12/54, 6. Dash from sleep, "Women in the GOC," AF, 8/58, 6. Farmwife, "Vigil in the north," AF, 12/57, 8. Pets, AF, 4/55, 6. AF, 10/55, 11. AF, 12/56, 10. AF, 2/57, 10.

33. Loving the work, AF, 4/56, 8. Then I thought to myself, "Women in the GOC," AF, 8/58, 4.

34. "GOC to ready reserve," AF, 12/57, 3. "GOC in transition," AF, 4/58, 4. Volan, 158.

35. Volan, 164, 165.
36. See "GOC phase out," AF, 1/59.
37. *Aircraft Flash* regularly featured articles about disabled people who volunteered for Sky Watch activities. Most of them read like bad jokes. A blind man and a deaf man team up to watch the skies, making out the whine of a turboprop, the blind man prods the deaf man to hoist his binoculars and look around for an incoming bomber. Boys in correctional institutions, AF, 11/53, 7. Girls in correctional institutions, AF, 12/57, 8. Inmates at the Detroit House of Correction, AF, 6/54, 6. Blackfoot teenagers in Browning, Montana, AF, 6/54, 6. Alaskans, AF, 2/56, 4. Teenagers, AF, 6/58, 5. Mothers of toddlers, AF, 6/55, 6. Jesuit mission in Arctic Circle, AF, 5/54. Federal, state, or military ground observers, Volan, 194, 195.
38. Samuel Williamson, Jr., and Steven Reardon, *The origins of US nuclear strategy, 1945–1953* (St. Martins, 1993), 141.
39. An NSC memorandum from 1950 suggested that the Korean War might be "the first phase of a general Soviet plan for global war." NSC 73/4, cited in Williams and Reardon, 141. See weekly summary excerpt, 7/7/50, in Woodrow Kuhns, ed., *Assessing the Soviet threat: the early cold war years* (Central Intelligence Agency, 1997), 412. Intelligence memorandum 301, 6/30/50, in Kuhns, 402.
40. No date is given for Truman's diary entry, but it must have been written in fall 1950, and most likely November or December. Williamson and Reardon, 143. "President warned of 'total danger,'" *New York Times*, 8/7/50, 9.
41. Williamson and Reardon, 140. "Matthews favors U.S. war for peace," *New York Times*, 8/26/50, 1, 6.
42. "Text of Stalin talk on world affairs," *New York Times*, 2/17/51, 3.
43. C. L. Sulzberger, "NATO lands agree on long vigilance to counter Soviet," *New York Times*, 2/22/52, 1, 4. Benjamin Welles, "Talks clear war for German army," *New York Times*, 2/23/52.
44. "Reds quote General's stolen diary to 'prove' U.S. plots world war," *New York Times*, 3/7/52, 8.
45. ORE 18–50 excerpt, 6/19/50, in Kuhns, 390.
46. Daily summary excerpt, 6/26/50, in ibid., 391.
47. Ibid., 392. Walter Waggoner, "Secretary says 'adventures' would divert hatred of Orient to Americans," *New York Times*, 1/13/50, 2. For an analysis of Soviet objectives in the war, see Intelligence memorandum 302, 7/8/50, in Kuhns, 409.
48. Daily summary excerpt, 6/28/50, in Kuhns, 394. Weekly summary excerpt, 6/30/50, ibid., 395.
49. Weekly summary excerpt, 7/7/50, ibid., 406. By the month's end, CIA analysts were still struggling to compass the scope of Soviet intentions. "The USSR has not yet given any firm indication of its intention to ex-

pand the Korean conflict and increase the risk of global warfare involving the Soviet Union." Weekly summary excerpt, 7/28/50, ibid., 425. Also see Intelligence memorandum 302, 7/8/50, ibid., 413. Weekly Summary Excerpt, 7/7/50, ibid., 407.

50. See Intelligence Memorandum 324, 9/8/50, ibid., 433. Weekly summary excerpt, 9/15/50, ibid., 437.
51. Weekly summary excerpt, 9/22/50, ibid., 440–441. Alexandre Mansourov, "Stalin, Mao, Kim and China's decision to enter the Korean War, September 16–October 15, 1950: new evidence from the Russian archives," *Cold War International History Project Bulletin*, Winter 1995/96, 105.
52. See Daily summary excerpt, 9/30/50, and Daily summary excerpt, 10/20/50, ibid. Daily summary excerpt, 10/30/50, ibid., 458. Weekly summary excerpt, 11/3/50, ibid., 462. Weekly summary excerpt, 11/10/50, ibid., 463.
53. NIE 3, 11/15/50, in Scott Koch, ed., *Selected estimates on the Soviet Union, 1950–1959* (Central Intelligence Agency, 1993), 170.
54. NIE 25, 8/2/51, ibid., 188.
55. NIE 48, 1/8/52, ibid., 193.
56. David Lilienthal's diary entry 5/30/48, cited in Lawrence Freedman, *US intelligence and the Soviet strategic threat*, 2nd ed. (Macmillan, 1986), 64.
57. Anecdotally Spurgeon Keeny disputes this. He recalls seeing detailed city plans of major cities in the Soviet Far East that had been prepared by General MacArthur's intelligence officers on the basis of reports from returned Japanese prisoners of war. Keeny interview, 1/30/01.
58. "Russians display balloons of U.S.," *New York Times*, 2/10/56, 3.
59. The flight-paths of the GENETRIX balloons also yielded precise information of the high-altitude wind patterns that would be exploited for the U-2 program. Gregory Pedlow and Donald Welzenbach, *The CIA and the U-2 program, 1954–1974* (Central Intelligence Agency, 1998), 87.
60. Pedlow and Welzenbach, 145.
61. Wizards, 162. Laurence Freedman, *The evolution of nuclear strategy*, 2nd ed. (Macmillan, 1989), 69.
62. Pedlow and Welzenbach, 72.
63. Ibid., 60. This is another example of American mirror-imaging. The CIA's belief that the U-2 missions would be undetectable to Soviet radar was based on a 1952 study of ten-year-old Soviet technology, as well as tests in 1955 on *American* radars, which could not match Soviet system's reach at higher-altitudes. Ibid., 97. In fact, the first mission of the U-2 in July 1956 was intercepted by Soviet air defense. MiG-15s and MiG-17s tried to pursue and attack the as-yet unreachably high aircraft. It would only be a matter of time before Soviet aviation engineers would redesign the next generation of fighters. On May 1, 1960, a surface-to-air missile disabled Francis Gary Powers's plane at 70,500 feet over the Sverdlovsk missile facility. The pilot survived the crash, was tried for espionage, and

was sentenced to ten years' imprisonment. He was released in a prisoner exchange in February 1962. See his memoir, Francis Gary Powers, *Operation overflight* (Holt, Rinehart & Winston, 1970).

64. Drew Middleton, "Khrushchev says Soviets will make H-bomb missile," *New York Times*, 4/24/56, 1. See Anthony Leviero, "Washington accepts claim by Soviets on guided missile," *New York Times*, 4/24/56; "Exaggeration is seen," *New York Times*, 4/25/56.

65. Pedlow and Welzenbach, 138.

66. "Khrushchev invites US to missile shooting match," *New York Times*, 11/16/57, 3.

67. NIE 11-5-57 in Donald Steury, ed., *Intentions and capabilities: estimates on Soviet strategic forces, 1950–1983* (Central Intelligence Agency, 1996), 59. NIE 11-6-57, ibid., 46.

68. NIE 11-5-58, ibid., 66, 67.

69. Pedlow and Welzenbach, 159.

70. Ibid., 164. Victor Marchetti and John Marks, *The CIA and the cult of intelligence* (Dell, 1974), 217–219. They based their story on an unnamed damage report of 1966 assessing the aftermath of Whalen's arrest and exposure.

71. Kaplan explained the significance of the lapse in testing. "If the Soviets were going to deploy 100 ICBMs by 1959 or 1960 . . . then they had to have fired more than six test missiles by August of 1958. There were lead times involved. In Convair's experience, a missile had to be tested at least twenty times before it could be declared operationally ready and reliable: then there was the additional time it would take to transport the missiles to their bases, set up launching sites, command-control centers and so forth. If the testing data were correct, then the National Intelligence Estimate must be wrong." Wizards, 164.

72. NIE 11-8-59, Steury, 72, 74n.

73. Ibid., 79, 82.

74. On estimates of monthly rates of missile production, see Freedman 1986, 74. NIE 11-8-59, Steury, 85. Their explanation is bewildering. On the one hand, they assumed series production had already begun at Tyuratam. "In the probable program," the plant would begin producing three missiles each month and, ascending the learning curve, within a year arrive at the production rate of 15 missiles each month. Hence they anticipated 100 missiles in the first year and 180 afterward. The expanded estimate posited a *second* plant, in which case 25 missiles could be delivered each month. "In actual practice, however," the authors conceded, "the Soviets would almost certainly not begin series production of ICBMs (or any other weapons at more than one plant simultaneously)." Instead they supposed that the second facility would begin series production a year or so *after* the start-up of the first. Ibid., 99.

75. John Prados, *The Soviet estimate, U.S. intelligence analysis and Russian military strength* (Dial, 1982), 84.

76. Ibid., 90. The analysts realized that in order to confirm an operational missile, they would have to find support facilities such as launchers, bunkers, and communications systems. Wizards, 165.

77. NIE 11-8-60, Steury, 109.

78. Ibid., 110n5. The question remained how to work out how many missiles would be needed for a surprise attack against America. The NIE authors conceded that their conjectures were too provisional to be illuminating. "Uncertainty regarding the inputs, and the sensitivity of the computations to variations in the assumptions made with respect to them, render the numerical results too various to provide a reliable basis for estimating Soviet ICBM force goals." Ibid., 110. They offered three different estimates of the Soviet missile forces. The air force tendered the highest program levels, 35 missiles in mid-1960, 200 in mid-1961, and 450 in mid-1962. The director of the CIA opined that the Soviets could produce 30 missiles in mid-1960, 150 at mid-1961, and 270 at mid-1962. Representatives of the Department of State, the secretary of defense, and the joint staff argued for levels between the medium and the low figures. The army and navy pushed for the lowest force levels, a few missiles in mid-1960, 50 in mid-1961, and 125 in mid-1962. Ibid., 111. These discrepancies unquestionably reflected the bias relative to each service's role in the strategic forces, rather than competitive competence in intelligence analysis.

79. Kevin Ruffner, ed., *CORONA, America's first satellite program* (Central Intelligence Agency, 1995), 24. Corona and Discoverer are code names for the same satellite program.

80. NIE 11-8-61, 9/21/61, Steury, 115, 116.

81. Ibid., 116n6.

82. NIE 11-8/1-61, 9/21/61. Ruffner, 140, 141. Freedman 1986, 73.

83. OTW, 201. Only Andrew Marshall and Joseph Loftus at RAND had access to better intelligence. Wizards, 206–219.

84. Fred Kaplan, "JFK's first-strike plan," *Atlantic Monthly,* 10/01, 84, 85.

5. HOW TO BUILD A WORLD WITH ARTFUL INTUITION

1. Frank Haak, "Formula for the future—operations research," *Proceedings of the US Naval Institute,* 4/62, 50. F. C. Brooks and L. W. Merriam, "CORG plans tomorrow's army today," *ARMY,* 2/56, 30. Gordon Rogers, "Battles without bloodshed," *Army Information Digest,* 12/60, 35. Malcolm Hoag, *An introduction to systems analysis* (RAND, 4/18/56), 20.

2. Vaughn Bornet, *John Williams, a personal reminiscence* (RAND, 8/12/69), 20. Italics added.

3. DoD News Transcript, 6/6/02, www.defenselink.mil/transcripts/2002. Testimony to Senate Armed Services Committee, 2/4/04, www.defenselink.mil/speeches/2004.

4. Wizards, 9–10.

5. OTW, 163. A year later, Kahn identified the motif directly. "The scenarios . . . facilitate the identification of 'branching points' of events that

are significant." Kahn, Mann (B). *Report to the MITRE Corporation* (Hudson, 10/31/61), 4. Richard Bellman, *What is dynamic programming?* (RAND, 7/31/59), 1.

6. "Conclusions will emerge," Arthur Raymond, *Talking outline,* 4/21/47, 3 in Jardini, 42. Murray Geisler, "Appraisal of laboratory simulation experiences," *Management Science,* 4/62, 240–241.

7. John McDonald, "The war of wits," *Fortune,* 3/51, 152, 156. Malcolm Hoag, *An introduction to systems analysis* (RAND, 4/18/56), 19.

8. Olaf Helmer, *The systematic use of expert judgment in operations research* (RAND, 1963), in E. S. Quade, "Methods and Procedures," in E. S. Quade, ed., *Analysis of military decisions* (Rand McNally, 1964), 150, 153. While the Helmer and Quade texts are from the 1960s, these quotes are distillations of ideas they conceived in the previous decade. Confirmation of the motif of intuition produced in the 1950s can be found in Chapter 6.

9. A. W. Marshall, *Experimentation by simulation and Monte Carlo* (RAND, 1/28/58), 1. See also Kahn, Mann (B). Albert Wohlstetter, *Systems analysis versus systems design* (RAND, 10/29/58).

10. Kahn, Mann (A), 77. Kahn, Mann (C), 2. Kahn couldn't resist unmasking the scientific pretensions of hypothetical models. In a 1955 briefing to the scientific advisory board of the air force, he stressed the fabricated quality of systems analysis. His remarks were repeatedly interrupted by audience laughter. "This [model] is sort of a toy, an educational toy, but still a toy, and we don't want anybody raising the question of realism. In fact, if anybody raises this question we'll send him home, wash his mouth out with soap, write a note to his mother, and see that he's really badly treated. I've already been told by the management that some people in this audience you can't do that to. Those people I'm asking to . . . give me a little courtesy. The rest of you, you take your chances." "This is essentially a classic systems analysis. It tells you how to allocate your money and what it buys you. A very good friend of mine says it's 'pure unadulterated crap.' That's actually a little bit unfair. It is not unadulterated. I mean a sparrow could get a lot of nourishment out of it. It doesn't answer the kind of question which a policy man would need in order to make the kind of decisions we hope he's trying to make. It really does give some information, not much, but some." SAB, 2–3, 17–18.

11. Kahn, Mann (A), 63.

12. Hoag, 18, 20.

13. "Still making bombs," *New Republic,* 12/31/45, 885.

14. Kahn, Mann (E), 12, 11. OTW, 125, 138, 312, 325, 326, 349.

15. Stanislaw Ulam, "John Von Neumann, 1903–1957," in J. C. Oxtoby, B. J. Pettis, and G. B. Price, eds., *Bulletin of the American Mathematical Society,* 5/58, 34. Kahn, 1961 (C). *War Scenarios: War in Europe Sequence* (Hudson, 10/31/61), xiv, draft manuscript.

16. See Kahn, *Determination of shield thickness for attenuation of air-scattered*

gamma radiation (RAND, 3/15/48). Kahn, *Elastic scattering of neutrons* (RAND, 8/3/48). Kahn, *Preliminary analysis of effective polarization gamma-ray transmission* (RAND, 12/23/48). Kahn, *Particle histories for plane slabs* (RAND, 12/24/48). Kahn and I. R. Latter, *Gamma-ray absorption coefficients* (RAND, 9/19/49). The first open conference on Monte Carlo took place in June 1949 in Los Angeles. Another set of meetings were part of the IBM Seminar on Scientific Computation in November and December 1949 at Endicott, New York. The third major conference was held at the University of Florida at Gainesville from 3/16 to 3/17/54.

17. At the beginning of the war, John Von Neumann was preoccupied with the motions of compressible gasses, especially the hydrodynamics of colliding shocks. The physics jargon of intuition that later played a prominent role in RAND futurology justified Von Neumann's move from solving partial differential equations to devising statistical approximations of phenomena with electro-mechanical calculators. He wrote, "We have to be guided almost entirely by *physical intuition* . . . [It is] impossible to be very specific about any point. And it is difficult to say about any solution . . . with any degree of assurance, that it is the one which must exist in nature." As he developed his new approach, he worked out a method for transposing mathematical operations into "a language of instruction" for computing machines. John Von Neumann, "Discussion of the existence and uniqueness or multiplicity of solutions of the aerodynamical equations," cited in Ulam, 29, 31.

18. The phrase "machine representation" comes from Peter Galison, "Computer simulations and the trading zone," in Peter Galison and David J. Stump, eds., *The disunity of science* (Stanford, 1996), 125. Nicholas Metropolis and Stanislaw Ulam, "The Monte Carlo method," *Journal of the American Statistical Association* (1949), 337, 339. Keith Roberts' remark in Galison (1996), 137. Also see Peter Galison, *Image and logic* (University of Chicago, 1997), 689–780. G. Goertzel and H. Kahn, *Monte Carlo methods for shield computation* (Oak Ridge National Laboratory, 12/19/49), 10.

19. R. W. Conway, B. M. Johnson, and W. L. Maxwell, "Some problems of digital systems simulation," *Management Science* 6 (1959), 95, 94.

20. Gilbert King, "The Monte Carlo methods as a natural mode of expression in operations research," *Journal of Operational Research,* 2/53, 50. See Kahn, *Stochastic (Monte Carlo) attenuation analysis* (RAND, 7/14/49). Kahn, *Modification of the Monte Carlo method* (RAND, 11/14/49). Kahn and Andrew Marshall, *Methods of reducing sample size in Monte Carlo computations* (RAND, 8/18/53). Kahn, *Use of different Monte Carlo sampling techniques* (RAND, 11/30/55). Kahn, *Applications of Monte Carlo* (RAND, 4/27/56). Kahn and Irwin Mann, *Monte Carlo* (RAND, 7/30/57). Kahn, *Multiple quadrature by Monte Carlo* (RAND, 9/5/58).

21. By the 1960s some physicists were inclined to dismiss Monte Carlo on these grounds. In the absence of immaculate empirical referents, "such computer simulations . . . [seemed] vulnerable to errors in fixing vari-

ous parameters . . . The programs were simply too sensitive to small changes in experimental parameters to be reliable." Peter Galison, *How experiments end* (University of Chicago, 1987), 227. More importantly, the validity of the pseudo-random numbers used to represent stochastic processes was seriously discredited. A "number-theoretical analysis" determined that the pseudo-random generators that succeeded the roulette wheel, "the multiplicative congruential generators," imposed regularities, or hyperplanes, on its strings of numbers. This meant that its sequences were *not*, in fact, reliably random. Consequently, citing one critic, "for the past 20 years such regularity might have produced bad but unrecognized results in Monte Carlo studies using these random generators, which sat in practically every major computer in the world." Galison (1997), 704, 21.

22. Digby, *Interview with Albert Latter*, 5.
23. Kahn, *Stochastic*, 7. For Kahn, this meant focusing on the most energetic neutrons that could penetrate the reactor shield very deeply, even to the point of exceeding the barrier altogether. Since he was helping to forge protective shielding for a cockpit crew from radiation emanating from a reactor in an airplane, this was worth amplifying. Kahn, *Applications of Monte Carlo* (RAND, 5/19/54, rev., 5/27/56), 124.
24. Kahn, Mann (D), 5.
25. Ibid., 11, 12. Kahn, *Stochastic*, 2, 7, 19.
26. Kahn and A. W. Marshall, *Methods of reducing sample size in Monte Carlo computations* (RAND, 8/18/53), 10, 11, 14, 23.
27. Metropolis and Ulam, 341.
28. Veterans of the Applied Mathematics Panel recruited by Williams made up the core personnel of the Evaluation of Military Worth section. In addition to Warren Weaver, who was its director, other important members of the AMP, Olaf Helmer, Melvin Dresher, and Samuel Wilks, were founding personnel (or consultants for Project RAND). Another member of the AMP, as well as the postwar US Strategic Bombing Survey, Edwin Paxson, was hired in spring 1947 to head the section. J. Williams, *Subjective account of the December meetings among Olaf Helmer, Frederick Mosteller, S.S. Wilks, Warren Weaver, and JDW* (RAND, 1/28/47). Jardini, 85. J. Williams, *Program for the evaluation section of Project RAND* (RAND,1/20/47), 1. Collins, 245.
29. *Defense and bombing systems sub-projects* (RAND 5/49, classified). Jardini, 59.
30. *Memorandum to file*, L. J. Henderson (RAND, 12/2/49, classified). Jardini, 58 (emphasis added).
31. To continue the story, see the well-documented histories of systems analysis at RAND in Jardini, Collins, and Hounshell.
32. See Charles Hitch, *Sup-optimization in operations problems* (RAND, 11/18/52), esp. 2, 9.
33. Roland McKean, *Sub-optimization criteria and operations research* (RAND, 4/22/53), 18, 6, 8, 10.

34. Armen Alchian and Reuben Kessel, *A proper role of systems analysis* (RAND, 1/27/54, classified), in David Hounshell, "The medium is the message, or how context matters: the RAND Corporation builds an economics of innovation, 1946–1962," paper delivered at the Dibner Institute Conference on the Spread of Systems Thinking, Cambridge, MA, 5/96. In Thomas Hughes and Agatha Hughes, eds., *Systems, experts, and computers* (University of Chicago and Dibner Institute, 1997), 269. "More competition, duplication, and 'confusion'" from Burton Klein, 1958, "A radical proposal for R and D," *Fortune*, 5/58, in Hounsell, 283. For more, see Philip Morowski, *Machine Dreams, economics becomes a cyborg science* (Cambridge, 2002).

35. SAB, 55–56. Also see OTW, 323.

36. Charles Hitch, "An appreciation of systems analysis," *Operations Research*, 11/55, 468, 474, 469.

37. Ibid., 475, 476.

38. Ibid., 477, 480, 481.

39. Charles Hitch, "Comments," *Operations Research*, 8/56, 427. Hounshell manuscript, 6. Hitch (1956), 430. In 1960 Hitch offered a solution to the puzzle of criterion specification. The problem coordinating future weapons systems with various budgets was an *economic* matter of resource allocation. Which system is "most efficient (maximizes the attainment of the objective with the given resources) or economical (minimizes the cost of achieving the given objective)." Charles Hitch and Roland McKean, *The economics of defense in the nuclear age* (Harvard, 1960), 3.

40. To the extent that the methodological comments of operations researchers exhibited motifs characteristic of the cold war avant-garde, they could plausibly be jostled into the circle of the simulationists. One finds the same motifs (provisionality, artfulness, intuition, the aspiration towards the totality) in operations literature as appear in the methodological comments of the systems analysts. For example, "Operations research is, by its very nature, the application of *all* forms of human knowledge to the solution of a whole problem. In this it differs from many of the other scientific disciplines: its tools and techniques are very diverse. *Anything goes . . .* as long as it leads to a better understanding of the problem." Thornton Page, "A Survey of operations research tools and techniques," in Charles Flagle et al., eds., *Operations research and systems engineering* (Johns Hopkins, 1960), 120. "It is by no means clear just what the method is other than that it is scientific (like all respectable methods, because operations analysts are typically resourceful and ingenious men who tackle their problems with no holds barred." Robert Dorfman, "Operations research," *American Economic Review*, 9/60, 575. "It seems oddly premature to speak of what 'operations researchers do' or 'try to do,' when the recent beginnings of operations research explicitly refused to accept the historical precedent of any field and the last decade has introduced so many different methods, all claiming to be 'cases' of operations research." C. West

Churchman, "Decision and value theory," Russell Ackoff, ed., *Progress in operations research*, vol. 1 (John Wiley, 1961), 44. "Understanding gained through simulation may enable human judgment to intuit a good solution . . . The analyst can see, understand, and develop more intuition for the operation being simulated than he can by reading computer outputs." George Morganthaler, "The theory and application of simulation in operations research," in Ackoff (1961), 374, 406. Kahn distinguished his work from operations research by its speculative sweep. "The techniques [of systems analysis] and philosophy are . . . similar to those of the Operations Analyst, but due to the breadth of the problems and the resulting increased uncertainties the role of mathematics and lengthy computations is subordinated almost (but not quite) to the vanishing point." OTW, viii–ix. I accept Kahn's distinction, but must add that insofar as operations researchers toyed with hypothetical systems, their work should be roped into the futurological aesthetic.

41. Daniel Belgrad, *The culture of spontaneity, improvisation and the arts in postwar America.* (University of Chicago, 1998), 7, 8, 9.

42. Ibid., 1.

43. While the artists flung themselves into improvisation "as a technique for bringing ideologically inadmissible possibilities into awareness," some people at RAND also tried ways of eliciting tacit knowledge of which the possessor was normally unaware. Belgrad, 9. For more on tacit knowledge, see the following experiments in forecasting: A. Kaplan, A. Skogstad, and M. A. Girschik, *The prediction of social and technological events* (RAND, 4/1/49). Norman Dalkey and Olaf Helmer, *The use of experts for the estimation of bombing requirements* (RAND, 11/14/51). Olaf Helmer and Nicholas Rescher, *On the epistemology of the inexact sciences* (RAND, 10/13/58, classified), revised and abridged in Norman Dalkey and Olaf Helmer, *An experimental application of the delphi method to the use of experts* (RAND, 7/62). Belgrad, 12, 142–150. In my discussion of war-gaming here and in Chapter 6, I am referring to role-playing games, not the eviscerated matrices of game theory. Joseph Goldsen, *The political exercise: an assessment of the fourth round* (RAND, 5/30/56), 54, 38. Olaf Helmer, *Strategic gaming* (RAND, 2/10/60), 1.

44. Richard Barringer and Barton Whaley, "The MIT political-military gaming experience," *Orbis,* Summer 1965, 454, 457.

45. Belgrad, 40.

46. Ibid., 149, 150, 152.

47. Obscure, 119. Belgrad, 110.

48. Mark Hedden, "If deterrence fails," *American Scholar,* Winter 1961–62, 90. Princeton briefing, 214.

49. Kahn, ed., *A paradigm for the 1965–1975 strategic debate* (Hudson, 11/22/63), 3, 79.

50. Belgrad, 111, 142, 39. Kahn (1963), 62.

51. Belgrad, 5, 212, 218.

52. His liking for lists was idiosyncratic, intricate, excessive, and repetitive. His family commemorated this by inscribing both faces of his gravestone with tables of his accomplishments. Marshall interview, 9/2/91.

6. FAITH AND INSIGHT IN WAR-GAMING

1. Bernard Brodie, *Strategy in the missile age* (Princeton, 1959), 162, 187. For greater depth, please see Sharon Ghamari-Tabrizi, "Simulating the unthinkable: gaming future wars in the 1950s and 1960s," *Social Studies of Science*, 4/00, 163–223.

2. Dr. F. C. Brooks and Colonel L. W. Merriam, "CORG plans tomorrow's army today," *Army*, 2/56, 29, 28.

3. Clayton Thomas, "Military gaming," in Russell Ackoff, ed., *Progress in operations research*, vol. 1 (John Wiley, 1961), 428, 430.

4. Francis McHugh, *Fundamentals of war-gaming*, 3rd ed. (United States Naval War College, 1966), 1–10.

5. Thomas McDonald, "JCS politico-military desk games," in Murray Greyson, ed., *Second war-gaming symposium proceedings* (Washington Operations Research Council, 1964), 67.

6. Bloomfield and Whaley reported that seminar games were perfectly realistic without "such superficial atmospherics as appropriate national symbols, i.e., flags or pictures of Lenin for the Soviet teams. Rewarding games can be played in bare rooms containing only the essential reference and writing materials." Lincoln Bloomfield and Barton Whaley, "The political-military exercise, a progress report," *Orbis*, Winter 1965, 867.

7. Paul Deems, "War-gaming and exercises," *Air University Quarterly Review*, Winter 1956–57, 108.

8. Sidney Giffin, *The crisis game: simulating international conflict* (Doubleday, 1965), 64, 65.

9. Herbert Goldhamer and Hans Speier, "Some observations on political gaming," *World Politics*, October 1959, 72, 73, 75.

10. Joseph M. Goldsen, *The Political Exercise: An Assessment of the Fourth Round* (RAND, 5/30/56), 1, 2. Also see E. Schnitzer, *Fourth RAND political exercise, summary and documents* (RAND, 5/25/56).

11. Goldsen, 32, 33.

12. Ibid., 35

13. Ibid., 32, 33, 35, 58, 54, 36.

14. Goldhamer and Speier, 80.

15. See Harold Guetzkow, "A use of simulation in the study of inter-nation relations," *Behavioral Science*, 7/59. William Coplin, "Inter-nation simulation and contemporary theories of international relations," *American Political Science Review*, 9/66. Arnold Hausrath, *Venture simulation in war, business, and politics* (McGraw-Hill, 1971), 230, 231.

16. Lincoln Bloomfield, "Reflections on Gaming," *Orbis*, Winter 1984, 784.

17. Lincoln Bloomfield and Normal Padelford, "Teaching note: three experiments in political gaming," *American Political Science Review*, 12/59, 1105.

Also see Lincoln Bloomfield, "Political gaming," *Proceedings of the US Naval Institute,* 9/60.

18. Bloomfield and Padelford, 1113, 1115.

19. "The initial purpose of the Pentagon games, which involved senior officials like the Joint Chiefs of Staff and Assistant Secretaries of State and Defense, was to improve interagency communication between the new defense intellectuals ('Whiz Kids') in Washington and the older professional military staffs." Letter from William Jones to Mandel, 2/26/75, cited in Robert Mandel, "Political gaming and foreign policy making during crises," *World Politics,* 7/77, 613.

20. With the aid of Kaplan's account of President Kennedy's exploration of a first-strike war plan, we can insert Schelling's games into the timeline of contingency planning in the Berlin Crisis of 1961. On 8/8/61 at a NATO Council meeting Secretary of State Dean Rusk announces the administration's new strategic concept of flexible response. On 8/13/61 East German soldiers begin to erect the Berlin Wall. On 9/5/61 Carl Kaysen and Henry Rowen send a 33-page memo to the chairman of the JCS, detailing combat options for Berlin, including a first-strike nuclear attack. From 9/8 to 11/61 the first Berlin game is played at Camp David, code-named "NATO Planning Conference." On 9/19/61 President Kennedy sends a written inquiry to his military advisers regarding a first-strike plan. Kennedy's questions remain unanswered. From 9/29/61 to 10/1/61 the second Berlin game is played at the Military Assistance Institute in Arlington, VA, code-named "ISA [International Security Affairs] Conference." Fred Kaplan, "JFK's first-strike plan," *Atlantic Monthly,* 10/01. Nitze's 33-page memorandum and other documents from the NSC, JCS, and SAC are in the Berlin Crisis section in the National Security Archive's website, www.gwu.edu/~nsarchive. Thomas Schelling, email message to author, 12/10/98. The players included DeWitt Armstrong, McGeorge Bundy, Alain Enthoven, Carl Kaysen, Henry Kissinger, Robert Komer, John McNaughton, Walt Rostow, Henry Rowen, and Seymour Weiss. The President and his brother did not attend.

21. Daniel Ellsberg interview, 6/19/99.

22. Schelling, email message to author, 12/10/98.

23. "World as theater" from Captain McCarty Little, "The strategic naval war game or chart maneuver," *US Naval Institute Proceedings,* 12/12, 1219. Bloomfield, 1984, 784.

24. I first became aware of this from Thomas Allen, *War games: the secret world of the creators, players, and policy makers rehearsing World War III today* (McGraw Hill, 1987), 30. Lincoln Bloomfield, email message to author, 12/9/98.

25. Three examples of serious play: (1) "Thus we define operational gaming as the serious use of playing as a primary device to formulate a game, to solve a game, or to impart something of the solution of a game." Clayton Thomas and Walter Deemer, Jr, "The role of operational gaming

in operations research," *Operations Research*, 2/57, 6. (2) "Without firing a shot or spilling a drop of blood, they test concepts for future warfare . . . by 'playing' in a very serious way, a large war game." Gordon Rogers, "Battles without bloodshed," *Army Information Digest*, 12/60, 33. (3) "Finally the game is closed and the teams start to play in earnest. They take on all the deadly purpose of a division war room in a real situation." Edgar Musgrove, "No game," *Marine Corps Gazette*, 8/65, 56. Lincoln Bloomfield, "Political gaming," *Proceedings of the US Naval Institute*, 9/60, 62.

26. Lincoln Bloomfield and Cornelius Gearin, "Games foreign policy experts play: the political exercise comes of age," *Orbis*, Winter 1973, 1027. R. D. Arnold, "Rules preparation and pre-game activities," in John Overholt, *First war-gaming symposium proceedings, November 30, 1961* (Washington Operations Research Council, 2/62), 17. Bloomfield and Gearin, 1012. Robert Chapman, *Simulation in RAND's system research laboratory* (RAND, 4/30/57), 3. Bloomfield and Gearin, 1025. McDonald, in Greyson, 65.

27. Martin Shubik, "Gaming, theory and practice, past and future," *Simulation and Games*, 6/89, 189. Thomas and Deemer, 6. Bloomfield 1960, 58. Bloomfield and Whaley, 870.

28. Bloomfield and Gearin, 1012–1013. Clark Abt, "War-gaming," *International Science and Technology*, 8/64, 29–31.

29. Robert Specht, "War games," in Max Davies and Michel Verhulst, eds., *Operational research in practice* (Pergamon, 1958), 149.

30. See, for example, E. W. Paxson, *War-gaming* (RAND, 2/63), 29. Hausrath, 10–11. Theodore Sterne, "War games: validity and interpretation," *Army*, 4/66, 68. Garry Brewer and Martin Shubik, *The war game: a critique of military problem solving* (Harvard, 1979), 12–13, 91. Barringer and Whaley, 451. James Cockrill, "The validity of war game analysis," *Proceedings of the US Naval Institute*, 1/66, 51, 53.

31. Behavioral Sciences Subpanel of the President's Science Advisory Committee, "Strengthening the behavioral sciences," *Behavioral Science*, 7/62, 282. W. L. Archer, "The techniques of modern war-gaming," *Canadian Army Journal*, Fall 1961, 23. Thomas 1961, 440.

32. Thomas and Deemer, 25. Taves in Greyson, 57. Barringer and Whaley, 451.

33. Norman Dalkey, *Simulation of military conflict* (RAND, 1/67), 14. Comprehending the game-problem was just as taxing to the analytic intelligence as formulating it in the first place. "In many instances phenomena are understood rather well in the small . . . but the over-all effect of the interaction of a complex set of such phenomena is not easy to grasp. This is particularly the situation where new, possibly nonexistent, weapons are concerned and where no operational experience exists." Ibid., 1. Olaf Helmer, *Strategic gaming* (RAND, 2/10/60), 1. Peter Perla, *The art of war-gaming* (Naval Institute, 1990), 184.

34. On a game's intensity see Deems, 124; Thomas and Deemer, 20; Kahn,

Mann (E), 5; Barringer and Whaley, 444; Bloomfield and Gearin, 1029; Barringer and Whaley, 449.

35. Bloomfield (1960), 61. Abt (1964), 29. See M. G. Weiner, "An introduction to war games," in Pierre Rosenstiehl and Alain Ghouila-Houri, eds., *Les choix économiques: décisions séquentielles et simulation* (Dunod, 1960), 270–271. Archer, 23. Alfred DeQuoy, "Operational war-gaming," *Armor* (9–10/63), 35. Hausrath, 22. Bloomfield and Whaley, 866. Deems, 126. Dalkey (1967), 2. The thesis, simulation as substitute for future experience, was a cornerstone of gaming apologetics. Sterne, 66. Also see McHugh, 1–25. Hausrath, 9, 20, 21. R. Rauner and W. Steger, *Game-simulation and long-range planning* (RAND, 6/22/61), 21.

36. The term "synthetic history" was often employed. Sterne, 64. McHugh, 1–25. Donald Meals, "Trends in military operations research," *Operations Research*, 3–4/61, 255. Hausrath, xvi. Bloomfield (1960), 63.

37. Herman Kahn, *The alternative world futures approach* (Hudson, 11/21/66), A1–12. Herman Kahn, ed., *A paradigm for the 1965–1975 strategic debate* (Hudson, 11/22/63), 77, 78.

38. Perla, 18.

39. Alexander Mood, *War gaming as a technique of analysis* (RAND, 9/3/54), 1. Rauner and Steger, 18. Kahn (1963), 78. H. Averch and M. M. Lavin, *Simulation of decision-making in crises: three manual gaming experiments* (RAND, 8/64), 3.

40. Thomas (1961), 439–440.

41. Mood, 9. Specht, 146. C. West Churchman, "Decision and value theory," in Russell Ackoff, ed., *Progress in operations research*, vol. 1 (John Wiley, 1961), 59. Walter Deemer, "A summing up," in Greyson, 173. Also see Archer, 18–19; Taves in Greyson, 59; Abt, 37.

42. Thomas and Deemer, 20. Thomas (1961), 460.

43. Thomas and Deemer, 21.

44. E. W. Girard wrote, "[War games] can function as *pseudo-experiments*, producing data for analysis after the plays are completed." E. W. Girard, "Reports, presentation of results, and analysis," in Overholt, 77. Sterne was even more emphatic in likening games to experiments. "A war game [is] no more nor less than a laboratory experiment in which the entire effort is designed to elicit facts for analysis." Sterne, 67. Thomas, Deemer, 21.

45. Archer, 18.

46. Paxson, 30–33.

47. Sterne, 67. Hausrath, 71. Also see: Meals, 253; Weiner, 279; Paxson, 25; Taves in Greyson, 61; Abt, 31.

48. Archer, 20. Abt, 37.

49. Pugh, "Discussion panel," in Greyson, 149. Girard in ibid., 150.

50. Senior officers had recoiled from computer-aided analysis. In 1960, we can read, "Many of us may intuitively distrust any assistance by a machine in making decisions." Commander John Davis, Jr., and Dr. John

Tiedeman, "The Navy war games program," *Proceedings of the US Naval Institute,* 6/60, 67. Col. Melvin Slate, "Discussion panel," in Greyson, 130.

51. Van Arsdall, 147.

52. Kornbluh in ibid., 144–145.

53. Captain O. S. Sigurdson, deputy assistant to chief of naval operations for war-gaming, in ibid., 133. Girard in ibid., 143. Deemer in ibid., 174.

54. Robert Davis, "Arms control simulation: the search for an acceptable method," *Journal of Conflict Resolution,* 12/62, 688AC, 695AC.

55. Bloomfield, Whaley, 862. Also see Davis, Tiedeman, 67; E. S. Maloney, "Modern war-gaming: state of the art," *Marine Corps Gazette,* 11/60, 12; McDonald in Greyson, 65–67; Cockrill, 49, 53.

56. Weiner, 275. Bloomfield (1960), 61. Archer, 21. Cockrill, 47.

57. Michael Banks, A. Groom, and A. Oppenheim, "Gaming and simulation in international relations," *Political Studies,* 2/68, 1–2, 13.

58. Bloomfield and Gearin, 1029, 1027, 1025.

59. Ibid., 1026, 1027, 1029, 1030.

60. Warren Weaver (1946), "Comments on a general theory of air warfare," in Collins, 230.

61. John Kemeny, "Games of life and death," *Nation,* 1/21/61, 50.

62. B. O. Koopman, "Fallacies in operations research," *Operations Research,* 8/56, 424. Deems, 106.

63. Specht, 150. Thomas (1961), 447.

64. Slate in Greyson, 130.

65. Robert Roy, "The development and future of operations research and systems engineering," in Charles Flagle, William Huggins, and R. H. Roy, eds. *Operations research and systems engineering* (Johns Hopkins, 1960), 25.

66. R. H. Crossman, "Western defence in the 1960s," *Journal of the Royal United Services Institute* (8/61), 324, 325.

67. Frank Haak, "Formula for the future—operations research," *Proceedings of the US Naval Institute,* 4/61, 51, 55.

68. F. O. Miksche, "The soldier and technical warfare," *Military Review,* 8/62, 73, 75, 78.

69. R. Duncan Luce and Howard Raiffa, *Games and decisions* (Wiley, 1957), 37.

70. Thomas Schelling, "Experimental games and bargaining theory," *World Politics,* 10/61, 55.

7. THE MINESHAFT GAP

1. Anatol Rapoport, "The sources of anguish," *Bulletin of the Atomic Scientists,* 12/65, 34. Eliot Fremont-Smith, "The last word and other illusions," *Village Voice,* 5/24/62, 12. Norman Thomas, "Roads that bypass peace," *Saturday Review,* 2/4/61, 19. Paul Johnson, "The new Schoolmen," *New Statesmen,* 5/12/61, 754.

2. Herman Kahn, *Some specific suggestions for achieving early non-military de-*

fense capabilities and initiating long-range programs (RAND, 1/2/58), 77, 101.

3. OTW, 517.
4. Spurgeon Keeny interview, 9/20/00. Wiesner, in Counsels, 117.
5. Kahn (1958), 109.
6. Kahn emphasized the arbitrary nature of his numbers. "The 'attacks' considered in evaluating various non-military defense measures should not be construed as . . . [well-grounded estimates.] They are hypotheses about threats that appear conceivable, some time in the future, and which provide a measure of the possible role of non-military defense systems." Kahn (1958), iv.
7. U.S. Strategic Bombing Survey, *The effects of atomic bombs on Hiroshima and Nagasaki* (Government Printing Office, 6/30/46), 36–43.
8. For its civil defense recommendations, see Technological Capabilities Panel [Killian Commission], in Marc Trachtenberg, ed., *The development of American strategic thought, 1945–1969: basic documents from the Eisenhower and Kennedy periods, including the basic national security policy papers from 1953 to 1959* (Garland, 1988), 373–374, 463–471. Memorandum, A. J. Goodpaster, 12/19/56, in David Alan Rosenberg, "The origins of overkill, nuclear weapons and American strategy, 1945–1960," *International Security,* spring 1983, 45.
9. Memorandum, S. Everett Gleason, 1/12/56, in Rosenberg, 40. Eisenhower's diary entry, 1/23/56, in ibid., 40.
10. Eisenhower's question was recalled by Jerome Wiesner, Counsels, 113.
11. Thomas Kerr, *Civil Defense in the U.S.: bandaid for a holocaust?* (Westview, 1983), 106.
12. Counsels, 79, 83 , 100. Paul Dickson, *Think tanks* (Atheneum, 1971), 110. In the 1950s moderate Republicans such as Nelson Rockefeller, liberals, the religious peace movement, and some radicals advocated civil defense.
13. Counsels, 117. Keeny interview, 9/20/00.
14. See A. Wohlstetter and F. Hoffman, *Protecting U.S. power to strike back in the 1950s and 1960s* (RAND, 9/1/56). Marshall interview, 8/16/04.
15. Andrew Goodpaster memorandum, 11/7/57, in Rosenberg, 47.
16. Wizards, 132–134. In an astonishing interview published in 1987, LeMay stated as a matter of fact that when he had commanded SAC in the 1950s, he would have launched his forces without authorization from the commander in chief: "If we got into a position where the president was out of action . . . I was going to at least get the bombs and get them to my outfits and get them loaded and ready to go—at least do that much." General Johnson interjected, "You couldn't release them, however." LeMay: "I would have, under certain circumstances." Johnson: "You mean after we had already been attacked?" LeMay: "If I were on my own and half the country was destroyed and I could get no orders and so forth, I wasn't going to sit there fat, dumb, and happy and do nothing . . . I may

not have waited until half the country was destroyed, but I felt I had to do something in case no one else was capable of doing anything." Interviewer: "If we were under attack?" LeMay: "Yes, if we were under attack and I hadn't received orders for some reason, or any other information . . . I was going to take some action at least to get ready to do something. Lacking orders and lacking the assumption that I was going to get some in the near future, I would take some action on my own." General Catton nervously interrupted, "The launch and execution procedures of the strategic forces are absolutely inviolable. You just cannot attack with atomic weapons without the proper kind of authority. This is very carefully safeguarded through all the procedures that were developed." LeMay retorted, "What I am trying to say is that SAC was the only force we had that could react quickly to a nuclear attack. We had no idea of what confusion might exist, or who the president might be or where, if a bomb hit Washington. I see nothing to be gained by discussing under what conditions I would have taken action in case of the destruction of Washington and loss of contact with the government. I doubt if I would have retaliated if Washington were the only target hit. But I certainly would not have waited until half the country were destroyed." Richard Kohn and Joseph Harahan, "U.S. strategic air power, 1948–1962: excerpts from an interview with Generals Curtis E. LeMay, Leon W. Johnson, David A. Burchinal, and Jack J. Catton," *International Security,* Summer 1988, 84, 85–86.

LeMay's intentions were doctrinally correct and permissible. President Eisenhower had predelegated to LeMay command authority to launch SAC bombers in retaliation for an attack against the United States in the event that he couldn't contact his commander in chief. "Retaliation for such an attack . . . will be on order of the president, except in circumstances where immediate communications have become impossible between the President and responsible officials of the Department of Defense." "Authorization for the Expenditure of Nuclear Weapons," 5/16/57, National Security File, Intelligence File, Box 9, Meetings, Records, Memoranda on Use of Nuclear Weapons. Lyndon B. Johnson Library. Another document qualified the terms of pre-delegated authority for nuclear use, "This authorization by the President is an emergency measure necessitated by the recognition of the fact that communications may be disrupted by an attack . . . Each authorizing Commander must insure that such delegation of authority is not assumed through accident or misinformation. Further, it should be regarded as an authorization effective only until it is possible to communicate with the President or other person empowered to act for him . . . It is essential that particularly strict command control and supervision be exercised and that the use of nuclear weapons be limited by circumstances of grave necessity." "Memorandum for Commander in Chief, Strategic Air Command, Instructions for Expenditure of Nuclear Weapons in Emergency Conditions," Office of Joint Chiefs of

Staff, nd, ca. December 1959. Office of Special Assistant for National Security Affairs, NSC Series, Subject Subseries, Box 1. Atomic Weapons, Background for Presidential Approval, Dwight D. Eisenhower Library. See "Documents on predelegation of authority for nuclear weapons use" at the National Security Archive website, www.gwu.edu/~nsarchiv.

17. Gaither, 25. The formal citation for the Gaither Report: is Security Resources Panel of the Scientific Advisory Committee of the Office of Defense Mobilization, *Deterrence and survival in the nuclear age*, November 1957. It was declassified and released in 1976 by the Joint Committee on Defense Production, 4th Congress, 2nd Session.

18. In Keeny's opinion, the efforts of the hundred people who worked on the Gaither Commission were highjacked by the steering committee and the author of the final report, Paul Nitze. "All of the people like myself who had been working on the details played no role in the final report." The picture of American strategic vulnerability reflected the views of Nitze, his co-author, and his cronies, and certainly not the consensus of the staff and consultants who had spent months drafting background papers. Keeny objected, "Nitze was nowhere in evidence when this study began. When it was quite far along, he got involved and sort of took over." Andrew Marshall surmised that the steering committee had recruited Nitze to write the final report on the strength of his memorandum, NSC-68. NSC-68 had become instantly canonical in elite policy circles for detailing the nature of communist hostility to the West, and the proper diplomatic and military postures that the United States should assume in response. Keeny interview, 9/20/00. Marshall interview, 8/16/04. Gaither, 25. The final report recommended the same measures put forward by the Killian Panel: improve strategic and tactical warning, disperse SAC bases, protect strategic bombers by parking them in 100–200 psi shelters, create a ring of missile defenses around SAC bases, increase the operational capability of land- and sea-based IRBMs and ICBMs, and plan for hardened ICBM bases. Gaither, 18.

19. Ibid., 19, 22, 19, 33.

20. Keeny interview, 9/20/00. Marshall interview, 8/16/04.

21. Dwight D. Eisenhower, *The White House years: waging peace, 1956–1961* (Doubleday, 1965), 221, 222.

22. In his farewell speech to the nation, he called himself a man "who knows that another war could utterly destroy this civilization which has been so slowly and painfully built over thousands of years." "Text of Eisenhower's farewell address," *New York Times*, 1/18/61, 22. Counsels, 116.

23. A. J. Goodpaster, 2/4/58, Rosenberg, 48.

24. Counsels, 117.

25. Keeny interview, 9/20/00.

26. Herbert York interview, 9/21/00. York in Marcus Raskin, "The megadeath intellectuals," *New York Review of Books*, 11/14/63, 7.

27. Keeny was hired as a technical adviser on nuclear weapons and arms control to a string of science advisers to the President: James Killian in 1958, George Kistiakowsky in 1959 and 1960, and Jerome Wiesner in 1961. He worked on arms control matters for the rest of his career. From 1976 to 1980, he was the deputy director of the U.S. Arms Control and Disarmament Agency. He subsequently became president of the Arms Control Association, a nongovernmental advocacy organization.

28. OTW, 10–11. Kahn (1958), 8.

29. While the report was the result of sixteen peoples' work, since Kahn laid claim to so many of its ideas, in what follows, for simplicity's sake, I shall write as though Kahn were the sole author. Kahn (1958), 1. In contrast to his study's $500 million proposal, Kahn had earlier recommended $200 *billion* to Keeny's working group, and the Gaither Report recommended $25 billion for civil defense.

30. Kahn (1958), 73.

31. Ibid., 74, 75.

32. Ibid., 81, 2, 6.

33. Ibid., 80, 79, 45, 79.

34. Ibid., 10. The idea of war damage insurance against atomic war had prominent advocates in Congress, academia, and RAND. Soon after the Korean War broke out, a Senate subcommittee convened hearings on the War Damage Corporation Act of 1951. The scheme was endorsed in a letter to the *New York Times* authored by the economists E. S. Mason, P. A. Samuelson, J. Tobin, and Carl Kaysen (7/29/51). Kaysen was especially enthusiastic, arguing that insurance compensating owners for the loss of their property due to atomic attack should be compulsory. Kaysen, "The vulnerability of the United States to enemy attack," *World Politics* 6(2) (1954), 203n11. Also see Jack Hirshleifer, *Compensation for war damage* (RAND, 4/29/54).

35. Kahn (1958), 8, 7.

36. Ibid., 19. For his breakdown for civil defense research, see ibid., 21.

37. Ibid., 23, 20. Regarding the mineshaft gap, the RAND study noted, "In the field of non-military defense . . . we are in a technological and quantitative race with the Soviets."

38. Ibid., 29.

39. Ibid., 29–33. Although this meant a "radical change" in industrial development.

40. Ibid., 36, 33, 47.

41. Ibid., 37.

42. Ibid., 42.

43. Ibid., 51. As a historical curiosity, algae cultivation as a synthetic food source shows up in a RAND paper delivered at the March 18 meeting of the American Rocket Society in 1958. The authors observed, "The implicit assumption is that the lunar base will be a closed ecology with an

environment not too different from that of our own earth." They concluded, "Insofar as respiratory exchange of the physiological gases O_2 and CO_2 is concerned, Chlorella appears to be the plan of choice. Its use as a sole food support is somewhat dubious however." I. Cooper, H. A. Lang, R. D. Holbrook, *Certain ecological aspects of a closed lunar base* (RAND, 3/6/58), 2, 6. Kahn (1958), 44.

44. OTW, 90–91. It is also worth noting that Kahn, along with his colleagues, slighted thermal effects in their calculations of the lethality of nuclear weapons. H. H. Mitchell, M.D., *Ecological problems and postwar recuperation: a preliminary survey from the civil defense viewpoint* (RAND, 8/1/61), 1.

45. Kahn (1958), 50.

46. Ibid., 48, 72.

47. Ibid., 107.

48. Kahn, "Why go deep underground?" in J. J. O'Sullivan, *Protective construction in a nuclear age: proceedings of the second protective construction symposium* (Macmillan, 1961), 6.

49. Ibid., 36.

8. ON THERMONUCLEAR WAR

1. OTW, 163.

2. Obscure, 126.

3. "Berlin Crisis Oral History Session #4, Contingency Planning during the Kennedy Administration, 5/7/91," in *NHP Berlin Crisis Oral History Project: Oral History Sessions #1–8*, Transcripts (Center for International Security Studies at Maryland School of Public Affairs, University of Maryland, 1994), 184–185.

4. Berlin #2, 104. Berlin #4, 185.

5. Armstrong recalled, "[I laid] . . . out what was likely to happen . . . under certain conditions. Alternative actions by both sides were considered." Berlin #2, 104. Berlin #4, 185. Berlin #2, 102, 103.

6. Ibid., 104.

7. Column I listed Soviet actions. NATO reactions were in Column II. Soviet responses to NATO were in Column III. Lee's group "tried to think up . . . the possible things the Soviets could do to interfere with communication to Berlin, and we wrote down each one of them in column I. For example, they could make the required documentation difficult . . . they could interfere with traffic on the *autobahn,* they could interfere with air traffic and the air navigation aids, they could shoot down an airplane, they could . . . deny traffic with ground and air forces, ultimately they could make a surprise nuclear attack. I think we had twenty or thirty possibilities." Berlin #4, 223.

8. "Text of Kennedy appeal to nation for increases in spending and armed

forces," *New York Times*, 7/26/60, 10. General Armstrong commented, "That text would probably be the key official document to which historians could point as a shift to a program of mounting pressures or a flexible response . . . By no means do I think that I invented, and by myself caused the change. It would have come to pass." Berlin #2, 108, 110. The State Department's political-military representative, Seymour Weiss, recalled, "We were arguing a bunch of abstractions as to what actions we should take in response to hypothetical Soviet actions. This became the poodle blanket . . . [The logic] was incrementally applying measures, from the political and economic through the military, up to nuclear [force]." Fred Kaplan, "JFK's first-strike plan," *Atlantic Monthly*, 10/01, 86. Berlin #4, 180. Berlin #2, 108.

9. Berlin #2, 104. Berlin #4 , 223.

10. During 1959 Kahn addressed audiences at the Lawrence Livermore Laboratory, the Weapons Systems Evaluation Group at the Pentagon, the Stanford Research Institute, the MITRE Corporation, the Air War College, Strategic Air Command, the Center for the Study of Democratic Institutions, the Foreign Policy Association at the World Affairs Center, and Henry Kissinger's foreign policy seminar at Harvard. Copies were sent to A. Wohlstetter, B. Brodie, H. Rowen, I. Mann, A. Bart, R. Eldridge, M. Peissakoff, W. Eisner, J. Williams, E. Oliver, A. Enthoven, T. Harris, J. Hirshliefer, M. Rush, F. Iklé, W. Capron, and D. Ellsberg. Memo, H. L. Moshin to J. R. Goldstein, 7/20/59, Chappaqua. Letter, Joseph Edgerton, director, Office of Security Review, Office of the Assistant Secretary of Defense, to Kahn, 10/19/59, Chappaqua. Letter, RAND Vice President J. R. Goldstein to Edwin McMillan, 12/9/59, in Jardini, 135.

11. Of the lectures making up *On Thermonuclear War*, the first two were based on his civil defense studies, which had been funded from a non–air force grant. And since they had been thoroughly revised, their continuity with RAND work "will grow more tenuous." Moreover, a full third of the book had been conceived at Princeton. Clearly, Kahn anticipated objections from the anti–civil defense faction in management and had hoped that asserting the book's private provenance would soothe institutional anxieties. Letter, from Herman Kahn to George Tanham, RAND, 4/28/59, Chappaqua. Even in his 1958 papers, *Some specific suggestion for achieving early non-military defense capabilities and initiating long-range programs*, and *Report on a study of non-military defense*, Kahn scrupled to declare, "Neither publication necessarily reflects the views of the RAND Corporation. The first two parts of this research reflect my own views, much influenced by those of my co-workers." *Some specific suggestions*, iii. Letter, L. J. Henderson, Jr., to Kahn, 6/19/59, Chappaqua.

12. "Dulles sets goal of instant rebuff to stop aggressor," *New York Times*, 1/

13/54, 1. The details of the new doctrine were specified in Basic National Security Policy (NSC-16/2) of 10/30/53.

13. "Text of Dulles' statement on foreign policy of Eisenhower administration," *New York Times*, 1/13/54, 2. Dulles had been understood to imply that the atomic bomb was America's favored weapon. On the contrary, he insisted, "Massive attack was one option among a wide variety in the means and scope for responding to aggression." John Foster Dulles, "Policy for security and peace," *Foreign Affairs*, 4/54, 363.

14. Letter, Richard Bellman to Herbert Bailey, 2/2/61, PUP.

15. MAG, 61. In the acknowledgments to his book, Kahn thanked Bernard Brodie, Thomas Schelling, Jack Hirshleifer, and Albert Wohlstetter for shaping his ideas. While they worked on the same topic, Brodie, Wohlstetter, and Schelling differed greatly from one another. Brodie balanced military means with political objectives. Wohlstetter heeded vulnerabilities of the offensive forces. Brodie had studied political science, Wohlstetter, mathematical logic. Brodie addressed the political exigencies of international relations, Wohlstetter, the systems analysis of the strategic mission. Brodie believed that the Soviets desired peaceful coexistence. Assuming an implacable will toward world domination, Wohlstetter extrapolated the enemy's war-making capabilities. Whereas Brodie and Wohlstetter wrote as colorlessly about nuclear catastrophe as is humanly possible, Schelling was disturbingly frisky. He contrived dazzlingly cunning moves for the game of war, exploiting ambiguous communication and the play of madness to buffet the enemy.

16. OTW, 19.

17. Ibid., 126.

18. Ibid. The burden of persuasion falls on the threatener to demonstrate the incentive that compels him to execute the threat. It's a weird dilemma. "How can one commit himself in advance to an act that he would in fact prefer not to carry out in the event, in order that his commitment may deter the other party?" Thomas Schelling, *The strategy of conflict* (Harvard, 1960), 36.

19. OTW, 137–138.

20. Ibid., 135–136.

21. OTW, 145. Kahn told the historian Gregg Herken that he had borrowed the notion of the Doomsday Machine from the physicist Leo Szilard. See Leo Szilard, "How to live with the bomb—and survive," in Morton Grodzins and Eugene Rabinowitch, eds., *The atomic age: articles from the Bulletin of the Atomic Scientists, 1945–1962* (Simon & Schuster, 1963), 231. This is similar to Kahn's Doomsday-in-a-Hurry Machine in OTW, 145–146. For *his* version of the Doomsday Machine, see Schelling, 197.

22. OTW, 145, 148, 149. MITRE, 64–65. Actually, he pondered the strategic implications of three imaginary weapons systems that correspond to Deterrence Types I, II, and III: the Doomsday Machine (Type I), the

Doomsday-in-a-Hurry Machine (Type II), and the Homicide Pact Machine (Type III). See OTW, 144–153.

23. MITRE, 64–65. OTW, 156–157.
24. OTW, 14.
25. Ibid., 16n6, 18.
26. Ibid., 24.
27. Ibid., 27.
28. Ibid., 159.
29. Schelling, 218–219. OTW, 159.
30. Ibid., 162–163
31. Ibid., 139.
32. Ibid., 155–156.
33. Ibid., 291, 282.
34. Ibid., 290.
35. Ibid., 290, 294, 287.
36. Ibid., 291, 306. He did acknowledge the risks in overdoing the madman act, cautioning, "We must resist the temptation to get off cheaply by overusing or otherwise abusing Rationality of Irrationality strategies." Ibid.
37. Princeton briefing, 191–192.
38. OTW, 60, 19.
39. OTW, 19, ix, 55. Sidney Winter, Jr., interview, 8/ 22/91.
40. OTW, 47.
41. Ibid., 306.
42. Ibid., 22, 19.
43. Ibid., 20.
44. MITRE, 9–10.
45. OTW, 21.
46. Ibid., 43. The Atomic Energy Commission promulgated radiation protection standards as a proposed rule in July 1955. By late February 1957 the AEC regulated exposure of atomic energy workers and the public living or working near a nuclear facility. Workers in AEC labs and production sites were henceforth forbidden to be exposed to more than three-tenths of a roentgen per week, or 10 roentgens from conception to age 30. "Government regulations protect against radiation," *Science News Letter,* 9/6/57, 110. (Also see National Committee on Radiation Protection in the National Bureau of Standards Handbook 52, *Maximum permissible amounts of radioisotopes in the human body and maximum permissible concentrations in air and water,* and NBS Handbook 9, *Permissible dose from external sources of ionizing radiation.*) But by 1959 disagreement surfaced between the National Committee on Radiation Protection and Measurement (NCRP) and the International Commission on Radiological Protection (ICRP). In an April 1958 publication, *Standards for protection against radiation,* the NCRP *doubled* the amount of strontium-90 a worker could absorb without injury. It also increased by one-quarter the maxi-

mum concentration of radioactive matter in water, food, and milk. Contrariwise, the ICRP recommended *lowering* the ceiling of maximum exposure levels to as low as one-tenth of current allowances. See "Reports disagree on radiation hazards," *Science*, May 1959, 1473. "Radiation standards, testimony at congressional hearings tends to be reassuring," *Science*, 5/10/60, 1723. In September 1960 the AEC reduced the maximum annual exposure level for atomic workers from 15 rems to 5.

47. OTW, 45. James Crow observed in 1958, "Medical radiation . . . adds appreciably to the total irradiation received. The average 30 year dose to the reproductive cell has been estimated . . . as 2 or more roentgens . . . By contrast, the 30-year dose from fallout if the rate of the last five years continues will be 0.1 roentgen more or less." James Crow, "Genetic effects of radiation," *Bulletin of the Atomic Scientists*, 1/58, 20. See also Karl Morgan, "Human exposure to radiation," *Bulletin of the Atomic Scientists*, 11/59, 387.

48. OTW, 45, 46, 47.

49. Ibid., 47, 54.

50. The same relation was postulated for potassium and cesium-137. The effortless palliatives of calcium and potassium supplements seem to be the basis for Kahn's expectations for ever-more powerful radiation antidotes.

51. OTW, 66. MITRE, 20.

52. OTW, 66, 67.

53. Ibid., 68. This found some support in experiments done at Los Alamos. One scientist reported to the American Chemical Society in 1958 that treating gardens with lime and learning to eat plants with deep taproots were "life saving proposals." "Diet can protect man from harmful isotope," *Science News Letter*, 4/26/58, 259. Also see, "Fruits shed strontium-90," *Science News Letter*, 9/2/60, 198.

54. OTW, 55. A word about these numbers. Kahn rarely cited references or justified his calculations in detail. While emphasizing the importance of quantifying significant phenomena in a post-attack scenario, his numbers were rhetorical, not measurements of testable processes.

55. OTW, 60. He conceded that weathering, uneven terrain, isotope decay, and protective gear might not adequately shield survivors working in farms, forests, or wilderness areas. Nevada test site data suggested that "it may be more difficult to decontaminate open land than was previously thought." Ibid., 61.

56. Ibid., 62, 74.

57. Ibid., 62.

58. Ibid., 114.

59. Ibid., 78.

60. Ibid., 92.

61. Ibid., 85.

62. Ibid.

63. Ibid., 84.

64. Ibid., 84, 649.

65. Ibid., 90, 646.
66. Ibid., 84, 91.
67. Ibid., 92.
68. Ibid., 94, 95.
69. Ibid., 311.
70. Ibid., 312, 313.
71. Ibid., 315, 316.
72. Ibid., 316.
73. Ibid., 318, 324, 325, 326.
74. Ibid., 325, 326.
75. Ibid., 326, 534.
76. Ibid., 484.
77. Ibid., 456–457n2.
78. Ibid., 457n2. He predicted that anti-radiation drugs, climate control, and weather control would be available by 1965. OTW, 483.
79. Bernard Brodie, ed., *The absolute weapon* (Harcourt, Brace, 1946), 27. In fact, Hudson Institute analysts prided themselves on scenarios that rivaled cold war thrillers. "[Many] scenarios we wrote were a lot better than the . . . movies." Frank Armbruster interview, 7/ 31/91.

9. COMEDY OF THE UNSPEAKABLE

1. Obscure, 124. Panero interview. Amitai Etzioni, "Our first manual of thermonuclear war," *Columbia University Forum,* fall 1961, 4
2. Letter, Major General Bruce Holloway, USAF, HQ, to Lawrence Henderson, 12/8/60, Chappaqua. Letter, Douglas Brooks, director of research, Naval Warfare Analysis Group, Massachusetts Institute of Technology, to Kahn, 12/5/60, Chappaqua. Letter, Elliot Baker, NBC News, to Kahn, 12/7/60, Chappaqua.
3. Newman, 197. "From a shocking new book," *Popular Science,* 7/61, 92.
4. In OTW he characterized his analysis as scientifically substantiated. The weight of "objective and quantitative" evidence had forced Kahn and his reluctant colleagues to accept the idea of a survivable nuclear war. OTW, 21. But in the 1958 study, after declaring that with inexpensive civil defense measures "the United States would be a pretty good place to live in even a year after the war," Kahn reversed himself absolutely. "However, we concede that the uncertainties are great enough to raise the question of sheer survival." *Report on a study of non-military defense* (RAND, 7/58), 8. For errors in his models, see OTW, 90–92.
5. Wizards, 222–223. MITRE, 5. Letter, Bernard Brodie to Kahn, 2/16/62, Counsels, 206.
6. Geoffrey Galt Harpham, *On the grotesque* (Princeton, 1982), 11. Erich Auerbach, *Mimesis* (Princeton, 1953), 278.
7. Harpham, 65. Mikhail Bakhtin, *Rabelais and his world* (Indiana, 1984), 163, 222. Obscure, 110.
8. Kahn argued that only by unhesitating quantification could one demon-

strate that in an environment subject to random danger, an individual's risks were generally tolerable. OTW, 375–376. Anatol Rapoport, "The sources of anguish," *Bulletin of the Atomic Scientists*, 12/65, 36.

9. One Man, 92–94. Bakhtin, 188. Paul Dickson, *Think tanks* (Atheneum, 1971), 112.

10. Bakhtin, 91. Michael Steig, "Defining the grotesque, an attempt at synthesis," *Journal of Aesthetics and Art Criticism*, Winter 1970, 256. Stephen Rebello, *Alfred Hitchcock and the making of "Psycho"* (Harper Perennial, 1991), 162–163.

11. John Springhall, *Youth, popular culture and moral panics* (St. Martin's, 1998), 5. Science Correspondent, "Nuclear warfare and after," *Glasgow Herald*, 4/27/61. George Kirstein, "The logic of no return," *Nation*, 1/14/61, 34. Letter, Herbert Bailey, Jr., director, Princeton University Press, to William Clifford, 3/6/61, Chappaqua. Letter, Herbert S. Bailey, to Richard Bellman, 4/24/61, Chappaqua.

12. *CBS reports: in case of war*, 11/9/61, CBS News archives.

13. Richard Kostelanetz, "The man who thinks about atomic war," *Popular science*, 7/61, 94.

14. Obscure, 114. Arnold Beichman, "Herman Kahn: questions and answers," *New York Herald Tribune Sunday Magazine*, 7/4/65, 4.

15. Anthony Caputi, *Buffo: the genius of vulgar comedy* (Wayne State, 1978), 66.

16. Princeton briefing, 55, 26. George Santayana, *Soliloquies in England* (Scribners, 1924), 132. Susanne Langer, "The comic rhythm," in Robert Corrigan, ed., *Comedy, meaning and form* (Chandler, 1965), 121, 127, 139.

17. MITRE, 39. Princeton briefing, 56, 27–28. OTW, 92.

18. Caputi, 130. *CBS reports*.

19. Caputi, 129–130. Langer, 133.

20. Caputi, 132, 135. John Davy, "The unthinkable war," *The Observer* (UK), 5/6/62, 15: "Advise and dissent," *Newsweek*, 10/9/61, 93. Laurence Barrett, "Face to face," *New York Herald Tribune*, Section 2, 11/26/61, 1. Myron Rosenthal, "Kennedy advisor blasts 'either-or' thinking, says civilization will survive nuclear war," *Trinity Tripod* (Trinity College Newspaper), Hartford, CT, 12/4/61, Chappaqua.

21. Frances FitzGerald, "Herman Kahn: metaphors and scenarios," *New York Herald Tribune Sunday Magazine*, 7/4/65, 3. "Planners for the Pentagon," *Business Week*, 7/13/63, 9. Joseph Kraft, "The war thinkers," *Esquire*, 9/62, 104.

22. One Man, 59, 82. Burch, 11.

23. Caputi, 204–5. OTW, 21.

24. Ron Goulart, *Cheap thrills: an informal history of the pulp magazines* (Arlington House, 1972). Lee Server, *Danger is my business: an illustrated history of the fabulous pulp magazines* (Chronicle Books, 1993). J. Fred Macdonald, *Don't touch that dial!* (Nelson Hall, 1979).

25. Geoffrey O'Brien, *Hardboiled America: the lurid years of paperback* (Van Nostrand Reinhold, 1981), 88. John Houseman, "What makes American movies tough?" *Vogue*, 1/15/47, 88, 120.

26. Goulart, 180.

27. Gerald Nachman, *Raised on Radio* (Pantheon, 1998), 311, 313, 314.

28. Goulart, 85. Server, 121. A brisk but memorable one-sentence scenario features "unidentified raiders, probably Soviet 'juvenile delinquent' Eskimos," dynamiting a radar installation. OTW, 216. "There is an enormous value to having the formulation of a new policy to meet a new challenge come out of one man's brain, insofar as one man properly advised can grasp the problem." Ibid., 584. Once he founded the Hudson Institute, Kahn circulated the idea in many guises. He exhorted every presidential administration thereafter to create a high-level office in the executive branch devoted to the future.

29. OTW, 649.

30. In 1936 the *New Yorker* cartoons of Charles Addams featured witches and monsters, psychopathic children, cannibals, murderers, and suicides. By 1938 his Addams Family characters regularly appeared in his cartoons. From 1949 on, collections of his drawings were published from time to time, and each one sold extremely well.

31. "A corrosion and heat-resisting metal tag . . . attached to a chain . . . [should be] worn permanently around the neck, wrist, or ankle," *Civil defense in California schools* (Sacramento, 10/23/53), 54, 67, 72–73.

32. *Report of the New York State Joint Legislative Committee to study the publications of comics* (Albany, 3/51), 18.

33. Philip Wylie, *Generation of vipers*, 2nd ed. (Pocket Books, 1955), 41. Gershon Legman, *Love and death: a study in censorship* (Hacker Art Books, 1963), 31–32, 49. Legman's book was originally published in 1949.

34. Mike Benton, *The comic book in America* (Taylor, 1989), 41, 44, 69, 155, 48, 51.

35. Digby Diehl, *Tales from the crypt: the official archives* (St. Martin's, 1996), 23, 129.

36. Maria Reidelbach, *Completely MAD: a history of the comic book and magazine* (Little Brown, 1991), 33, 76, 51.

37. "Unfunny comic books barred in Los Angeles," *New York Times*, 9/23/48, 38. "50 cities ban off-color funnies," *New York Times*, 10/5/48, 29. Edward Feder, *Comic book regulation* (Bureau of Public Administration, UC Berkeley, 2/55), 11–12.

38. US Congress, *Juvenile delinquency (comic books): hearings before the Senate Subcommittee on Juvenile Delinquency*, 83rd Congress, 2nd Session, 4/21–22/54 and 6/24/54 (Government Printing Office, 1954), 82. Peter Kihss, "No harm in horror, comics issuer says," *New York Times*, 4/22/54, 1.

39. Diehl, 90, 91.

40. Amy Kiste Nyberg, *Seal of approval: the history of the comics code* (University Press of Mississippi, 1998), 109, 93.

41. "Crime comic sales reported dropping," *New York Times*, 1/3/56, 29. Peter Bart, "Advertising, Superman faces new hurdles," *New York Times*, 9/23/62, Section III, 12.

42. Hilton Kramer, "Look! Allover! It's esthetic . . . It's business . . . It's supersuccess!" *New York Times*, 3/29/66, 33.

43. T. E. Murphy, "Progress in Cleaning Up the Comics," *Reader's Digest*, 2/56, 108. Richard Gehman, "It's just plain *Mad*," *Coronet*, 5/60, 103.

44. "Sassy newcomer," *Time*, 9/24/56, 71. J. M. Flagler, "The Mad Miracle," *Look*, 3/19/68, 46. Also see "Now comics have gone *Mad*," *Pageant*, 6/54. "International advertising," *Mad*, 1/59.

45. "Pravda," *Mad*, 7/58.

46. "Maddiction," *Time*, 7/7/58, 63. Jack Skow, "*Mad*, wild oracle of the teen-age underground," *Saturday Evening Post*, 12/21/63, 64.

47. Dwight Macdonald, "Profiles, a caste, a culture, a market, II," *New Yorker*, 11/29/58, 76. Gehman, 97. T. J. Ross, "The conventions of the *Mad*," *Dissent*, autumn 1961, 504.

48. Charles Winick, "Teenagers, satire, and *Mad*," *Merrill-Palmer Quarterly of Behavior and Development*, 7/62, 191, 198–199.

49. "Bloody Mary, anyone?" *Time*, 10/21/57,70. Max Rezwin, ed., *Sick jokes, grim cartoons and bloody marys* (Citadel Press, 1958).

50. Little Willie jokes were originally published in 1899 as *Ruthless rhymes for heartless homes*, but they were fresh enough to be included in a 1936 joke anthology edited by Lewis Copeland. (*The world's best jokes*, Halcyon House). Little Audrey jokes were popular during the Depression. One folklorist collected them in the mid-1930s from high school and college students in Texas. Cornelia Chambers, *From straight Texas* (Publications of the Texas Folklore Society, #13, 1937). Gerald Walker, "The way those joke cycles start," *New York Times Magazine*, 10/26/58, 36.

51. Brian Sutton-Smith, "Shut up and keep digging, the cruel joke series," *Midwest Folklore*, 10(1) (1960), 12. Roger Abrahams, "Ghastly commands, the cruel joke revisted," *Midwest Folklore*, 1961–62, 236, 240. An appreciation for Lenny Bruce's comedy plied the same formula, "Although 'sick' humor appears to be [an] . . . unfeeling reaction to misery . . . it actually is an oblique protest against the enforced repression of . . . revulsion, anxiety, and guilt evoked by deformity. It [is a] . . . rebellion against the piety that demands automatic sympathy for . . . every . . . human limitation." Albert Goldman, "The comedy of Lenny Bruce," *Commentary*, 10/63, 315.

52. Rezwin, *The best of sick jokes* (Pocket Books, 1962), i, ii. Also see Rezwin, *More sick jokes and grimmer cartoons* (Citadel Press, 1959). Rezwin, *Still more sick jokes and even grimmer cartoons* (Citadel Press, 1960).

53. Alta Jablow and Carl Withers, "Social sense and verbal nonsense in urban children's folklore," *New York Folklore Quarterly* 21 (1965), 244, 245, 248, 249, 251, 253.

54. William Douglas, "The black silence of fear," *New York Times Magazine,* 1/13/52, 7.

55. Frank Sullivan, "Well, there's no harm in laughing," *New York Times Books Review,* 12/16/51, 1, 10.

56. "Time out from thinking," *Time,* 1/4/54, 48. "Imp of the blue angel," *Newsweek,* 4/22/57, 70.

57. Winick, 191.

58. Jules Feiffer, *Boy, girl, boy, girl* (Random House, 1959).

59. Dick Gregory, *From the back of the bus* (Avon, 1962), 67, 70, 71.

60. "An electronic comic and his TV tricks," *Life,* 4/15/57, 176, 179.

61. Kenneth Rexroth, "The decline of American humor," *Nation,* 4/27/57, 375, 376.

62. Jerome Beatty, Jr., "Humor vs. taboo, the sorrowful story of the cartoon," *Saturday Review,* 11/23/57, 11, 12, 13.

63. See Herbert Block, *Herblock's special for today* (Simon & Schuster, 1958).

64. James Reston, "The unfamiliar sound of laughter," *New York Times,* 3/16/58, Section 4, 10. Lenny Bruce, *How to talk dirty and influence people* (Playboy, 1965), 232.

65. Robert Osborn and Ronald Searle, "The emasculation of American humor," *Saturday Review,* 11/23/57, 17. John Sisk, "No offense intended," *Commonweal,* 3/14/58, 613, 614.

66. Frank O'Connor, "Is this a dagger?" *Nation,* 4/26/58, 371, 372.

67. Gore Vidal, "The unrocked boat," *Nation,* 4/26/58, 371, 372.

68. Harold Clurman, "No time for comedy," *Nation,* 4/26/58, 376.

69. Jules Feiffer, "Couch-as-couch-can school of analysis," *New York Times Magazine,* 5/18/58, 20. Jules Feiffer, *Sick, sick, sick: a guide to non-confident living* (McGraw Hill, 1956).

70. "Sick, sick, well," *Time,* 2/9/59, 52. "Oh-so-sensitive," *Time,* 11/13/61, 93.

71. Nat Hentoff, "The iconoclast in the night club," *Reporter,* 1/9/58, 36. Robert Rice, "Profiles," *New Yorker,* 7/30/60, 32. "Free association," *New Yorker,* 11/30/57, 36, 44. Hentoff (1958), 35. The state of the nation's humor, 26.

72. Rice, 31. Herbert Mitgang, "Anyway, onward with Mort Sahl," *New York Times Magazine,* 2/8/59, 32.

73. Nat Hentoff, "Where liberals fear to tread," *Reporter,* 6/23/60, 50. "The wit in the mirror," *Newsweek,* 1/2/61, 62. Gilbert Millstein, "Man, it's like satire," *New York Times Magazine,* 5/3/59, 30. Bruce, 127–138.

74. Hentoff (1960), 52. Martin Williams, "The comedy of Lenny Bruce," *Saturday Review,* 11/24/62, 60. Bruce, 233.

75. Malcolm Muggeridge, "Another world shortage—humor," *New York Times Magazine,* 9/11/60, 56. Nat Hentoff, "Satire, schmatire," *Commonweal,* 7/7/61, 376. Goldman, 312.

76. DeMott, 109, 110, 118, 114, 119, 118. Even Lenny Bruce's admirers

affixed an approving note of mental hygiene to sicknik bravura. "This public display of the ugly, the twisted, the perverse . . . gives the audience a profound sense, not only of release, but of self-acceptance. Again and again, Bruce violates social taboos—and he does not die!" Goldman, 316.

77. Goldman, 312.

78. Hentoff, 1961, 377. James Reston, "Bourbon in your grits and all that," *New York Times*, 4/22/62, Section 4, 10.

79. Russell Baker, "Observer," *New York Times*, 12/13/62, 6.

80. Victor Navasky, "Introduction," in Leonard Lewin, *Report from Iron Mountain* (Free Press, 1996), vi. Victor Navasky interview, 9/11/00.

81. Otto Friedrich, "The ultimate solution," *Monocle*, preview issue, 1962, 40–41.

82. Editorial, *Outsider's Newsletter*, 1962, 3. "Col. C. C. Chestnut's Column," *Outsider's Newsletter*, 1(14), 1963, 5. "Col. C. C. Chestnut's Column," *Outsider's Newsletter*, 1(18) 1963, 2.

83. Ed Koren, "Introducing SuperKahn," *Outsider's Newsletter*, 1963.

84. Goldman, 312.

85. Bosley Crowther, "'Dr. Strangelove,' a shattering sick joke," *New York Times*, 1/30/64, 24.

86. TAU, 27, 283. Loudon Wainwright, "The strange case of Strangelove," *Life*, 3/13/64, 15. "Direct hit," *Newsweek*, 2/3/64, 79. Not only did Kubrick cross paths with Kahn, but the author of the novel on which *Dr. Strangelove* was based struck up a brief, fawning correspondence with Kahn. Having just finished devouring OTW, that "massive and magnificent . . . brilliant piece of thinking" for the third time, Peter Bryan George gushed, "May I stress again the great admiration I have for your book. It seems to me to represent the first real and rational effort to get to terms with a monster which, unless we can conquer it, will surely conquer [us]." Letter, Peter Bryan George to Kahn, 7/20/61, Kahn Correspondence 1961, NDU. Kahn returned the favor by inviting George to write scenarios for him. Letter, Kahn to Peter Bryan George, 8/8/61, NDU. While he couldn't entice George to work for Hudson, he successfully wooed the novelist William Gaddis to polish Hudson reports and Ralph Ellison to be a nonresident consultant. Arthur Herzog, "Report on a 'think factory,'" *New York Times Magazine*, 11/10/63, 35: One Man, 105.

87. Peter George had been an RAF officer when he got the idea for *Red Alert*. "He was on an air base which was full of US B-47s. They were in the officer's club. Someone had a cup of coffee which was very close to the edge of the table. The B-47 took off and roared over head, and the whole building vibrated and the coffee cup fell on the floor, and somebody said, 'You know, that's the way World War III's going to start.' Peter George went out and called his publisher and said, 'If you'll give me an advance,

I'll take three weeks leave and write you a book about how World War III got started.' The publisher said, 'You're on,' so he took 3 weeks off, and wrote the book." Thomas Schelling interview, 9/5/00. Letter, Schelling to author, 10/12/98.

88. Peter Bryant, *Red alert* (Ace, 1958), 74. For details of the opening of the war, see pp. 36–40, 50. (George used the pseudonymn Peter Bryant). In *Dr. Strangelove* a mad general makes use of an emergency war plan that authorizes a base commander to launch his bomber force in the event that communications with his superiors are cut off by the enemy. The general telephones SAC and announces, "Yes gentlemen, they are on their way in and no one can bring them back. For the sake of our country and our way of life I suggest you get the rest of SAC in after them, otherwise we will be totally destroyed by Red retaliation. So let's get going, there's no other choice." Peter George, *Dr. Strangelove or, how I learned to stop worrying and love the bomb* (Bantam, 1963), 37–38.

89. Schelling interview, 9/5/00.

90. The Doomsday Machine was Kahn's idea. "Since Stanley lifted lines from *On Thermonuclear War* without change but out of context," Kahn told reporters, he thought he was entitled to royalties from the film. He pestered him several times about it, but Kubrick held firm. "It doesn't work that way!" he snapped, and that was that. One Man, 94. See pp. 49, 97, 98, 115, 123, 142, 143 in George's novelization of the screenplay for either direct quotations or close paraphrases of passages from OTW.

91. Bosley Crowther, "'Dr. Strangelove,' a shattering sick joke," *New York Times*, 1/30/64, 24. Peter George was troubled by the reception of *Dr. Strangelove*. He wrote Schelling a letter soon after the film's release asking whether he had been outraged by the screenplay and begging his pardon. Schelling recalled, "I wrote him a nice letter back saying No I thought it had turned it out beautifully. That they had resolved the issue the right way by making it a comedy. I said I didn't find it the least bit offensive." Soon afterward, Schelling received a note from George's wife informing him that he had committed suicide.

92. "Direct hit," *Newsweek*, 2/3/64, 79. "Detonating comedy," *Time*, 1/31/64, 69.

93. DeMott, 114. Hentoff (1961), 376.

94. Philip Hartung, "What five-sided building?" *Commonweal*, 2/21/64, 632. Loudon Wainwright, "The strange case of Strangelove," *Life*, 3/13/64, 15. Moira Walsh, "Films," *America*, 3/28/64, 462, 464.

95. OTW, 85–86.

10. MASS MURDER OR THE SPIRIT OF HUMANISM?

1. One Man, 92–94. Friedrich Nietzsche, *Beyond good and evil* (Penguin, 1973), 42.

2. Letter, Walter Marseille to Kahn, 6/20/59, Chappaqua. Marseille renewed his criticism in *Bulletin of the Atomic Scientists*. "What Kahn has to say is hard to take in any case, but he compounds the difficulty further by antagonizing his reader with a careless and unskillful use of the English language . . . On every other page he exhibits some little, or not so little, gaucherie." Marseille, "On Thermonuclear War," *Bulletin of the Atomic Scientists*, 5/61, 166.

3. Kahn, *Three lectures on thermonuclear war* (Lawrence Radiation Laboratory, University of California, 8/17/59), ii, iii, iv. Kahn said much the same thing in the preface to OTW. He justified the informality of his prose "in order to feel freer . . . advancing tentative or speculative notions," and offered his ideas only provisionally, as "suggestions for work to be done." OTW, viii.

4. Kahn 1959, vi.

5. "I have long felt that there are many at universities and elsewhere who could contribute but do not, perhaps, because they feel the problems are futile." Ibid. Marshall Windmiller, Commentator, "Nuclear Strategy and Herman Kahn," 3/8/60, KPFA Berkeley; 3/10/60, KPFK Los Angeles, Chappaqua.

6. Walter Marseille, "Marshall Windmiller and the Truth," manuscript and cover letter, no date, Chappaqua.

7. Hubert Humphrey, Foreword, in Herman Kahn, *The nature and feasibility of war and deterrence* (Senate Document No. 101, 86th Congress, 2nd Session, United States Government Printing Office, 5/24/60), iii. Kahn, his editor, and the marketing department of Princeton University Press liked Humphrey's endorsement so well that they cajoled him to contribute a blurb for the book jacket. In it, Humphrey equably framed thermonuclear war as a proper topic for disagreement among a free people. "New thoughts, particularly those which appear to contradict current assumptions, are always painful for the human mind to contemplate." The book jacket was girdled with paeans from other opinion leaders. Robert Sprague, the acting director of the Gaither Commission, affirmed its significance for moderate and conservative cold warriors. "OTW is the most comprehensive and valid analysis I have read on what we need to do to strengthen our deterrence and insure our survival as a nation in the nuclear age." To mollify liberal readers, Harrison Brown, a geochemist at CalTech and author of several books on disarmament, contributed a tribute to Kahn's importance to the national debate. "I urge all persons to read it . . . This book will influence history more than any which I have read in the last 20 years." Book Jacket, OTW, 1st ed. (1960).

8. "An editorial note," *History Book Club Review*, 1/61. The book was also adopted by the Air Force Book Program. Letter, Barbara Huber, Princeton University Press, to Kahn, 11/23/60, PUP Archive. Walter Millis, "On Thermonuclear War," *History Book Club Review*, 1/61, 3.

9. Gerard Piel interview, 5/16/99.

10. Newman, 197, 200.

11. Piel interview.

12. James Newman, "A moral tract on mass murder," *Washington Post*, 2/26/61, E7. "The Nightmare World," Letters from William Kent and Mortimer Taube, *Washington Post*, 3/5/61, E4.

13. Letter, Kahn to Donald Brennan, 3/8/61, Chappaqua. Letter, Kahn to Gordon Hubel, 3/5/61, NDU. The advertisement featured excerpts from the reviews of John Norris in the *Washington Post*, Norman Thomas in the *Saturday Review*, Max Lerner in the *New York Post*, Jerome Spingarn in the *New York Times*, and endorsements from Harrison Brown, Senator Hubert Humphrey, and a cablegram from Bertrand Russell, who wrote, "Respect Kahn's candor as to facts but deplore his obedience." Memorandum, John Criscitiello to Herb Bailey, Subject, Advertising on KOTW, 3/9/61, PUP Archive.

14. Letter, Kahn to Dennis Flanagan, 3/6/61. The original letters are in Kahn papers, Chappaqua. Kahn typed out a complete set of his correspondence with Flanagan and sent it to scores of his colleagues. While he could not persuade his editor to publish it as an appendix to *Thinking about the unthinkable*, he invited his readers to write to the Hudson Institute for a copy of the letters. Herman Kahn, *Thinking about the unthinkable* (Horizon Press, 1971), 280n2.

15. Letter, Dennis Flanagan to Kahn, 3/15/61.

16. Letter, Kahn to Flanagan, 3/18/61. Letter, Flanagan to Kahn, 3/20/61.

17. Letter, Kahn to Flanagan, 3/28/61.

18. Letter, Herbert S. Bailey, Jr., to Flanagan, 3/23/61.

19. Letter, Flanagan to Kahn, 4/4/61.

20. Letter, Kahn to Flanagan, 5/29/61.

21. Piel interview, 5/16/99.

22. Ibid.

23. Letter, J. D. Williams to Editor, *Scientific American*, 3/6/61, NDU. Letter, Robert M. Lerner, D. C. Maclellan, C. L. Mack, Jr., and J. Max, to Dennis Flanagan, 4/27/61, NDU.

24. Letter, Herbert Bailey, Jr., director, Princeton University Press, to William Clifford, 3/6/61, Chappaqua. Letter, Herbert S. Bailey, Jr., to Richard Bellman, 3/24/61, PUP Archive.

25. Letter, Gordon Hubel, assistant to the director, Princeton University Press, to Kahn, 7/13/62, PUP Archive. OTW sold 18,381 copies, not including book clubs and copublishers. Letter, Walter H. Lippincott, director, Princeton University Press, to author, 10/11/94. The History Book Club sold 9,431 copies. The Aerospace Book Club sold 1,600 copies. A total of 29,412 copies sold in its first ten years, not including overseas sales. Royalty statements from PUP, Chappaqua. Greenwood Press published a reprint edition in March 1979 and had sold a total of 501 copies

as of September 27, 2000. Interview, Norma Johnson, Rights and Permissions Coordinator, Greenwood Press, 9/27/00.

26. Marseille (1961), 158, 166. Geminus, "It Seems to Me," *New Scientist* (UK), 4/27/61, 192. William Lee Miller, "Which unthinkable thoughts do we think?" *Worldview: A Journal of Religion and International Affairs,* 4/61, 10. Kahn, Letter to Editor, *Worldview,* 10/62, 11.

27. Spingarn, Letter to the editor, *New York Times Book Review,* 2/12/61, 43. Gabriel Kolko, Letter to the editor, *New York Times Book Review,* 2/12/61, 43.

28. Irving Louis Horowitz, "Arms, policies and camps," *American Scholar,* Winter 1961–62, 97.

29. Ibid., 100, 102.

30. Anatol Rapoport, "The Sources of Anguish," *Bulletin of the Atomic Scientists,* 12/65, 31, 36.

31. Ibid., 36.

32. Mark Hedden, "If Deterrence Fails," *American Scholar,* Winter 1961–62, 91, 89.

33. John Strachey, "On thermonuclear war," *Survival,* 5–6/61, 147.

34. "The military intellectuals," *Times Literary Supplement,* 8/25/61, 559.

35. Ibid., 558.

36. Frank Meyer, "Policy for victory," *National Review,* 3/25/61, 189.

37. Robert Paul Wolff, "The game of war," *New Republic,* 2/20/61, 13, 10. Also see Arthur Waskow, "The Game of Strategy," *New Republic,* 2/26/62.

38. Walter Goldstein and S. M. Miller, "Herman Kahn, ideologist of military strategy," *Dissent,* Winter 1963, 78, 85, 75. Alastair Buchan, "A cold look at the holocaust," *Reporter,* 8/17/61, 53.

39. P. M. S. Blackett, "Critique of some contemporary defence thinking," *Encounter,* 4/61, 9.

40. John Polanyi, "Armaments policies for the sixties," *Survival,* 3–4/62, 77. For a similar argument see Rudolf Peierls, "Agonizing misappraisal," *Spectator* (UK) 4/28/61.

41. Paul Johnson, "The new schoolmen," *New Statesmen,* 5/1/61, 754. By 1968 Kahn's penchant for compressing bodies of knowledge into graphical form resembles this classificatory impulse. In answer to the question, What had the Hudson Institute done to earn its 10 million dollars' worth of contracts? he remarked, "Look at the charts . . . All the knowledge of the world is here, like Diderot's encyclopedia . . . Some of these charts are worth in the billions." Obscure, 124.

42. Marseille (1961), 158, 159.

43. Letters to the editor, *Bulletin of the Atomic Scientists,* 9/61, 294.

44. Ibid.

45. H. Stuart Hughes, "The strategy of deterrence," *Commentary,* 3/61, 192.

46. Ibid.

47. John Fry, "What are the shades of black?" *Presbyterian Life,* 5/15/61, 42.

48. Donald Michael, "On Thermonuclear War," *Science*, 3/3/61, 635.

49. John Bennett, "Ethics, the bomb, and Herman Kahn," *Christian Century*, 3/28/62, 384, 385.

50. Roy Wolfe, "A geographer looks at Herman Kahn," *International Journal*, Winter 1961–62, 57, 50, 52, 53.

51. Ibid.

52. David Lilienthal, "Skeptical look at 'scientific experts,'" *New York Times Magazine*, 9/19/63, 79, 82.

53. Marcus Raskin, "The megadeath intellectuals," *New York Review of Books*, 11/14/63, 7, 6. Not surprisingly, the hidden objectives of the warfare state for whom the abject scientist-strategists toiled appeared with regularity in the radical press. The venerable British Marxist scientist J. D. Bernal denounced Kahn in the *Daily Worker*. In the teeth of the international peace movement, Kahn's book was meant to "put a stop to such an unpatriotic and unprofitable arrangement" by demonstrating nuclear survivabililty. J. D. Bernal, "Salesmen for the horror war," *Daily Worker* (UK), 5/31/61, 2. The review of OTW in the Socialist Labor Party Newspaper, avidly collected by the RAND library, reflected much the same attitude. OTW articulated the "the grim thoughts of the 'planners' of decadent capitalism . . . The more the capitalists become convinced that they may 'prevail' in a thermonuclear war with the Soviet bloc, the more eager will they be to prepare for it." "U.S. capitalist class beset by feelings of growing desperation," *Weekly People*, 1/28/61, 6.

54. Norman Thomas, "Roads that bypass peace," *Saturday Review*, 2/4/61, 18, 33. Letter, Norman Thomas to Editors, Princeton University Press, 4/17/61. Press Archive.

55. William Lee Miller, "Which unthinkable thoughts do we think?" *Worldview: A Journal of Religion and International Affairs*, 4/61, 10. Sumner Rosen, "Bulletin books," *AVC Bulletin*, 7–8/61, 2.

56. Midge Decter, "The strangely polite 'Dr Strangelove,'" *Commentary*, 5/64, 76.

57. Lionel Rubinoff, "Author-reviewers symposia," *Philosophy Forum*, Fall 1970, 113. Herbert Marcuse expressed the same idea, "When the whole is at stake, there is no crime except that of rejecting the whole, or not defending it." Herbert Marcuse, *One dimensional man* (Beacon, 1964), 82.

58. Rubinoff, 113.

59. Ibid.

60. "Herman Kahn speaks," Letters to the Editor, *San Francisco Chronicle*, 4/27/61, Chappaqua.

61. Herman Kahn, "We're too scared to think," *Saturday Evening Post*, 9/16/61, 12.

62. Ibid., 14.

63. Alain Enthoven interview, 6/4/71, 2. Oral History Collection, John F. Kennedy Library. Jardini, 155, 154.

64. Paul Dickson, *Think tanks* (Atheneum, 1971), 111. Counsels, 98. Gustave Shubert offered the opinion that "Collbohm had no great distaste for Kahn. He was against civil defense on emotional and philosophical grounds. He thought it was a refuge for scoundrels, knaves, and cowards." Gustave Shubert interview, 5/13/99. Andrew Marshall confirmed, "Herman could easily have stayed at RAND, not if he wanted to continue working on civil defense, but [if he studied] other sorts of things. Collbohm thought very highly of Herman." Andrew Marshall interview, 9/3/91.

65. "Face to Face," *New York Herald Tribune*, 11/26/61, Section 2, 1.

66. "Advise and dissent," *Newsweek*, 10/9/61, 93.

EPILOGUE: A COMIC PHILOSOPHY

1. OTW, 646–647.

2. G. W. F. Hegel, *Lectures on Aesthetics*, vol. 2 (Clarendon Press, 1975), 1202, 1220, 1221. Undoubtedly drawing on the same notion, Herbert Marcuse characterized Kahn, and indeed the organizational culture of RAND, as an expression of the "Happy Consciousness" in his book, *One-dimensional man* (Beacon, 1964). He wrote, "[Happy Consciousness] reflects the belief that the real is rational, and that the established system, in spite of everything, delivers the goods. In this . . . guilt has no place. One man can give the signal that liquidates hundreds and thousands of people, then declare himself free from all pangs of conscience, and live happily ever after." The happy subject administers a technological apparatus that appears to be rational, neutral, and apolitical. Getting ahold of a RAND corporate newsletter describing a strategic war game, Marcuse reflected, "The Happy Consciousness has no limits—it arranges games with death and disfiguration in which fun, team work, and strategic importance mix in rewarding social harmony. The RAND Corporation, which unites scholarship, research, the military, the climate, and the good life, reports such games in a style of absolving cuteness." Marcuse, 79–80.

3. OTW, 646.

4. Ibid., 110. These were amino-ethyl-thiouronium (AET) cysteine, mercaptoethylamine (MEA), serotonin, and p-amino-propiophenone (PAPP).

5. "Protection method found," *Science News Letter*, 5/6/61, 256. Also see "Looking for a fallout pill," *Business Week*, 12/2/61. "Anti-radiation drug," *Science News Letter*, 4/7/61, 222. "Sulfur gives protection against radiation harm," *Science News Letter*, 5/9/62, 366. "Radiation death delayed," *Science News Letter*, 3/16/61, 164.

6. "Fallout lollipops . . . a doctor tries to lick radiation," *Life*, 2/8/63, 54.

7. OTW, 484. Also see vol. 5 of *Proceedings of the Second Plowshare Symposium*, UCRL-5679, cited in OTW. John von Neumann, "Can we survive technology?" *Fortune*, 6/55, 108. William Kotsch, "Weather control and national strategy," *Proceedings of the U.S. Naval Institute*, 7/60, 80.

8. "Colonize space! Open the Age of Reason" was the jolly title of conference proceedings published two years after Kahn's death. The conference honored the German-American rocket engineer Krafft Ehricke who "was convinced . . . that only when man lifts up his eyes away from the Earth, looks into the stars and actually thinks what his role can be, can he achieve what Schiller called the dignity of men. And only if we start to think about space, and the colonization of space, will the Age of Reason that the great humanists of European cilvization were thinking of accomplishing be possible." Helga Zepp-LaRouche, "Krafft Ehricke and the age of reason," in Fusion Energy Foundation and the Schiller Institute, *Colonize space! Open the age of reason: proceedings of the Krafft A. Ehricke memorial conference, June 15–16, 1985* (New Benjamin Franklin House, 1985), 10–11. Kahn's space-centered perspective projected "the eventual establishment of large autonomous colonies in space involved in the processing of raw materials, the production of energy and the manufacture of durable goods—both for indigenous consumption and as exports back to earth or to other solar-system colonies." Herman Kahn, William Brown, Leon Martel, and Hudson Institute staff, *The next 200 years, a scenario for America and the world* (Morrow, 1976), 5. Kahn and his coauthors returned to the theme in the conclusion of the book. "A capability for self-supporting existence in space would make possible the continuation of earth's civilization and the resuscitation of human life on the planet following an irreversible tragedy in the case of thermonuclear war or ecological catastrophe." While the possibility of a planetary-wide catastrophe was unlikely, nevertheless "the potential disutility [of such a disaster] is so enormous that a concerted international effort to create extraterrestrial self-sustaining communities, in concert with other space objectives, would probably be well warranted." Ibid., 223, 224, 10.

9. OTW, 515. Norman Moss, *Men who play God: the story of the hydrogen bomb* (Victor Gollancz, 1968), 264. In his interview with Gregg Herken, Kahn remarked cryptically that he regarded the issue of using nuclear weapons as "akin to a religious issue." He added, "At some psychological level I find nuclear war unthinkable." Counsels, 205.

10. Norbert Weiner, *The human use of human beings: cybernetics and society* (Houghton Mifflin, 1950), 141.

11. Kahn, Mann (B), 18.

12. Blaise Pascal, *Pensées* (Penguin, 1966), 150.

13. OTW, 430, 432.

14. Andrew Wilson, *The bomb and the computer: wargaming from ancient Chinese mapboard to atomic computer* (Delacorte, 1968), 129.

15. Some words about Kahn's later life. In 1972 the Club of Rome published a report entitled *The limits to growth*, which cautioned that the needs of the global population would exceed available resources by 2000. Kahn spent much of his final decade rebutting its ideas. In 1976 he published *The next 200 years*, which declared that the potentials of capitalism, sci-

ence, technology, human reason, and self-discipline were boundless. The planet's resources set no limits to economic growth; rather, human beings would "create such societies everywhere in the solar system and perhaps to the stars as well." He predicted that "200 years from now we expect almost everywhere, [human beings] will be numerous, rich, and in control of the forces of nature." Herman Kahn, William Brown, Leon Martel, and Hudson Institute staff, *The next 200 years: a scenario for America and the world* (Morrow, 1976), 1. He continued to work on military affairs. From 1966 to 1968 Kahn consulted with the Pentagon on the direction of the Vietnam War. He believed U.S. strategy had erred "by constantly offering to negotiate." He suggested "a sharp, potentially uncontrollable increase in threat, which might raise anxiety about points of no return." *New York Times,* 3/10/67, 35.

Kahn died on July 7, 1983, of a heart attack. He was 61 years old. For more futurology, see Herman Kahn, *The world of 1980* (Hudson, 1969); Herman Kahn and Barry Bruce-Briggs, *Things to come: thinking about the seventies and eighties* (Macmillan, 1972); Herman Kahn, "Thinking about the Unthinkable," *Forbes,* 11/22/82; Herman Kahn and Michael Redepenning, *The coming boom: economic, political, and social* (Simon & Schuster, 1982). For military topics, see Kahn, *On escalation, metaphors and scenarios* (Praeger, 1965); Herman Kahn, Frank Armbruster, Raymond Gastil, William Pfaff, and Edmund Stillman, *Can we win in Vietnam?* (Praeger, 1968); Herman Kahn, William Pfaff, and Edmund Stillman, *War termination issues and concepts: final report* (Hudson, 1968); Herman Kahn, *The nature and feasibility of war, deterrence, and arms control* (Hudson, 8/82); Herman Kahn, *A case for low-level civil defense* (Hudson, 7/83); Herman Kahn and Owen Cote, *Mobilization and deterrence* (Hudson, 1/10/84); Herman Kahn and Neil Pickett, *Alternative central war strategies* (Hudson, 1/10/84); Herman Kahn, Frank Armbruster, Owen Cote, Kurt Guthe, and Doris Yokelson, *Mobilization and defense planning* (Hudson, 8/84); Herman Kahn, *Thinking about the unthinkable in the 1980s* (Simon & Schuster, 1984).

Acknowledgments

Martin Collins, David Hounshell, David Jardini, and Andrew May were the first historians to peruse RAND's archival holdings in the 1990s. I have relied on their research for important source material. The National Defense University at Fort MacNair in Washington, D.C., has a Hudson Institute archive. There are more than a dozen boxes of Kahn's papers and correspondence in this collection, dating from 1961 to his death in 1983. The rest of Kahn's papers remain in his family's possession in Chappaqua, New York. In 1991, Kahn's widow graciously allowed me to examine a half dozen boxes of her husband's papers from the late 1950s. I am grateful to the late Jane Kahn for hosting my visit so long ago, and to Drs. Collins, Hounshell, Jardini, and May for sharing their research with me.

This book has been sponsored by so many institutions, has been helped along by so many friends, it gives me great pleasure to acknowledge them. I am indebted to the following:

- A Humanities Division Graduate Research Grant, University of California at Santa Cruz for travel, as well as the extraordinary expenses of transferring kinescope negatives of two television programs featuring Kahn in 1961 to videotape.
- A Smithsonian Graduate Student Fellowship, Space History Division, National Air and Space Museum, summer 1991, sponsored by Martin Collins and Space History Division Director Gregg Herken. Collins's expertise in RAND matters guided my early years of research. His generosity and friendship remain dear to me.

- An Institute for Global Cooperation and Conflict Dissertation Year Fellowship and UC Regents Dissertation Year Fellowship, 1992–1993. I happily acknowledge Barbara Epstein, who encouraged me to pursue the topic; Andrew Feenberg, who offered theoretically fruitful suggestions; and especially Donna Haraway for encouraging my attempt to conjoin the history of science with critical theory, and for befriending me at a critical time.
- A Postdoctoral Fellowship in the History of Science, History Department, Northwestern University, 1993–1994. Thanks to David Joravsky for sponsoring my fellowship, and Ken Alder and Bronwen Rae for their affectionate hospitality.
- A Postdoctoral Fellowship in American Studies, The Commonwealth Center for the Study of American Culture, The College of William and Mary, 1994–1996. Thanks to Chandos Brown for sponsoring my fellowship; to fellows Grey Gundaker and Patrick Hagopian for their staunch friendship; and to Arthur Molella of the National Museum of American History for his friendly interest.
- A Postdoctoral Fellowship in the History of Cold War Science and Technology, Carnegie Mellon University, 1996–1998. Thanks to David Hounshell for sustaining me with two years of fellowship, for generously entertaining my ideas which were as far in taste and temperament from his as could be imagined, as well as for his insights into RAND's organizational culture and the social role of the cold war entrepreneurial scientist-administrator. Thanks to the members of the cold war research group, Glen Asner, Jennifer Bannister, Doug Davis, Gerard Fitzgerald, Joshua Silverman, and Ruud Van Dijk, who astounded me with their generosity, energy, and collegiality; and to CMU's librarians, Joan Stein and Geraldine Kruglak, for their persistence.
- A Senior Research Fellowship at the Center for the Humanities at Wesleyan University during 1998–99. Thanks

to Elizabeth Traube for sponsoring me, and to the other Center fellows, and to the Center staff, Jackie Rich and Pat Camden, for a memorable year. Thanks also to the Wesleyan interlibrary loan librarians, Kathy Stefanowicz and Kate Wolfe, for their labors.

I am happily obliged to the friends and scholars who have offered corrections, suggestions, and editorial wisdom: the late Susan Abrams, Laurence Badash, the late David Edge, Lawrence Freedman, Peter Galison, Grey Gundaker, Patrick Hagopian, Gregg Herken, Susan Lindee, Everett Mendelsohn, Charles Nathanson, Michael Sherry, and Fred Turner. I am especially grateful to my editors at Harvard University Press: Michael Fisher for gambling on me, Sara Davis for patient assistance with the art program, and Susan Wallace Boehmer for her sagacity, flexibility, exacting expertise, and appreciation for the finer points of the sick joke.

Heartfelt thanks are due to the men and women who allowed me to interview or correspond with them: Frank Armbruster, Lincoln Bloomfield, Sam Cohen, James Digby, Richard Frykland, Olaf Helmer, Jane Kahn, Carl Kaysen, Arnold Kramish, Bradford Lyttle, Irwin Mann, Francis McHugh, Everett Mendelsohn, Robert Panero, Gerard Piel, Steuart Pittmann, Walt Rostow, Henry Rowen, Gustave Shubert, Sidney Winter, Jr., Roberta Wohlstetter, and Herbert York. I am obliged to Irwin Mann, Thomas Schelling, Max Singer, and Anthony Wiener for allowing me to interview them at length. Separate and special thanks are reserved for Daniel Ellsberg, Spurgeon Keeny, and Andrew Marshall, who read parts of the manuscript repeatedly and carefully, alert to errors, omissions, and overstatements. Their critical suggestions and their willingness to explore this material with me thoughtfully helped make the book more accurate and more pointed.

Thanks to Victor Navasky and Richard Lingeman for sharing their collection of *The Monocle* and *The Outsider's Newsletter;* to J. Fred MacDonald for hosting a week-long scurry through his archive; to Peter Hornick for his hospitality in Manhattan; to Zhan Li and Doug Davis for research tips and help; to Barry Bruce-Briggs for the drive from the city; to David Kahn and Deborah Kahn Cunningham for their pleasant conversation in 1991; and to David Kahn for his later interest in the book.

David Kahn and Deborah Kahn Cunningham have given me permission to quote from their father's unpublished papers in their possession. However, they wish to make clear that they do not endorse the views, interpretations, and opinions that I have set forth in this book. Permission to quoted copyrighted material was also given to me by: Frances Burwell, Executive Director, Center for International and Security Studies at Maryland, for the Berlin Oral History Transcripts; Hudson Institute, for Herman Kahn/Hudson Institute Archive materials in the National Defense University; MITRE Corporation Archives; the National Air and Space Museum; Princeton University Press Archives; and the RAND Corporation.

Tim Haggerty has earned my awestruck gratitude for gamely reading the *long* version of this book. And for their beautiful constancy, thanks flow out to Diane Bennett, Christine Collins, Sharon Josepho, Carol Kirk, and Barbara Powell. The love of my parents, Harvey and Randi, my brother, Charles, my other family, Maman, Bijan, Behdad, and Behjat, and the children of my heart, Megan, Donya, Jodi, and Mana, have fortified and inspired me.

Finally, this book is dedicated to my wise and gallant husband, Behrooz. Without the benefit of his witty, affectionate conversation over the years, the tempo of this book would have been more plodding, and the pleasures afforded by it surely fainter. With great love and respect, I offer my thanks to you.

Index